A RELIABLE ACCOUNT OF THE COAST OF GUINEA (1760)

by Ludewig Ferdinand Rømer

Translated from the Danish and edited by
SELENA AXELROD WINSNES

DIASPORIC AFRICA PRESS

This book is a publication of

DIASPORIC AFRICA PRESS
NEW YORK | WWW.DAFRICAPRESS.COM

© Diasporic Africa Press, 2013

All rights reserved. No part of this publication may be reproduced or distributed in any form or by any means, or stored in a database or retrieval system, without the prior written permission of the publisher.

ISBN 978-1-937306-07-6 (pbk.: alk paper)
Library of Congress Control Number: 2013948733

To

My grandchildren, in order of appearance,
Ina, Henning, Linn, Samuel, Martine, Henriette, Jacob, Hannah

For their patience

Contents

Editor's Introduction ix
A RELIABLE ACCOUNT OF THE COAST OF GUINEA (1760) conflated with
A RELIABLE ACCOUNT OF TRADE ON THE COAST OF GUINEA (1756) 1
Verse (by C. E. Engmann) (1760) 3
Foreword: To the Reader (by Erik Pontoppidan) (1760) 5

1. About the Guinea Coast in general 15
   The climate: some insects 17; The inhabitants: Cape Mount rulers 21; Benin influences: aggrey beads 23; Ignorance regarding Africa: man-eaters 27

2. With which nations trade is carried on, and in what manner, as well as in what it consists (1760) 30
   The Guinea Trade (1756) 30; The nations involved (1760) 32; The Dutch (1760) 36; The Dutch (1756) 46; The English (1760) 55; The English (1756) 57; The French (1760) 63; The French (1756) 65; The Danes (1760) 69; The Danes (1756) 69

3. About the Negroes' religion in general (1760) 78
   Religious queries 79; A trickster spirit 80; Other spirits: the Labode fetish 83; A New Year ceremony 87; The fetish oracle 89; Women possessed 91; Sacred objects 93; The Fante fetish 95; Propitious days: sacred animals 98; Circumcision: oaths and tests 100; The Labode fetish again: a fetish anecdote 102; Prophecies 103; Death beliefs 107

4. About the Negroes' history, customs, and way of life (1760) 110
   Territories and peoples of Gold Coast 111; The history of wars: the Benin era 113; The rise of Aqvamboe 116; Accra under Aqvamboe 118; The Akims threaten Aqvamboe 120; The Accras as brokers for the Aqvamboe 121; War customs 125; How the Aqvamboe captured Accra 128; Aqvamboe policies 130; A Danish governor 132; Aqvamboe conquered by the Akim 136; Accra under Akim 139; Akim and Asante 143; Gold mines 147; Akim conquered by Asante 150; Asante and the Europeans 157; Gold Coast products 161; African-European relations on Gold Coast 162; Gold Coast warfare 166; Aqvamboe survivors 169; Asante wars 170; Future conditions? 175; Some cunning Africans 176; Gold Coast ceremonies 182

5. About the trade of the Danes, as well as about their forts and establishments on the Guinea Coast 188
   Monopolies and forts as trade hindrances 188; Trade from ships 190; The Man of the Line 193; Discipline in ships and forts 194; Foodstuffs 196; Future dispositions on Gold Coast 199; The Danes on River Volta 204; River Volta described 207; Qvitta 209; Fort Christiansborg and Accra 211; Labode 218; Ponni and Prampram 219; Fort Fredensburg 221; Export trade in slaves, etc 225; Import trade 228; Danes and other Europeans on the Coast 230; Fauna of Gold Coast 235; Excursus 240

Editor's Appendices
A   The West Indies trade of the French, English and Danes (1756)   243
B   The 1744 Christiansborg rebellion   255
C   A 1760 Danish account of a Gold Coast warrior   261
Glossary   265
Bibliography   267
Index   277
Addenda et Corrigenda   291

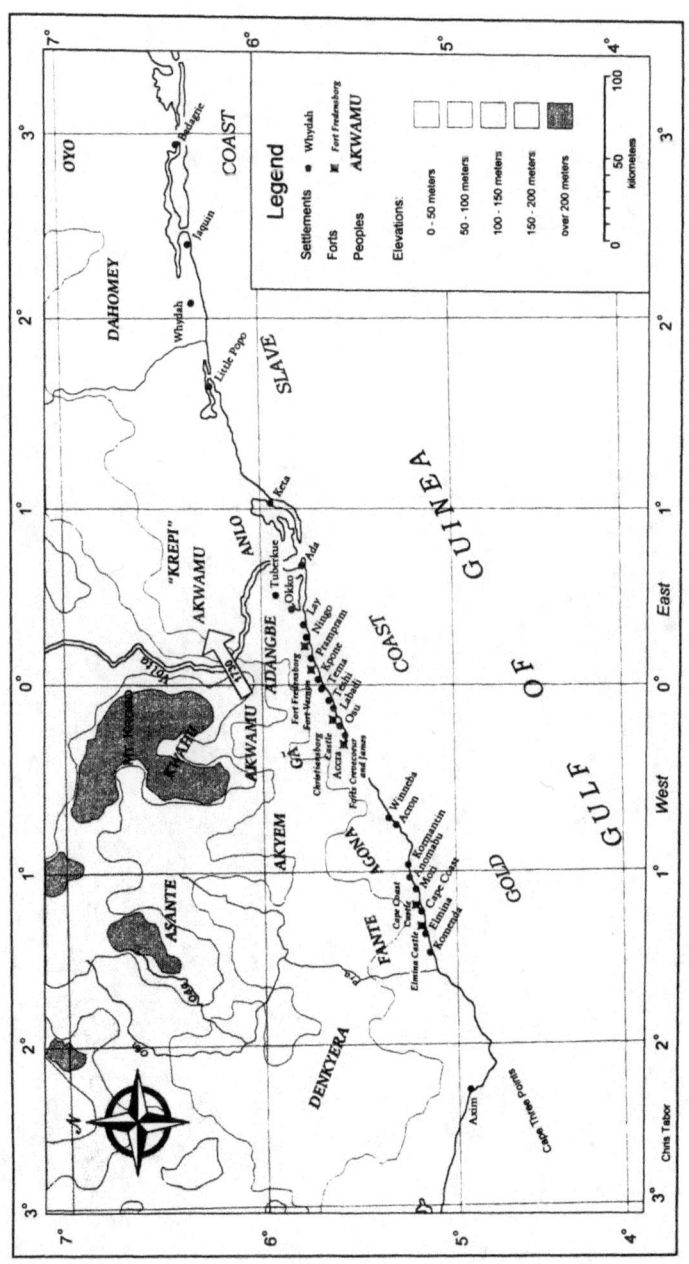

Editor's Introduction

In 1756, at Copenhagen, Ludewig Ferdinand Rømer (1714–1776) published a 64-page quarto booklet entitled, in translation, *A Reliable Account of Trade on the Coast of Guinea and the Nations trading there, and in what Manner it is practised by each Nation in particular, together with humble Suggestions about how Our Trade there and to the West Indies could be improved.*[1] Four years later, in 1760, also at Copenhagen, Rømer published a longer work with a shorter title, a 348-page octavo book entitled, in translation, *A Reliable Account of the Coast of Guinea.*[2] Each work dealt with contemporary African-European relations on the coast of Guinea, especially on 'Gold Coast', as witnessed by Rømer himself. While the shorter work concentrated on the operation of various national companies trading on Gold Coast, the longer work had much more to say about the African traders and customers, their societies and traditions. The present edition therefore takes the 1760 work as its primary text but includes the 1756 text, the two being conflated. Each work appeared in a contemporary German translation, and the 1760 work has latterly been reprinted in a modern transcription and appeared in a French translation. But the 1756 work has not previously had an English translation, and the 1760 work has not previously had a complete one.[3]

---

[1] In Danish, *Tilforladelig Efterretning om Negotien paa Kysten Guinea, Af hvilke Nationer den drives, og paa hvilken Maade den er indretted af enhver Nation især, tilligemed Uforgribelige Betænkninger, hvorledes vor Negotie derhen og til Vestindien, bedre kunde indrettes.* The work has no foreword, illustrations or index. It is hereafter referred to either as 1756 or as *Negotien*.
[2] In Danish, *Tilforladelig Efterretning om Kysten Guinea.* The work includes a Foreword, three engravings, a map and a poem, but no index.
[3] Ludewig Ferdinand Rømer's *Nachrichten von der Küste Guinea, mit einer Vorrede D. Erich Pontoppidan, aus dem Dänischen übersetzt* (Copenhagen and Leipzig, 1769) 304 pp.; translator unnamed, a close version of the Danish original but variation in details makes attributing it to Rømer questionable; includes the Foreword, the three engravings and the map; pagination of the original not shown; no index. The French translation: Mette Dige-Hess, trans. and ed., *Le Golfe du Guinée 1700–1750: récit de L.F. Rømer, marchand d'esclaves sur la côte ouest-africaine* (Paris 1989); a close version but slightly abbreviated and original pagination not shown; includes the three engravings but not the original map, instead three other maps, with annotation and index. English translation of single chapters: chapter 3 (by Kirsten Winther, 1977, typescript, Balme Library, Legon, Accra [hereafter BLL]); chapter 3 (by Irene Odotei, *Institute of African Studies Research Review*, 3/2 (1987), 115–58); chapter 4 (by Karen Berthelsen, 1965, typescript, BLL). The Foreword to 1760 speaks of an 'immediate German translation' of the earlier work (/5/ below). There seems to have been such a translation, entitled *Die Handlung verschiedner Völker auf der Küste Guinea* (Copenhagen 1758), but no copy has yet been traced. A transcription of 1760, from gothic into roman script, including the Foreword and the entire text, was published in 1997 by Frifant Forlag, Nesodden, Norway.

The first Europeans, the Portuguese, having reached Guinea in 1444, arrived in 1471 at the stretch of eastern coast later known as 'Gold Coast'. Thereafter, for one hundred and fifty years, the marine import/export trade of Gold Coast remained in Portuguese hands, with only infrequent and temporary challenges from other European nations. Imports were mainly of metal and ceramic goods, and textiles, the export mainly of gold. The major Portuguese base was the fort of São Jorge da Mina, at a locality which eventually came to be known in Europe as Elmina. Built in 1482 to store goods between voyages from Portugal, and to defend the trade against other European nations, the fort was captured by the Dutch in 1637. Although Portugal retained bases in the islands at opposite ends of the Guinea coast, the Cape Verdes and the equatorial islands of Príncipe and São Tomé, Portuguese trading on Gold Coast declined sharply.[4] Nevertheless, the long period of Portuguese control of the seaward side of the gold trade led to a degree of Portuguese cultural influence on African societies of the coast, most notably in the trade language.

The seventeenth century saw the arrival on Gold Coast of traders representing several nations of northern Europe. Because of sharp rivalry, their trading places or 'lodges' were backed up by a series of newly constructed forts. In general, the European bases were established with the encouragement and permission of local African polities, partly because of the rivalry among the latter to control, on the landward side, the rich import/export trade. While the export trade in gold continued throughout the seventeenth and eighteenth centuries, an export trade in slaves gathered momentum, as the relevant Europeans nations gained sugar plantations in the Caribbean requiring slave labour.

Although Brandenburg and Sweden had earlier possessed momentary interests in Guinea, by the mid-eighteenth century the European land-based rivals on Gold Coast comprised the Dutch, the English, and the Danes, all of whom owned forts. Apart from the lingering Portuguese interest, the French attempted to break into the trade but gained no permanent land base on Gold Coast proper. Following the example of the Dutch, the other nations endeavoured to work through chartered companies, although these were often ephemeral and were always weakened by the interloping of excluded nationals. This was the general situation when Rømer served in Guinea between 1739 and 1749.

* * *

---

[4] In 1679–1683 the Portuguese temporarily occupied Christiansborg Fort at Osu (Accra), renaming it Fort Xavier (Erick Tilleman, *A Short and Simple Account of the Country Guinea and its Nature* [1697] (1994) 26).

Denmark-Norway[5] entered the Guinea trade in the 1650s. Chartered by King Frederik III, the Glückstad Company was founded in 1659, and a fort named Frederiksborg was built in 1661, on Mount Amanful, overlooking the English base of Cape Coast Castle (built 1665), in the country of Fetu, an Akan polity.[6] The company did not prosper, and in 1685, on the verge of bankruptcy, sold the fort to the English, who renamed it Fort Royal.[7] From then on, the Danes had their headquarters at a fort built in 1661, farther east, at Osu, in Gã country. Enlarged later, it became known as Christiansborg Castle, and served as the Danes' headquarters for the rest of their 165-year stay on Gold Coast.[8] In 1697 the Glückstad Company was merged with the Danish West India Company to form a chartered West India and Guinea Company.[9] This was Rømer's employer, but its rules and restrictions were a constant source of frustration to him. His service in Guinea was mainly at Christiansborg, and his account deals largely with the vicissitudes of company trade and government there, as well as with the history and culture of the African peoples in that eastern part of Gold Coast. These peoples were the Gã on the coast (with the various neighbouring sections of their linguistic cousins, the Adangbe), and also, but to a lesser extent, the Akan, located on the coast to the west and in the interior to the north and NW.

By the mid-eighteenth century Gold Coast had become the major focus of European interest in West Africa. The topography of that section of the Guinea coast, with its bays and rocky promontories, allowed for relatively safe anchorage in the roads and for the construction of permanent buildings

---

[5] Norway was one of the realms of the House of Oldenburg, and the 'twin monarchy' was Denmark-Norway, but referred to by Rømer, and hereafter, as simply 'Denmark'.

[6] For a description of Fort Frederiksborg, see Müller [1673] in Adam Jones, ed., *German Sources for West African History* (1983) 148–9 (Müller lived in the fort). See also reports of visits to the fort in N. Villault, *Relation des Costes d'Afrique appellées Guinée* (1669) 195–7; J. Barbot, *Barbot on Guinea* [1732] (1992) 399–401. The Danes followed to Gold Coast the Swedes, whose chartered company operated from lodges in 1649–1663, but then withdrew, forced out by the Danes (Tilleman [1697] (1994) 3).

[7] Albert van Dantzig, *Forts and Castles of Ghana* (1980b) 31.

[8] It now serves as the headquarters for the government of the Republic of Ghana.

[9] The name of the new company was Vestindisk-guineisk Kompaniet, hence the abbreviation V-gK applied to the company's records in the Royal Archives in Copenhagen [hereafter CRA]. The company was granted a monopoly in respect of Danish trade in Guinea and at the West Indian island of St. Thomas. In both his books Rømer called for a relaxation of monopolistic restrictions and the opening of the Guinea trade to private shippers. The company was eventually dissolved in 1754, as Rømer joyfully noted, and all its assets were taken over by the Crown. The government managed to keep the finances in balance, but no great profit was shown, so, in 1765, a new, privately-owned company was formed, but this suffered serious losses and was liquidated in 1776. In 1779 another monopoly company, the Baltic-Guinea Company was formed and survived until 1786. The next year a 28-year contract for the continuation of the trade was signed between government and a group of private merchants known as the Guinea Entrepeneurs, and this operated until the ending of the Danish transatlantic slave trade in 1802 (Georg Nørregård, *Danish Settlements in West Africa 1658–1850* (1966) 143, 150–51).

nearby, in contradistinction to other stretches of the surf-ridden coast where offshore sand banks and reefs generally predominated, allowing only limited and dangerous landings. On Gold Coast, the most desirable exports of gold and slaves were readily available, the local Africans having had long experience in forming trading networks, originally with the far interior and then with European shippers and resident traders. Between the Africans and the Europeans communication was eased by the lingua franca of 'Coast Portuguese'. Some twenty-five stone or brick forts and an equal number of lodges, or factories, came to exist along an approximately 320-kilometre stretch of coast. The major forts, as noted by Rømer, were the following. Elmina Castle, the earliest fort, hence originally built by the Portuguese, was now the headquarters of the Dutch company, the WIC (West India Company). But when the Brandenburgers withdrew in 1720, their fort, Gross Friedrichsburg at Pokesu, in western Gold Coast, also came into the hands of the Dutch. The English, in the form of the rapidly decaying Royal African Company, had headquarters at Cape Coast Castle;[10] the Danes at Christiansborg Castle.

Whereas the export gold trade had linked Africa and Europe, the Atlantic slave trade, soon to be at its height, linked Africa and America. Each of the European powers trading on Gold Coast had acquired colonies in America, mostly in the Caribbean, and the demand for Africans as slave labour on Caribbean plantations underlay much of the feverish European rivalry on the coast which Rømer describes. The extent to which it also fuelled the more dramatic and bloody rivalry of the local African polities which Rømer also relates, is less clear and somewhat controversial. With the decline of imperial Spain, the Dutch, English and French had acquired Caribbean colonies early in the previous century; the Danes, later arrivals, acquired the small islands of St. Thomas in 1671, St. John in 1712, and St. Croix in 1733 (by purchase from the French), as well as the islet of Vieques, acquired in 1694.[11] In both his writings, Rømer adds to his account of Gold Coast lengthy references to the Danish position in the West Indies.

The forts on Gold Coast were intended to channel and protect the trade of each individual European nation. Their limited resources and distance from home normally prevented them from exercising a significant military influence on the local African polities, although the economic nexus led both sides to indulge in elaborate diplomatic and social manoeuvring. However, on the seaward side the forts and their associated lodges did not wholly control the

---

[10] Established under English law, the Royal African Company was an English company. But by the mid-eighteenth century its employees were, strictly speaking, British. On the coast, however, and by Rømer, they were generally still termed 'English', and for consistency this use will be followed.

[11] As further evidence of Spanish decline, under the terms of the 1713 Treaty of Utrecht Britain acquired the exclusive rights to supply 4,800 African slaves per year to Spanish America.

import/export trade of the coast, since the companies involved did not wholly control the seas. The French, although without forts and lodges, at times carried on an extensive trade from the roads, profiting from the saving on the expense of maintaining land bases, a situation which Rømer, like his Dutch and English colleagues, found unfair and deplorable, complaining about it at every opportunity. The Portuguese also continued a certain amount of trade, although they tended to be under the shadow of the Dutch, who required them to pay a tax at Elmina.[12] But eventually the greatest threat to the companies with forts was not the competition of foreigners but that of their own nationals. Ports, businesses and individuals excluded from the charter system supported interloping voyages, taking from the state monopolies more and more of their trade. Being normally without the costs of shore establishments, the interlopers attracted African traders by their lower prices for imports and higher prices for exports. By Rømer's day, as he relates, all the companies were in the slow process of retreat from monopoly, their licensing of non-company shippers leading to eventual open trade.[13] The arrangements by his competitors to permit progressive elements of private trade were viewed with envy by Rømer, but the Danes eventually followed suit.[14]

* * *

Rømer was born at Elsfleth, on the River Weser, in Oldenburg in northern Germany. It has not been possible to discover when he moved to Denmark. Well-educated and comfortable with English, French and Dutch (as well as knowledgeable in Latin), he was employed by the Danish West India and Guinea Company and sent to Gold Coast in the capacity of assistant clerk, or 'copyist'. He was then twenty-five years of age. Sailing on the *Laarburg Galley*, he arrived at the Danish headquarters, Christiansborg Castle, on 23 October 1739. There, in addition to his language skills — enhanced by his learning Coast Portuguese and gaining some capacity in the local African languages, Gã and Akan — he revealed a talent for trade

---

[12] Cf. P. Verger, *Trade Relations between the Bight of Benin and Bahia* (1976) 21–8.

[13] The Dutch Governor Barovius, upon his installation in 1740, instituted a system of permitting private trade, conditional on payment to the company of a fixed fee for every slave bought and sold. However, the system was plagued by circumvention and there were constant complaints about interlopers disturbing the trade. Yet the Dutch West India Company continued to hold a legal monopoly of the Dutch trade on Gold Coast until the end of the century (Harvey M. Feinberg, *Africans and Europeans in West Africa: Elminans and Dutchmen on the Gold Coast during the Eighteenth Century* (1989) 31). The English Royal African Company was licensing private traders when Rømer was working on Gold Coast, but required to be subsidised by the government. The company was finally dissolved in 1752, and replaced by private capital, under the name of the Company of Merchants Trading to West Africa (Eveline C. Martin, *British West African Settlements 1750–1820* (1927) 7–9).

[14] It would be of interest to know if a comparable shift from strictly controlled trading took place within polities on the African side, the traders breaking free from regulation by the ruling group, but the sources are not helpful on this subject, preferring to concentrate on inter-ethnic substitution (p.c. P.E.H. Hair).

and was promoted several times during the next five years, finally attaining the rank and title of 'Merchant'. He states that he travelled extensively along the eastern Gold Coast and into the neighbouring 'Slave Coast', on behalf of various governors.[15]

In 1744, five years after his arrival on the Coast, a rebellion on the part of the Danish and Norwegian soldiers and some of the administrative staff at Christiansborg was mounted against the Governor, Jørgen Billsen.[16] Between Billsen and his subordinates trouble had been brewing for some time. Rømer, an old hand at trading when Billsen arrived, had attempted to instruct the new governor in trading practices on the Coast. Perhaps the old hand was undiplomatic, but whatever the cause Billsen and Rømer were soon on a collision course. Finally, when Rømer and a colleague, Klein, disagreed vehemently with a judgement Billsen handed down against a sergeant for trading privately, the governor suspended both subordinates. He accused Rømer of involvement in a rebellion against the governor and the Company, adding that he was inept and incompetent in trade. The accusation of trading incompetence was absurd, considering that Billsen himself had earlier sent reports to Copenhagen praising Rømer's skill as a trader.

Tempers ran so high that Rømer had to flee Christiansborg Castle precipitously, taking refuge first at the Dutch fort Crevecoeur (the closest fort to Christiansborg) and then with the English at Cape Coast Castle. He had always been on particularly friendly terms with the Englishmen on the coast, and they urged him, as they had done before, to leave the Danish service and work for them. Rømer refused their offer because he wished to return to Copenhagen, in order to plead his case and be cleared of Billsen's accusations. Since he was in poor health at the time, he stayed for about six months at Cape Coast Castle, where he passed the time by studying the local records of the Royal African Company. At some point he moved on to Elmina Castle and remained there, studying more records, those of the Dutch West India Company, until he was given passage to Europe on a Dutch ship.[17] Sailing first to Vlissingen in the Netherlands, he disembarked and travelled overland to Amsterdam, where he joined another Dutch ship sailing to Denmark.

The last leg of the journey ended catastrophically. On 4 November 1745, the ship ran aground at Målen, near Arendal, off the southern coast of Norway.[18] Barely managing to save his own life, Rømer lost all his belongings, including the savings accumulated during those first five years in West

---

[15] 1756, 32, within Chapter 2 below.
[16] For the history of this rebellion, especially as reported by Rømer, see Appendix B below.
[17] As reported in 1756, 6, within Chapter 2 below. His perusal of those records provided him with much material for the 1756 publication.
[18] Ships sailing to and from Denmark always sailed along the southern Norwegian coast to take advantage of the bays and out harbours there before entering, or after leaving, Skaggerak and Kattegat, areas of sea characterized by storms and sand banks.

Africa — except for a few parrots.[19] He was given free passage to Denmark on an Icelandic ship, and complained that he even lacked the money to protect his body against the winter's cold. However, once in Copenhagen and armed with excellent testimonials from the English staff on Gold Coast, he was not only able to clear his name but was promoted to the post of Chief Merchant, and in 1746 sent back to Gold Coast. In the meantime Governor Billsen and his two successors had died in rapid succession.

Rømer remained in West Africa until 1749. In that year he was offered the post of Governor, but refused in order to return home, pleading poor health. Having purchased a number of slaves for private sale in the West Indies, Rømer sailed from Gold Coast, this time on the triangular route.[20] It was his first and seemingly only visit to the West Indies, but it produced in his books a variety of comments on the management — or mismanagement, as he saw it — of the Danish trade between Guinea and the West Indies.[21] His refusal to accept the offer of the governorship on Gold Coast may very well have been due to his growing frustration with company rules, but he was also planning to form and run a business of his own in Denmark. Clearly he did not return empty-handed since he was soon able to establish what became a profitable sugar refinery in Copenhagen (at Nyhavn 11, where a plaque still commemorates the enterprise). On 2 June 1751, Rømer married Anna Catherine Wedderkamp, the nineteen-year-old daughter of a municipal surgeon, and in the course of their nineteen years of marriage she bore him fourteen children, of whom five outlived their father. She died in 1770 at the age of 38, and Rømer himself died of tuberculosis on 17 April 1776 at the age of 62.

In the later 1750s, by now well established in trade, Rømer was eager to make his views on the Danish Guinea trade known to the public at home. This resulted in 1756 in his first publication, *Negotien*. The booklet was well received, and in 1758 was translated into German. Then, having regaled his friends with tales of his life in Guinea, he was urged to record his personal experiences. Accordingly, Rømer wrote and published in 1760 his longer account, *Efterretning*. He showed a draft of the book to Bishop Erik Pontoppidan, one of the leading literary lights in the kingdom,[22] and received unstinting approval and encouragement to publish the material, even in its very rough and rambling state (a decision for which we have ample cause to reproach the good bishop). Not only did Pontoppidan urge

---

[19] This is described in Appendix B below. The mythology of this Norwegian locality has it that, on particularly stormy nights, Rømer's ghost wanders around the rocks looking for his sea chest.

[20] An English factor at Accra wrote as follows. 'The Danish factor Mr. Rømer, who has now decided to go home, and is trading a good number of slaves for himself, to take to the West Indies, also does great injury for he pays 6½–7 ounces [of gold] for a good slave' (BLL, Furley N46, 30.9.1749). The going price for 'a good male slave' at that time was 6 ounces of gold.

[21] For the section of 1756 on the West Indies, see Appendix A below.

[22] Erik Pontoppidan (1698–1764), for whom see note 1 of the Foreword below.

publication, he also wrote a long foreword to the book, in which he seized the opportunity to argue that the forced migration of the enslaved Africans was ultimately for their own good, on two counts: first, by their being removed from the horrors of life in Africa—as so vividly described by Rømer—and secondly, by their conversion to Christianity in America. A German translation of *Efterretning* appeared in 1769.

The interest of Rømer's writings is likely in the future to lie less in his views on the management of Guinea trade — his statements about the rival national companies reflect his bias and may not be always fully correct — and more in his descriptions of the African context, in particular the history of events on Gold Coast during his time on the coast, or, as he learned about them, preceding events. For whereas the detailed history of the several companies may yet be revealed from exploration of their copious archives, and may produce challenges to Rømer's contemporary claims, his writings represent a primary and uncommon source on a specific segment of West African history. This is not to say that what he recounts can be accepted as comprehensive or unbiased, or indeed more than at times somewhat simplistic. His perspective on Africa, howbeit unusually well-informed, was essentially that of the alien trader, as is clear from his concentration on dramatic political and military events, since these were likely to have immediate repercussions on the marine import/export trade. Before discussing Rømer's response to the African context, it is necessary to sketch the ethnic and political situation on Gold Coast, summarizing the episodes narrated by the Dane. Fuller and wider accounts of the local history are available in the recent studies cited in the notes and bibliography.

* * *

The region about which Rømer wrote was linguistically in two parts. Speakers of the Gã language (together with those of the closely related Adangbe language) occupied the most eastern stretch of the coast of Gold Coast, from James Town eastwards to Kpong. Immediately to the north and west were speakers of Akan languages, in various dialects, their numbers far outweighing those of the speakers of Gã-Adangbe. Cultural and political divisions to a large extent followed these linguistic divisions, which therefore may be considered ethnic divides. Akan-speakers, in specific dialects, were found on the coast to the west of the Gã, in the polities of Fetu and Fante, and to the north, in a number of polities of fluctuating fortunes and sizes, named below. But when Rømer writes about local behaviour patterns he is mostly describing the Gã.

At the beginning of the eighteenth century there were several powerful states on Gold Coast, all of them in the interior. From then on, and hence throughout the mid-century decades, wars of expansion occurred. It is conventional to relate these essentially to competition among the relevant nations and polities for control over trade with and on the coast. But this is partly because little is known about their earlier histories and internal power structures, and the normal degree of traditional inter-ethnic confrontation cannot, for instance, be totally ruled out. The coastal trade was twofold: a long-established domestic trade in which the salt and dried fish of the coast, articles much desired by the inland countries, were exchanged for agricultural products, cloths, and metals (gold and perhaps brass); and the more recent African-European trade generated by ocean shipping reaching the coast, a trade whose effects nevertheless stretched back far into the interior. The former trade is, inevitably, less adequately documented.

At first, Denkyira, an interior Akan polity located north of the western Gold Coast, exercised control over the supply of gold to the coast, particularly the supply to the Europeans at Elmina and Cape Coast. In 1701, however, this nation was totally defeated by Asante, another inland polity whose power was growing rapidly.[23] Following on from the subjugation of Denkyira, Asante went to war in 1717 against an ally of the former, Akyem, a wealthy gold-producing polity located somewhere NW of Gã-land. But Asante suffered a stunning defeat in this attempt.[24] Meanwhile, further to the east, another inland polity, Akwamu, also originally located to the NW of the Gã, had grown strong enough by conquests between 1677 and 1681 to take over control of the most or all of the Gã coast, and Akwamu retained suzerainty of that area until 1730.[25] The Gã had been under the overlordship of Akwamu for nearly fifty years before they were able to form an alliance with elements of the Akyem (and apparently even with some dissident Akwamu). In 1730 this alliance attacked and routed the Akwamu nucleus, driving their leaders and seemingly much of the population to what then became their new home on the eastern bank of River Volta. With Akwamu driven off, Akyem now had a measure of control over the Gã coast. But in 1742 Asante resumed its assault on Akyem and this time succeeded.

Thus, between 1681 and 1750 the Gã were successively under the notional rule of three interior polities, or, as Rømer says it, three separate peoples, the Akwamu, the Akyem and the advancing Asante. This then is the story told by Rømer — one of kaleidoscopic changes in the interior affecting the Gã coast. While in outline the story seems true enough, it is difficult now to assess the

---

[23] For the defeat of Denkyira, see K.Y. Daaku, *Trade and Politics on the Gold Coast* (1970) 66–70; J.K. Fynn, *Asante and its Neighbours* (1971) 37–9; T.C. McCaskie *State and Society in Pre-Colonial Asante* (1995) 2.

[24] Cf. Fynn (1971) 44–8; McCaskie (1995) 313, 416 and note 160. Rømer, like contemporaries, uses the term 'nation' to describe Gold Coast polities, with the disadvantage for the translator that sometimes the term is singular (Asante = 'it') and sometimes plural (Asante = 'they'). In the Introduction 'polity' is substituted but in the texts 'nation' is retained.

[25] See Tilleman [1697] (1994) 102–5. For maps showing the changes in location of Akwamu as a result of wars, see I. Wilks, 'The rise of the Akwamu empire', *Transactions of the Historical Society of Ghana* 3 (1957) 103, 110, 115, 130. See also /120/–/23/ below.

extent to which the Gã were in detail controlled by the conquerors and their behaviour influenced. What instead seems clearer is that, throughout this history, the Gã, and their cousins the Adangbe, worked to turn the competition for the coastal trade to their own advantage, by becoming brokers and middlemen for the inland peoples when they sent their gold and other commodities, including slaves, to the European forts, lodges and ships. And meanwhile, during all these upheavals and changes of fortunes the Europeans, who seldom themselves went inland, struggled to decide which side to support—or in doubt, affected neutrality—anticipating that a wrong decision would affect their trade, both in the short and the long run. This was not because the conquering Africans would cease to trade in general—the trade was too useful for total withdrawal—but lest they should then favour a European rival and competitor.

* * *

Rømer not only had long commercial experience of the Coast, a total of ten years, but he also had a close relationship with the coastal Africans. He probably took a local wife (he practically says as much),[26] enjoying a familial network as a result. His friendship with Odoi Kpoti (in the text 'Putti'), the Chief Priest and Caboceer (headman) of Labode, a Gã town near Accra, is made clear in the 1760 text, as is his nurtured acquaintance with other African leaders and merchants. The impression given is of a man who could establish rapport easily, and who was therefore as equally at ease in the world of trade as in the sphere of everyday life. There is evidence that his relationships were not simply pragmatic and ephemeral but more lasting and genuine, as indicated by a letter he wrote, a decade after his return to Denmark, sending fond greetings, accompanied by gifts, to Ashangmo, the King of Popo, and mentioning gifts sent to Caboceer 'Ursu' in Accra.[27]

Turning to Rømer's two texts, when they are compared, apart from the different focuses certain significant differences in tone appear. In 1760 Rømer portrays the European traders neatly categorised. The French were inhuman and gullible; the Dutch were coarse, totally untrustworthy, and unscrupulous; the English were such paragons of virtue as to be more than human; the Danes were pragmatic, somewhere in between the best and the

---

[26] See /246/ below. Given R.'s procreative powers, as shown by the size of his subsequent family in Denmark, it is odd that the name 'Rømer' does not appear in the Accra area today, as do very many other Danish names. However, a Rømer has been traced by Adam Jones in Christian Protten's manuscript journal, where Protten notes that he had visited 'Ferdinand Rømer's Mutter' and received a visit from 'eine Negerin, Ojeba, des Ferdinands Mutter Schwester' (Herrnhut, Archiv der Brüder-Unität, R 15 N 8.1a, 'Prottens Reise-Diarium 1756–1761', 6.11.1757, 8.11.1757). And in 1850 a Mulatto named Rømer, aged 30 and 'wounded', was listed as a pensioner of the Basel Mission station (G. Nørregård, *Guvernør Edward Carstensens Indberetninger* (1964) 387).

[27] I am indebted for this last reference to Adam Jones (Herrnhut, Archiv der Brüder-Unität, R 15 N 5/13, 27.11.1767, copy of a letter of Rømer to 'meinen Freund, Koenig bey Popo').

worst. Yet, in 1756 a more nuanced picture had been given. In the case of the French, having described the capriciousness and naiveté of French traders in general, he made a point of naming individuals — his personal friends — who deported themselves with sobriety and reason. He praises the French establishments and system in the West Indies. Writing about the Dutch, he reports on the attempts of the company directors to find ways of combating the infighting and corruption on the Coast; he reports how the Dutch bullied the Portuguese to purchase otherwise unsaleable goods; he describes the Dutch sending deserters to isolated lodges where they had to fend for themselves — and sometimes became wealthy. As for the English, he supplies a fairly detailed description of the English system of government at Cape Coast. None of this fuller information on the other European nations trading on Gold Coast appears in 1760.

The Dutch were very serious competitors in trade, receiving many more ships from Europe than the Danes did. Their Fort Crevecoeur was the closest neighbour to Christiansborg, and at times during Rømer's time on the Coast, or just prior to it, altercations between the two sets of Europeans regularly occurred, often instigated or encouraged by some of the factors.[28] A specific area of contention was the rivalry between the Danes and the Dutch over the establishment of out-stations to the east, at the mouth or on the lower course of River Volta. Since by this period the coast to the east of Gold Coast proper, known significantly as Slave Coast, provided European shippers with a large proportion of their slaves, interest in establishing forts and lodges there was strong. Furthermore, control over the navigation on a great river which allowed access into the interior — an interior which was currently imagined, quite wrongly, to be replete with exportable products — was an extremely tempting goal for both nations. Rømer and his colleagues claimed that River Volta was solely a Danish trading area, by treaty with the inhabitants.[29] Yet, despite all the opportunities for friction, Rømer has to admit that members of the Danish and the Dutch staffs were not infrequently friends. This came about the more easily because so many of the staff at the Danish forts were actually Dutchmen, indeed so many that a modern Dutch historian has referred to Rømer's colleagues as 'the so-called Danes'.[30] Moreover, when fleeing in 1745 from Governor Billsen, Rømer spent some time — exactly how much is not known — at Elmina, before returning home on a Dutch ship. At the Dutch headquarters he was allowed to peruse the company books freely, evidence of a lack of animosity between himself and the Dutch (although the latter may have nourished the hope that Rømer would now desert the Danish cause and join the rival company).

---

[28] E.g., /148/–/149/ below. See also Governor Wærøe's long list of complaints of constant, even life-threatening, harassment (CRA, V-gK, 122, 30.10.1730).
[29] See /277/–/280/ below, and Appendix B.
[30] A. van Dantzig, *The Dutch and the Guinea Coast* (1978) 239.

If Rømer exhibits something of a love/hate relationship in respect of the Dutch — and his criticism of them can be very severe — his attitude to the English was extraordinarily simple. For whatever reason, he admired the English to excess.[31] Not only were some of the English on the coast personal friends, so that he spoke highly of the English character, but he was notably sparing of criticism of the English trading system and its operation in Guinea. However, he did, in all honesty, reproach the English at Cape Coast for harbouring the heads of African warriors in a chest.[32] Perhaps the relevant factor was a belief that the English were leading the way in breaking down monopoly and opening the Guinea trade. The extent to which the Royal African Company competed on the Coast with the Danish company is not made clear because Rømer tends not to highlight it. His admiration of the English must, however, have been reciprocated, since the English agents on Gold Coast frequently urged him to come and work for them.

* * *

The present edition contains the text, in translation, of both of Rømer's writings. This is necessary because of their curious relationship. Each contains material on the Guinea companies and on the African scene, 1756 concentrating on the former and 1760 on the latter. Each contains information on each subject not to be found in the other, but the works also overlap, that is, certain topics are found in both. However, in many instances a topic is treated differently, being either fuller in 1756 than in 1760, or vice-versa. While this is understandable, it is puzzling that occasionally the two works do not agree on information. It rather looks as if, when writing his later work, Rømer forgot to check what he had said earlier. The possibility that he thought he was writing for a different readership, or alternatively that his views changed between 1756 and 1760, does not seem to meet the case, since no pattern emerges in the contradictions. In general, it has to be conceded that the writings are works of occasion and not solid treatises, much of their content falling into the category of reminiscences, with all the faults thereby. Yet they are works of significant value as sources, particularly the later work.

Efterretning was published a good ten years after Rømer's return to Denmark. We should, then, envisage Rømer as settled in Copenhagen, a successful businessman and paterfamilias, writing from notes, and from memory. He admitted that his notes were inadequate, perhaps also in disorder, and he included an appeal for further and confirmatory information from his readers. His frame of reference was ostensibly his past experience but also to some extent

---

[31] It is not known whether he had ever visited England. However, in the mid-eighteenth century English political institutions were often regarded with envy by Continental thinkers, and commended, perhaps unduly. Rømer, although not an original thinker, may have shared in the Zeitgeist.

[32] See /135/–/137/ below.

his sharing of contemporary Copenhagen, and European, mindsets. In the latter respect, the Foreword by Bishop Pontoppidan is of special interest. As noted above, Pontoppidan discountenanced trade in human beings in general but found special reasons for the continuance of the transatlantic slave trade, a major one being the condition of Africans in their home continent. On his reading of Rømer, he concluded that nothing could be more miserable or inhuman than social relations in Africa. Consequently life in the West Indies offered the African assurance of a much better condition — provided he had not been separated from his wife and children — and furthermore, he would there learn about God and His kingdom.[33] Although disagreeing fervently with the theology of the Moravian Brethren, Pontoppidan felt constrained to approve the work they did in the West Indies, producing slaves who 'neither lie, steal, rebel or do anything else evil'.[34] Whether in fact this was altogether a fair conclusion to draw from Rømer's writings is one issue. Another is whether the bishop was entirely influenced by what he read, or whether he read into the text aspects and approaches of the general European mindset, which seems plausible considering that Rømer himself did not treat of the slaves' condition in the West Indies in his writings.

A final, if largely uninvestigatable issue, is the extent to which Rømer himself wrote to the agenda of that current mindset. It is not unreasonable to suggest that Rømer's critical and condemnatory appraisal of many aspects of behaviour of Gold Coast Africans and the mores of their societies was what was expected of a respected gentleman in his new, bourgeois milieu. It might even be argued that he had accepted many of the practices he now condemned and even mocked when he was living in Gold Coast, but later, writing from a hazy, warm memory, he had regularly to pull himself up short in order to conform to the prevailing ideas in Copenhagen. This is not to say that Rømer was making a deliberate play to the gallery. He was no intellectual, probably not particularly well read, his writing was rough and rambling. But he was a shrewd businessman, and as such, an individual who automatically adjusts to the situation in which he finds himself — which, in turn, contributes to his success in business. We are dealing here with Rømer in two different worlds, and he himself describes the condition. Among the Europeans in Guinea, 'the [normal] European mildness, friendly manner of speaking, sensible behaviour, [and] innocent pastimes are totally lacking. A

---

[33] This was, of course, not a novel view, but a traditional one. The Portuguese chronicler, Zurara, writing c. 1450, balanced the lamentations of African slaves brought to Portugal against the better life they subsequently enjoyed and their Christian faith (C.R. Beazley and E. Prestage, trans. and eds., *The Chronicle of the Discovery and Conquest of Guinea* (1896), chapters 25–26).
[34] Foreword to the Reader at /16/ below. The Moravian Brethren, a pietistic movement started in 1722 in Saxony and in frequent conflict with the established Lutheran church, organised and ran a series of schools in the Danish West Indies. For a contemporary account, see C.G.A. Oldendorp, *Geschichte der Mission der evangelischen Brüdern auf den caräibischen Inseln St. Thomas, St. Croix und St. Jan* (1777), passim.

barbaric spirit, a barbaric manner of speaking, pastimes and association have instead taken over in us [Danes] and others... I should like to know if they can put aside these habits equally quickly when they return to Europe. They must certainly be able to adopt another attitude, otherwise I do not doubt there would come times in public company when they would be, if not beaten, at least ridiculed.'[35] Accommodation is the operative term.

Nevertheless, when all allowance is made for the circumstances of the production of the writings, Rømer's untypically long experience in Guinea, where the average career of a European employee at the forts was one of sickly months rather than of active years, and his senior role, particularly in contacting African notables, give his recollections special value, even if they are not to be regarded in every instance as the only possible truth.

* * *

As the few scholars who have wrestled with Rømer's writings through the years have noted, they are not of high literary quality. Terms used to describe the man and his books have included 'quaint', 'hardly reliable', 'credulous', 'hysterical'. There are indeed many statements that draw the reader up short. For example: lacking iron, the people in old Benin made tools of gold; [36] black women were raped by apes;[37] in the Qvitta area the entire population of the town went to the beach at night and all buried themselves in the sand, except for a portion of their faces, to avoid being bitten by mosquitoes;[38] a slave with pointed teeth took a bite out of the arm of another and chewed it greedily.[39] Rømer exaggerated freely, particularly with numbers (among earlier observers on Africa he was not of course alone in this). It would appear that his 'a million' simply means a great many.[40] The distances he cited in 'miles' are totally unrealistic, considering that he apparently had in mind the long Danish mile.

Given such faults, what is there to recommend the books? There is, indeed, a great deal. First, they are largely original. Although many of the topics had been mentioned by preceding writers on Gold Coast, Rømer borrows very little.[41] He makes reference, by name, several times to

---

[35] See /329/–/330/ below.
[36] See /115/ below.
[37] See /343/ below.
[38] See /298/ below.
[39] See /21/ below.
[40] For those interested in analysing numbers there is a separate listing in the index of all the places where numbers appear.
[41] This judgement and what follows relates specifically to the African aspect of the writings. As regards the general history of the various national trading companies, their detailed operation on Gold Coast, and even the internal history of the Danish company, I am not competent to assess the extent to which, if at all, Rømer drew on public sources. Not only are the printed sources often in the form of rare pamphlet literature, but the manuscript sources which he claimed to have consulted on Gold Coast are not necessarily extant.

Bosman (published in Dutch 1704, in English 1705), but mostly to take issue with him.[42] One episode related by Rømer is clearly taken from either Villault (1669), or as borrowed from Villault, from Labat (1730).[43] Otherwise there is no indication of borrowing.[44] A related reason for interest in Rømer's books is that, because they are original, they have been used by a number of later historians and their information repeated, in certain instances without acknowledgement. In particular, many stories in Reindorf (1895), often regarded as the first African historian of Gold Coast and therefore a prime source when recounting traditions, are borrowed from Rømer.[45] The evidence of much earlier collection of the particular 'traditions' may well be considered to enhance their overall veracity. But the major recommendation of these works is that, as a result of their author's length of stay on the Coast, his personal involvement with life both inside and outside the forts; his capacity for communication with acquaintances both European and Africa, and above all his genuine interest and curiosity, they contain much information not available elsewhere. This is particularly true for the information on the Gã, about whom only a limited amount has appeared in the subsequent two and a half centuries. Rømer gives us glimpses into the lives and attitudes of this people, into their customs and their inter-relationships, including the inevitable confrontations with other African groups in the vicinity; into the interdependency necessary between the Europeans and the Africans as both sides operated opportunist co-existence; and, finally into the activities—including occasional skulduggery—of the Europeans at the establishments and on the ships.

We may start with Rømer's most important source, Odoi Kpoti ('Putti'), who was both chief priest and secular head of Labode, one of the six major towns of the Gã people. Rømer was privileged in having this man as a friend, colleague, and confidant. Because of his position in Gã society Kpoti had a wealth of knowledge and experience concerning his people, their customs, their religion and, above all, their history. Rømer clearly respected him and was alert and inquisitive enough to question him on all

---

[42] William Bosman *A New and Accurate Description of the Coast of Guinea* (1705).
[43] This is the incident of 'Father Bahourd' in /3/ below, taken from either Villault (1669) 269–75; or J.B. Labat *Voyage du Chevalier des Marchais en Guinée* (1730) 324–6.
[44] It is perhaps curious that he does not borrow from a very full account of Gold Coast in Barbot (1732), a fairly recent work which one might have expected to have been on hand at the English fort where Rømer stayed, as well as available in Copenhagen. Even more curious is his neglect of the writings of two former employees of Danish companies, Müller (1673) and Tilleman (1697).
[45] C.C. Reindorf, *The History of the Gold Coast and Asante* [1895] (1966), passim; cf. Nørregård (1966), passim. Not to multiply instances of the same, I have cited Reindorf in only a proportion of the cases where he repeats Rømer's text. I would have treated Reindorf at greater length and with greater respect had I had access earlier to Paul Jenkins, ed., *The Recovery of the West African Past: African Pastors and African History in the Nineteenth Century. C.C. Reindorf and Samuel Johnson*, Basel, 1997.

manner of subjects. He has preserved the answers for posterity, as well as he could. Remembering, however, that Rømer wrote years after leaving the Coast, allowance must needs be made for lapses of memory, as well as for lacunae in the body of information. It is unlikely that the Dane anticipated writing a book when he queried Kpoti, although it is not inconceivable that on some matters he was seeking information to put into an official report. With other informants he had problems gleaning information, since some of the Africans he questioned gave it to him piecemeal and in haphazard fashion, while other refused, for various reasons, either to answer questions or to elaborate on and clarify what they had already told him.[46] Moreover, there is no indication concerning the language or languages employed in these sessions. Was it Gã, Akan, or Coast Portuguese? Was Rømer sufficiently fluent in these languages to be able to discuss abstract matters, or to pick up nuances? Was an intermediate interpreter employed? How often was the answer a response to a leading question from Rømer, and how often was the information given selected or shaped principally to please the White? In one of Rømer's anecdotes the 'fetish' was said to declaim — 'Be obedient to your Whites!' (upon which the Europeans gratefully presented the shrine with a gift of brandy). Answers to all these questions are of course not forthcoming, but the questions serve as a reminder that what Rømer writes must be received with not less than the due caution given to all historical sources. In some instances a degree of confirmation can be obtained from latter-day practice and information, in others this cannot be done.

The 1760 work, with its fuller African content, calls for further comment. While its contents tend to represent the same range of subject as do earlier printed sources, it does so more comprehensively and from a closer, more involved viewpoint. We are informed about religion, trade practices and ethnography, and given descriptions of plants and animals. History is regularly invoked, as derived both from documentary sources and from oral tradition. The oral traditions recorded in Rømer's text, often allegedly ancient, are perhaps of special interest. Appearing for the first time in print, they were not only repeated by Reindorf, frequently in Rømer's own words (although sometimes embroidered), but have been retold by the Gã since. At least in a few instances it appears that the modern Gã may have learned their traditions, via Reindorf, from Rømer. One of the most notable and tenacious of current traditions is that of Gã provenance in Benin.[47] This notion may even have been initiated by Rømer, although probably arising from his misinterpretation of something he had been told. A century and more later, repeated by Reindorf, it was fed back into oral tradition by literate Gã

---

[46] See /50/ below.
[47] See /15/–/17/, /114/–/115/ below.

reading their Reindorf.[48] But other Rømer traditions reflect reality, whether or not they directly represent it. The story of the circumcision of the Akwamu prince by the Gã king who had him in his charge for training gives an insight into cultural differences between the Gã, who practice male circumcision, and their neighbours the Akwamu who, as Akan, do not. The actual circumcision and the fatal consequences of that act — according to Rømer's telling of the tale — sound like myths, nevertheless they touch on important issues among the Gã, the court training of a prince and his participation in the ritual and rules of office. Again, Reindorf picked up this story and repeated it as tradition, this time without citing Rømer as his source.[49] Another story tells of the origin of the Akwamu. A prince from the interior, called Akwamu, having stolen the prospective bride of another notable, fled with her to Gã territory where they took refuge with the king of Accra, and there produced a family of descendants who formed the new ethnicity called Akwamu. Here we have a historical justification for a later close relationship between the Akan and Gã peoples. Rømer related the tale in the eighteenth century, and Reindorf, citing Rømer, repeated it at the end of the nineteenth century.[50]

But in certain of the episodes narrated the extent of historicity is considerable. Important historical events such as the defeat of Akwamu by Akyem and the defeat of Akyem, in turn, by Asante, events which occurred either just before or during Rømer's stay on the Coast, are well documented elsewhere. Informed by those who had participated in them, or at times from his own first-hand experience, Rømer industriously recorded details of both military and civilian contributions to these events. His friends also told him about the history of the conflicts that had occurred before their own time, identifying leaders, citing chronologies and explaining treaties. It is, however, a moot point whether the importance attached to dramatic, and even sensational reversals of fortune, in military, political and ethnic terms, genuinely represented the African concept of the past, or else, given that a European was making specific inquiries, merely a contemporary European view of how things must have been in the African past. But we must leave it to modern historians to discover the slow tides of cultural change underlying and to some extent determining more dramatic events.

Observations on the Gold Coast life of Rømer's time are not lacking. His more or less first-hand account of the power and performance of various local oracles, notably those of the Fante 'fetish' *Nananom Mpow*, provides important material for study of a religious phenomenon that was an impressively

---

[48] Cf. Reindorf [1895] (1966) 3–6/18–21; D. Henige, 'The problem of feedback in oral tradition' *Journal of African History* 14 (1973) 223–35; 'Truths yet unborn' *Journal of African History* 23 (1982) 405–11.
[49] Reindorf [1895] (1966) 20/32–3; cf. /117/–/120/ below.
[50] Reindorf [1895] (1966) 13/25; see also /116/–/117/ below.

social force until its decline in the later nineteenth century.⁵¹ Another well-nigh unique set of observations relates to the tales of *Ananse*, their social expression, and their propagation of myths of origin. Where other writers ignored a commonplace activity, or at best ridiculed it, Rømer invites us to an evening performance of one of the *Ananse* stories, providing a description that could have been written today since that type of theatre is still very much alive.⁵² In another instance, Rømer describes certain rituals and associated customs relating to the chief Gã annual festival, *Hɔmɔwɔ*, which are strikingly similar to those still practised today.

Turning to African-European relations, Rømer is untypically frank about the most intimate. Miscegeny, though everywhere and always practised by Europeans on the Coast, as a domestic as well as a sexual necessity, was not a subject for discussion by other Europeans writing about Africa, who either looked the other way, or mentioned it with distaste.⁵³ Rømer's attitude is refreshing in his honest treatment of the practice and its implications.⁵⁴ He pointed out not only how widespread it was but enumerated the advantages and disadvantages for both partners, the European men and the African women. Then, having mentioned the fact that, on certain conditions the marriages would be considered bona fide by the Bishop of Copenhagen, he closes that section with the statement, 'each one of our nation has his mistress' — and he does not add, 'apart from myself'.⁵⁵

Rømer's reports on the marine trade are important. Commerce was, after all, his reason for being on Gold Coast. He clearly showed a talent in conducting trade, and there is no doubt of his overriding interest. An expert businessman, time and time again he tried to persuade the company to avail itself of his expertise and change its system. His detailed references to both the trade in gold and the trade in slaves, their organization and commercial value, together with his suggestions for changes in each, carry much authoritative weight.

Like any honest person, Rømer's views were sometimes uncertain and could therefore be ambivalent. Occasional unease can be detected. Thus, he comments approvingly that some slaves coming into European hands had been obtained by the Akyem king by purchase rather than by seizure, although this was of course to ignore that in the first instance many of them had been seized. He noted, with some relief, that the Europeans could

---

⁵¹ See /84/–/85/ below; T.C. McCaskie '*Nananom Mpow* of Mankessim: an essay in Fante history', in D. Henige and T.C. McCaskie, eds., *West African Economic and Social History* (1990) 133–50.
⁵² See /152/–/157/ below.
⁵³ Miscegeny of course took a particular form on Gold Coast as almost all the Europeans were male. However, male sexual relations with local foreign women were nothing new, having been standard with seamen and soldiers, no doubt since the beginning of time. It was therefore otiose for Europeans to comment censoriously on miscegeny on Gold Coast.
⁵⁴ See /245/–/248/ below.
⁵⁵ See /246/ below.

now be called mere tradesmen, able 'with good conscience, [to] carry out our commission, while, in earlier times we were called 'fences' and accomplices to murder and robbery'.[56] Again, although presenting a case for legalized miscegeny and proposing a plan for educating the children resulting from mixed unions, he did not hesitate to term all the African partners 'mistresses'.[57] In a trade context, he conformed to normal practice and frequently referred to the captives as 'goods'. Undoubtedly Rømer sometimes reports in a demeaning manner on Gold Coast religious ideas and practices, yet at other times he speaks of them without comment, even when one might have expected an ironic remark. Hence, it is often in his omissions that we sense ambivalence. A stance he shared with other Europeans was to deplore the bloody wars between Africans, affirming them highly disruptive of trade — while on the other hand admitting the self-interested benefit, in that they could provide a flood of slaves for sale to the shippers. A further glimpse is afforded by the poem at the beginning of the 1760 text — surprisingly, a harangue rather than a plaudit. He had requested his friend and colleague, Carl Engmann, with whom he had worked for several years at Christiansborg, to write an introductory poem for the book, and after he had read the text Engmann complied and wrote of the warmth of their friendship. But he reminded Rømer, in rhetorical anger, of the promise they had made each other that when they returned to Denmark they would not write about certain of their experiences in Africa. Yet Rømer had done just this. Although it is not clear which experiences Engmann had in mind it cannot be said that the reference to the author is altogether complimentary. Notwithstanding this assault, Rømer published the poem, apparently unaltered. He did, however, rebut the criticism at the end of the last chapter citing the encouragement of 'a patron and learned gentleman' — meaning Pontoppidan — 'to serve the public here, and perhaps in other places'.[58] Rømer was honest, with a readiness to concede his imperfections, limitations and failures, over against the achievements, efforts and good intentions claimed in the text.

* * *

A word about the translation and scholarly apparatus. The Danish text is at times awkward and even obscure and the translation cannot be guaranteed at every point. However, difficult passages and terms have been noted in the

---

[56] See /169/ below.
[57] There may, in fairness, have been a problem in terminology. While with the church's permission some African partners could be considered 'wives' — or at least 'temporary wives', since almost all Europeans hoped in the end to return home, to existing or future European wives — it is by no means certain that even these women were regarded by the African societies as 'wives' in the same sense as wives of Africans, where the union involved property and social complexities inapplicable to relatively short-term unions with Europeans.
[58] See /346/.

original language. These and other editorial insertions are in square brackets. All round brackets are Romer's. Because the texts are imperfectly written and organized, and obscure in places, for clarity the original sentences are often divided and the paragraphing adjusted. The style of eighteenth century writing is not that of modern writing, and Romer's sHghtly crabbed style increases the differences. While the translation has been kept as close to the original as possible, it adopts style and language which conveys to the modern reader what Romer is endeavouring to communicate, rather than a hteral word-for-word sequence.

The original pagination of both texts is inserted in double slashes /-/ and in bold type, thus /78/. In the notes, reference to the texts is always to this original pagination (and not to the pagination of the present volume). The pagination of the 1760 work is indicated by, e.g. /78/-/V9/, usually followed by 'above' or 'below'. Citation of the 1756 work states '1756' and then merely repeats the original page number, e.g. 1756, 78.

The original texts are in gothic script, with italic for toponyms and bold face for personal names. These typeface variants have been dropped, as has the capitahzation of nouns. Instead, Romer's Danish terms when untranslated or noted, and all other foreign terms, including those in African languages, are in italic. Four frequent terms, **Negere, Sorte, Invaanere, Naturellerne,** have been translated respectively 'Negroes', 'Blacks', 'inhabitants', 'natives'; and initial capitals have been given to Whites, Blacks, and Mulattos. General toponyms have been reproduced in their modern form and spelling. But ethnonyms (which do not necessarily represent the modern look-ahke equivalents) have been kept in Romer's form, although on first introduction the look-alike equivalent is normally added in square brackets. In certain African terms special characters appear, as is the current usage in modern Ghanaian languages, having been introduced in the 1920s to replace characters with accents (these being disliked by printers). Readers may care to note that the backward c (o) is sounded as 'aw' in 'law'; the epsilon character (s) as the 'e' in 'get'; the elongated 's' (J) as 'sh'.

The placing of footnotes has raised problems because events are mentioned in widely dispersed locations; and long asides of great import often interrupt chronological narratives. Limited cross-referencing is supplied, but for minor topics reference needs to be made to the Index. Dates for archival references are given numerically, as day/month/year. The scholarly apparatus concentrates on the African aspects of the text and does not attempt to deal in any detail with the history of the European companies, whether at home or on Gold Coast. Although Romer has understandably much to say about the Dutch, Enghsh and Danish companies, and the present editor could justify or is perhaps likely to have available. As a result the annotation on the 1756 work, which concentrates on the companies, is somewhat limited.

* * *

ACKNOWLEDGEMENTS

A critical translation of Rømer's works could not be accomplished by one person. The language can be difficult, the range of subjects wide; the type of information often obscure. It has been my privilege and pleasure to have friends and colleagues who gave unstintingly of their expertise whenever I cried out (usually electronically) for help.

Archival sources present a problem when access is limited by geography. Two travel grants made it possible for me to spend time at the National Archives in Copenhagen — but never enough. However, I was fortunate in having Erik Gøbel as a life-line to those archives. Per Hernæs provided much material that he had photocopied, and Finn Fuglestad made available to me a collection of excerpts which, again, Per Hernæs had transcribed and typed in the roman alphabet, a great time-saver.

Always available were the African historians Adam Jones, René Baesjou, Stanley Alpern and Ivor Wilks, the last-named a scholar to whom Rømer was an 'old friend'. They were quick to respond and provided me with invaluable material. For aid and advice in linguistics I am deeply indebted to Mary Esther Kropp Dakubu and Seth Allotey, and for ethnographic material on the Gã I thank Irene Odotei. On zoology assistance was always forthcoming from Alan Tye, and on geography from Daniel Hopkins, while Millicent Cobblah commented on entomology. For Scandinavian maritime history and related matters I thank Johan Kloster. Karsten Bundgaard provided me with much biographical material, and Leif Svalesen gave me photographs. Christopher Tabor made the map for me.

I wish to express special thanks to the librarians who hunted tirelessly for sources; Nancy Frank and Frøydis Haugan at the Ethnographic Museum and Svein Helge Birkefelt at the School of Theology, both in Oslo; also Hans Jørgen Hinrup at the Research Library in Aarhus.

Financial support and aid were indispensable to this project and I am deeply indebted to the Translations Program of the National Endowment for the Humanities (NEH) of the U.S.A., for one year's salary support. Several trips to Ghana and Copenhagen for research were made possible by two travel grants, one from The Norwegian Institute for Comparative Research in Human Culture, and a second from The Norwegian Non-fiction Writers and Translators Association.

My son, Peer Winsnes, was always on hand to help out when technology failed me.

Finally, and most of all, I must thank Paul Hair, who, as advisor and informal copy editor, has spent countless and wearing hours as a mentor and guide, explaining, arguing, listening — as we both practised international 'e-mail', learning of its joys and disappointments. He succeeded at last, by pleas and threats, in making me write finis to a work that began to appear unending.

Selena Axelrod Winsnes
Rælingen, Norway
31 March 1999

A RELIABLE ACCOUNT OF THE COAST OF GUINEA (1760)

conflated with

A RELIABLE ACCOUNT OF TRADE ON THE COAST OF GUINEA (1756)

by Ludewig Ferdinand Rømer

[Verse addressed to L.F. Rømer by C.E. Engmann][1]

Betænk, hiertelskte Ven!
    Hvad i Guinea mig
Du lovet har, igien
    See Du erindrer Dig
Det Forset, samme Tiid
    Af Dig betænkt var fattet,
Jeg havde dertil Liid,
    Og Dig lyksalig skattet.

Men, ach! mit Haab jeg seer,
    Desværre svækket er,
Det jeg ey ventet skeer,
    Du Ord ey holdte her.
Af de Forandringer
    Du udi Hedenskabet
Har seet, hvor Sandhed er
    Af Løgnen efterabet.

Du paa en salig Viis
    Dig saadan Lærdom tog,
At Sandhed holdte Priis,
    Og intet Dig Bedrog,
Ved saadant lovede
    Du altid fast at blive,
Og aldrig lade see
    Forandring her i Live.

Remember, my beloved friend,
    what in Guinea.
you promised me. Now
    take care to recall
the resolution made by you
    at that time.
I believed you then,
    And held you in high esteem.

But, oh, I see my hopes
    sadly impaired,
What I did not expect has happened.
    You did not keep your word.
Among those aberrations
    which you in heathendom
have seen, are those where Truth
    is mimed by Lies.

By divine providence you
    were granted the knowledge
to set great store by Truth
    and not be misled.
And you promised
    to be firm,
and never in your life
    falter in this resolve.

[1] Carl Gustav Engmann, a Swede, was the Governor at Christiansborg Castle 1742–1757, and Director of the Guinea Company 1766–1769. He was originally sent to the Coast as a surgeon, but his astuteness in trade led him to concentrate his energies in that area. Among other things he improved the Castle and built the famous cistern still visible today. He and Rømer were close friends, and, having discussed the matter of what they should or should not make public of things they had seen and experienced during their service, had obviously agreed to keep discreetly to themselves a number of matters. But exactly what is unclear. If the discretion applied mainly to activities on the part of Africans (cf. verse 2), could it be that what was being objected to was R.'s acceptance of the reality of a supernatural element in African fetish? In these heathen practices 'Truth is mimed by Lies'. That is, they are really fake. An alternative view is that Engmann was upset, perhaps more generally, by R. describing the sexual and other foibles of previous governors, whose relatives might still be alive and prominent in Denmark. Engmann stayed on at Christiansborg for eight years after Rømer left, and the latter may have written much, or all, of the book while Engmann was still in Africa. The poem, although commissioned by Rømer, while declaring lasting friendship clearly berates Rømer for having broken his promise by writing about matters the two of them had decided should be kept from the public. Most remarkable is the fact that Rømer, nonetheless, included the poem in his book. He makes a manner of apology at the end of the book /346/, admitting the earlier promise made, but falling back on Pontoppidan's 'urging' him to publish the book as it was. I am indebted to Sverre Øygarden for helping me with translating the Danish text of the poem.

Med saadant Dig og mig
    Jeg gratulerede,
Og ventet visselig
    Den beste Frugt at see,
Du loved', aldrig meer
    Sligt Galskab paa at tænke.
Men, ach! mit Haab jeg seer
    Mig tvungen at indskrænke.
	Therefore I congratulated
	    you and myself,
	And expected so certainly
	    to see the finest fruits.
	You promised never more
	    to think on such madness.
	But, alas!, I see myself
	    forced to quench my hopes.

Du, paa Tilskyndelse
    Af Venner, noget skrev,
Mens, uforvarende,
    Fortrydeligt det blev,
Thi, skiønt ey nogen Tiid
    Man Sandhed bør forglemme,
Saa bør man dog med Fliid
    Den undertiden giemme.
	On the urging
	    of your friends, you wrote
	Of things which - unintentionally -
	    were most blameworthy,
	for even if one should never
	    forget the truth,
	yet one should, at times,
	    conceal it.

Jeg veed, der mange I
    Forkeerte Verden leve,
Meer, end endogsaa vi
    Beskrive kand med Breve,
Men! mon ey samme skeer
    Endog i beste Lande?
Jo! meget meget meer,
    End burde troes for sande.
	I know that many [things] exist in
	    a mad world,
	more than you or I can
	    describe in words.
	Yet, who knows, perhaps the same is so
	    In even the finest of lands?
	Indeed, much, much more so than
	    we could believe to be true.

Her mine Tanker seer
    Du da, som Du begierer,
Jeg kand ey skrive meer,
    Viid, jeg Dig have kiær.
Hold Dine Løfter! Nu
    Jeg ey vil meer skrive
Kom stedse det ihu
    Som os til (Lyst) (Gavn) kand blive.
	Here you read my thoughts,
	    as you yourself desired.
	I can write no more.
	    Know that I hold you dear.
	Keep your promises. Now
	    I shall write no more.
	Remember always those things
	    which can be (pleasing) (gainful) to us.[2]

Carl Gustav Engmann

---

[2] Alternative adjectives are placed thus, in brackets, within the text. Presumably either Engmann could not decide which to present, or the printer could not decipher what Engmann wrote.

Foreword: To the Reader[1]

One of the advantages of latter-day times, it is particularly considered, is that the inhabitants of the world have come to know one another better than they did formerly. It is true that they all had their origin in Adam, and, later, Noah, and according to the words of the Apostles all the people living on the surface of the earth are of one blood. The size and bounds of the living space of each of them were determined by God, but in the course of time, and by constant emigration, the first family's descendants have spread, in many branches, in all directions, with such differences in language, customs, and ways of living that most nations have become complete strangers, and alien to one another. A few thousand years ago, the most advanced peoples knew only little about their neighbours, and as near as nothing about all the rest. Not until the conquests of Alexander the Great did even the wise Greeks learn about Persia and India, as well as, in the times following — also through campaigns of war — did they learn about Africa, Italy and Spain. As for the rest of Europe, for a long time the inhabitants had a sadly incorrect and confused idea, as seen everywhere in their literature, about the Hyperbores [Far North], the people and lands which lay north of the Alps and the Riphaean Mountains.

Yet that was no wonder, considering the extremely few opportunities which existed formerly for contact, commercial intercourse and trade with distant countries. The invention of the compass, having made voyages by sea easier, has enriched the world, if not merely by costly metals and by means of enjoying life (which in certain aspects must be reckoned as impoverishing the world), yet with a richer knowledge and understanding about life in countless foreign countries, in natural and human affairs. Thus the Great Master's wise and mighty dispositions have become very much better known to us Europeans, and this has also increased our desire to discover the unknown, which is still probably the greater part of these dispositions.

The unknown can especially refer to that part of the world commonly called Africa. If we except those parts which border on the Mediterranean Sea, namely Egypt and the so-called Barbary shores, our knowledge of the

---

[1] The writer of the Foreword was Erik Pontoppidan (1698–1764), a professor of theology and by 1760 a leading figure in the Lutheran church of Denmark-Norway. His interests and writings were not confined to religious matters and he published extensively on history, geography, natural history and education. While Bishop of Bergen he published his *Glossarium Norvagicum*. In 1755 he became pro-chancellor of the University of Copenhagen, and in 1763–1781 he produced, in seven volumes, a basic geographical work, *Den danske atlas*. His catechism was still in use in Norway until recently.

remainder is not nearly as full as is our still incomplete knowledge of America, a country which was discovered only two hundred and fifty years ago. But since America is less wide and long, as well as being cut through by a number of inlets and rivers, we have visited there and had more opportunity to learn about it. Furthermore, its rivers are more convenient for sailing than are the broad and everywhere interlocked ones in Africa. In Africa lie lands which are far larger than any European country, yet all we know of them are their names, and of those, again, only the common, descriptive names. We know as little about them as about that distant *terra incognita australis* [unknown southern continent], which we assume, purely by deduction, to be situated near the South Pole, and which we must leave to our descendants to discover.

Yet it is surprising that the innermost or most central part of Africa is still hidden from us, given that the seacoasts have been visited by European ships for three hundred years — and not just calling here and there — so that the coasts have become somewhat familiar to us. This is especially the case with regard to the Guinea coasts, because of the [printed] reports of Bellefond, Bosman and other travellers.[2]

What we know about the Guinea Coast has now been enlarged and improved by the pen of Mr. Rømer, in the present work which is both remarkable and reliable. This good man, today one of our most esteemed and most valuable citizens, lived there for several years as a trader and official in the service of the former Company, and has now taken the opportunity to record numerous observations about certain matters that appear most strange and wondrous but were least remarked upon by other writers. Once returned to our Fatherland, he took upon himself the trouble of writing a draft, yet only for his own recollection and the enjoyment of some private friends. Hence, he paid little attention to the order in which things were presented — something not expected, either, in what the French call *Mémoires*. The draft concentrated on the information of interest to himself and his friends, rather than on the method or the order of presentation. He was kind enough to entrust his text to me for perusal, and I persuaded him to have it published, since there were many truly strange observations concerning, in part, the study of nature; in part, the history of the wars of those distant barbaric nations, their customs, superstitions, and means of sustenance; and in part, also, information about the other Europeans there, as well as about the trade and conditions of our Danes on that particular Guinea coast.

---

[2] Pontoppidan is referring to two specific works: Nicolas Villault, sieur de Bellefond, *Relation des Costes d'Afrique appelllées Guinée* (Paris, 1669; English translation 1670), and Willem Bosman, *Nauwkeurige beschryving van de Guinese Goud-, Tand- en Slave-kust* (Utrecht, 1704; English translation 1705). Villault had voyaged along the Guinea coast in 1666–1667, but Bosman, a merchant who worked for the Dutch Company and lived on Gold Coast 1688–1702, was not a 'traveller'.

As regards the last topic, a few years ago Mr. Rømer, without his mentioning it here, provided us with a useful little treatise under the title *Adskillige Folkes Handel paa Kysten Guinea og i Vest-Indien* [The Trade of the Various Nations on the Guinea Coast and in the West Indies].[3] This first work of his received such a good reception among many Danish readers that a German translation of it was published immediately. Both nations then found themselves much better informed than previously about these matters, but they also wished that the author's intention had taken him somewhat further, and that he had supplied us with information concerning a number of other things, such as the [state of the] country and the inhabitants of the Guinea coast.

The degree of public interest, together with the urging of several friends, has convinced our author that he should please readers with the present assortment of observations, which, as I said before, were written as reminiscences for his own pleasure. I consider that this was a good decision, since it rarely happens that any of those who have stayed on the coast only for the purpose of trade so decide, or take such trouble as he has done, both before and after his homecoming, which took place in the year 1744.[4] Since that time the Danish Guinea trade has changed much, and has, we hope, been improved following the dissolution of the Company and the opening of trade to all of our seafarers who now industriously travel there, especially in respect of the trade in slaves which is necessary for our colonies on St. Croix and the other [West Indies] islands.

As for the last-mentioned matter, namely the slave trade, which Mr. Rømer also to a certain extent discusses, we must reflect seriously on it when we consider the moral aspect. It might seem that the spirit of Christianity would not permit the practice of trade in human beings created, just as we are, in the image of God, and redeemed by the same great Broker between God and Man. The opportunity for my plucking on this string has arisen because I know that a certain Christian-minded person of rank recently revealed his serious doubts about contributing anything to the progress of that trade unless, at the same time, trouble was taken to offer those poor African slaves in the West Indies some form of advantage that could balance the hardship inflicted on them by carrying them so far away from

---

[3] In fact, the title of the work published at Copenhagen 1756 and included in its entirety in the present edition is *Tilforladelig Efterretning om Negotien paa Kysten Guinea, Af hvilke Nationer den drives, og paa hvilken Maade den er indretted af enhver Nation især, tilligemed Uforgribelige Betænkninger, hvorledes vor Negotie derhen og til Vestindien, bedre kunde indrettes* (A Reliable Account of Trade on the Coast of Guinea and the Nations trading there, and in what Manner it is practised by each Nation in particular, together with humble Suggestions about how Our Trade there and to the West Indies could be improved). Presumably Pontoppidan was citing the title from memory and was deliberately summarizing it.

[4] Rømer returned home briefly in 1744, to clear his name of accusations made by Governor Billsen. He returned after a few months, in 1745, and stayed on the Coast until 1749. See Appendix B.

their Fatherland. Hence more attention must be paid to their immortal souls, and we must seek, by teaching them Christianity, to help them approach somewhat closer the bounds of the kingdom of God.

Truly the greatest Christian law is love, and the first degree of love is equal treatment. Yet equal treatment forbids us to change the status of an inferior to a poorer or worse condition, unless, at the same time, we can provide him with an equally great or a greater advantage. When the matter is thus considered, I agree with the complaint of that Christian person, but, on the other hand, there are two important things to be remembered. First, that the condition of the Guinea slaves in their own land, at least as regards their physical condition, is so very miserable that it cannot be much worse — it is insecure and inhuman because they steal, mistreat, indeed murder one another, as Mr. Rømer reveals, so that nations are nearly wiped out, and the entire land will soon be quite deserted. Consequently, I feel that that the Negro who is transported to the West Indies, as long as he is not separated from his wife and children, will be far less miserable, as well as far more secure concerning his life and sustenance. His condition is not made worse, unless by chance because of a bad owner, since a sensible owner would care for his Negro just as he cares for his money.

The second important thing is this. Provided these heathens do not hear or observe much that is scandalous on the part of the Christian gentlemen, most of them will come to a better understanding of God and His kingdom. Thus they will be liberated in Christ, even though servants of man. Our most merciful king, here too not wishing to be lacking in paternal concern, has sent out, at his own cost, ten or more catechists and school masters, whose main purpose will be to implant the knowledge of Christ in those heathen planting sugar. Whether they have succeeded, God alone knows.

In my opinion it is enough that, at least there, if not in their own fatherland, the Negroes approach the Light. I might add that the so-called Moravian Brethren [of Herrnhut] — of whose utterances and behaviour in Europe I can in no way approve — apparently have deserved the gratitude and praise of many who have been eye-witnesses to their work as evangelists in America, and particularly in St. Croix.

You might say that that their kind of antinomian gospel, often preached here in such a way that the evangelical call gives offence, as it did during the Reformation — indeed, I may say, as early as the time of St. Paul — would abolish the law governing Communion, so that the latter state would frequently be worse than the former.[5] I answer that this was also my fear,

---

[5] The pietistic enthusiasm of the Moravian Brethren, with less concern for the traditional structures of the Lutheran Church, was often considered by traditionalists to encourage social anarchy. The antinomian doctrine re-emphasised good works, albeit only as the fruits of redemption, but their opponents accused them of substituting good works for divine grace and election, and therefore reverting to the supposed theological defects of the medieval Church (p.c. P.E.H. Hair).

until I conversed with some of our brave Christians who had returned from the West Indies, and who were not precisely Herrnhuter-minded gentlemen. To my surprise, I was assured that, regardless of how the Herrnhuters act or do not act in other places, in St. Croix they produce far greater and more recognizable fruit than is seen in parishes elsewhere which have orthodox teachers. And since even among the wildest and coarsest Negro slaves, who in their own land appear to have lost all humanity, one finds a great many examples of honest and permanent turning to Christ Himself, it behoves us to follow His example and follow the rule (when He referred to prophets) that 'By their fruits ye shall know them'.[6] Then we must acknowledge the truth, praise God, and admit that in many normal parishes one does not often find so many blessed fruits of the ministry as among the slaves in those Danish colonies. This, among other things, may serve as proof that many a gentleman and farmer out there, who by his life-style shows that he and his household do not fear God, and truly does not love or care for the Herrnhuters for the sake of God, nevertheless loves them for another reason, namely his own temporal advantage, just as Laban loved in Jacob a happy and useful domestic servant.[7] One master prefers these Brothers on his plantation rather than any other ministers, since they convert his slaves to Christianity, with the result that, from that time on, they do not lie, steal, rebel, or do anything else evil, but become their master's most competent and best workers. This is a testimonial which I am pleased to present on this occasion — stating the truth impartially and with frankness, and as proof I quote those brave men now [returned and] living here. If any doubt their testimony, I can only say that it honours God alone.[8]

From this chance, but not unserviceable, digression I come back to Mr. Rømer's text concerning the coast of Guinea and the things there which deserve attention. These are certainly many, and a lover of knowledge about the world, especially of the study of nature, will find much which he did not know, or, at least, had not believed to be so. The information is assuredly reliable, based as it is on Mr. Rømer's own extensive experience. But instead of my dwelling on this (especially since the author presents the information clearly enough to give the discriminating reader ample food for thought), I would rather use a few lines — which in a Foreword may yet be justifiable — in order to explain the meaning of a term which often appears in this text, but being only quoted might leave some uncertainty in the mind of the reader as regards its true meaning. The term is used very frequently, and the observations referring to it are difficult to understand,

---

[6] Matthew 7:16.
[7] Genesis, chapters 29–30.
[8] The same sentiments as those of Pontoppidan had been earlier expressed in print by John (Jean) Barbot. But Barbot regretted that in the West Indies the Protestant powers had not carried out this Christian duty as thoroughly as the Roman Catholic ones had done (J. Barbot, *Barbot on Guinea* [1732] (1992) 550–3).

since the author does not expound the meaning each time. Furthermore, as employed the term varies in meaning in different contexts.

The word is *Fetis*. It belongs, not to the language of the Africans, but to that of the Portuguese, since the latter appeared on these coasts, as well as on those of India, before any other foreign nation, and with their authority established their language. Because it was found to be far easier for all the Europeans to learn Portuguese as a common and useful language everywhere on the coasts [rather than the local languages], it is still commonly employed, even after the Portuguese [have been replaced]. However, the term is now often used in a way which gives it a totally different meaning, one far beyond its original definition. It is made to serve in many contexts where it has a somewhat distant semantic relationship to the original meaning, indeed one far removed. Also, there are a number of other and more suitable terms used by the inhabitants of the land, for instance, the word *Wong,* denoting God Himself.[9] However, in the mouth of the European the common word *Fetis* must serve for many uses, even when it only vaguely fits the use.

The term in question is *fetis*, correctly *fedes,* from the Latin *fides* ['faith'].[10] The term is used to signify not only belief or trust in something invisible, but also the invisible Great Being himself, of whom Cicero says that the concept has captured the most savage nations.[11] When, then, their *fetis* priests and priestesses claim that they receive answers from God about things which people wish to know, they call their supposed oracles by the same name, and the images of their idols as well. Moreover, according to an explanation which I have requested from Mr. Rømer, *fetis* means every act of worship of a god or form of religion, indeed everything which can be said to belong to religion in any way at all.[12] For instance, when a Negro goes into a field to do whatever it was that the *fetis* priest ordered him to do, be it to pound a sacred pole into the earth and bind raffia around it, or to place a sacrifice of an egg or something else for the idol, it is expressed as 'He has gone off to make *fetis*'. In the same way, he keeps a *fetis* day, which is a holy day. And in the same way, this or that animal is *fetis*—it is holy and must not

---

[9] The Gã term *wong* 'spirit, god' is not given as such by Rømer, but might be deduced from the name *Giemawong* (Chapter 3, /58/, below).

[10] Pontoppidan was wrong. 'Fetish' is actually from Medieval Portuguese *feitiço* 'fashioned, man-made' (the modern meaning 'magic spell, etc' influenced by 'fetish'), ultimately from Latin *facere* 'to make, etc', via *factitius* 'man-made, artificial'.

[11] *Nemo omnium gentium tam est immanis, cujus mentem non imbuerit Deorum opinio,* 'No one in the world is so barbaric that the concept of gods has not penetrated his mind' (Cicero, *Tusculanae disputationes*, I, chapter 13) (p.c. Gunn Haaland).

[12] It should be understood that there are separate terms in all African languages, as in all European languages, for each aspect and item of religious devotion. In this period, however, Europeans tended to lump together all references to African religious belief and practice under the head of 'fetish', and Africans conversing with Europeans in European languages or in pidgins tended to accept the simplification, perhaps not caring to apprise the aliens of sacred terms.

be killed lest it bring great offence to God. The Negro wears a decoration in his hair or around his arms or legs, be it of beads, elephant hair, horns of certain small animals, or other dubious things — all these are considered to be sacred objects, or a kind of phylactery, which will preserve him from evil and must therefore be preserved and defended even at the cost of his life. Yet they themselves freely make changes in this *festis*, often, and wear now one, now another, absurd object, especially in their hair on their heads, which always must have something or other hanging from it. If asked what it, is they answer that it is *fetis*, and a European expects no further explanation, as if the Black is not capable of explaining the secret which he blindly believes lies in it.

The most permanent *fetisses* are the poles which are found pounded down into the ground in their houses or outside the doors, and there they must stay, bound around with raffia, until they rot. If a European wants to break that pole, or remove some of the raffia, likewise if he wants to tear from the Negro's head the small things hanging there, it would be seen as an act of violence and unjust, and hence as provocative as if the Negro were being threatened with a drawn sword. He must defend his *fetis* with all his might, since he believes that there is a kind of bond between himself and his *fetis*, and that when it is destroyed it will be the end of him.

It was briefly mentioned above that the sacrifice which is set out for the spirit, be it hens, chickens, eggs or other things, is also called *fetis*. No Negro dares to eat these sacrifices, but our people often do. If they inquire whether the patient or supplicant will tolerate the Europeans treating themselves to their sacrifices, the Negroes answer that it is enough that they had done the bidding of the *fetis* — the *fetis* knew that it was there and he knew that your people would take it, [otherwise,] why did he not come and take it himself? For them, moreover, it is extremely blasphemous to eat the *fetis*. This is done [only] by an accused individual in trials involving very serious offences — to offer [to eat] an egg on [the outcome of] a case means to call God to witness the individual's innocence. This is no different [from the practice of] superstitious Christians, who, in earlier times, misused the Holy Communion as a *juramentum purgatorium* [purgatory oath]. Thus, to eat *fetis* to prove the truth of a case is to claim it with all one's might.

As far as Mr. Rømer has been able to discover, after many years of contact, this *fetis* practice alone represents the religion of those poor people. About their oracles or divine answers, given in the *fetis* hut, and the wicked abominations practised there, he reports in his text as much as he could say with certainty. The young, perverted Negroes were willing to tell him a load of absurdities about these matters, especially when he gave them a glass of brandy as payment. Their stories would then continue endlessly until he had to ask them to stop. If he wanted to hear something not quite as absurd it had to be from an old Negro who had been a friend of the Company for a long time. One of the latter sort was offended, wondering greatly why certain Europeans often went to the *fetis* hut and asked about future and secret things. His words to the author of this text were approximately as follows: 'we Blacks have, from time immemorial, submitted to the yoke of the *fetis* and there we must remain. But why would those who come from another country, and have lived long without the *fetis*, submit to him?'[13]

In matters of religion, a Negro is not concerned about the opinions of others. Even less would he try to convince others to believe and accept his own opinion. If you ask him [about anything], he answers so briefly and in such a way that you realize that previously he has not given much thought to the matter. A Danish priest, newly arrived in Guinea, had as a servant one of the Blacks who spoke Danish well. The priest gave a talk to several Negroes, using this servant as his interpreter. After the talk had lasted a long time, but the Negroes had not been given brandy, they impatiently left and told the interpreter (as Mr. Rømer who had his room next door, heard): 'Another time you must warn us when the priest does not have brandy so that we will not have to sit here with dry mouths and listen to his chatter.'[14] Such little taste, desire, or willingness to learn leaves no hope that these poor people, in the depths of superstition and blinded by it, would receive the richer offer of truth even if it were done in their own land and according to their customary way of life.

The disorder of these nations, and their uncertainty and coarse barbaric form of life, are among the main truths which, along with many others, are perfectly revealed in the following pages, the reading of which will without doubt please many others as they have pleased me. Moreover, in my mind they have renewed the great truth that heathendom is in fact more wretched than the very poorest degree of Christianity, and that even where the Gospel, both in learning and way of life, is the very farthest away from its possible truth and degree of purity, yet it acts far better than heathendom in respect of man's morality and earthly bliss. I shall not speak here of the eternal blessedness which God desires for all His sensible creatures, and offers earlier to some, later to others, but leave it to Him alone Who judges rightly and is unfair to no one. This boundlessly good God who wants all people to be blessed, also wants them first to come to a recognition of that truth, and allows none of those who read this work to be ignorant of personal blessedness — having been born and brought up in Christianity — or to be ignorant of his duties to strive worthily after a mightier mission and a brighter light.

Written in Copenhagen 3 April, 1760
Erik Pontoppidan

---

[13] The statement about the young telling interminable tales, and the quotation at the end of the paragraph, do not appear in R.'s texts, so presumably came from conversations Pontoppidan had with Rømer.

[14] This again must have come from conversations since it does not appear in the texts.

A Reliable Account of the Coast of GUINEA

Containing a
DESCRIPTION

1	Of the Coast in general	1
2	Of the Trade of the European Nations	23
3	Of the Religion of the Negroes	49
4	Of the History, Customs, and Way of Life of the Negroes	107
5	Of us Danes, our Forts, and our Establishments	249

by

Ludewig Ferdinand Rømer

Copenhagen
Printed by the Widow of Ludolph Henrich Lillie
1760

Chapter 1

About the Guinea Coast in general

The greatest part of Africa, one of the four continents of the world, was unknown in early times before the 14th century, when the Spaniards discovered the so-called New World, and the Portuguese the African coasts. Bartolomeu Diaz, a Portuguese, was the first, who, with the help of the improved compass, sailed past the Cape of Good Hope, an event which occurred in the year 1487. He was followed by Vasco de Gama, who reached East India, or, at any rate, took possession of the most important coasts. Finally, the Dutch were the first to sail around Africa, /2/ thus showing all the other Europeans an easier and shorter route to East India than the one which had been known earlier.[1]

The Pope [blank] divided the entire world into two parts, and the dividing line was the *Linea Longitudinis* [line of longitude], which passes over the Peak of Tenerife. He gave all that lay west of this *Linea* to the Spaniards, and what lay east to the Portuguese. These two nations followed different rules in their new dominions. The Spaniards murdered all the nations whom they found in their presumed property and papal gift; the Portuguese, on the other hand, let them live. We know that the former still own the greatest part of the conquered lands which they acquired in earlier times in such a detestable manner, yet to no profit or use, either for the Europeans or for the Spaniards established in the New World. The Portuguese, however, who dealt leniently with their new subjects, kept their properties to themselves for barely a half century. Apart from a few places, they were driven out of Africa and Asia by the inhabitants, with the help of other Europeans. What they now have in their possession [in those continents] is of no importance, since we know that it is only Brazil that makes them richer than other nations, but by no means happier. /3/ I have read authors who have found fault with the Portuguese for not having treated their subjugated people and countries in the same

---

[1] In the first few paragraphs of the book R. attempts to set the scene by giving a very general historical background. His presentation is not only confused and occasionally contradictory, but it contains some curious notions about the decline of the Portuguese influence in Africa. He clearly has on his mind the 1637 capture of the Portuguese fort (Elmina) on the Gold Coast by the Dutch, and the latter's subsequent replacement of the Portuguese as the leading traders on that coast.

way as the Spaniards did. Regardless of how unchristian it might have been, they are of the opinion that the Portuguese should have acted in the same way, which would have resulted in the same permanency as with the Spaniards. But these authors have not been on the Guinea Coast, or if they have been there, they have only sailed along the coast and perhaps for a time satisfied their curiosity at a single place or a few places. Among these authors I count a certain French Father, by the name of Bahourd, who zealously scolds us Protestants for not converting the Negroes to Christianity. This good Father, it is said, already in the course of a couple of days at Cape Coast has made a good beginning by tearing down and destroying the so-called fetishes of the Negroes, and by giving them instead small crosses, which the Blacks received willingly and promised to honour.[2] We could wish that the Negroes' nature was quite as Father Bahourd describes it, but anyone who has been on the Coast does not at all believe this. Rather, it is certain that if this good Father had treated /4/ a Negro's fetish thus, he would undoubtedly have got a bloodied head and been wiser.[3]

We must admit that Africa (the sea coasts excepted) is still wholly unknown. The Europeans established there often see and hear of nations which they have neither seen nor heard of before. How would it have been possible for the Portuguese to subjugate nations living in such a wild as well as trackless land, a land which Nature herself has so enclosed in forest and bushes that the inhabitants have to cut them down at least once a year in order to retain a slight path to their neighbouring towns and the coast? Had they attempted any hostile assaults, would [even] the brave Spaniards, who with a couple of hundred horsemen killed so many Mexicans and Peruvians, have been able to make any headway in Africa? It was impossible for the Portuguese to achieve more command over the inhabitants than the European nations now living there have achieved, namely, no more than what the Negroes themselves allow them, and no farther than the cannons at their forts can reach.

---

[2] It has not been possible to trace any Father Bahourd. However, this particular incident is related in Nicolas Villault, sieur de Bellefond, *Relation des Costes d'Afrique, appellées Guinée* (1669) 269–75, in the first person; and in Jean Baptiste Labat, *Voyage du Chevalier des Marchais en Guinée* (1730) 342–6, in the third person, without mentioning Villault. R. probably picked up the tale from Labat. The name Bahourd does not appear in these sources, but French *balourd* signifies an oaf, a coarse character, so perhaps R. has played with the term and dubbed the priest Father Balourd, either a printer's error changing one letter, or else R. disguising the term slightly (p.c. Thierry Rivière).

[3] The term 'fetish' is derived from the Portuguese *feitiço*, Coast-Portuguese *fetisso*. From an original meaning of anything manufactured it came to be used generally by Europeans for all religious objects, rituals and beliefs among polytheistic West Africans. For 'fetish' as a concept and its particular usage during the eighteenth century, see William Pietz. 'Bosman's Guinea', *Comparative Civilizations Review* 9 (1982) 3–22; and 'The problem of the fetish', *RES: Anthropology and Aesthetics* (1985) 5–17.

Fate itself has, in fact, arranged matters better for the Europeans and the Portuguese. Africa is /5/ still full of people, apart from the Gold Coast where the Europeans have been established for over a hundred years, as will be shown later. If the African nations were as co-operative as the Americans, undoubtedly there would be more gold and silver mines [opened] in Africa than there are in America, and just as rich ones; but where, then, would the people come from who would work in the mines? And if Spain, in former times so powerful and heavily populated, is now emptied and sparsely populated, what would become of little Portugal if it sent Europeans to the African or Brazilian mines, and saw them die of the poisonous underground fumes?[4]

[The climate: some insects]

Most of the west coast of Africa between Cape Mount and River Volta is, at the coast, flat land. The mountains and bush begin two to three miles inland. From the Accra road,[5] when it has rained and the air is cleared of mist, you can see three ranges of hills stretching from SW to NE, the last higher than the first [sic].[6] It is in every way a blessed and fertile land, which, in this respect, is far superior to the West Indies. At the coast there is only one rainy season, which begins in April and lasts until the end of May, in most years with such violence that all the salt lagoons run out to the sea. /6/ It is then difficult to travel, partly because the earth is soft, and partly because of the many streams which flow over our route. Inland, a few miles from the coast, rain falls twice a year, namely in the months of May and September. The inhabitants plant and harvest twice, and are so blessed that they are rewarded more than a thousand fold for their labour. However, at the coast, in the dry season, all the grass turns almost to ashes, and fresh water is very scarce. If, then, an army of many thousand Europeans were to conquer the land, how would they manage in such a country?[7]

---

[4] From his own experience R. is aware that the European traders were to a large extent the clients of African polities. His account, however, indicates an unwillingness to accept that the particular nationality of specific European traders played no great part in the Africans' choice of whom they traded with.

[5] 'road', that is, 'roadstead', a harbour where ships ride at anchor, just offshore.

[6] The hills to which R. is referring are the Akwapim-Togo ranges. These highlands, with an average altitude of 500 m. in the Akwapim section, extend from Pokoase, north of Accra, through to Togo, and ultimately north to River Niger (E.A. Boateng, *A Geography of Ghana* (1970) 161). River Volta cuts through the ranges at Ajena (A.T. Grove, *Africa* (1978) 71).

[7] Since Accra has a much lower mean rainfall than the coastal areas to the west, access to water became of strategic importance to trade. At watering places, local Africans and the Europeans were able to exercise control over watering. Winnebah, for example, was a frequently used watering place where both Europeans and local inhabitants controlled access to water, a situation which had political and economic consequences; and the area attracted many ships, to the advantage of both the Africans and the Europeans. For examples of problems related to the acquisition of water, see BLL, Furley N44 (9.3.1731), (4.12.1741); N45 (22–23.3.1742). See also Chapter 4, /184/–/188/, below.

Along the whole Coast a constant southwesterly wind blows, except when the so-called travados occur.[8] The travados are truly a terrible sight. They generally rise up when the wind is from the NE. You might be out in the field, a half *fierding*[9] distance from the fort, or wherever else you might be able to take shelter, and although these black clouds, just the size of a hand, are visible over the horizon, yet all your haste will not be sufficient to find refuge before that cloud has darkened the entire horizon, producing a violent rainfall. accompanied by thunder and /7/ by lightning flashes from these travado clouds. In such a case there is nothing else to be done than to lie down flat on the ground or take shelter behind a tree. At times, ships under sail cannot secure their sails quickly enough but must cut them loose and let them fly, otherwise the violent wind would overturn the ship, instances of which have been known. The best thing about these storms is that they last scarcely an hour. A cloudburst and thunderstorm in Europe cannot be compared to this terrible sight. Our travel accounts have little to say about this, or about other similar matters, for example, the Easterlies (as we Danes call it) or *Trompe de Mer* in French, which nevertheless are worth research by the learned.[10]

The *Oriental Tiid* [season of the easterly winds] on the Coast is also something special and worth describing.[11] In the middle of December or at the beginning of January a strong east wind of a particularly dry and strange character arises and lasts for eight days or longer. If you spill water, or (ṣ v) [pardon me][12] spit on the floor, it dries in less than a minute. Our European oak and fir beams and boards crack and split, so that you can put a finger into the crack; but as soon as the wind is over, they draw together again so /8/ tightly that it is not possible to see where the cracks were. We

---

[8] The travado (Port. *trovoada* 'sudden thunderstorm'), now known as the line squall, was described, and feared, by many early travellers (Olfert Dapper, *Naukeurige Beschijvinge der Afrikaensche gewesten* (1676) 89; Jean Barbot, *Barbot on Guinea* [1732] (1992) 29–33; Thomas Phillips, 'A journal of a voyage made 1693, 1694', in A. and J. Churchill, [publishers], *A Collection of Voyages* (1732) VI: 189; William Bosman, *A New and Accurate Description of the Coast of Guinea* (1705) 112; Paul Erdmann Isert, *Letters on West Africa* [1788] (1992) 210). For an explanation of the phenomenon, see Boateng (1970) 32.

[9] A *fjerding* is one quarter of an old Danish land mile, or 1.9 km.

[10] *Trompe* 'tube, jet' may be a misprint for *trombe* 'water spout'. R. is wrong in claiming that these marine phenomena were ignored in earlier writings. It would, in fact, be difficult to find an earlier source that did not mention these storms. Cf. note 8 above.

[11] The phrase refers to the season when the wind is from the east. The description is of the *harmattan*, when the NE trade winds, dust-laden from the Sahara, blow down to the coast (Boateng (1970) 23–6, figs. 8, 9). This dramatic change in weather can occur sporadically between December and February, and the phenomenon was regularly discussed by the early writers (e.g. Dapper (1676) 90; Barbot [1732] (1992) 456–7; Phillips (1732) 198–9; Bosman (1705) 114–5; Johannes Rask, *En kort og sandferdig Rejse-Beskrivelse til og fra Guinea* (1754) 198). For measurements of the drop in humidity, see Isert [1788] (1992) 210–11.

[12] R. inserts, here and in other places, '(s.v.)', apparently meaning 'pardon the expression'. It seems to be an abbreviation of the archaic term *saa til viis*, represented in modern Danish by *således* 'thus, sic'.

experience an extreme dryness in our throats, mouths, and noses, which is intolerable. The Blacks are not willing to leave their huts during this period, and you can see that the skin on their entire body cracks and splits, in the same way as the Europeans' noses and mouths dry up. The air is darkened by flying insects, especially winged ants, large and small; and the stronger the wind, the more the air fills with these ants. You can see ants on the surface of the sea several miles from land. A French captain has assured me that, 50 miles from land, the sea was so thick with them that one kept another from drowning, but they lay almost like a crust on the sea.[13]

In the walls of our fort and the other forts there are many ant mounds, and the ants, during that time, can be seen outside their mounds, as thick as a swarm. If you observe them carefully, the true ants are occupied with pulling the winged ants out of the mounds.[14] Two true ants have got hold of one winged ant which tried to enter the mound again, but the others hold him until the wind blows him away. /9/ The delightful author of *Spectacle de la Nature* notes that these seven-year ants are useless citizens in their little republic, and only a burden for the others, therefore they are cast out, and must serve on the Guinea Coast as food for the fishes. The fish are indeed fatter during that period than otherwise, and are caught in great quantities. In my opinion it would truly be worthwhile for philosophical eyes to observe these phenomena.[15] If it were the case that these insects remained in the country, they might, perhaps, cause plague, or other discomforts; thus, Nature's Master has devised this wind, which, like a broom, cleanses the land.

No author, apart from Bosman, has written about a strange variety of ant which is found on the Guinea Coast. The English call them *Box a Box*, the Dutch and we ourselves call them *fotter*.[16] They do not stay underground

---

[13] R. is probably referring here to termites (*Termitidae*). Both ants and termites swarm, but the description of the swarms as large, dense, and forming a crust on the sea sounds more like a reference to termites because ant swarms are not usually so prolific (p.c. Alan Tye).

[14] This could refer to either termites or ants (p.c. A. Tye). The phrase 'in the walls' and the term 'mounds' may denote mounds on the ground within the area of the walls, protruding trails and spoil-heaps within wooden walls, or the visible trails made by termites on their foraging trips along masonry walls.

[15] The reference is to Abbé Antoine Pluche, author of *Le Spectacle de la Nature, ou Entretiens sur les particularités de l'histoire naturelle* (9 vols, Paris 1732–1750). Well received and widely read, the work was translated into English, German, Spanish, Italian and Dutch (p.c. René Baesjou). The 'seven-year ants' are probably the winged castes which although they are supposed to appear once in seven years actually appear almost annually and swarm at least once a year. Their high fat content does indeed make nourishing food, both for animals and humans (p.c. A. Tye).

[16] Bosman gives no special name for these ants, which are undoubtedly termites, known inaccurately as 'white ants' (Bosman (1705) 276–7). He was, in fact, not the only author who wrote about termites (cf. Barbot [1732] (1992) 447 n. 16, 477; Rask (1754) 199–200). The English term R. is repeating is Coast-English *bug-a-bug/s* 'ant/termite/s' (p.c. P.E.H. Hair).

like other ants, but build towers of red clay 16–24 feet high, and if you break into one with a crowbar, you see actual streets and living quarters. A Black would be unwilling to break one of these unless he was provided with a pair of boots, since these *fotter* would soon drive him away from their home, and bite or cut his /10/ legs until they bled. These ants are quite white, larger than any other variety of ant, but have shorter legs. They seem to have a pair of scissors in the front of the head. If you irritate them, and then hold a finger out to them, they can bite or attack with the scissors until they draw blood. If you continue to break the tower down to the ground, or to a little way underground, you come to their storehouse or pantry in which you find all kinds of grass seeds weighing up to 1–1½ *skieppe*.[17] Under that is a longish, rectangular box made of clay, about a knife-blade's thickness, a half span long, two fingers high and three fingers wide, almost like a coffin, in which are a king and queen (in my opinion). They are lying on their backs and there is a divider between them. If you want to see them more clearly you must break off the upper part of the case since there are only two small holes in the box. Perhaps the ordinary *fotter* go in and out this way in order to feed these creatures, who can be as fat and long as a thick silk worm, but cannot walk, and resemble a child in swaddling. They are alive, as you can see since they open their mouths when you touch them with your finger.[18] Under the case, and perhaps a span farther underground, there is usually a /11/ black resin in a lump or in rods. Snakes are very fond of this resin and you frequently see the marks of their teeth in it, so you should have a loaded musket or pistol with you, to kill them. More than a hundred of these towers can be counted in a single piece of ground. The *fotter* are very harmful when they get into our warehouses, where, in a single night, they can damage goods to a value of several hundred *rixdaler*. All creatures fear them and instances have occurred when they have completely devoured a sheep, a goat, or some other creature without leaving anything behind, other than the bones.[19]

---

[17] The tower and the physical description of the insect certainly refer to termites. Prior to swarming, workers make exit holes in the mound, and they and the soldiers congregate around these apertures whilst swarming is in progress. The soldiers are equipped with huge mandibles, and their attack is indeed vicious (p.c. M. Cobblah). A *skieppe*, an old measure for grain, comprised 17.39 litres.

[18] R.'s description of the 'king and queen', the breeding male and female, is correct. The termite community is made up of a caste system of reproductives, workers and soldiers. The king and the egg-laying queen live in a 'royal chamber'. The queen has a grotesquely swollen abdomen, while the king is much smaller. The workers, pale in colour, leave the colony in large groups daily, to forage for food (p.c. M. Cobblah).

[19] The description of termite damage is generally correct, but the indication of great speed ('in a single night') is not true of termites. R. has here confused termites with driver ants (*Anomma arcens*), which are indeed so feared. Driver ants attack sluggish or tethered animals, and they also invade warehouses en masse (p.c. A. Tye).

It must be admitted that the country itself is in no way unhealthy. It is true that after the rainy season, in July and August, when the mists rise up out of the ground, most of the deaths among the Europeans occur. But I think that their manner of living causes this, by their eating many oily fish and much fruit, since game is not available at all, or hardly at all, at least in this rainy season. It does not seem that this season is more dangerous for the Negroes than any other [season]. Europeans commonly get chills during this period, and it is strange that although the sun is in the zenith precisely during those months, yet it is so cold that at times one must have a brazier with embers brought in, in order to warm one's self.[20] /12/

[The inhabitants: Cape Mount rulers]

Surely this wonderful land lacks nothing more than better inhabitants who would understand in what an earthly paradise they have been placed; who would thank the Creator with hands and eyes raised to Him, and submit to His reasonable laws. But this is far from the case. We see that the Greenlanders in their cold land fare better than the Negroes in Africa, and that the inhuman wars of the Negroes, fought because of their hatred of one another, inherited from their ancestors, have made them into wicked creatures.[21] A slave is more certain of his life than his king or master. For the latter does not know on which day or night a neighbour, gravely insulted by him earlier, may sneak up on him with his armed men — sneaking through paths that seem to have been made especially for the neighbour by wild animals — to kill both him and his whole family.

On the Upper Coast, from River Galinhas to River Sess and Cape Palmas, the Negroes are much more friendly and of service, and not as murderous or false as those on the Gold and Lower Coasts.[22] Big men [*sc.* prominent individuals] usually have European names, so that the king at Cape Mount is called King William and his queen Queen Anna.[23] On this side of Cape Mount is a Duke of Marlborough. /13/ The Dutch do not give prominent Negroes who demand titles such noble names, but generally some such as Groote Peter Passop [Big Peter Passop] and Kleine Peter Passop [Little

---

[20] Deaths were probably caused by malaria or yellow fever because the rainy season would provide more stagnant pools where the carrier mosquitoes could breed.

[21] The prevalence of revenge and vendetta among the local Africans is a recurrent theme in R.'s account. The reference to the Greenlanders is explained by the fact that Greenland was much in the news in Denmark-Norway in R.'s day. The Norwegian missionary, Hans Paulsen Egede, dubbed the 'Apostle of Greenland', settled in that land in 1721, established the colony of Godthaab, and was eventually appointed Bishop of Greenland.

[22] R. is probably referring to what he later (in Chapter 2, /25/, below) calls the 'Costa de Malagens', Coast of the Bad People.

[23] 'Big man/men', in Twi *abirempɔn/ɔbirempɔn*), was (and is) a title used for men prominent on account of their wealth and power but not 'caboceers' (head-men) or kings (T.C. McCaskie, *State and Society in Pre-Colonial Asante* (1995) 275). The Gã, however, use the term *abilempɔn* as an appellation rather than as a title (p.c. I. Odotei).

Peter Passop].[24] We Danes follow the English in this, and have now, at a couple of places, given them the name of a distinguished noble family in Denmark. King Martin rules several miles before Cape Mount. When the inhabitants visit the Europeans on their ships, or the Europeans visit them on land, they usually wear European clothing, which, however, they only vaguely know how to use.[25] In 1743, which was the last time I was there, Kings William and Martin had made peace shortly before, following what was said to have been a bloody war. I was amused to hear each party explaining the reason for the war, which was that King Martin had tried to make out that he was as great a king as William, although William's father had been king over Martin's father, the latter having been, in effect, the vassal of the former. The war had lasted two years, and, according to their own account, had been very bloody, in that five on Martin's side and three on William's side had been killed. Apart from that, I gained the impression that the war had consisted principally in their ruining one another's /14/ plantations, since at that time there was neither rice nor other food to be had.

The articles of the peace treaty are altogether too remarkable for me to refrain from reporting them here. They comprised:

(1) That Martin would relinquish the title of king and take only the title of captain.

(2) Captain Martin was not to wear shoes or stockings, as was his habit when he went out on the Europeans' ships, or when the Europeans came to him on land, but that honour was to be left to King William alone.

(3) Captain Martin was to give his most beautiful daughter to King William to marry, and she would rank above all his former wives, and bear the title of Queen Anna.

It was obvious that Captain Martin was annoyed with the dishonourable peace to which he had agreed. Several times when he came on board our ship wearing only a red scarlet smock, without shirt or trousers, I asked him why

---

[24] For the use of European titles, cf. John Atkins, *A Voyage to Guinea* (1735) 57. Dutch *passop* merely means 'take care, look out'. Whether *groote* 'big' and *kleine* 'little' refer to status or physical size is not clear. R. implies that the nickname was in general use, presumably by the Dutch. However, there is only one other person evidenced with the name Pieter Passop — his proper name, according to Accra tradition, being Otu Ahiakwa (Ivor Wilks, 'Akwamu and Otublihum', *Africa* 29 (1959) 394; Kwame Yeboa Daaku, *Trade and Politics on the Gold Coast 1600–1720* (1970) 105–7; Albert van Dantzig, *Les Hollandais sur la Côte de Guinée* (1980a) 145; Harvey M. Feinberg, *Africans and Europeans in West Africa* (1989) 82, 109).

[25] Articles of European clothing were used in trade as well as given as gifts, and hats were particularly popular. For an illustration, see Paul Roussier, *L'Établissement d'Issiny 1687–1702* (1935) plate IX; and in general see Müller [1673] in Adam Jones, *German Sources for West African History 1599–1669* (1983a) 205 (listing a number of articles); Bosman (1705) 120 (old sailor's hats); Jean Barbot, *Barbot on Guinea*, [1732] (1992) 725; William Snelgrave, *A New Account of some parts of Guinea* (1734) 35; Atkins (1735) 55, 64–6; Isert [1788] (1992) 94; Adam Jones, *Brandenburg Sources for West African History, 1680–1700* (1985) 153–4.

he had not put on those garments which he was allowed to do according to the peace treaty, /**15**/ to which he answered that love for his subjects and children had forced him into this condition. Since, however, his daughter Queen Anna would soon present King William with an heir to the latter's throne, he felt that his daughter's son would not deny him and his descendants full royal regalia.

William loved his queen very much and bought for her all the silk cloth we had on board. Since one of our ship's officers had brought along an officer's round collar and a grenadier's hat (I know not for what occasion), King William bought these, too, for his queen, who was also on board with him. She was immediately adorned with these gifts, and King William assured her that in this attire she was far more beautiful than before. He invited us ashore as his guests, saying that he also wished to grant her father the pleasure of seeing his daughter so adorned. Captain Martin also came to the festivities and was as pleased as the other guests; and the former enemies associated with each other as if there had never been any enmity between them. It happens quite differently on the Lower Coast, where /**16**/ a war never ends until one party is down and completely ruined.

[Benin influences: aggrey beads]

Before the Portuguese or other Europeans came to the Coast, the king at River Benin was emperor over the entire Guinea Coast, all the way to River Gambia; and some say that his rule extended the same distance southward from River Benin. It was, therefore, a greater kingdom than China.[26] I believe that only a few Europeans on the Coast know this, although they can see vestiges of it daily. The red *contreterre* which the Negroes wear was an imperial symbol of honour.[27] The old-fashioned swords, which the Negroes consider to be great objects of splendour in their families, are proof that they are descended from a royal field marshal or captain. But it strikes me as strange that the Negroes' languages differ so much from each

---

[26] The Benin kingdom, at its widest extent, was bounded on the east by River Niger, on the south by River Benin, and on the north and west by Yoruba country (with purportedly, by latterday 'tradition', some control over a limited area further west, leading to the nationalist renaming of the territory previously known as Dahomey as Bénin). This is a far cry from the extensive suzerainty R. claims for it. For a map showing the approximate limits of the Benin empire, see A.I. Asiwaju and Robin Law, 'From the Volta to the Niger, c.1600–1800', in J. Ajayi and M. Crowder, eds, *The History of West Africa*, 3rd edition (1985) I: 417. Extension to the River Gambia to the north, and equally as far south, which would be roughly to Angola, was a claim unprecedented, and one never made since. Although a myth of the Benin empire extending as far as the Gold Coast is occasionally publicized today, R.'s claim, if not mere fantasy, would seem to derive from some misunderstanding of what he was told.

[27] 'Contreterre' is clearly the same as *conta da terra*, Portuguese for 'bead/s of the earth/land' (but *conta de terra* in Bosman (1705) 119). This may mean beads found in, rather than fashioned of, earth — an idea which is an important part of the mythology of aggrey beads (see note 39 below). But it is more likely that the term means 'country beads', that is, local beads, as distinguished from imported beads (A.F.C. Ryder, *Benin and the Europeans 1485–1897* (1969) 187 note 4).

other.²⁸ They have never had any literature. Signs of this rule can also be seen on the Upper Coast, but not as many as on the Gold Coast, where some families really can reckon their origins from these great Benin generals or viceroys.²⁹ As great tokens of splendour they display their horsetails, which have been, and still are, a great sign of honour (just as among the Turks). You can see that these tails are a couple of hundred years old.³⁰ /17/ Their spears, or assegais, are of the same type, and their iron is much harder than the European.³¹

For information, not only on this, but on other matters, such as their ceremonies and religious practices, I have to thank an Englishman who has stayed and traded at River Benin for several years, and who has often visited the royal palace.³² When you hear this about Benin and see their ceremonies on the Gold Coast, it is clear where their religion (one can

---

²⁸ Perhaps R. is saying that, after all, the language of Benin (Edo) is not the same as the language(s) of Gold Coast. This is correct, but it is not clear how he would know this. Alternatively he is showing an understanding that the languages of the Gold Coast he knew, that is, the dialects of Akan and those of Gã-Adangme, differ between themselves (between Akan and Gã-Adangme to a considerable extent), a fact patent to anyone living there.

²⁹ The notion of Gold Coast, and especially Accra (Gã), subjection to Benin, is today represented in frequently cited oral tradition, and hence in some writings, in the form of an alleged migration from Benin, and this latterday day myth may well derive from the passage in R.'s text. For the myth, see C.C. Reindorf, *History of the Gold Coast and Asante* [1895] (1966) 3–6/18–21; M.J. Field, *Social Organization of the Gã People* (1940) 142; W F F Ward, *A History of Ghana* (1969) 57. A nineteenth-century Gã or European individual who could read Danish, possibly Reindorf himself, may have accepted R.'s statement as historical truth and spread the idea, which then fed back into oral tradition (David Henige, 'Truths yet unborn?', *Journal of African History* 23 (1982) 405–11). The origin of the notion can be explained in a number of ways. First, R. may have deduced it from his belief that certain religious practices and ceremonial artefacts were common between Benin and Gold Coast. Secondly, the anonymous Englishman may have postulated the connection and convinced R. Thirdly, since R. cites local families who lay claim to origins in Benin, the myth may have already existed in oral tradition by his day. But if he was told this, it may only indicate that he received a polite reply when he asked a leading question ('Are you descended from Benin generals?' 'Indeed!').

³⁰ By 'horse tail' R. is referring to fly whisks, which could be made of elephant's tails as well as horse's tails, and are still widely in use as ceremonial regalia for chiefs in Ghana (A.A.Y. Kyerematen, *Panoply of Ghana* (1964) 87; Ryder (1969) 40, 80, 340; Ivor Wilks, *Forests of Gold* (1993) 140 ff). Horse's tails were imported into Guinea from the early days of European trade, and have no connection with Benin, where there are no horses (p.c. P.E.H. Hair). As for the great age attributed to the whisks, R. either deduced this from their condition or was told this by their owners, who could not have given an exact age. Possibly it is one of his exaggerated guesses.

³¹ Presumably he means that the spears looked old. They may well have been made of local iron, since iron-working had been long known in West Africa, and the blacksmithing technology was equal to making spears. But that local iron goods were 'much harder' than imported iron goods seems a dubious generalization (p.c. P.E.H. Hair).

³² Assuming that the Englishman existed, he was probably either an agent of the Royal African Company, or a private trader, operating from a trading base such as Whydah. Trade between Benin and Gold Coast, via the coastal lagoons, was certainly known at some periods (Robin Law, *The Slave Coast of West Africa 1550–1750* (1991) 20–1).

hardly call it that) comes from. But even so, on account of the Blacks' carelessness and negligence in all religious affairs, their religion remains so murky and unrecognizable that you could live among them for many years without noticing that; in the form that the Negroes' forefathers have practised it, it has in it something of Judaism, as well as of the old Chalderian [*sc.* Chaldean] or fire worship. Our Accras, more than any other nation, are close to Judaism in their ceremonies of circumcision and those in relation to the slaughter of sacrifices, when they must saw away at the throat of a cow, sheep or other creature with a sharp stone, and never use a knife since that would desecrate the sacrifice. At Benin both of these religions are very recognizable.[33] /18/

This Englishman was irritated by a Dutch author (Bosman) who, in his description of Guinea, when also describing the capital city Benin, depicted it so disdainfully, saying that the country's form of government and the [chief] city were not much better than those of the kings on Gold Coast. Therefore the Englishman wanted to assure me that Bosman or his assistant had never been there, but that he had written this according to what he had been told by Negroes who lived fifty miles before or beyond the mouth of the lagoon, and who knew the capital city Benin no better than Bosman.[34] According to what is said, the Benin Negroes are very courteous and well mannered. Moreover, they have a sort of literature, which consists of many hieroglyphic figures and images in stone, by which they can record and narrate their entire history and that of the country.[35] The above-mentioned

---

[33] On being confronted with the practice of male circumcision and the method of slaughtering animals, many early writers on Guinea assumed that the Africans must have learnt these practices from Jews or 'Mohammedans', as a result of trade contacts (e.g. Bosman (1705) 210). On male circumcision, see Ulsheimer [1616], Brun [1624], and Müller [1673], in Jones (1983) 40, 58, 79, 218; Isert [1788] (1992) 131. Similar rituals could, of course, have been adopted among different peoples independently. Nor would trade contacts necessarily foster adoption of rituals: witness the Asante who had had long-standing contact with Muslims but who never practised circumcision. As regards the stones used for slaughtering animals at Benin, in 1651–1652 a Capuchin missionary in Benin described a table on which he saw scimitars used in ritual decapitation of men and animals but made no mention of sharpened stones (Ryder (1969) 105). R.'s mention of 'Chalderian or fire worship' is probably a reference to the Chaldeans mentioned in the Bible, although there they were described as sorcerers and astrologers, not as fire worshippers (Daniel II: 2).

[34] Neither the Englishman or R. can have read Bosman carefully since he never claimed to have visited Benin. The section of Bosman's book on Benin was contributed, as stated, by David Van Nyendael — perhaps, however, the individual described as Bosman's 'assistant' — who claimed to have visited the city twice (Bosman (1705) 423–68). There is no reference in Bosman to the comparison between the government and capital of Benin and those of 'the kings on Gold Coast'.

[35] Perhaps R.'s 'hieroglyphic figures' refers to decorative patterns of symbolic import (Paula Ben-Amos, *The Art of Benin* (1980) 11, plate 20). While Benin had no 'images in stone', the bronze plaques which hung in the royal palace might be 'read' with reference to former rulers and historical events.

Englishman had once taken the liberty of asking the emperor if he did not have the wish to conquer the lost countries which his forefathers had owned and ruled. The emperor smiled and answered, that since these nations could do without him, he could do without them as well. His forefathers had never concerned themselves with them, and he would not either. /19/

There is still no one on Gold Coast who knows where their *aggrier* [aggrey beads] are made.[36] It can be seen that they are porcelain, and, in proportion, heavier than our Chinese porcelain. They are longish pipe-corals [*sc.* beads], with a hole through them, as thick as a man's little finger, and as long as the joint of a finger, with beautiful colours all the way through. This is the difference between them and our Chinese porcelain, which is white inside, and whose colours are doubtless overlaid as a finish. On these beads, however, the colours go right through.[37]

I have counted four or five of the loveliest colours on one *aggrey*, [for instance,] a bright red, a lovely green, and a Saxon blue; another one [is] yellowish and white, either flame-like or striped. One such *aggrey* is priceless in the eyes of the Blacks. Some have only one colour, of which the yellow ones are the poorest.[38] An African king, when he is in his complete finery, usually has many strings around his neck, on his arms, around his waist and on his legs. Pendants and lumps of gold are then far too poor for him. It is known that such *aggreys* are still found in the earth in Benin, where the inhabitants dig them up, and they are of the opinion that in olden times a prominent corpse was buried in that spot, since /20/ several score beads usually lie in a row or circle, as if a person had been wearing them when he was buried. Yet there are found no human bones. But it may have been so long ago that these bones had long since turned to dust.[39]

---

[36] The term *aggrey/akori* has been used both specifically to identify a particular type of bead, usually one of translucent blue, as well as more loosely to refer to several types of beads of high value, as R. appears to be doing here. The term undoubtedly changed its meaning over time, and was used differently in different areas, and also by different writers (p.c. C.R. DeCorse). The origin and substance of 'true' *aggreys* have long been shrouded in mystery and are still the object of research (J.D. Fage, 'Some remarks on beads and trade in Lower Guinea in the sixteenth and seventeenth centuries', *Journal of African History* (1962) 343–7; Milan Kalous, 'Akorite', *Journal of African History* 20 (1979) 203–17; J.D. Fage, 'More about aggrey and akori beads', *2000 Ans d'Histoire Africaine* (1981) 207–8; Christopher R. DeCorse, 'Beads as chronological indicators in West African archaeology', *Beads* (1989) 44, 48).

[37] The beads may, in fact, have been Chinese porcelain beads, which were brought to Africa in significant amounts from the sixteenth to the eighteenth century (DeCorse (1989) 44). However, R. may also be describing some locally made glass beads which also have colours that go right through, as opposed to surface decoration (p.c. C.R. DeCorse). The term 'coral' is in general ambiguous because it meant either 'beads' or actual coral, but in this context it is clearly 'beads'.

[38] In fact, certain yellow beads were, and are, highly valued, such as the *bodom* beads of West African manufacture (p.c. C.R. DeCorse).

[39] For beads found in the ground and fashioned of natural glass or of tektites, see Kalous (1979) 206 ff.

The Negroes on the entire Coast know, by reason of tradition, of the common Flood.⁴⁰ They believe that the sea has been land. There are found many traces of the Flood. Two hundred miles inland, namely in the Akim gold mines, I have found petrified eggs of considerable size, as well as mussel shells, etc.⁴¹ The Negroes consider large fish, such as whale fish, *Terniner*, and others, to be their relatives, and they believe that those people who have lived in and inhabited the land which is now sea have been changed into fish of the largest variety. They have, therefore, a sort of respect for them.⁴²

[Ignorance regarding Africa: man-eaters]

How laughable it is that our geographers give the appearance of being as equally knowledgeable about Africa as about Europe itself, a map of Africa being just as closely covered with the names of countries and places as the best known kingdom in Europe! Hübner (if I recall correctly) describes for us /21/ Bilidulgerid, etc., as a powerful and advanced kingdom.⁴³ Similarly, he describes the Coptic Christians, or the kingdom of Prester John which, in his opinion, lies in the middle of Africa. It would be desirable if Prester

---

⁴⁰ Knowledge of the Flood is more likely be an indication of the infusion of Christian and Islamic beliefs into oral tradition (Henige (1982) 399–400, 403). However, questions on the subject put by Europeans may have been misunderstood by African informants, and/or their answers further misunderstood by the Europeans.

⁴¹ R. writes '*200 Miile op i Landet har jeg havt petrificered Æg*' (my emphasis) The underlined words translate—'I have found', which implies that R. himself was in Akyem and visited the gold mines. In his earlier publication he had claimed to have travelled inland (*Negotien* (1756) 32, in Chapter 2 below), and given the contact he had with the Akyem leaders it is possible that he did in fact visit Akyem. But that he actually visited the gold mines is less likely, since Europeans were rarely permitted to do this (Timothy F. Garrard, *Akan Weights and the Gold Trade* (1980) 130–1). Moreover, the distance stated, 200 Danish miles, representing 1,500 km (1 *miile* (12,000 *alen*) = 7.5 km), would place the mines north of Timbuktu. Perhaps this was a misprint for 20 Danish miles, that is, 150 km, indicating somewhere in Asante—but nowhere does R. state that he ever went as far north. Perhaps he had merely seen some uncrushed ore containing fossil material that had been brought down to the coast (p.c. Ivor Wilks).

⁴² The vague but comprehensive description, large fish or whale-fish, most likely covered several varieties of whales, as well as dolphins, porpoises, and perhaps the African manatee (sea cow). I have not been able to identify R.'s *Terniner*. He misunderstood the reverence shown by the Gã for these and other sea creatures. It was as gods, not as ancestors, that they were, and are, revered, the swords of swordfish at times being put on shrines. For *Bonsu* (an Akan term, 'whale') as the reincarnation of the sea-god, see M.J. Field, *Religion and Medicine of the Gã People* (1937) 69.

⁴³ Johannes Hübner (1668–1731) was a geographer in Nürnberg who worked under Johann Baptist Homann (1664–1721). In 1754 Hübner published his *Bequemer Schul-Atlas*, based on Homann's *Atlas Scholasticus* of 1712. Homann himself copied maps of Dutch and French origin. 'Bilidulgerid' is *Bilad-al-jarid* 'the land of the palms', referring to Southern Tunisia and the Algerian Sahara. Hübner probably found this information in Dapper, where it is given as Biledulgerit (Dapper (1676) 366).

John were to be found there, but I would not accept a commission to look for him.[44] Indeed, they have placed an entire island in the African Sea, namely St. Mattheu, which has never existed.[45] I think they should draw it as they do the South Pole: *Regio incognita* [unknown region].

We have bought slaves at Accra who were Mohammedans, and were born north of River Gambia. They could write Arabic.[46] We have met slaves brought at third hand to [the region] SE of River Volta, who were, according to the Blacks' explanation, born in nations at least five hundred miles inland. But the farther up in the land the slaves come from, the more stupid they are. Among these slaves, we have seen those of nations whom one could hardly call human. They have a particularly wild nature, a physiognomy like that of a tiger and comparable teeth in their mouths. We have placed them among other slaves, and they have sneaked up and bitten a large piece of flesh from an arm or thigh, and eaten it quite greedily.[47] Believing that those of this nation file their teeth, we therefore forbade all the factors from buying man-eaters with filed teeth. /22/ Actually they have such teeth and were born thus, by Nature's hand.

A so-called man-eater was once on board many ships in Anomabu road during a period of more than half a year. The Negroes had broken the points off his teeth and sold him to a ship. On the very first day, the captain noticed what sort of person he had aboard, so he got some Negroes to sell him at night to another ship. And so it continued. One captain was unlucky enough to buy him twice. He tied a couple of cannon balls to the neck of the man-eater and cast him into the sea.[48] On the

---

[44] Inasmuch as Prester John was the European reference name for the emperors of Ethiopia, which, being an inland state by the seventeenth century, was in the interior if not quite in the 'middle' of Africa, and also inasmuch as the Ethiopians were indeed Coptic Christians, R.'s mockery was unjustified.

[45] The non-existent island of St. Matheus appeared on maps of the South Atlantic between the sixteenth and the eighteenth centuries. In all cases the island was drawn on the same latitude as the island of Annobon (Pigulu), but its longitudinal placement due south of Cape Palmas. Conceivably the error arose through a miscalculation of longitude, very common before the development of a reliable chronometer, and the existence of the island was considered factual by constant repetition in writings and on maps.

[46] While the sale of Moslem slaves at Accra is plausible, it is less plausible that they came from as far away (although Islamic traders and clerics from far west did occasionally arrive in the Asante hinterland: Wilks (1993) 58.) Moslem slaves might well be able to recite Koranic texts, but only a few would be, to any extent, literate in Arabic.

[47] It has been argued that the degree of bizarre behaviour attributed by Europeans to groups of Africans tended to increase in direct proportion to any group's distance from the coast (Philip D. Curtin, *The Image of Africa* (1973) I, 36–45; Adam Jones, *Zur Quellenproblematik der Geschichte Westafrikas 1450–1900* (1990) 67).

[48] The story is not altogether convincing and may well be apocryphal. The cost of an individual slave being high, it is not very likely that a healthy slave would be thrown overboard. However unruly or objectionable a slave, a captain is more likely to have detained him securely, in anticipation of selling him later.

Upper Coast there also occur slaves who have pointed teeth, but they are good people. Their teeth join one another in the same way that one sees the teeth in a fox-trap.[49] /23/

---

[49] The phenomenon of pointed or filed teeth always excited comment. Many reports linked pointed teeth to cannibalism (Ulsheimer [1616] and Brun [1624] in Jones (1983) 71, 201; Phillips [1693] (1732) 197; Bosman (1705) 487). But for the view that pointed teeth did not necessarily indicate cannibalism, see C.G.A. Oldendorp, *Geschichte der Mission der evangelischen Brüder auf den caraibischen Inseln* (1777) 305; and for a neutral view, Isert [1788] (1992) 139–40. The matter is discussed in detail in Jones (1990) 61–7.

Chapter 2

With which nations trade is carried on, and in what manner, as well as in what it consists
[*Negotien* 1756 conflated]

We continue with our project of explaining with which nations trade is practised on the Guinea Coast, and in what manner. But before I go further, I must first introduce the reader to the Guinean slave trade as the driving power behind the entire West Indian trade, since, without Guinean slaves it would not be possible for us to obtain West Indian products. Indeed, without these slaves all the gold and silver in Peru, Mexico, and Brazil would remain in the earth, or, at least, not a thousandth part would come to light. And Europe would soon be poor in silver, if we continued to send to the great Mogul and the Chinese emperor the considerable sums annually which we now do.[1] /24/

[The Guinea trade (1756)]

/3/ It is well-known to all that, before America was discovered, and even for some time after that, Europeans acquired coffee, sugar, etc. from Turkey and the Canary Islands. We were forced to pay the prices decided and set by the countries which produced those products. After America was discovered, nearly every nation tried to gain possession of land in that clime, by transporting people of their own nation there, and through their labours, obtaining products needed in Europe, thus preventing great sums of capital from being taken out of their country.

The Spaniards were the first to discover the West Indies, and to establish themselves on the mainland as well as on several large islands — where the English have not driven them out, areas still in

---

[1] Alarm about the export of bullion to the East was a recurring theme in eighteenth-century European commercial discourse (p.c. P.E.H. Hair). Moreover, the Danish trade with China (in exchange for exotic Asian products) involved a system of toll and customs payments to the Viceroy of Canton, through an established group of businessmen (Ole Feldbæk, 'The organization and structure of the Danish East India, West India and Guinea companies in the seventeenth and eighteenth centuries', in Leonard Blussé and Femme Gaastra, eds, *Companies and Trade* (1981) 141–2).

their possession. From time to time England has acquired large provinces on the mainland in the north, as well as a few considerable islands. Except in the north, France owns nothing on the mainland, but it does own a number of islands which are large and well populated. /4/ [*mispaginated* /3/] The Dutch have only a few small islands and one area of the mainland, called Suriname [Surinam]. We have three islands, namely St Thomas, St Jean, and, since 1734, St Croix.[2]

At the start, the Europeans thought that the people sent to the West Indies would be [permanently] there as farmers cultivating the land. But they discovered that Europeans, due to the change of climate, also experienced changes in their own constitution, and because of constant labour in the hot climate died like flies. Hence all the expense and trouble was in vain. The European nations were in a dilemma for a long time before they arrived at the perfect solution. Only a very few slaves were being taken from the Guinea Coast, since the intention of the African Companies was simply to acquire gold, ivory, dye-wood of all sorts, gum, and so on. Navigation had not reached the heights of excellence it enjoys today. At that time, the slaves on the Guinea Coast were a good buy; for a knife, a mirror, or other trivia, the Europeans could obtain from the Blacks a slave who had been sentenced to death for his crimes. The planters in the West Indies gradually found it more convenient to let the Blacks work for them rather than work themselves, and the Blacks, having been born in the same climate, could tolerate it better than the Europeans.

This opportunity created the great and famous Guinea trade, which has brought many advantages to those nations seriously involved in it. First, it improved European manufacturing, since so many kinds of cotton and woollen textiles were sold [in Guinea]. Secondly, the improvement extended to the East Indian trade, /5/ for those nations which formerly had managed with a single shipload of East Indian goods later had to have ten or more shiploads, because the Negroes so much desired those goods. Next, such quantities of sugar, indigo, coffee, cotton, etc. from the West Indies were bought that these nations could offload their surplus to other nations who had no colonies in America, as well as to the nations who had not organized their system of trade so successfully. By this means the Dutch brought a great amount of capital to their country.

It being clear to these nations that the source of this wealth was the Guinea Coast, the Guinea trade therefore gave rise to great envy

---

[2] St Thomas was the first island permanently settled by the Danes, in 1672; St John ('St Jean') was claimed in 1683 and settled in 1716–1717; St Croix was purchased from France in 1733 (W. Westergaard, *The Danish West Indies under Company rule* (1917) 2).

between the European powers. Each wanted to exclude the others, and this caused bloody wars. French subjects were not free to bargain on Gold Coast before England granted the right to them after the War of the Spanish Succession, at which period, during the reign of the Regent, the Duke of Orleans, the first ships from France came to Gold Coast.[3] However, they earned little profit for their owners since the French nation did not know as much about this kind of trade as did the English and the Dutch. Yet, what they did not then understand they learned later, as is shown by the fact that, because of the remarkable establishments in the French West Indian colonies, they have, between 1730 and 1743-4, conveyed more slaves from the Guinea Coast than all the other trading nations put together. As a result, they have forced all the other nations out of the sugar trade.[4]

[The nations involved (1760)]

The Portuguese, who were the first [European nation] to be established in the western region of Africa, now own nothing at all in that region, apart from their Angola, a few degrees south of the equator. They were everywhere [else] driven away by the Dutch, who in turn became so arrogant that they desired to exclude all other nations. It is well known that they drove away from Cape Coast first the Swedes, and, after that, us.[5] At Christiansborg there can still be seen what the Portuguese, and then the Swedes, built.[6] When anyone wants to negotiate a deal with the Negroes, it definitely must be done in the Portuguese language, or, more correctly, in Negro-Portuguese. We Danes, as well as the Dutch, must learn this before we can be trusted to

---

[3] This is inaccurate. For French ships trading on Gold Coast in 1679 and 1682, see Jean Barbot, *Barbot on Guinea* [1732] (1992), passim; and there were earlier instances. But R. presumably has in mind regular French trading, not merely occasional voyages.

[4] French trade is further discussed below (1760, 47-8) briefly, and was discussed more fully in the earlier publication — see below (1756, 25-32).

[5] Henrik Carlof, a former employee of the Dutch West India Company, in 1652/3 established Carolusburg fort at (the later-named) Cape Coast for the Swedes, but in 1658 drove them out, on behalf of his new employers, the Danes. A year later, the fort was handed over to the Dutch by the Danish merchant Schmidt who had been left in charge. The Danes were then forced to build Fort Frederiksborg above Cape Coast Castle. For the Dutch expansion on Gold Coast in the second half of the seventeenth century, see Erick Tilleman, *A Short and Simple Account of the Country Guinea* [1697] (1994) 2-5, 22; Georg Nørregård, *Danish Settlements in West Africa 1658-1850* (1966) 32-3; W.E.F. Ward, *A History of Ghana* (1969) 77-9; Kwame Yeboa Daaku, *Trade and Politics on the Gold Coast 1600-1720* (1970) 75 ff.; Adam Jones, ed., *German Sources for West African History 1599-1669* (1983) 135, 146-7.

[6] The Portuguese, during their occupation of Christiansborg in 1679-1683, built a chapel, a building which still existed in R.'s day (A.W. Lawrence, *Trade Castles and Forts of West Africa* (1963) 203, 211). But there could have been nothing left of the Swedish lodge built, at nearby Osu, by Henrik Carlof in 1652 and taken over by the Danes in 1661, the same year they built Christiansborg Castle (Tilleman [1697] (1994) 25-6; Nørregård (1966) 10, 42-3).

carry on any trade with them. The English, on the other hand, usually learn the Negro language, or have an assistant with them who speaks Negro and is their interpreter.[7]

Before the Dutch gained their present main castle of Elmina, Fort Nassau at Mourée was their chief fort. Built of European bricks, it is nearly as large as Elmina. I believe that they used more than 200 shiploads of bricks, so you can see what advantage they were enjoying on the Guinea Coast at that time.[8] Elmina (meaning 'mine', or 'gold mine') /25/ was so named by the Portuguese because of the quantities of gold they received by trading with the Blacks.[9] But they have never possessed their own mines.[10]

The English are established in some places on the Upper Coast, which is called by the Portuguese the *Costa de bonos Gentes* [Coast of Good People] and stretches from Cape St Mary to Cape Palmas. From there to Cape La

---

[7] Like other European writers, R. makes it clear that trade was by negotiation with Africans, not by mere haggling. The conduct of trade seems to have been a fairly elaborate and formal business. As for the use of 'Negro-Portuguese', when the Portuguese vocabulary of social relations and religion that appears in all these writings is considered, it is clear that although the Portuguese spoken on the Gold Coast may have been different from metropolitan Portuguese and limited in vocabulary, it was more than merely a simplified jargon, as often assumed (p.c. M.E. Kropp Dakubu). For the use of Portuguese in important documents between Europeans and Africans, see BLL, Furley N44 (25.4.1734), (5.5.1734). R.'s remark about the English is not convincing, it being very unlikely that the English were unduly proficient in any Gold Coast language. But R. seizes every opportunity to exalt the English above all the other nations on the coast, especially over his enemies, the Dutch. None of the Europeans resident on Gold Coast in R.'s time showed any interest in studying the local African languages, not even to the extent of recording vocabulary. But a Frenchman who in the 1680s merely visited the coast recorded a vocabulary of Akan/Twi which was eventually published in an English work in 1732 (John Barbot, *A Description of the Coasts of North and South Guinea*... (1732) 413–4; Jean Barbot, *Barbot on Guinea* [1732] (1992) 746–7; P.E.H. Hair, *Barbot's West African Vocabularies of c. 1680* (1992)). There were, however, earlier vocabularies in print of both Akan/Twi/'Fante' and Gã/Adangbe (numerals only), collected by a Dutchman, De Marees (published 1602), a German, Müller (published 1673), and a Dane, Rask (J. Rask *Rejsebeskrivelse til og fra Guinea* [collected during service at Christiansborg 1709–1712] (1754) 169–73. But there is no evidence that R. knew any of these works. Given the short time that most Europeans remained (or survived) on Gold Coast, it is likely that in local contacts interpreters were generally used and very likely that there was often no need because the contacted Africans had some command of a European language.

[8] Fort Nassau was built at Mori in 1612 at the invitation of the king of Asebu, who sent ambassadors to the States-General to request aid against the Portuguese (Daaku (1970) 12). It was built in a European style which was unsuited to a tropical climate (Albert van Dantzig, *Forts and Castles of Ghana* (1980b) 13). On the fort, see also Lawrence (1963) 242–4. Presumably the Dutch 'advantage' refers to the number of their ships which in a short period visited the coast to trade and conveniently brought out the bricks, but the number of ships involved is probably exaggerated.

[9] For the name 'Mina' and its evolution to 'Elmina', see P.E.H. Hair, *The Founding of the Castelo de São Jorge da Mina* (1994) 43–4, notes 3, 4.

[10] For local gold mining, see Chapter 4, /177/–/180/, below.

Hou is called the *Costa de malos Gentes* [Coast of Bad People].[11] No European goes ashore in the latter, yet considerable trade is carried on, and easily ten times as much as on the Coast of Good People;[12] In truth, the nations which wage such subtle wars as King William and Captain Martin have done cannot be expected to provide many ships with slaves. They do not know about gold.

Yet, fifty to sixty years ago, the whole Gold Coast, from Cape Three Points to River Volta, could have been called a gold mine. The reason that not a thousandth part of the gold formerly brought from there is not brought today is not that the land is no longer as rich in gold as it was in former times, but that millions of people have been beaten to death, that entire nations have been destroyed, and that the Akim people,[13] who had

---

[11] R. is in a muddle. He writes *Captamarin*, which presumably stands for Cape St Mary. But the only Cape St Mary in Guinea is at the mouth of River Gambia, hence his reference to the 'Upper Coast' includes English activities, these being in fact at James Fort on River Gambia as well as in the Sierra Leone estuary and at Sherbro Island. But in normal coast terminology the 'Upper Coast' extended westwards beyond River Gambia, as far as River Senegal. Furthermore, R. is confused about the 'Coast of Bad People' and the 'Coast of Good People'. The former was normally considered to stretch from Cape Palmas to Lahou (thus comprising the western coast of modern Côte d'Ivoire), and the latter from Lahou to Cape Three Points (thus comprising the eastern coast of Côte d'Ivoire). R. reverses the order of the coasts. These terms were recorded as early as c.1500 and subsequently transmitted from one map to another (Adam Jones, *Brandenburg Sources for West African History 1680–1700* (1985) 34, note 22). It has been suggested that the terms may have had their origin in propaganda, to keep people away from the places where the most profitable trade was to be had (Lars Sundström, *The Exchange Economy of Pre-Colonial Tropical Africa* (1974) 18). But the argument is unconvincing, since the Portuguese invented the names before they had any rivals.

[12] On the correctly-located Coast of Bad People (western Côte d'Ivoire), European traders did not normally go ashore but conducted trade from the ships, and thus had a limited contact with the people (Brun [1624] and Hemmersam, [1683] in Jones (1983), 64–5, 103; Nicolas Villault, sieur de Bellefond, *Relation des Costes d'Afrique appelleés Guineé* (1669) 176–7; Olfert Dapper, *Naukeurige Beschrijvinge der Afrikaensche Gewesten* (1676) 61–3; Thomas Phillips [1694] in [A. and J. Churchill, publishers], *A Collection of Voyages* (1732) VI: 196–7; Tilleman [1697] (1994) 16, 18; Barbot [1732] (1992) 308, note 11, 309, note 12, map plate 25; William Bosman, *A New and Accurate Description of the Coast of Guinea* (1705) 486–90). European trade on both coasts was much more limited than European trade on Gold Coast, but it is unlikely that trade on the western coast ('of Bad People') was greater than that on the eastern coast ('of Good People'), since the latter coast contained the trading locality of Assini and (on some reckoning of its extent) a fort at Axim. On R.'s own geographical terms, the contention that trade between Cape Palmas and Cape Lahou was 'ten times' as much as that between Cape St Mary and Cape Palmas was hopelessly wrong, the opposite most probably being nearer the case. For the kings, actually at Cape Mount, see Chapter 1, /13/–/14/, above.

[13] Following the usage of the archival sources, R. terms the people of Akim the 'Akenists'. This is out of line with his other ethnonyms, e.g. Accras, Assiantes. To aid the reader, the translation hereafter uses the more obvious term, 'Akims'.

actual expertise in digging gold, have, in fact, since 1747, all fled from their country.[14] /26/

Old Negroes on the Gold Coast, when they become confidential with a European, can philosophize quite sensibly over the state of their country. 'It is you, you Whites', they say, 'who have brought all the evil among us. Indeed, would we have sold one another if you, as purchasers, had not come to us? The desire we have for your fascinating goods and your brandy, bring it to pass that one brother cannot trust the other, nor one friend another. Indeed, a father hardly his own son! We know from our forefathers that only those malefactors who had thrice committed murder were stoned or drowned. Otherwise the normal punishment was that anyone who had committed a misdeed had to carry to the injured party a large piece of firewood for his house or hut, and ask on his knees for forgiveness, for one, two, or three days in a row. In our youth we knew of many thousands of families here and at the coast, and now not a hundred individuals can be counted. And what is worse, you have remained among us as a necessary evil (*malum necessarium*), since if you left, the Negroes up-country would not let us live for half a year, but would come and kill us, our wives and our children. That they bear this hatred for us is your fault. Formerly our fetish (or oracle) was asked for advice /27/ when something important was about to happen. We followed his advice, and thereby felt contented.'[15]

---

[14] For the destruction of Akyem, a dramatic episode which made a deep impression on R. and influenced his viewpoint on Gold Coast affairs, see Chapter 4, /183/ ff, below. It is less than certain that the gold trade did in fact decline during the eighteenth century (Timothy F. Garrard, *Akan Weights and the Gold Trade* (1980) 57-8; Harvey M. Feinberg, *Africans and Europeans in West Africa* (1989) 53-8); Per O. Hernæs, *Slaves, Danes, and African Coast Society* (1995) 320-7). The loss of 'millions of people' refers to local wars and R. does not specify loss by export as slaves.

[15] This striking passage presents an Arcadian view of the local past not uncommon among group myths across the world. Outsiders are to blame for all family breakdown and all social evils. R. repeats the myth and apparently takes it seriously as wholly true history. In actuality, slavery and slaving among peoples on the Guinea Coast preceded the European presence, albeit arguably in different forms and less extensively (p.c. P.E.H. Hair). For instance, in the 1480s the Portuguese began carrying slaves from Benin to Gold Coast, to meet demand from local merchants (Daaku (1970) 24; John Vogt, *Portuguese Rule on the Gold Coast 1469-1682* (1979) 71-2; Paul E. Lovejoy, *Transformations in Slavery* (1983) 661 ff.; Robin Law, *The Slave Coast of West Africa 1550-1750* (1991) 116, 124; Hair (1994) 58-9, note 44). European trade is blamed for the growth of avarice and the desire for luxury goods, and certainly it increased the availability and quality of many goods previously in limited supply (cf. Feinberg (1989) 41-2). Of particular note is that this passage, inasmuch as it represents a genuine local viewpoint, does not explicitly object to the export of Africans as slaves but instead only to the related import of 'luxury' goods. The final sentences seem to be saying, not only that increased trade has brought on the coastal peoples the attacks of their interior neighbours, which may well be correct (although inter-ethnic wars were of course not unknown before), but also that the new wars were caused by the clumsy diplomacy of the Europeans replacing traditional modes of reconciliation between neighbours, with divine guidance — a point more difficult to judge.

Thus, according to their own account, the Negroes have lost much of their former integrity, and have not gained anything by having helped the Dutch to drive the Portuguese away.[16]

[The Dutch (1760)]

The Dutch are now the strongest [European nation] on the Guinea Coast, which they let us feel, and not only us but, at times, the English, too.[17] They have fourteen fortresses, and no nation acquires as many recruits at one time from Europe as they do.[18] On the other hand, more die among them than among any other nation, especially at Elmina.[19] The cause is the inhumane miserliness of the officers, because instead of the good gold or the goods which they should give the garrison as a monthly salary for their sustenance, they give them filed copper, or filed copper dust which has been gilded. The Black merchants who sell provisions can in no way trade this copper dust further, and thus will not trade their goods for [such] false coin; yet at times they are forced to do this by the soldiers, which often results in

---

[16] R. reverts from accusations about the general European presence to hostile comments on a specific nation, the Dutch. For relations between Dutch and Africans in opposition to the Portuguese, see Daaku (1970) 54–57.

[17] Treating of the main rival nation to the Danes, R. writes at length about the Dutch, but with few dates. The following chronological table may help the reader.

1730 or 1731	interlopers allowed on per cent payment to the Company (1756, /18/; 1760, /34/).
1736–1740	Director-General de Bordes, dies 1740 (note 59).
1740	Elmina besieged (1760, /34/).
1740–1741	Director-General François Barovius (note 59).
1741–1747	Director-General Jacob Baron de Petersen (notes 22, 57).
1741	factors permitted to trade in non-Company goods (1756, /7/; 1760, /37/), but they cheat (1760, /8/).
1742	de Petersen's agent travels to Europe with R. (1756, /12/).
1747–1754	Director-General Jan van Voorst (notes 22, 56; R. says 1746, corrected note 64).
1747	clash between Van Voorst and Fiscal-General (1760, /28/–/29/).
1749	Van Voorst cheats Frenchman (1756, /14/–/15/).

[18] There were fifteen forts of varying sizes: 1 St Anthony at Axim; 2 Hollandia at Princes Town; 3 Dorothea at Akwida, which had fallen into decay but was still standing at the time R. was writing; 4 Batenstein at Butri; 5 Witsen at Takoradi; 6 Orange at Sekondi; 7 St Sebastian at Shama; 8 Vreedenburgh/Vredenburg at Komenda; 9 St George d'Elmina; 10 Coenraadsburg (St Jago) at Elmina; 11 Nassau at Mori; 12 Amsterdam at Kormantin; 13 Leydsaamheid at Apam; 14 Goede Hoop at Senya Beraku; 15 Crevecoeur at Accra (Van Dantzig (1980b) passim; Feinberg (1989) 41).

[19] While mortality at Elmina was not quite as high as was at times reputed, it averaged in 1714–1760 nearly 20% p.a. for Europeans, a high contemporary rate in Europe for young males (Feinberg (1989) 36–8; Johannes Menne Postma, *The Dutch in the Atlantic Slave Trade 1600–1815* (1990) 66).

arguments.[20] False gold has thus become so common that the Negroes copy it in great quantities, and try to pass it off on inexperienced /28/ Europeans.[21] This fraud has even gone so far among the Dutch that two Directors-General have swindled and distressed many people. Indeed, we know that one of them ordered many hundredweight [of false gold] from Europe and gave it in payment for goods purchased from all those nations who came to the Coast! As a result, the French tradesmen in Rochelle, Nantes, and other cities have posted, not only once but frequently, the names of General de Petersen and General van Voorst on the customary blacklist in the *Bourse*, where all swindlers are listed.[22] When, then, the most prominent Dutch behave this way, you can well conclude what sort of people the minor servants become when they witness such conduct. There was nothing in the world which they were incapable of doing—religion and all morals having totally died out among them.[23] Hence, once no foreign nations wanted to have anything to do with them, they wronged and betrayed one another. As an instance of this, we now report a clash that occurred in the year 1747 at Elmina between Director-General Jan van Voorst and General-Fiscal van Ryk.

Fiscal van Ryk had twice previously irritated his fellow servants by pretending that he was going to return home, and demanding that they /29/ buy the remainder of his goods (as was the custom when an officer

---

[20] The soldiers were regularly paid in *kakraas* (Twi for 'little [things]'), that is, small irregular metal pieces notionally of beaten gold but often of brass and copper scraps containing gold filings. For their early uses, see Hair (1994) 52, note 30. There appear to have been different sorts with different values; for a reference to *Achantynse kakraas*, that is, Asante *kakraas*, see BLL, Furley N44 (1–2.9.1740). Although *kakraas* were a regular currency along the Coast (Garrard (1980) 88, 93), they were not acceptable in local markets during a particularly precarious situation in 1738–1740 when the Elminas were at war with the Fante. The military were then being forced, on threat of punishment, to accept *kakraas* (BLL, Furley N45 (1.7.1742); Feinberg (1989) 145–50). The 'arguments' R. mentions were most likely the result of the serious conflicts at the time, rather than merely over the value of the *kakraas*. But this situation was not typical of the normal relationship which obtained between the Elminas and the Dutch, as R. would have us believe. For the text of the document containing all the grievances of the Elminas, see Albert van Dantzig, *The Dutch and the Guinea Coast, 1674–1742* (1978) 345–6.

[21] On the adulteration of gold on Gold Coast, see Hemmersam [1663] and Müller [1673] in Jones (1983) 121, 250; Phillips [1694] (1732) 206; Tilleman [1697] (1994) 32; Bosman (1705) 81–5; Barbot [1732] (1992) 485, 490, note 8; Paul Erdmann Isert, *Letters on West Africa and the Slave Trade*, [1788] (1992) 86–7; Garrard (1980) 58, 66, 86–9, 176; Jones (1983) 90, notes 267, 268.

[22] Following de Bordes (7.4.1736–16.3.1740), Jacob Baron de Petersen was Director-General from 8.3.1741 to 10/12.4.1747; Jan van Voorst succeeded him and held office until 14.7.1754 (Feinberg (1989) 163). For more on Van Voorst and false gold, see below (/41/, also 1756, /12/–/13/). I have found no other source that reports the export from Europe to Africa of adulterated gold.

[23] For the types of men who worked at the Dutch establishments on the Coast, especially at Elmina, see Feinberg (1989) 86 ff.; Postma (1990) 65–6. On the arbitrary power of the Governor and the weakness of the Council at Elmina some fifty years before R.'s description, see Bosman (1705) 100–03; Albert van Dantzig, *Les Hollandais sur la Côte de Guinée* (1980a) 154–6; Feinberg (1989) 32.

returned home). Truly wishing to be rid of him, they had agreed to this and bought such goods as he himself probably could not so readily have exchanged for gold. The third time General van Voorst bought everything, and since he knew that the Fiscal's arms had become powerless due to an illness, and that he was, moreover, very weak and because of this normally took a midday nap, the General arranged to have the payment sent to him at that time of day. The men who were to carry the gold had orders that if van Ryk was asleep they were to set it down on the Fiscal's table. This was done, and two hours later van Ryk woke up. His servants reported to him that the General had sent him so many chests of gold. The Fiscal, suspecting a trick, immediately went to the table and saw that he had not been mistaken, it all being false gold. With all the chests carried behind him, Van Ryk went to the General and requested him to take this false gold back again, and give him good gold instead. The General admitted that these were his chests but denied that it was his gold and accused van Ryk of having exchanged the gold. The Fiscal ordered his men to set the chests on the General's table, but the General would not allow that, so the Fiscal's /30/ men threw them on the floor and prepared to leave. The General collected them up and threw them out of the room. The Fiscal, who was standing outside, as well as he could threw them back in again. The chests fell apart and these two most prominent Dutchmen on the entire Coast of North and South Africa threw the false gold into each other's eyes, swearing most coarsely at one another and behaving like the poorest specimens of humankind. All the minor servants came to the scene and saw this unedifying battle and duel.[24]

Many such occurrences could be related. Yet no Negro brought up in evil ways has such a desire, or such eagerness, to swindle people, or is as shameless in denying his fraud, as is a Dutchman on the Guinea Coast. There is nothing in the world which bothers the conscience of the Dutch when profit by any means is concerned. It might be said that they allow a great number of their soldiers to die of hunger, since if the soldiers could use what the Company allows them, which is one *rixdaler* more a month than what our soldiers receive, they could subsist[25] But this would not fill the purses of the civil servants, and when /31/ the soldiers die (it is said on the Coast) the bookkeeper allows them to go on living for a while in the books, so that he can profit by them after their death — as others did while they were

---

[24] This anecdote does not appear in 1756. The departure of Fiscal van Ryk is documented in quite different terms in the Dutch archives (I am indebted to René Baesjou for this information). There is no indication of an altercation between van Ryk and Governor van Voorst, and instead the latter assisted the former to return home without delays, by purchasing merchandise from him (ARA, WIC 113, 10.10.1748, 23.12.1748).

[25] What R. implies is that the Dutch soldiers regularly failed to receive their due pay in acceptable currency. According to R., the Dutch soldiers received 8 *rixdaler* (= 20 fl.) per month, since the lowest-ranking Danish soldiers received 7 *rixdaler* per month, although also free uniforms (Nørregård (1966) 166). Elsewhere R. claims that when the Dutch soldiers were given adulterated gold with which to purchase provisions, the Africans refused to accept it (1756, 13, below).

alive.²⁶ Things have occurred which enable one to see, as surely as $2+3=5$, that they poison one another, and after a rich factor's death manipulate the figures to show him to have been in great debt to the Company.²⁷

An instance of this was the case of a Dutch factor at Creve-Coeur fortress at Accra, named Baltazar Coymans, who was born in the West Indies.²⁸ He was no doubt related to our deceased Dutch envoy, a gentlemen who was beloved by the high and low here in Copenhagen, and I deduce this relationship not only because of the name but because I have seen the same coat of arms on the factor's seal which was on that gentleman's coach.²⁹ In 1747 this factor, who often had an attack of gout, wrote to Elmina for some medication, which was then sent to him, together with written instructions on how to use it. The medicine came too late, since he had already recovered. In the afternoon, at tea, his assistant (a Frenchman from Bordeaux, by the name of du Puis) said to him /32/ that he should take some of this mixture anyway, it being, no doubt, also a palliative. He did so, taking 40 drops according to the directions, but scarcely a quarter of an hour passed after he had taken it before he fell off his chair with convulsions, and he died three hours later.³⁰

---

²⁶ R. is alluding to the private trading of Dutch officials which he goes on to describe. For private trade and personal enrichment among the Dutch, see Feinberg (1989) 38–40; Postma (1990) 67–8. It is, however, difficult to distinguish between private trade, which was accepted by the Company to a degree, at least in the case of officials, and corruption. Great differences existed in the estates of the Dutch dying on the coast, the officials leaving considerably more than the military and artisans. Clearly, access to Company funds for use in private trading contributed to the officials' personal enrichment, their gains being far beyond what soldiers and artisans could make by the same activity.

²⁷ Presumably R. is claiming that the bookkeepers help themselves to a dead man's goods and then doctor the books to show that he owned none but was in debt to the Company, perhaps even transferring their own debts to the account of the deceased.

²⁸ This anecdote does not appear in 1756.

²⁹ Balthazar Coejmans was a mulatto from Surinam and undoubtedly related to the brothers Coejmans, who were influential bankers (Van Dantzig (1980a) 120–1; Jones (1985) 181, note 2; Postma (1990) 33, 38, 42–6).

³⁰ Coejmans' death is recorded as having occurred in 1748, not 1747, after a serious illness (BLL, Furley N46, 2.9.1748). However, poisoning could easily have been arranged, and Coejmans death at that point was extremely convenient for the Dutch on the Coast. In November 1746 he had seized a number of Africans who had sought refuge at the lodge at Kpone, and this had caused the Dutch Company much embarrassment (CRA, Vestindisk-guinea Kompagniet [hereafter V-gK] 888, folder 1747/111, 1748/157–9). Other convenient deaths of European officials on the Coast likely to attract accusations of poisoning, in this case officials of the Danes, were those of Governor Jørgen Billsen, who died on 11.3 1745, in the midst of a rebellion on the part of his staff (see Appendix B); of his successor, Thomas Brock, who intended to launch an inquiry into the situation at Christiansborg twelve days later; and of Brock's successor, Johan Wilder, who died one month later, on 23.4.1745 (see Appendix B). But there were other deaths of Europeans in this period, and, given their unhealthy situation, sudden death among the Europeans could be expected at more or less any time (Nørregård (1966) 103–4). Accusations of poisoning as explanations of non-violent deaths were commonplace in West African societies, being part of the witchcraft cult, and it rather looks as if resident Europeans were influenced (although accusations of poisoning important individuals were of course not unknown in Europe).

On the following morning I and others at our fort, together with the English factor, James Hopkins, were invited to accompany Coymans to his grave.[31] Mr. Hopkins, who had heard about this cure from the Blacks, as we had done, but who did not understand Dutch or French, took me aside privately and asked me to enter into conversation with this assistant when the burial finished and try to obtain the bottle of the drops.[32] We two would put our seals on it and he (Hopkins) would send it to the [medical] faculty in England in order to take revenge on a man as lacking in conscience as General van Voorst, who had often committed such murders. Hopkins was himself a medical man, and had been the doctor for several years at the main English castle. I began what I had agreed to and the assistant showed us the bottle, but when I requested that he give it to me, before our very eyes he threw it out of the window. /33/

No nation could have challenged the Dutch in the trade on the Coast if great hatred had not existed among the Dutch themselves. They distinguish between a Hollander and a Zeelander, so that it is a fault among them to have been born ten miles south or east of Amsterdam and The Hague. On the other hand, it is a great honour among them to be able to say that one was born *in't Haart van Holland* [in the Heart of Holland] — although a baboon as regards reason and morals. And since the entire Council is made up of Hollanders, they would rather aid a true foreigner whom a *Ziel-Verkooper* [recruitment agent] has sent to the Coast than a Zeelander, unless absolute orders have come from Europe about him.[33]

Apart from their fourteen fortresses on the Gold Coast, the Dutch also have many places on the Lower Coast where they have factors, the Negroes in no way allowing them to build forts.

Even though their goods are priced lower than those of the other nations are, the Dutch Company suffers considerable losses on the Guinea Coast.[34] Dutch interlopers on the Coast have sold 14 or 16 muskets for two ounces

---

[31] James Hopkins, a factor at James Fort, was a medical doctor. He was also called to practise medicine at the Dutch forts when needed, and perhaps at the Danish ones. 'The English Dr. Hopkins came by hammock from Cape Coast to attend the very ill *Equipagemaster*' (BLL, Furley N45 (30.7.1742)).

[32] R. therefore spoke English.

[33] Since Zeeland dominated the trade, once it had been opened to private traders jealousy on the part of the Hollanders may have been behind the situation to which R. refers (Postma (1990) 132–4). *Ziel-Verkooper* 'seller of souls' was a derogatory term (the English equivalent being 'crimp') used to identify an agent who recruited seamen, allegedly sometimes by decoying them aboard or forcibly impressing them.

[34] The interlopers are mentioned again below (/18/). For the decline of the Dutch Company due to competition from private traders and the English, see Feinberg (1989) 137. An increase in French shipping was also a factor (Van Dantzig (1978) 343, doc. 409). Moreover, African traders received better prices from ships than they did from forts, the latter in setting prices having additionally to cover their upkeep and the cost of the garrison (Postma (1990) 203–4).

of gold [equalling 32 *rixdaler*], while our muskets cost three *rixdaler* each in Europe. /34/ They have sold us 100 lb. of gunpowder for [only] 16 *rixdaler*.[35] I dare say that the Dutch private traders bring more gold and elephant tusks from Guinea than the Dutch Company and all the other nations together.[36] Nearly all private trade which takes place from Holland to the Coast is simply for gold and tusks. Slave ships rarely go there. Private traders pay a certain per cent to the Company, and are thereby given permission to remain away for 16 months; and a slave ship may stay for 18 months. Only since 1730 have Dutch individual shippers had permission to go there on these conditions. Not that they did not go there before. But the ship and its goods were confiscated if a Dutch Company ship seized an interloper.[37]

In 1740 Elmina was besieged by its own Negroes.[38] The Dutch General had forbidden anyone to sell gunpowder and muskets to enemies, but two Dutch interlopers put in at the Elmina road and sold their entire cargo to the Blacks.[39] /35/ General de Bordes enticed one of the captains ashore and placed him in irons and the Fiscal was to bring charges, threatening capital punishment. But the ship's crew got hold of two of the members of the Elmina [fort] Council and threatened to hang them if de Bordes did not release their skipper, which was done. Even the Dutch factors on the whole Coast, or most of them, privately sent considerable quantities of gunpowder and guns to the Blacks at Elmina, so that they could make things hot for their

---

[35] R. always refers to *Flinter*, that is, flintlock muskets, a type of gun replacing the matchlock musket in the last two decades of the seventeenth century (Ray A. Kea, *Settlements, Trade, and Polities in the Seventeenth-Century Gold Coast* (1982) 161). The price of gunpowder on the Coast in 1725 was fl. 0.87 per lb or fl. 87 per 100 lb., and in 1727 was fl. 0.75 per lb. or fl. 75 per 100 lb. (Feinberg (1989) 52). Compared to a purchase price in the Netherlands of fl. 25 per 100 lb., the mark-up was considerable, although certain costs, such as those of transport and garrison maintenance, made the actual profit much less. R.'s purchase from interlopers of 100 lb. for 16 *rixdaler* gives a price of fl. 40 for 100 lb. (one *rixdaler* being worth fl.2.5 at the time).

[36] According to Bosman, at the beginning of the century the amount of gold bought by the interlopers equalled that bought by the Dutch Company (Bosman (1705) 89–90). But Bosman had reasons for exaggerating.

[37] For more on the interlopers, see below (1756, 18). For the extent to which the gold trade exceeded the slave trade for the Dutch West India Company (WIC), see the chart in Van Dantzig (1980a) 166. For the slave trade of the WIC on Gold Coast, see Daaku (1970) 23; Feinberg (1989) 62–4. As early as 1710, the Governor at Elmina suggested that the Dutch desist from buying slaves on the Gold Coast because of the great expense it entailed (Van Dantzig (1978) 156). For Dutch private traders, see Van Dantzig (1980a) 17, 104; Postma (1990) 78–82.

[38] That is, Elmina fort was besieged by the inhabitants of the African town which had grown up close to the fort, many of them being dependants of the fort or otherwise economically involved in its activities. This episode is not mentioned in 1756.

[39] For the General, de Bordes, see note 17 above. In 1756, R. claimed that the only credential of de Bordes for appointment as Governor was that a brother of his was one of the Directors of the Company in Amsterdam (below, 1756, /7/).

General in his fortress, he having made himself so hated among both Europeans and Blacks by his devilry.[40]

Here is an instance.[41] Mr. de Bordes once convened the entire Council, and after the Council meeting was over there was considerable drinking, as was the custom. In the merrymaking it was discussed whether a Director-General on the Coast, who had the authority to inflict capital punishment in respect of the Company's servants, could equally pass judgement on, and punish with death, a member of the Council. Those present debated the pros and cons. De Bordes, once he had heard what their dispute was about, ordered a black servant to fetch a dozen spikes and as many ropes of raffia, together /36/ with a ladder. He had the spikes fastened under the beams in the room. The guests noted these arrangements without knowing what it all meant. Finally de Bordes asked which of those present doubted that a General could punish a Council member with death. But there was no longer anyone there who doubted it. Had one or more of the those Council members responded positively to the question, it would have been interesting to see whether de Bordes would actually have done it.[42]

By treaties, the Portuguese must pay a tithe in toll at Elmina before starting to trade. This toll must amount to a considerable sum in a year. For, although according to the orders of the King of Portugal, no more than four ships should arrive quarterly, in practice nine or ten arrive each three months. They come directly from Brazil and have nothing other than gold and tobacco with which to buy slaves. They use these slaves in the mines, but those they use for their plantations they fetch from Angola.[43] The manner in which both Portuguese and Spaniards treat their slaves, namely those who are destined for the mines, is inhuman. They are sent underground,

---

[40] R. is referring to the period of the confrontation brought about by de Bordes between the Elminas and the Fantes (Feinberg (1989) 145–7, 164–8). He may be specifically referring to an incident when H. Raems, the factor at Shama, on instructions from de Bordes, sent a boat loaded with gunpowder to Elmina fort, but the boat was seized by the Elminas between Komenda and Elmina (BLL, Furley N44 (3.11.1739, 24.11.1739)).

[41] This anecdote is not in 1756.

[42] There are numerous reports in the archives complaining of de Bordes' activities and asserting how greatly he was hated by the Africans (e.g., BLL, Furley N44 (17.9.1739, 3.11.1739, 17.11.1739, 16.12.1739)). On de Bordes' claim to absolute power, see a letter from English officers to Cape Coast, in BLL, Furley N44 (7.9.1739). Other tales of de Bordes' wild behaviour include one of his placing his Chief Factor, François Barovius, in a small cage and throwing bones to him (Feinberg (1989) 148). Upon his death in 1740, he was succeeded by that same Barovius, who was installed as President 'to the joy of everybody': BLL, Furley N45 (22.3.1740).

[43] Treaties forcing Portugal to pay a tithe (10% of a cargo) in toll were in existence from the mid seventeenth century (Pierre Verger, *Trade Relations between the Bight of Benin and Bahia from the 17th to 18th Centuries* (1976) 21–8). For the triangular trade between Portugal, Angola, and Brazil up to the end of the seventeenth century, see C.R. Boxer, *The Golden Age of Brazil 1695–1750* (1964) 4–5, 24–29. Governor van Voorst reported the boarding of a Portuguese ship over the issue of toll (BLL, Furley, N46 (27.12.1748); Van Dantzig (1978) 240–3; Postma (1990) 76–8). Further references to the Portuguese/Brazilian trade are made below, in 1756, /10/.

and never come /37/ up to see daylight again. Since, however, there are certain times when they are free from work, priests go down into the mines, to baptise them and teach them Christianity. They are also given some entertainment down there.[44] The usual price for a Guinean slave in Brazil is 16 ounces of gold.[45] I know that [some of] the Dutch have loaded ships, acquired a Portuguese passport and captain, and have, at their own expense, also sent slaves to Brazil, where they have profitably recovered their costs.[46]

In former times, right up to 1741, the Dutch Company forbade its factors to trade with other goods than Company goods — just as we also did. If the General wanted to ruin a man, it was up to him alone to send the Fiscal, together with his assistants, to the [particular] fort, without warning, where the Fiscal never failed to find contraband goods bought from interlopers. A [guilty] factor had then to try to come to an agreement with the General and the Fiscal by paying a fine; otherwise he would be thoroughly ruined. Indeed he had, at times, to carry the musket [*sc.* become a mere soldier] at Elmina. This did not happen without the Company losing considerably by it, since often the factor had lent his goods /38/ to Black merchants [to sell for him], and when the factor was removed they did not have to pay up.[47]

After de Bordes' death, their chief merchant, Barovius, became president.[48] He instituted free trading for all the factors on condition that they paid an eight-rixdaler fee to the Company for every slave bought and sold. Further, they had to report, under oath, to the Elmina office at the end of every month how many slaves they had bought and sold. The Company's goods were so [favourably] priced that when Company ships arrived the factors would prefer to deliver slaves to the Company, it being to their advantage to do so. The Dutch Company profited considerably by these arrangements, and I believe they would have never changed any of them

---

[44] The Brazilian gold was largely alluvial, so R.'s accusation that Portuguese slaves worked continually underground was incorrect, but it probably represented a confusion with the labour in the silver mines in Spanish America, much of which was subterranean. Even so, the notion that slaves were continually underground was part of the *Leyenda Negra* fondly believed by many enemies of Spain and the Roman Catholic Church. For Brazilian gold mining and the labour therein, see Boxer (1964) 35–39, 182–83.

[45] According to R. (Chapter 5, /318/–/319/, below), the price of a male slave on land in Gold Coast was 96 *rixdaler* (representing 6 oz. of gold), while the ship's price varied from 128 *rixdaler* (8 oz. of gold) to 160 *rixdaler* (10 oz. of gold). Given a price in Brazil of 16 oz. of gold, that is, 256 *rixdaler*, the mark-up was considerable. But again it is difficult to calculate profits since the uncertain additional costs need to be taken into account.

[46] On the practice of acquiring a Portuguese passport, see Bosman (1705) 89–90; Verger (1976) 24–6.

[47] Although R. seems to be continuing his remarks about the governorship of de Bordes, he states that the practice of inspecting for illegal goods happened 'right up to 1741'. But de Bordes died in 1740. By 'lent his goods' R. must mean that the goods were handed over on credit, a not uncommon practice in Afro-European trading. On the relationships between factors and the higher officials, cf. below (1756, /7/).

[48] Barovius is referred to but not named in 1756, /7/, below,

had the factors not become lukewarm in paying their fees. But after a year, hardly any of the Dutch factors reported more than ten slaves, although they had bought and sold 100. The Directors noticed this and asked the private shippers in Amsterdam and other places to lend them their ship's books, which they did. The Directors compared these /39/ to the books kept at Elmina, and they saw the differences, thus revealing the degree of embezzlement. They could conclude how many slaves must have been sold to other nations.[49] The Directors in Holland informed the Director-General and all the chief merchants of their calculation of what could be shown to have been unpaid, yet that was all the revenge they took on their servants on the Coast.[50]

However, the Dutch on the Coast did not forget to pay out their countrymen adequately, in particular those private shippers. No one was willing to sell slaves to their ships, or to have anything to do with the interlopers' captains. Indeed, the Dutch were so unscrupulous that they set the Negroes on them, to harm them in every way they could, with the result that many of these ships had to return to the Upper Coast in order to complete their trade.[51]

These Dutchmen make use of such titles as 'Director-General', or 'Council of the North and South Coast of Africa'. Such meaningless titles are the product of their imaginations, since in reality they have no more say over the Negroes than we do, that is, only as far as their shot can reach. Moreover, the Dutch are so hated by the Negroes in general that it would be easy to make the natives enraged against them, although not so easy /**40**/ to drive them away, as they drove the Portuguese away in earlier times.[52]

The Directors in Holland have realized that on most occasions when the Fiscal, on the General's orders, attacked a factor, always resulting in injury to the Company, a private quarrel was involved. They have, therefore, made their factors as good as free of the General, by decreeing that, when the

---

[49] Regarding the state of the books, there had been complaints during de Bordes' administration that frequent arrests and transfers of personnel created difficulties in bookkeeping (BLL, Furley N44 (20.9.1739), letter to WIC from Bookkeeper-General Verscheuren): Van Dantzig (1978) 343, doc. 408).

[50] Since this was 'all the revenge' taken for doctoring the books, perhaps certain Directors had an interest in the defalcations of some of the traders on the Coast. For the earlier and more extended version of this episode, see below (1756, /7/–/8/).

[51] For English relations with Dutch interlopers, and the Dutch Company's protests, see Van Dantzig (1980a) 155, 176, 179.

[52] The title 'Council of the Coast of North and South Africa' dated back to the time during the mid seventeenth century when the Dutch had almost complete control of the coast from Cap Blanc to the Cape of Good Hope (Feinberg (1989) 31). Bosman had found the title amusing because meaningless (Bosman (1705) 101). Between the Dutch and the Elmina Africans there was in fact a high degree of interdependency, but R.'s intention is to present the Dutch in the worst possible light and he therefore implies that they held their position only by force, and within the narrowest of geographical bounds.

factors overstepped their bounds, a trial should be held but no execution take place before the Directors had been informed of the case.[53]

It is not news that *Ober-Betientere* [Chief Assistants] in the Dutch service, given the advantages they enjoy and such dissolute consciences as they usually have, leave the Guinea Coast with more than a million guilders, a sum a Director-General normally earns [only] in five or six years.[54] It also appears that it is recognized in Holland that the Coast is only a good place for those servants who stay on there. For when a rich servant like this comes home, they regularly get him to /**41**/ buy stocks and receive him on the Board of Directors, yet they have not achieved their goal.[55]

An *Over-Commissarius* [Chief Factor], or Council member, receives in subsistence pay 20 guilders a month, and an ordinary factor 16, although twice that amount is expended daily at table. The individual dare not touch his salary because that would put him in discredit [sic] in Holland.[56] There is nothing in the world that such a man is incapable of doing, whether in accordance with religion, honesty, and humanity, or otherwise — it matters not to him. In Mr. de Petersen's time, the factors began to return to each other their original letters concerning their private affairs, together with the answers, for this reason — that if one of them were to die or were to initiate a betrayal, there would be no evidence. Mr. de Petersen employed a Jew by

---

[53] For a bitter comment, fifty years earlier, on the lack of freedom on the Council, of which the factors were also members, see Bosman (1705) 100–03. For an instance of conflict between the factor at Accra and the Governor, see note 30 above. Cf. Postma (1990) 63, 134.

[54] This seems to be another case of R.'s penchant for exaggeration. A Director-General's salary in the eighteenth century was 300 guilders a month, plus a subsistence allowance of 320 guilders a month, making 7,440 guilders p.a. In five years this would be 37,200 guilders, and in six years, 44,640 guilders. To increase his earnings to a million guilders, a Director-General would have had to make in private trade more than twenty times his salary. For Dutch Company salaries, see Feinberg (1989) 32. The practice of private trading by Company officers was not limited to the Dutch, but R. was eager to besmirch the Dutch reputation at every opportunity. For salaries supplemented, either legally or illegally, by private trade at the English stations, see K.G. Davies, *The Royal African Company* (1957) 111. Nor were the Danes averse to supplementing their salaries. A number of their governors were charged with profiteering at the expense of the Company, e.g. Anders Petersen Wærøe and Christian Glob Dorph (Joe Reindorf, *Scandinavians in Africa* (1980) 136). In his earlier work, R. had made a strong case for the practice, and necessity, of private trade — see below (1756, /43/–/44/).

[55] R.'s final remark is to some extent explained by the statement in his earlier publication that 'the Company loses considerable capital every year despite the purchase of stocks by the servants who have returned from the Coast' (below, 1756, /11/).

[56] A factor was paid 36 guilders a month, plus a subsistence allowance of 20 guilders a month, while an *Oppercommies* (Chief Factor) received 50–100 guilders a month, plus the subsistence allowance (which seems to have been the same for all ranks) (Feinberg (1989) 33). R.'s amounts are too low. However, he is saying that the subsistence amount is insufficient, hence the recipient had to resort to various other means to earn enough for food. This situation obtained at the other establishments too. For similar difficulties among the English staff at Cape Coast, see John Atkins, *A Voyage to Guinea* (1735) 90–1. Why the salary was not to be touched is unclear, but perhaps it was the normal arrangement, as was the case with sailors, that most or all of the amount was only paid to Company servants on return home.

the name of Alexander, whom he had made hospital manager at Elmina, to cast false gold for him. Mr. van Voorst, who was his successor, ordered it from Europe in entire hundredweight and swindled in this way all the nations.[57] /**42**/

No nation has such a great turnover in trade as the Dutch have, the result of their having their forts supplied with goods at all times, so that the Blacks there have a choice among many hundreds of articles of every kind.[58] Although this is not advantageous for the Company, it is for its servants. One sort [of stock] replaces another, the Chief Assistants buying and ordering entire shiploads, and yet all are sold. Thus a Chief Assistant may advance a very large sum to a trustworthy soldier to allow him to trade, and thereby prove that he can be a good Coastman by being in a position to trade when the opportunity arises.[59]

[The Dutch (1756)]

Since, as has just been shown, the Guinea trade, with its profitable branches, has been the source of wealth for England, Holland, and France, I must now explain on what basis each nation has carried it on. I shall begin with the Dutch, /**6**/ they having been the first to drive the Portuguese from the Guinea Coast. Indeed, they have even tried to exclude England, this twice leading to war. The Dutch have fourteen forts on Gold Coast, and it might be said that no enemy is able drive them out by force. In earlier times they had a Guinea Company and a West Indian Company, but they realized that the latter could have no advantage without the Guinea Coast, or the former without the West Indies. They combined their stocks, forming a West Indian and Guinea Company. This was divided into four classes, or chambers, namely, of Amsterdam, Zeeland, Rotterdam and Utrecht. I never encountered any ships on the Guinea Coast from the last two places, although I have seen, in the office of the Dutch chief castle, Elmina, separate account books for each chamber. It may well be that the Utrecht and Rotterdam trades send ships to the Guinea Coast using commissioners from Zeeland and Amsterdam. No nation has been able to do business on the Coast as well as the Dutch, since their better establishments in the West Indies, their many forts, and the enterprise and experience of this nation have certainly combined to enable them to become masters there. But it is a stroke of luck for the other nations

---

[57] Jacob Baron de Petersen succeeded Barovius in 1741; Jan van Voorst became Governor after de Petersen, and was in office 1747–1754 (Feinberg (1989) 163). For imported false gold, see note 22 above.

[58] For imports at Elmina, see below (1756, /13/–/14/); also Feinberg (1989) 49–52; Postma (1990) 103–5.

[59] R.'s argument appears to be that maximizing sales benefits the factor, who takes for himself so much of the profit that the Company does not gain.

that the Dutch harbour such great envy among themselves, sometimes setting aside religion, conscience, and all Christian virtues in order to injure one another. On the other hand, the Directors in Holland have done all they could to prevent such [in-fighting and] corruption, making the factors as good as independent of the Director-General, yet this has not helped much. An ambitious Director-General can still be seen attaining his goal by the death of one or other factor, and counting the factor, after his death, to be in debt to the Company to the extent of many thousands of guilders. /7/

Until 1740 the Dutch Company placed limitations on their factors, forcing them to depend exclusively on the Director-General. If the Director-General wished to ruin a man it was done by sending a Fiscal-General and an Assistant to the factor's fort without warning. They never failed to find foreign goods, and then the factor had to come to an agreement with the Fiscal-General, to give him what he wanted, or see himself totally ruined—indeed, forced to become a [mere] soldier at Elmina. I said this was the situation until 1740, being the period during which they had a Director-General named de Bordes, whose merit wholly consisted in what is said above, and who was there by virtue of having a brother who was a director in their Company in Amsterdam. He was, in general, an unreasonable and brutal man who conducted himself so coarsely that his factors rebelled against him, each one making himself sovereign at his own fort. When De Bordes died, their Chief Merchant succeeded him as President, as was the custom on the Coast.[60] And he established free trade for all the factors, on condition that they paid eight *rixdaler* in gold as a fee for each slave they bought or sold. Thus it can be seen that formerly a Dutch factor was in a weak position when a Director-General felt no good will towards him, but now the factors are better off. The Dutch company sent a Director-General to the Coast again, and he approved of everything the President and his council had decided.[61] Furthermore, the Company decreed that the Director-General and the Council should not have the power to dismiss the factors or to trouble them in any way. But, if it could be proved that they had not reported honestly about purchases and sales, this should be made known to the Directors in Holland.

It came about that, after the very first year /8/ when the factors had the freedom described above, the Directors in Holland saw that, instead of suffering an annual loss of a great sum for the maintenance of the forts on Gold Coast, they now enjoyed a considerable profit. And what was most remarkable was that, although they had sent no goods to the

---

[60] The successor, as Director-General, was François Barovius, March 1740–March 1741 (Feinberg (1989) 163).
[61] The 'President' here seems to be the president of the Council at Elmina.

Coast, yet they received payments for goods the factors evidently had had in storage at their forts from an earlier period, when they had not been able to trade them for slaves, gold or ivory. A number of Company ships sailing to the Coast at that time were immediately supplied with as many slaves as the captains wished to take on board, since the Council had put such a price on the Company's goods that all the factors competed to see who could deliver the greatest number, whereas formerly they had been forced [individually] to deliver [only] as many as 50 slaves for each ship's load. The price for one male slave paid by the Dutch factors was 96 *rixdaler*, which was a common price. But the Council at [Dutch] Elmina had set a price of 3–6 *rixdaler* for certain goods we sold at Christiansborg for 5–10 *rixdaler*. Their Viopœl [*sc.* ? best] brandy sold an anker of 50 *potter* for 4 *rixdaler*, while we at Christiansborg sold an anker of Flensborg brandy holding 35–6 *potter* for 8–10 *rixdaler*; and all other sorts of goods *advenant* (accordingly).[62] So, even though the French at that time paid 160 *rixdaler* and more for a slave, the Dutch factors preferred to deliver their slaves to the [Dutch] Company rather than to others, since they saw their own profit therein.

The Dutch Company was well satisfied with this arrangement, and I believe they would never have changed it if the factors had not become lukewarm in their undertaking to pay their fees — it is certain that, after three years, no factor on the Coast was paying for more than ten slaves when they actually had bought and sold one hundred. /9/ The Directors in Holland noticed this, and took the trouble to examine the books of a particular Captain who sailed as a slaver for a certain owner in Amsterdam. There they saw that both the Director-General and the factors had not paid over even a tenth of what they had sold to the Amsterdam firm, even although they had recorded their payments, under oath, at the Elmina office every month. From this the Directors were able to calculate how great their loss had been in relation to what had been sold to the French, English, and other ships. They therefore ordered the ship-owners in all the provinces to send them the account-books kept on their ships and this was done. When they then compared these books with the account-books kept at Elmina, they immediately saw the difference, a large sum. The Directors in Holland then sent to each of the factors, as well as to the Director-General, a bill for what each still owed the Company. This was all the revenge they took on their servants. But when the Dutch on the Coast discovered they had been found out, they did not

---

[62] For the term translated 'accordingly', R. wrote *Advenant*, which seems to represent the French *à l'avenant* 'appropriately, accordingly'. The argument in this paragraph is not easy to follow. But presumably R. is arguing that all Dutch goods were cheaper, hence the African sellers of slaves did better with the Dutch because they received more of the cheaper Dutch goods. But precisely why this benefited the Dutch factors is not so obvious — perhaps as intermediaries in the transaction they took a proportional cut.

forget to adequately repay their countrymen—the particular shipowners [who had supplied evidence against them]—by refusing to sell slaves to their ships. In fact, they were so unscrupulous that they set their Negroes on them, in order to do them all the harm they could, with the result that most of the Dutch slave-ships coming to Gold Coast, in order to trade had to sail off to the Upper Coast, with great difficulty.[63] Since then only a few Dutch slave-ships venture to come to Gold Coast, unless the General himself, or one of the most prominent officers, has also in interest in the company owning the ship. At the installation in 1746 of Director-General Jean van Voorst[64] the previous system of payment of fees was abolished, and the factors were again to trade for the Company, as earlier. /10/ But the independence of the factors was confirmed by the Company, and the General and Fiscal dared not rob them as they had done before.

You might think that the Dutch Company has profited enormously on the Guinea coast when you consider the following. First, their factors are so well supplied with goods at all times that occasionally they have more goods in a lodge (or Negro hut) than we have at Christiansborg [castle]. Secondly, no assortment of goods brought to the Coast can be unmarketable for them because, along a stretch of 100 miles from Axim to Chaqvin [Jackin] on the Lower Coast, they have factors who can communicate and negotiate with each other at will, and if any of their goods deteriorate, a Portuguese will [still] buy them in exchange for his gold or tobacco. Since he would place his life in danger, I would not advise a Portuguese to refuse [to buy rotten goods from a Dutchman]. However, a slave could not display greater obedience to his master than a Portuguese does to the worst Dutchman on the Guinea Coast. Thirdly, the Portuguese, by virtue of treaties, must pay a sizeable toll at Elmina, amounting to a tenth. Even so, they are not let off so easily, for although, with the Company's permission, from each ship the General receives only 16 oz. of gold, the Fiscal 8 oz., and the Chief Merchant 8 oz., I would be willing to bet that thrice that amount is the total they take from each Portuguese ship, in addition to the goods they are allowed to bring from Holland.[65] And the Portuguese pay them shilling for shilling for what, in turn, the Dutch take to Brazil, where the latter still sell them to their own profit. The King of Portugal has often

---

[63] Because of the prevailing wind and the Guinea current, sailing westwards along the coast, that is, from Gold Coast to the 'Upper Coast', presented difficulties, particularly at certain seasons (Tilleman [1697] (1994), 44). Why the Dutch ships had to backtrack westwards when slaving was difficult on Gold Coast, rather than proceed to the 'Slave Coast', is not explained.

[64] R. appears to have his dates wrong here. Jan van Voorst was Director-General from April 1747 to July 1754 (Feinberg (1989) 163). But it is just possible that R. was reporting a date of appointment in Amsterdam rather than the date of assuming office on Gold Coast.

[65] A particularly obscure reference, the whole sentence being crabbed.

forbidden the Brazilian merchants, under severe penalties, from sending more than one ship a month to the Coast, but the merchants could not do without more, their slaves dying in great numbers /**11**/ in the mines. In return for allowing the merchants more ships, the Viceroy [of Brazil] demands from them large gifts. Every month five ships arrive [on Gold Coast], and sometimes nine or ten. Indeed, I have known the Dutch to buy up the old ships the English had used for many years on the Coast, and, with the help of Brazilian merchants, acquire a Portuguese pass, install a Portuguese captain on these ships, and send them, full of slaves, to Brazil, where they were paid 16–20 oz. of gold for each slave.

Considering all this, you might assume that the Dutch Company made a profit on the Guinea Coast, yet the opposite is the case. The Company loses a considerable amount of capital every year, and if they did not benefit from a certain percentage on each ship sent as an interloper to the Coast by the private merchants in Holland, I feel certain that they would not be able to hold out for long—or else would have to make many changes on the Guinea Coast. In Holland they recognize that the Coast is of benefit only to the Company's servants, and rarely does a General or Chief Commissioner leave there without being in possession of a million guilders. When such a person arrives in Holland, they see to it that he buys stocks [in the Company], and they place him on the Board of Directors—which is how a number of persons whom I knew on the Coast are now Directors;—yet the Directors have not achieved their purpose [of controlling their employees and making the trade pay].

To describe adequately the Company servants on the Coast and the unchristian measures they take to enrich themselves is an impossibility. The Board of Directors in Holland pays its commissioners and factors only a small salary and a food allowance. As the commander of a fort, a commissioner receives as table allowance 16 guilders a month, while he expends twice as much each day. He dares not touch his salary, since that would be a humiliation and would, moreover, /**12**/ place him in discredit in Holland. So he must look for other ways to enrich himself, which would be impossible were he to follow [strictly] the instructions of the Company. In consequence, there is nothing in the world such a man is not capable of doing. Whether the deed is in accord with honesty and conscience, or otherwise, is of no account to him. I dare write this openly because, together with many French and Englishmen, I can prove it. I shall report briefly on the last two Directors-General at Elmina, namely de Petersen and van Voorst.[66] The former had in his service a Jew named Alexander whom he had installed as the manager of the hospital

---

[66] Jacob Baron de Petersen was Director-General from March 1742 to April 1747 (Feinberg (1989) 163).

at Elmina. This Jew produced false gold for him. The same Alexander left the Guinea Coast in 1744 on a ship to Middelburg, in company with me,[67] and he assured me that de Petersen had never provided gold more than half of which was pure, but had included gold adulterated with brass. It was especially the French who carried large amounts of it from Elmina, and they were unable to discover its quality before it was placed in a crucible for smelting. Mr van Voorst, on the other hand, operated in another way. The Jew, mentioned above, had left, and although some Blacks had learned the craft, he felt that a European artist could do a better job. He therefore sent a sample to Holland [for adulteration] and ordered a few pounds at first. But when he discovered that the European craftsman had a better understanding of the art, he ordered entire hundredweights [of false gold], in which any good gold was entirely lacking. Van Voorst used this to pay the French and Portuguese captains for their goods. The Fiscal-General was nearly as good at this as the General, and I have been told by two French captains that the names of both Dutchmen have been black-listed at the Bourses in Rochelle, Nantes and St Malo, not once but several times, by those captains /13/ who had been cheated by them. These two ruined their own credit to the extent that no French captain was willing to go ashore there [at Elmina] in order to trade. But before this occurred, many hundredweights of that false gold had been put into circulation in place of good gold. The Elmina garrison, numbering 100 men, is [still] paid in that same currency for their food allowance and salary, although according to Company rules they should have been paid in good gold. It is impossible to say how many people die of hunger there. Company ships bring some 60–80 soldiers to Elmina, and before the ship has left five or six are already near death, because the Blacks refused to sell them provisions [for bad gold] and the soldiers have to seize some by force — which the General has allowed them to do.[68]

In trading, the Dutch garrison surpasses the military personnel of the other nations. You might assume that, for fear of losing out on the sale of their own goods, the staff would prevent the lowest ranks of servants from trading, but experience has shown that this is not so on the Guinea Coast. The more trade that is carried on at any place, the more trade is attracted there, and this is certainly true of Elmina, where not only does the Dutch Company have a great warehouse, but the General, the Fiscal, the Chief Merchant, the Chief Bookkeeper, and the Secretary buy and order from Holland entire shiploads [of goods], and everything is sold. You can see the great difference if you spend one day at Cape Coast (the English chief

---

[67] R.'s return was because of the rebellion against Governor Billsen. See Appendix B.
[68] Early deaths of Europeans arriving in Guinea were not uncommon but were usually ascribed to onboard ailments or the local diseases. In this instance a degree of malnutrition might have weakened the soldiers, but unless the ship stayed long after arrival, the poor or unsuitable feeding is as likely to have been aboard ship as on shore. R.'s anecdote is not altogether convincing.

fort) and the next day at Elmina. At Cape Coast you might be there an entire day without seeing the factors go into the warehouse. At Elmina, on the other hand, you cannot have a quiet conversation with the employees mentioned above, for as long as half an hour, before their black domestic servants interrupt them, to /14/ announce either that a black trader has come with a few ounces of gold and wants a certain type of goods, or that a slave has been brought in for sale, and so on. It is certainly not just because of this situation that more trade is carried on at Elmina than at all the other forts. No! It is because all the Blacks, even though they may live 100 miles inland, know that at Elmina they can find any type of goods they desire, indeed, they can choose from among some hundred pieces of each kind.

If you wish to know how the Dutch deport themselves when anyone complains of having received false gold from them, I shall here briefly report an incident which happened several months before I left the Coast—an incident related to me first by several Englishmen and then by the Frenchman himself. You may know that the French export great quantities of all kinds of silk cloths, chiefly to the Guinea Coast, after that to the West Indies. These are goods that have gone out of fashion in France, and the French manufacturers are happy when a captain or naval officer is willing to take them [off their hands], and they share the profit with him. A captain from Nantes had just such an arrangement or 'bottomry',[69] in respect of what the French call *pacotille* [cheap goods, junk]—and had among his assortment of goods a great quantity of brocade textiles. It was his misfortune that on the Upper Coast he did not meet any Portuguese, to whom he had planned to sell these textiles. So he had to anchor in Elmina road, thinking that those at the fort could sell the silks more easily than he could. Being himself sick, the captain sent the surgeon ashore with all the silk goods. The surgeon sold them all with good profit, to the satisfaction of the captain—[and to the satisfaction of the Dutch,] yet not to that of the General alone, but to that of many other Company employees there. The captain weighed anchor and sailed away /15/ that same day to Cape Coast, where he had acquaintances and could enjoy a few days of relaxation. The next day, at dinner, the conversation turned to his trade, and the captain told those there about the good price he had received for his silk textiles. The chief agents at Cape Coast could not believe this, realizing immediately that the poor man had been cheated by the Dutch, and they then asked him to have the gold brought ashore. This was done, and they showed him that it was false. The captain immediately sent his surgeon back to Elmina with

---

[69] Bottomry was a system of lending money to shipowners for the purposes of a voyage on the security of the ship, the lender forfeiting the money if the ship was lost. R. appears to extend the meaning to cover lending goods against a return from future overseas sales.

the false gold, still packed in the same paper in which he had received it from the General and the other employees. Mr. van Voorst ordered him to come forward, and the surgeon complained of having received false gold from the Dutch serving at the Fort. The General, in order to administer justice, summoned one Company servant after the other to his upper room, and asked the Frenchman to point out which packet he had received from which employee. The Frenchman had a good memory and without hesitation showed the packets for each one, whereupon the General asked his servants if they had represented this as good gold, and they answered, 'Yes'. The General ordered them to fetch good gold immediately. This was done by four of the servants, who either did not have the impudence to deny their cheating or thought that their Governor seriously intended to help the poor man. Up to then the Frenchman had said nothing about the General's own gold. However, after he had received the [good] gold from the servants, he said, with tears in his eyes, that modesty had thus far not permitted him to ask the General also to *troquere* [exchange] his gold, but since he saw His Excellency treating him with such prompt justice, he felt assured that he dared ask this without fear of dire results, since His Excellency would find no enjoyment in the total ruin /16/ of a poor man, a man who shortly before had been ransomed from English captivity. The surgeon promptly brought out a large box apparently containing eighty ounces of gold. Mr. van Voorst, who had listened gravely to him, responded by saying that if he did not leave the fort immediately the batons of three corporals would accompany him out! And in this way he was cheated. I could report many such affairs, but will pass over them, leaving the difference there is between those [Dutch] there and those in Europe to your judgement. Those here [in Europe] know that trade increases when customers are treated fairly; those there have no such concept.

Earlier I spoke about the jealousy and envy of one another the Dutch display, but this is cancelled out when it comes to insulting or oppressing the English or us. We have examples of a Dutch factor and his entire garrison of some twenty men swearing an oath about something which was patently a lie, and could be proved to be so. But what would their military personnel not do for a glass of brandy? — men owning [only] one pair of shoes who have served three or four *potentater* [masters]. Is there anything such desperate people cannot be persuaded to do? They have settled in all of the most difficult places on the Lower Coast, such as Little Popo, Great Popo, Appe, Eppe, Chaqvin, etc.[70] These deserters come in droves from Holland, and when they arrive at Elmina they realize that they must

---

[70] Little Popo [Anecho], Appe [Apa], Eppe [Epe], and Chaqvin [Jakin] were all localities on the Slave Coast (that is, east of River Volta and therefore beyond the normally accepted limits of Gold Coast), the last three in modern Dahomey/Bénin.

undertake desperate actions in order to improve their ill fortune. This means that three or four of them are taken to places such as those just mentioned, and left there to perish or be beaten to death by the Blacks — otherwise they must die a lingering and miserable death by starvation /17/ at Elmina. If any of them dared to remark that it is unchristian to treat people this way, he would be hanged as a rebel. Such examples are made, often on flimsy excuses, in order to strike fear into the other deserters. On the Coast these individuals cannot desert, because the English and we ourselves have made an agreement with the Dutch to hand them back, and if they try to desert to the Negroes, they are then sold to their forts again. Thus it is their *non plus ultra* [this far and no further]

All of the places on the Lower Coast under Dutch control have come into their hands in the following way. Sometimes twice or thrice a year, they send new people after the Negroes have taken the lives of the former ones. They do this until the Negroes themselves have become bored with killing them but have, *peu à peu* [little by little], learned to dance to their tune. That is to say, the Negroes deliver slaves, etc, to the Dutch [agents], and they, in turn, sell the slaves to the ships, living off the profit, since from Elmina they do not receive the least thing, in terms of goods or anything else. The Council at Elmina knows that this results in some loss, yet they are sure that they will never see the offender again. However, if it happens that one or another of these fellows survives, he cannot fail to become a rich man. Then the Dutch no longer send their silenced deserters to those places where the Negroes have been tamed. If such a man wishes to be relieved and to go to Europe, he is not allowed to leave, but, instead, is made a factor, and is sent five or six soldiers to keep beside him, for safety's sake. The Portuguese go to such places on the Lower Coast in droves, having discovered that the Negroes they purchase there are very hardy and best suited to work in their [Brazilian] gold mines, and, although they have paid their toll at Elmina, the Dutch /18/ do not want them to trade directly with the Negroes, but to buy slaves from the Dutch employees.

This, I feel, is enough to give you an idea of the Dutch situation on the Guinea Coast. Despite the sums lost to the Directors in Holland by such behaviour on the Coast, they earn double that amount [in fees] from other merchants in Holland who wish to send ships to Guinea, to trade either for slaves or just for gold and ivory. These so-called gold-traders are ships which usually carry a cargo worth 30,000 guilders, and they sail along the Coast to sell their goods, for gold or ivory, to the Europeans and the Blacks. The English from London and other places have often tried to get rid of them, but they have never succeeded without loss, so we must admit that there are arts in which no one can emulate the Dutch. Only since 1730 or 1731 have the merchants in Holland been given permission to trade on the Coast on these terms. Before then they were called 'sly foxes', and whenever a Dutch Company ship encountered a sly fox and could overpower it, such ships were declared legal prizes. However, that rarely happened because the interlopers normally travelled two to three together, and when they saw a Company ship they did not wait to be attacked but fired on it first, [often] inflicting great damage. Otherwise, they were informed by the Dutch factors themselves when a Company ship was present, so the interlopers usually sailed to other places [and stayed away] until the ship was gone.

[The English (1760)]

The English are not as strong on the Guinea Coast as are the Dutch.[71] They have only seven fortresses.[72] It may generally be said that they live in accordance with the morals by which they were brought up, and never in any way bring shame to their countrymen in Europe. We have never seen an instance of an Englishman cheating anyone with false gold, or in any other way.[73] The English also have an entirely different form of government from the Dutch. There are three chief agents, who can be described as Chief Governor, Chief Merchant, and Chief Bookkeeper.[74] All three have equal authority, and switch rank every week. Yet it must be /**43**/ admitted that no other Company's affairs are in such poor shape as those of the English. Ships come out from England only rarely, and when they do come the factors are given nearly the entire cargo as payment for the advances they have had to make for the maintenance of the garrison and forts. Each of their forts has a fixed staff, and whether they are actually present or not, the factors and agents enjoy their salaries, and thus profit quite considerably. The same practice applies to their warships, and it might be called 'perks'.[75]

---

[71] In his earlier publication, R. gave a much fuller account of the English 'Royal African Company' on Gold Coast, see below (1756, /18/–/25/).
[72] The seven English forts were as follows: Dixcove, Komenda, Cape Coast Castle, Tantumquery, James Fort (Accra), Fort Vernon (Prampram), Fort Charles (Anomabu) — the last abandoned and demolished in 1731 but reconstructed in 1737 (Van Dantzig (1980b) 58–9).
[73] For opinions about the English on Gold Coast diametrically opposed to the opinion of R., see Barbot [1732] (1992) 393–5, 407, note 19; Bosman (1705) 48–53. The Dutchman described the English as illegal protectors of Dutch soldiers who had deserted, also as being besotted, slovenly, greedy, and immoral, the last in the sense of having African 'wives' (which was, of course, general among the European residents in Guinea). For the realities of life at the European forts, see Davies (1957) 253–8.
[74] Repeated below (1756, /19/, /21/), with the English agents named. For a slightly different version of the division of authority in an earlier period, see Davies (1957) 244.
[75] Reference here is to the Royal African Company (RAC), established in 1672, which continued until 1752. For difficulties experienced by the RAC, see Eveline C. Martin, *British West African Settlements 1750–1820* (1927) 7–9; Davies (1957) 344–7. For an example of the cost of maintenance of the English forts and lodges, see Elizabeth Donnan, *Documents Illustrative of the History of the Slave Trade to America* (1930–1935) II: 109–12. R. earlier supplied a fuller account of the manning of the English forts: see below (1756, /19/–/20/). That English warships had 'dead souls' as officers seems unlikely, and the earlier work does not mention this.

The English let no European starve to death, as the Dutch do. They have Mulattos as soldiers, and if their pay, which is half brandy or *kieldyvel* [kill-devil], and half water, does not suit them, they can be dismissed.[76] They have no Europeans as soldiers, apart from the officers at Cape Coast, and if they are sent anyone from England, or anyone who has been released from our fort, he becomes a sergeant straight away, and receives 20 *rixdaler* a month as salary.[77] If there are goods or gold in storage for the Company, the man can choose which of these things he wants [as capital for trading] but if not he must take what the factors care to grant him; since this /**44**/ is an advance and when the ships come in the factor takes [from him] goods at [the local] gold price in return.[78] If an *Under-Betient* [Assistant] has the means for his own maintenance, he can, upon the arrival of the ships, take goods on credit himself, or on assignment to the directors in England.[79] Up to 1741 the English Company received £10,000 sterling annually for the maintenance of their establishments, but this was not sufficient so it applied for more.[80] In 1742 three chief agents were stationed there. They managed things so that, although they had no goods with which to trade, yet they could fully support the forts with the sum mentioned above—indeed the forts were twice as strongly manned as before.[81]

Unprofitable as the situation was for the English Company on the Guinea Coast, the conditions organized for its staff were, in general, good, and of advantage to them. For the traders on the Gold Coast splendid arrangements exist. When they have sick slaves, a factor must take them into the fort. A captain allows his sailors to go ashore with his slaves, in order to /**45**/ buy from the Negroes the type of refreshment they desire.[82] At nearly all the English forts there are gardens which are kept up by the Company, using a certain number of Company slaves. A captain can get as many vegetables as he wants for his people, and a couple of *lod* of garden seeds are used for

[76] For a view of the treatment by the English of the 'White Negroes', that is, the 'Mulattos', see Atkins (1735) 90. In 1772 there were reports of cruelty and 'the miserable state of the ill-treated soldiers as one of the scandals of coast management' (Martin (1927) 38). This situation was probably not new and may have obtained in R.'s time. *Kieldyvel* was rum or cheap brandy, the nickname originating in the Danish West Indies. For more on the payment of Mulatto soldiers, see below (1756, /20/).

[77] For rapid advancement in rank, partly due to deaths, see Martin (1927) 39.

[78] In the eighteenth and nineteenth centuries, the traders operated with two prices for gold, the coastal or currency price of £3 12s per ounce for unrefined gold as it was purchased on Gold Coast; and the world price of £4 per ounce for gold refined in Europe to coinage standard (Davies (1957) 253; Garrard (1980) 258–9).

[79] R.'s remarks refer to the private trading permitted to European staff.

[80] Fuller references to the financing of the English forts appear below (1756, /20/–/21/). The £10,000 annual subsidy actually continued until 1743. It was doubled in 1744, then reduced, and finally cancelled (Davies (1957) 345).

[81] Cf. below, 1756, 18–19. For Company staff and their salaries at an earlier period, c.1680, see Davies (1957) 252–3.

[82] These slaves were perhaps Company slaves, and for that reason receiving preferential treatment (Martin (1927) 52–3).

payment.[83] Most of the watering places being in English hands, the English can obtain fresh water without paying for it, provided their own people draw it. The other nations, on the other hand, must pay dearly, and, at times, can obtain none, not even for payment.[84]

Until 1730 the English acquired most of the slaves purchased on the Coast. But since that date French ships have become thrice as many as English, thereby putting the French colonies in America in a very flourishing condition. The French have also tripled the amount of West Indian produce brought to Europe [by them] compared with what the English bring.[85]

[The English (1756)]

The English have seven forts on the Guinea Coast, and these are only poorly manned. Normally we see [only] one or two Europeans at their forts, the rest being Mulattos (that is, individuals born of a European and a black woman). /19/ Their chief castle is more fully manned, having a staff of fifteen Europeans, both military and civilian, and an approximately equal number of Mulattos. The English form of government is entirely different from that of the Dutch, the English council consisting of three people, the Governor, Chief Merchant and Chief Bookkeeper, who are collectively called Chief Agents. Each has equal authority and it cannot be said that one has a higher rank than the others. They alternate every week, so that the one whose week it is puts the first signature on documents and the account books, sits himself in the highest position, and gives orders to the garrison, etc. This lasts until Saturday, then one of the other two takes his place. The English forts on the Guinea Coast are so poorly maintained that ten years ago the buildings were threatening to fall on their heads. The Directors in England do not manage affairs on the Guinea Coast in a just manner. Thirty years ago the Government, against the will of the Directors, gave three places the liberty of trading on the Coast, those places being London, Bristol and Liverpool. Since these cities traded there

---

[83] One *lod* = 15.5. grams.
[84] For a description of water supplies at Cape Coast, and the gardens in the 1690s, see Phillips [1694] (1732) 204–5. See also Chapter 1 above, note 7.
[85] 1730 was the year in which dues to the RAC were replaced by a parliamentary subsidy. After this, the Company no longer held a monopoly for the slave trade, but it maintained the forts and collected fees from individual traders. That English trade with Gold Coast actually declined is uncertain and perhaps doubtful. In the relevant decades there were frequent complaints about the constant presence of French ships and their trading. For instance, in 1730 Pranger, the Dutch Director-General at Elmina, reported many French ships trading with the Fante and the Asante, and in 1739 and 1749 there were complaints about the number of French ships in the road (BLL, Furley N43 (16.4.1730), N46 (30.9.1749—a letter from Accra); Van Dantzig (1978) 343, doc. 409). The chief French West Indian colonies in mid-century were Martinique, Guadeloupe, and Saint-Domingue (J.H. Parry, P. Sherlock, and A. Maingot, *A Short History of the West Indies* (1987) 51, 57, 94). The claim that the French had overtaken the English was earlier stated by R.—see below (1756, /25/).

without paying anything, the Parliament in England gave the African Company in London £10,000 sterling annually.[86] It should be noted that the West Indian and Guinea Companies were not combined in England but remain different companies.

Strange to say, in earlier times a decision was made as to the extent of the manning of each English fort on the Coast, and whether the entire staff were present or not, the [actual] factors enjoyed the [total of the fixed] salaries. For instance, it was determined that a fort should have a staff consisting of one Factor, two Assistants, one sergeant, two corporals, one constable and 20 foot soldiers. The Factor could enter all their wages in the Company books, these being £100 sterling annually for himself, /20/ £60 for each Assistant, £50 for the sergeant, £40 for each corporal and 10 *rixdaler* monthly for each soldier — when in fact, the actual staff present consisted only of himself and two or three Mulattos.[87] These Mulattos received 10 *rixdaler* monthly in [the form of] 10 *potter* of *kieldyvel* ['kill-devil', brandy] mixed with an equal amount of water, making up 10 bottles.[88] This could be sold for as many *rixdaler*.[89] The same situation obtained at Cape Coast, where that fort was supposed to have a staff of one hundred persons, yet sometimes there were not as many as twenty military personnel, made up of Mulattos who were paid, as in other places, with half brandy and half water as salary. (I have explained earlier what a Mulatto is, and although these individuals have mostly Dutch fathers they are not taken into [Dutch] service.[90] We Danes do not take any of them [into service] unless they were born under our fort and christened. The others must seek work in the English service, where they are normally accepted for employment.) In this way an English factor might earn £3,000-£4,000 sterling in the course of four or five years. Then, when he has enough money to his credit with the Company in London, he shows proof of having maintained the fort and garrison for so many years and thus having the [accumulated] sum to his credit. Thereupon he travels to London. The Directors make their apologies [for their lack of immediate funds to pay him] (as is to be expected), but the factor

---

[86] For an extended and more correct account of the rise and success of the interlopers, and the changes in the monopoly of the RAC, see Davies (1957) chap. 3.

[87] Given the high mortality, it is plausible that this abuse existed, although R. instances it to an implausible extent.

[88] For *kieldyvel*, see note 76 above.

[89] If the full value had been always obtainable, the payment was a fairly reasonable one, but probably it was not. On the other hand, it is unlikely that the Mulattos would have continued to serve if they had been grossly and regularly underpaid.

[90] It is highly unlikely that the main RAC fort, staffed with a number of Englishmen, was ever so affected by mortality that no Englishmen remained; but possible that among them, at a particular time, none counted as 'military personnel', thus justifying R's claim that the only soldiers were Mulattos.

makes claim to the funds allotted annually by Parliament [which the Company now applies for], and the Company receives none of this money until the factor is paid. It is easy to detect the weaknesses inherent in such an arrangement, particularly since a couple of factors, or a Chief Agent, leave the Coast every year.

The Directors requested more funds from Parliament, otherwise, they declared, they neither could nor would send more ships to the Guinea Coast, and would let all the English establishments fall into ruin. /21/ They then received (as I was told on the Coast in 1744) £20,000 sterling annually, on account of the claims of the factors, which they increased, in order to earn money to balance the losses of the Company. The factors wrote in that, at times, because of the visits they had had in a single week, they had had to expend from six to eight dozen bottles of Madeira wine, 20 gallons of rum (one gallon = 4 *potter*), and so on, and when they themselves had not had sufficient Company funds, so they wrote, they had had to use their own good gold.[91] When a man advanced to the post of factor in the English service and was given command of a fort holding Company goods worth £500-£1,000 sterling, he was able, after two years, to reckon that not only had the [sale of] goods covered his living costs, but that he even had a couple of thousand pounds sterling to his credit. If the Directors received money from Parliament which was not claimed by the agents and factors who had returned home, they sent out ships with goods. Normally, as soon as the ships arrived at the Coast all the factors gathered at Cape Coast, and each one had so much debt outstanding to his credit that the entire cargo, consisting usually of two ship-loads, went in meeting those debts, indeed in the end even that was not enough. This continued until 1744 when the English directors installed as Chief Agents Mr. David Crichton, Mr. Thomas Chalmer and Mr. James Cruix. If they had had support from the Directors in England these men would really have done their Company a great service. They took charge of the English forts, and noting the actual strength of the factors' garrisons, they examined the localities carefully. But most of the factors who had been personally profiting, together with the former chief agents, returned to England, and what they were owed [in credited salaries] for several years was more than the Directors could pay out of the money allotted to them by Parliament. /22/ The result was that the Chief Agents named above did not receive more than two shiploads [of goods] during a period of five to six years. They sent the returns of the trade in slaves and gold [to the Company], leaving themselves empty-handed, so in spite of all their honesty, they could accomplish nothing. On their return home, most of the former agents have been able to present to the Government in England [claims]

---

[91] The visits referred to might be from African traders and potentates, or from ship's officers — or from both.

of their service on the Coast as having been so outstanding that, in addition to their earnings, they have been placed in high positions, some in England, some as governors in the West Indies. However, the three gentlemen [named above] showed little profit on the Coast, and since the African Company in London is as good as dissolved, they have gained little regard (so unjustly can things sometimes happen in this world.)

As bad as things are for the affairs of the African Company on the Guinea Coast and in England, they are correspondingly good and advantageous for the [English] nation in general. Remarkable systems for the [independent] traders exist in London, as well as on the Guinea Coast. East Indian goods are not sold at auction, as they are here [in Copenhagen], but are stored in the East Indian houses, and lists are printed so anyone can see the price at which each piece of goods will be sold. The wholesalers have an excellent supply of all the kinds of goods manufactured in England which are marketable on the Coast. In this way, when they have been informed that there are not too many ships [there already], or when they receive information that two [African] nations on the Coast are preparing to go to war, the merchants can, in one week, supply 50–60 ships for the Guinea Coast. The [information on war preparations] indicates, first of all, that the Blacks will need guns and powder, and then that many slaves will be available. On the Coast the merchants have their own establishments, and whenever an English ship arrives and demands something of a factor, /23/ the latter must immediately help and serve him. If the captain wishes to put sick slaves ashore, the English factor must immediately take them into his fort and the captain sends along some sailors in order to purchase from the Negroes whatever refreshment the sick slave wants. The ships are provided with water for next to nothing, while other nations must pay dearly for it, and often receive none at all.

As I said earlier, the English have seven forts on the Coast, but this refers only to the Gold Coast.[92] On the Upper Coast they possess a large river, called River Gambia, where they can sail 100 miles upstream with their ships. They have forts and lodges on both banks, and they keep out all other nations.[93] The French have River Senegal, 20–30 miles to the north, but they dare not come here [to River Gambia] if they wish to keep their ships and goods. Here the African Company has made some profit every year, which is no wonder, because if one nation were to own [all] Guinea and were able to exclude others, it would be

---

[92] Most of what follows relating to the English on the 'Upper Coast' was not repeated in the later work. Cf. 1760, /25/.

[93] The English did not 'possess' River Gambia but they did to some extent control its export trade, by means of James Fort. R. continues with material on his 'Upper Coast', especially on the Sierra Leone region, but his vagueness and inaccuracies suggest that his acquaintance with this stretch of the Guinea Coast was limited.

better [for it] than it is in Peru and Mexico [for the Spaniards]. The gold and silver in the American mines there would never come up to the light of day if the Spaniards did not receive some 1,000 slaves annually from Africa — and did not let them die in the mines.

The English have five or six other places along the Upper Coast owned by some merchants in London, and it is interesting to learn how they came to [acquire] these establishments. It should be understood that the Negroes of the Upper Coast are friendly and generous by nature, so Europeans are safer in a Negro hut among them than they are on Gold Coast in a fortress with 30-40 cannon. When you travel along the [Guinea] Coast you notice a great difference among the peoples. The farther downcoast you come, the more morose and malicious are the inhabitants. Moreover, the Upper Coast is a more comfortable place, with great groves of palm trees, and large fields of rice, which /24/ seed themselves without the least trouble on the part of the inhabitants.[94] *Pisang* [plantain] and *bacco* [banana] (as we Danes call them)[95] and other delicious fruits are to be found in abundance. All of these wonderful things are lacking on the Lower Coast, where, during the dry season, nothing can be seen other than sun-scorched land and dry mountains. What I mean here by 'the Lower Coast' must not be taken to encompass more than the seashore or two miles inland from the sea, since I should, in truth, say that three to four miles inland is the most wonderful land in the world, and equal in every way to the Upper Coast — a land surpassing the West Indies in fertility and products. Some English captains have found the land on the Upper Coast so attractive that, at five or six places, they have from time to time settled there.[96] That is, when they have chosen such a place — which they had undoubtedly visited several times before and had already favoured — they set about things in the following way. They give orders to the officers and crew to unload all the goods, and when that has been done, they say to their first mate, 'Go home now, and give my greetings to the owners!' Some of them have been living in those places a long time, becoming wealthy and elderly there. In their old age most of them have a desire to end their lives in Christendom, but this is impossible unless they are willing to settle with the ship-owners and their heirs. This is normally done by the captain not only paying the

---

[94] Rice was certainly cultivated in western Guinea but does not sow itself, if that is what R. was intending to state. His knowledge of western Guinea and its crops seems to have been limited and perhaps slight.

[95] The term *pisang* for the plantain is still in use in Denmark. For *bacco/baccofen*, see Isert [1778] (1992) 68, 205; Jones (1983) 320.

[96] In the early decades of the eighteenth century a number of English pirates settled in the Sierra Leone estuary, and these seem to be the individuals to whom R. is referring. Stories about the pirates mingle fact and fiction, and it is difficult to say whether what R. narrates is factual or mere embroidery on contemporary reports (e.g. in Charles Johnson [= Daniel Defoe] *A General History of the most notorious Pyrates* (1724–1726), passim).

capital and interest on the place, but also ceding it to his ship-owner or heirs. If there are no living heirs, the captain is pardoned by the Government in England, and he cedes the place to the crown. All of the Englishmen who have been on the Coast know that the forts and establishments they have in Sierra Leone, and which have been so advantageous for trade, /25/ have been acquired in the way which I have just described, including the entire Island Bannanna [Banana Island], whose size is 20 miles.[97] I have also heard of other places but have not myself visited any others than the ones [sic] mentioned here. However, I have been at River Galinas, acquired by the English in the same way.[98] The Dutch are also said to have a place [there] still in their hands, but that began with an East Indian ship whose whole crew, except for five men, were close to death. Knowing nothing of navigation, they grounded the ship on purpose, saving as many goods and cannon as they could, and they built a small fort as protection against the Negroes. I do not know where this place is, although I am very well acquainted with the Upper Coast, but some Dutchmen have told me this story.[99] Who could imagine that the English nation, in possession of so many advantages and enjoying such encouragement both in England and on the Coast — being so experienced in trade and owning the most powerful colonies and islands in different climates in the West Indies, and, most of all, having captains, to whom they entrust their trade, who are experienced and sensible men, having travelled on the Coast since boyhood — who could imagine, I say, that they would be entirely forced out of the sugar trade by the French? (N.B. When we speak of 'the sugar trade' the term must be understood to cover all West Indian products, notably sugar, coffee, indigo, and cotton.) That the English now ship only a little of these goods compared to what they did earlier is because the French offer a better price for them [in France], therefore other nations [than the English] go there to buy them.[100]

---

[97] The major English bases in the Sierra Leone district, on Bunce Islands and Sherbro Island, belonged to the Royal African Company and its successors. Independent traders had establishments at other points but it is not known that any were acquired in the way R. describes. Other trading points were in the hands of Mulatto descendants of Portuguese and English traders. The two Banana Islands are small and jointly measure at the fullest extent only two miles. Almost certainly, R. has confused these islands with Sherbro Island, whose extent is about 30 miles. The above assumes that R. was using the English mile, but if the Danish mile of 4.7 English miles, he grossly exaggerates the size of his island.
[98] The English never 'acquired' River Galinhas but English ships traded there (Adam Jones, *From Slaves to Palm Kernels: A History of the Galinhas Country (West Africa) 1730–1890* (1983b) 21-4).
[99] No source for this story has been traced.
[100] The implication is that the English ship only to England and not to France, whereas 'other nations', including of course the French themselves, can ship to France.

[The French (1760)]

The French have no establishments on the Guinea Coast other than those at River Senegal and at Whydah on the Lower Coast, both of which /**46**/ are, however, not of any importance.[101] Yet in recent years they have done considerable shipping [of slaves].[102] They have often tried to get a foothold on this Coast, but have not taken the right course, as happened in 1744, when they attempted to establish themselves at Annamaboe. They thought it was enough that for several years they had supported in Paris, as a prince, a Negro boy from Annamaboe, the son of Corrantrin, calling him *le Prince [et] l'Empereur de la Côte de Guinée* [Prince and Emperor of the Guinea Coast].[103] What an incorrect report the captain who had brought him to Paris had presented is shown by the fact that Fante, where Annamaboe lies, is by no means the most powerful kingdom on Gold Coast. Indeed, there are cities in Fante which are much larger than Annamaboe, and in Annamaboe city itself there are caboceers, or kings, who are ten times more powerful than Corrantrin, father of the boy whom the French captain took to France with him.[104]

---

[101] In his later work R. omits the mocking comments on French behaviour of his earlier publication — see below (1756, /24/–/27/).

[102] The French who from the sixteenth century had traded in western Guinea, especially in Senegal, in the eighteenth century attempted to break into the trade in eastern Guinea, mainly in order to obtain slaves for their new West Indian colonies. They established no forts but had trading stations on Côte d'Ivoire and Gold Coast, and also at Whydah on the Slave Coast. For French establishments on the Slave Coast, see Barbot [1732] (1992) 635; John D. Hargreaves, *West Africa: The former French States* (1967) 61–2; Law (1991) 126 ff. For the French on Gold Coast, see Van Dantzig (1980b) 47; Albert van Dantzig, 'English Bosman and Dutch Bosman VIII', *History in Africa*, 11 (1984) 329 note 50. R.'s dismissal of the value of French trading activities in Senegal and at Whydah was not well founded.

[103] A very much fuller account of the French at Anomabu and the episode of the boy taken to France appeared in the earlier work — see below (1756, /29/–/31/). For an earlier French attempt to obtain a footing at Anomabu, see Van Dantzig (1980b) 58–9. For the French elsewhere on the Gold Coast, at Assini and Komenda, see Paul Roussier, *L'Établissement d'Issiny 1687–1702* (1935) xxx–xxxii, 73–7, 79–80, 96–103; Daaku (1970) 17, 61, 80–1.

[104] The French targeted Anomabu for several reasons: the large African settlement there could provide water and provisions; extensive trade in slaves from there already existed; the old Dutch fort had been demolished by the English and there was nothing yet to replace it; finally, they believed that they had a personal connection with the caboceer. (With variations, 'Caboceer' is derived from the Portuguese *cabeça* 'head, leader'.) Corrantrin (Koranteng) was Eno Baisee (Ano Bassi) Kurentsi, otherwise known as John Currantee, a merchant of Anomabu and, despite what R. says, a 'Great Cabuseer', according to de Petersen writing from Elmina (BLL, Furley N45 (2 7.1741); T.C. McCaskie, 'Nananom Mpow of Mankessim: an essay in Fante history', in David Henige and T.C. McCaskie, eds., *West African Economic and Social History* (1990) 141). In 1752 the RAC urged Governor Melvil to gain and keep the support of Currantee (J.J. Crooks, *Records relating to the Gold Coast Settlements from 1750 to 1874* (1923) 19–20). It was not uncommon for African notables to send their sons to Europe for education, as the guests of a host country with which they had relations on the Coast. Koranteng, profiting by the competition between the English and the French at Anomabu, also had two sons studying in England (Margaret Priestley, *West African Trade and Coast Society* (1969) 12–15, 40; Van Dantzig (1980b) 59).

64   *Chapter 2*

In 1744 the captain brought the boy back again, and thought that with his father's help he could build a fort there. The French brought a load of goods with them to the value of 30,000 *rixdaler*, which they stored in Corrantrin's house. But the caboceer himself, with his people, stole most of the /47/ goods from the French, by undermining their house at night. At first the French had wanted to guard their goods, and therefore they stayed at night at the place where the goods were locked up, yet somehow Corrantrin broke in at night, bound them hand and foot, and stole everything there. After that, they had to work out how to stay alive. Finally, they proposed to leave, but Corrantrin set fire to the house and let it burn down, only to have a reason to keep them there. He claimed that he had hidden many treasures and a great quantity of gold in the walls, and that this fire had damaged many thousand ounces of gold which the French had to pay for before they could leave. Doubtless he thought that the French would again send him another juicy steak. In the end, they got away at night and fled to the English at Cape Coast, and in that way escaped from the so-called emperor of the Guinea Coast.[105]

Outfitting of their ships costs the French more than outfitting costs other nations.[106] I believe that no nation can outfit ships for trade better than we do, and no nation takes on more freight than we do — which is difficult to understand.[107] /48/ The crews of the English ships must have their *caks* [cakes], the French their *biscuit*, which are hard twice-baked rusks of fine wheat flour. The officers and those who are ill are given fresh bread twice a week, for which they have a baking oven on board.[108] Our sailors bite with joy into their mouldy rusks, so that a cloud of mould floats about their ears. They tap or brush the worms out — to some extent — and everyone is then satisfied. They are fortunate if the food is not already spoiled when packed here in Copenhagen, in which case they must eat rotten provisions for six months

---

[105] R. considerably heightens what he said about the same episode in his earlier publication, where he gave a more sober, and detailed, narrative of the boy's stay in France, of the harrowing experience of the governor La Cour, and of the fate of the boy — see below (1756, /31/). His melodramatic improved version was no doubt intended to shock the lay reader. Nevertheless, the episode occurred while R. was on the coast, perhaps even while he was in refuge at Cape Coast, close to Anomabu, so the anecdote seems reasonably trustworthy. Other anecdotes about Corrantrin appear below, Chapter 4, /224/, /233/-/234/.

[106] Repeats a statement made in 1756, /25/, below.

[107] By the mid eighteenth century, the outfitting of ships in the Guinea trade, especially slave ships, in almost all respects was in fact fairly standard for all nations (Herbert S. Klein, 'Economic aspects of the eighteenth-century Atlantic slave trade', in James D. Tracy, ed., *The Rise of Merchant Empires* (1990) 304–5; Leif Svalesen, *Slaveskipet Fredensborg* (1996) 92). For the types of ships used by the Dutch and their adaptation to different types of cargo, see Postma (1990) 142–4. R.'s last remark is itself 'difficult to understand', but perhaps he means that despite the advantages of the Danes, they made smaller profits than other nations.

[108] The earlier publication does not limit the provision of fresh bread to the officers, but on the contrary states that it was for the able-bodied seaman — see below (1756, /25/-/26/). For citrus fruit carried on board French ships to prevent scurvy, see Isert [1788] (1992) 105.

or longer.[109] Now you can understand why scurvy appears among them, and thus, lamentably, they must [die and] be thrown overboard.[110]

[The French (1756)]

The French, on the other hand, have no establishments on the [Gold] Coast. Their ships are more costly to equip and run than those of other nations. Their sailors must have their warm bread twice a week, their /26/ pot of wine every day, their garlic, etc., otherwise they die like flies. Most of the goods they have for trade on the Coast are bought in Holland. I know of no more than three or four varieties of their own East Indian goods which are suitable for trade on the Coast. Their *Bougers, Indiennes* [Indian cloths], *Limenias*, and white and blue *Salempures* [cloths] are all purchased in Holland.[111] If they are anchored on the Coast alongside an Englishman and the Englishman pays seven or eight ounces [of gold] for a slave, the Frenchman must pay nine or ten ounces. But do we not see that the Englishman [despite paying less] completes his trade more quickly and acquires better slaves than the Frenchman![112] The French officers dress like cavaliers, and you even see an apprentice [*sic*] staining a couple of lace-trimmed cloaks in the Guinea surf.[113] Instead of having a captain and a first mate on a ship, as we do, they have a captain, a second-captain, a lieutenant, a second-lieutenant, an ensign, and pilots or apprentices,[114] while the surgeon is a major. If you ask a French officer how many trips he has made to the coast, he answers that he has made so and so many 'campaigns'.[115] An Englishman can finish his business in one hour, for the purchase of as many as one hundred slaves. But with a Frenchman it requires several ceremonies. If

---

[109] For the rations of both crew and slaves on board Danish ships, see Svend Erik Green-Pedersen, 'Om Forholdene på Danske Slaveskibe', in *Handels- og Søfartsmuseet på Kronborg Årbog* (1973) 47–50. Bread is not specifically mentioned but it would appear that the rations were rather better than R. suggests.

[110] R. presumably meant to say that seamen who died of scurvy were 'buried at sea'.

[111] 'Bougers' is probably an error for 'bouges' (derived from Portuguese *buxios*), that is, cowries.

[112] R. is leading up to criticism of the French traders for dawdling.

[113] For a drawing showing Frenchman in Guinea in full dress, see Barbot [1732] (1992) frontispiece. But Frenchmen were not alone among Europeans in 'dressing up' to impress Africans, as they doubtless thought.

[114] Since 'pilots' cannot have been 'apprentices', these are not alternative terms for the same persons, yet ships cannot have carried the latter as alternative personnel to the former, so the meaning is obscure.

[115] The explanation is probably that earlier French trading voyages tended to be also exploratory expeditions on behalf of the government, for instance, seeking out sites for bases on Gold Coast, and therefore were 'campaigns' directed against hostile rivals. Note G. Thilmans and N.I. de Moraes, 'Villault de Bellefond sur la côte occidentale d'Afrique. Les deux premières campagnes de l'*Europe* (1666–1671)', *Bulletin de l'Institut Fondamental de l'Afrique Noire*, série B, 39 (1976), 257–99.

a French captain hears there are slaves at a fort, he normally comes in a *chaloup* [sloop] as far as the breakers, where the factor at the fort has him picked up in a Negro boat, called a canoe. He brings three or four braid-trimmed *monsieurs* with him. They then walk through the courtyard of the fort where the slaves are sitting. Expertise in trading should then enable the captain to do business immediately, were he to only show a list of his goods, since every one is knowledgeable about them. But after the first compliments have been exchanged, he normally requests that /**27**/ a boat be sent out to his ship to fetch several bottles of champagne and Burgundy wine. When that has been done and the factor asks him if he wishes to buy slaves, the captain may answer, '*Nous ne parlerons point de négoce ni aujourdhui ni demain, Monsieur!*' [We will not discuss business either today or tomorrow, Sir!] The wine is then brought ashore, and the *messieurs* dine. They normally disdain all our foods and have their own cook brought ashore so he can prepare better food for us. They tell us that their cook has been trained in Paris at the home of a prince or duke, and they dilate on the types of *paté* or *fricassée* he prepared for them the last time. Nor does the captain forget to order a number of spices not found here on the Coast. All this is done, and then the *messieurs* at the forts drink cheerfully with *Messieurs les François*, and so everyone becomes very merry. The Frenchmen demonstrate the new *Caprioler* [turns] and *Krumspring* [leaps] their dance-masters in Paris have devised recently. They tell us of their amours, etc., and if we so wish, our neighbours, English or Dutch, are invited in to observe this remarkable trade. Should they accept, and the captain's wine come to a hasty end, he must again request a canoe to fetch another dozen [bottles] of each kind.

If you think I am presenting an exaggerated picture, I must admit that differences do indeed exist among the French. I have known a Bancio from Rochelle, a Courchamp from St Malo, a Boisandre from Nantes, men whom, in truth, no European could surpass in good conduct and experience in trade. What I have said applies to the majority, and should I [be thought to] include those for whom that picture is much too severe, anyone who has known le Chevalier de la Bretagniere also knows that many of his like are to be found among the French captains. It is said that when /**28**/ those who have lived on the Coast for three or four years become very solemn, some of them almost morose, it is due to the illnesses of the land, but I believe it comes from the way of life. When young [inexperienced] boys come among them, they have different dispositions and these may serve as an excuse for poking fun at the newcomer. If he wants any kind of refreshment he may have to pay double for it. An English captain, as soon as he sees a factor who has slaves for sale, takes his papers out of his pocket, shows what and how much he will pay for a slave, and on the spot, with a yes or no, the transaction is done. He scarcely stops to sit down if there is nothing more for him to do. This kind of conduct suits the temperament of the Guinea factors best.[116]

All this was only to show the differences between the business methods of the English and French slave-traders. When a Frenchman has brought his slaves to the West Indies he will prepare his overall costing, and an Englishmen will do the same. Should it appear that the Frenchman's slaves come to 20–25 *rixdaler* per head more than those of the Englishman, would you not assume that the Englishmen could deliver their [West Indian] products for a better price here in Europe than the French could? The English sell the Gold Coast slaves for £40 sterling, Upper Coast slaves for £30, Angola and Lagoon slaves for £20–25. The French, on the other hand, never receive less than 1,200 *livres*, and for an extra fine slave, 1,400–1,600 *livres*.[117] The reason for this must be sought in the West Indies. In fact, their remarkable laws, handed down by their king, are what make it possible for the French to carry so many products from the West Indies. And their islands are governed by reasonable men, normally individuals who /29/ have already, in Europe, proved by their courage and reason that they are worthy of running a government. They are normally *Chefs d'Escadre*, commanders, men who have shown their merit and to whom the Court wishes to give an opportunity to enrich themselves, which they usually do within a period of five to six years. I shall let this matter rest until I come to speak of the colonies of all the nations in the West Indies.

The French have often tried to establish themselves on the Gold Coast, seeking especially to settle at Annamaboe in Fante, where until now the Negroes have not cared to have [resident] any Europeans. It is true that the English once had a fort there, but they were so plagued by the Negroes at that place that they thanked God to be able to get away. The Negroes then tore the fort down completely and negotiated directly with the ships. It is this place that has given rise to jealousy between the French and English courts, but at the present time, since the recent peace of 1748, French ships are chased away from there, as from Gold Coast in its entirety.[118] Sensible Englishmen say that the Article [of the treaty] blocking the French slave trade is more advantageous for the nation as a whole than it would have been to retain Cape Breton. The French arrived there [at Anomabu] in droves before the last war, and for every single Englishman there were ten Frenchmen. The Negroes at Annamaboe would like to trade with the French, from whom they receive higher prices for their slaves and provisions.

---

[116] It is not easy to follow R.'s somewhat rambling line of thought in this paragraph.

[117] 300 *livres* = £25 (Law (1991), 174). This makes the ordinary price £100 and the higher prices £117–£133. But all these figures seem implausible.

[118] The reference is to the Peace of Aix-la-Chapelle of 1748, at the end of the War of Austrian Succession.

Corrantryn (one of the small Negro kings) receives more custom or toll from them than from the English.

This Corrantryn was one of the oldest caboceers in Fanteland, and he wielded a great deal of authority. The English at Cape Coast persuaded him to allow his heir — whom we have seen entitled Prince of Annamaboe in our official journals /**30**/ and about whom a novel has been written which we have read — to go to England.[119] The Chief Agents reported to some important people in London that this Negro boy might, at some time in the future, be useful to the English nation, and people of high status collected money for his education and sustenance. This happened a few years before the French received one of Corrantryn's sons in France. An English journalist had, without hesitation, given the boy who came to England the title of 'prince', so a French captain also wished to bring a prince from Annamaboe. He described to Corrantryn the advantages that one of his sons could enjoy in France, if he took him there. But this would have been of no use if the captain had not given Corrantryn the value of three to four slaves. This was [merely] to console Corrantryn in the event of the boy being lost, since he still had 30–40 sons living with him and he could purchase four or five slave boys with the goods received. Any Coaster knows that a Negro acts no differently in respect of his slaves and in respect of his children. The captain took Bassi (the boy's name) aboard, and during the voyage he taught him how to deport himself in his fine braid-trimmed clothing, and how to act when he arrived in France. Bassi played his role excellently, and the captain showed him great respect on board ship. The boy became accustomed to being called 'Monsieur le Prince'. On his arrival in France, the captain personally took Bassi to the Court and presented him to the ministers, telling them that he himself had such high status with the King of Annamaboe that the latter had entrusted to him his prince and successor. The captain made a long speech, claiming that the King of Annamaboe informed the French King that he had sent his prince to France because of the affection he felt for the French, and /**31**/ so that the boy should be given Christian instruction. The captain also spoke of the national advantage when, in the future, a king who had been in France, and was a Christian, ascended the throne of Fante. Bassi was instantly treated in a manner fitting for a prince, being given four lackeys, a *hofmester* [chamberlain], and so on. He was then christened by the Archbishop of Paris, the King himself acting as his godfather, and given the name 'Louis Bassi, Prince de Corrantryn'. He could write this much and the name was written in all the books given him to take home from France. He read French well. In 1744 the French sent a Governor and two other officers to Annamaboe, together with this

---

[119] The novel is *The Royal African, or memoirs of the young prince of Annamaboe* (London, n.d. [1749]). The 'prince' was William Ansah, son of Eno Baisie Kurentsi, alias John Currantee.

'prince', in order to build a fort. The Governor was M. de la Cour, who had served earlier for a few years at Fida [Whydah]. He brought with him a cargo worth 100,000 *livres*, and since a fort could not be built quickly he had to store all these goods in Corrantryn's house. The English made threats, and their warships shot cannonades at Annamaboe, to no avail. The Negroes did not want to lose such rich pickings so easily. M. de la Cour was admired along the entire Coast, and I believe no other man could have held out as well for four years among the Negroes as he did. His Company sacrificed their employees, since from his nation he received neither more men nor more ships. Corrantryn himself stole all the goods during the first year, and in the three following years de la Cour had to struggle to remain alive. The French [finally] left for Fida, leaving the prince behind at Annamaboe. His father not liking him, because Bassi could not tolerate seeing the French being treated so badly, rejected him. After that Bassi was in my service, and was paid the same salary and given the same type of work as any other Negro boy. /**32**/

[The Danes (1760)]

In a separate chapter I shall deal with us (the Danes), the third nation [at present] established on the Guinea Coast.[120] I must first report something about the religion, nature, and customs of the inhabitants. /**49**/

[The Danes (1756)]

Before I leave the Guinea Coast I must report on the third nation established on the Gold Coast, which is ourselves, the Danes. I wish I could honestly praise us for always having sensible governors, always capable factors, and always warehouses so full of quantities of goods that, on the strength of their quality and fair prices, we had the most trade at Accra, where we have our chief castle. But that would be not be telling the truth. Let no one take offence if I speak truthfully about us. I believe no Dutchman reading here what I have written about the English, and no Englishman reading what I have written about Dutch methods, could add more from their own experience. No Dane has been on the Coast who has had to travel around as much as I have, first up the Coast, then down the Coast, then up River Volta, then inland. If any of my poor Governors lacked wine or brandy, I had to take off with slaves or gold — be it day or night, whether I was risking my life or not, whether there were ships in the roads or not — and travel 20–30 miles up or down the coast in a small Negro boat. It mattered not to the Governors. And the strangest thing about it all was that I was the only one capable of keeping the Company's books, and had I died the

---

[120] References to the Danes are scattered through the remaining chapters but are fullest in Chapter 4.

Company's affairs would have fallen into confusion — yet during that period I was paid only an Under-Assistant's salary.

Our Governors slept off drunken spells at least twice a day, our bookkeeper drank himself blind, and our chief assistant could not reckon up to four *specier*. We had one decent person there, but the merchant at /33/ Friderichsborg [Fredensborg][121] had to keep him at that fort, otherwise all the bookkeeping would have gone wrong. I was later promoted to Bookkeeper, but things remained the same: I had to flit around as before, until finally I was banished and had to stay at [English] Cape Coast for nine months before I could find the opportunity, in 1744, to return to Europe.[122] At that time I considered all this to be an unfortunate and a troublesome affair visited upon me by evil people, but now it is over I realize that the Almighty arranged things for the best I learned to know people, I observed their methods in trade, I visited the offices at both [Dutch] Elmina and [English] Cape Coast. To pass the time, at the latter place I copied out a number of their trade books, and sometimes examined their archives. I voiced my opinions to reasonable people, and they gave me theirs. By this means I feel that the conclusions I present here are correct. I could cover more ground but I fear it would be boring to the reader. I had to write something about the foreigners in order to be better able to compare us to them, and to give a true report of our condition on the Coast and in the West Indies. What I finally wish to write about is how our trade could be improved by leaving it to the judgement of sensible people.

I said above that I passed the time at Cape Coast by reading through the archives, and when I visited a good friend at Elmina, the General Bookkeeper, he was so kind as to allow me the same [privilege]. Before this, I had spent many hours in the office at Christiansborg, passing the time there with the old account books, from which I felt I could learn about /34/ the trade, procedures and correspondence, character and merits [of predecessors]. From 1712 the books were easily legible, and since it concerns our own nation I beg to be allowed to go that far back and comment upon the character of each Governor, their care for procedures, their arguments, their reports to the Directors here in Copenhagen, their resolutions, and so on. I will not guarantee that the dates and periods are accurate, I beg the reader to consider that I have been away from the Coast for four years, and during the last five years I was there I had other things to do than to leaf through old books.

---

[121] 'Friderichsborg' was a strange slip for R. to make, since the Danish fort of this name, in Fetu, was no longer in existence in R.'s day, whereas Fredensborg, at Ningo, was already in use although its construction was continuing.

[122] See Appendix B.

From 1710 to 1718 our Company had a Governor at Accra named Franz Boye.[123] During that period we were at war with Sweden, and the Directors had not sent ships to the Coast for seven years. Our chief fort at that time was closer to Cape Coast, a fort called Fort Royal, a fitting name, whose ruins can still be seen. An impregnable fort, it was set on a high hill, from which one can recognise any individual at Cape Coast as they move from room to room.[124] Still visible is a high tower left standing by the English, time not having been able to destroy it. A Danish Director-General named Grönberg, who was born in Emden, was buried there in 1704, as can be seen on a gravestone. In addition, we have a fort up-coast ten miles from that one, called Accada.[125] These two forts were sold to the English by the Director-General at that time.[126] Our nation was then concerned with other things than protecting its rights, and the Directors sold it to the English Company for £20,000 sterling. /35/ Frantz Boye managed affairs far better, and rather than leaving or selling his fort, he sent, by way of England or Holland, 10,000 *rixdaler* in gold home every year, even though he received no goods from the Company for several years.[127] Nearly all the co-workers who could have helped him with trade and bookkeeping died, so he had to pick out a young soldier, teach him to write, and install him as bookkeeper at the fort. This young man was called Østrup, and he proved most ungrateful to his benefactor. He had been Bookkeeper for scarcely a year before he secretly left the fort, travelled to Copenhagen, and informed against Franz Boye, claiming he was not acting in the Company's interest and other such charges.[128] The Directors sent a ship commanded by Captain Werröe [Waerøe][129] to the Coast, and promoted the Chief Merchant at Christiansborg to the governorship, Østrup being installed as Bookkeeper and as prosecutor in the case against Franz Boye. He was supplied with an indictment a hands-breadth thick, this booklet being neatly written and full of [the details] of this case, while the ship was to remain there until the case had been completed. The

---

[123] R. now lists and discusses a series of Governors, praising his favourites and criticizing others, the latter particularly those he served under and fell out with.

[124] This was originally Fort Frederiksborg on Amanful (Manfro) Hill (Müller [1673] in Jones (1983) 148–9; Tilleman [1697] (1994) 4–5, 22–3; Van Dantzig (1980b) 29–31).

[125] R. seems to be mistaken here. Fort Dorothea near Akwida (Accoda) was a Brandenburg possession. This was indeed located 'up-coast' from Cape Coast, but there is no indication of the Danes ever being in possession of it (Tilleman [1697] (1994) /58/; Van Dantzig (1980b) 38–9).

[126] Governor Hans Lykke pawned Fort Frederiksborg to the English at Cape Coast in 1684: cf. Tilleman [1697] (1994) 4–5, 23.

[127] For a far less complimentary description of Franz/Frantz Boye, see Nørregård (1966) 69–72.

[128] Boye eventually sacked Østrup, but, things being as they were on the Coast, the latter wound up as Governor in 1720, when Boye's successor died. Østrup was removed in 1722 and died on the way back to Denmark (Nørregård (1966) 71–2).

[129] Anders Pedersen Wærøe himself became governor in 1728 (Nørregård 1966, 76).

case lasted for thirteen months, and yet was not fully completed. Remarkably, this booklet is still at Christiansborg where it serves not only as a model for young assistants to learn to write, since the scribe in this instance had a fine hand, but also as a model for hearing all the legal actions undertaken since then at the Fort. It includes summons, interrogations, replies, duplicates, pleas, voting, judgements of all sorts, and, if I have understood correctly, the final interrogations regarding the return home of Svane.[130] It is still very serviceable. Having been forced to stay on the Coast such a long time in order to take Boye away, and so that the ship's officers /**36**/ could appear in court, the ship had become half rotten before the West Indies was reached, and it had to be left there. It had brought no goods to the Coast, and no slaves were purchased. Frantz Boye went to England, and from there returned to the Coast as Chief Agent in the English service. He lived there for several years, and finally died there.

Shortly after Frantz Boye's death his successor at Christiansborg died and Mr. Østrup succeeded him. He still lives in the memory of the Blacks on the Coast and they call him Mad Østrup because of the insane and terrible things he did there. The Directors could then see what a good man they had had in Frantz Boye, because the Company sent Østrup shiploads of fine goods but received nothing in return. Not even account books or the slightest records of trade can now be found. One document, however, states that he has been chosen [to be governor], and on the same page we find a resolution by his successor, David Herrn, dated two years later. Herrn had great difficulties when he came to the Fort since Østrup refused to relinquish his post. Finally he was enticed away to a Dutch fort, hands and feet bound, and shortly thereafter he died.[131]

The Directors had no better service out of David Herrn however. They had ordered him and the rest of the Council to keep their books in Italian. The literate members mastered it but could not fathom where they could find Italians to act as scribes. But nothing was

---

[130] This must refer to Frederik Svane, formerly Frederik Pedersen, a Mulatto, who apparently adopted the name of the chaplain who sponsored him, Elias Svane (p.c. M.E. Kropp Dakubu). The chaplain established a school at Christiansborg for Mulatto children, and was instrumental in sending several boys to Denmark for education, among them Frederik Svane, who was sometimes considered to have been the chaplain's son, or at least his adopted son and protege. After completing his education, Frederik Svane worked on the Coast for several periods, and acted as chaplain at Christiansborg. But his life there was exceedingly turbulent, and after a number of incarcerations he was sent back to Denmark, where he became a schoolmaster on the estate of the great dramatist, Ludvig Holberg (Nørregård (1966), 72). On the Svanes, see CRA, V-gK 890, Justisprotokol; 285 (1717–1746) *Forhørs- og domsakter* fra Guinea.

[131] David Herrn was installed in January 1722, after the forcible removal of Østrup (Nørregård (1966) 72).

recorded, either in Danish or Italian, as is revealed in Governor Suhm's interrogation of David Herrn's successor. During this inquiry, both the [Chief] Merchant and the Bookkeeper testified that they had often gone to their Governor and asked him if they should not record, as was usual, /37/ the trade they had carried out, what it had cost, and more information. The Governor had responded angrily — did they understood Italian? etc. Herrn lived in the country for eighteen months and his successor was relieved by Captain-Commander Suhm, who chased Østrup, in his miserable state, out of the Fort.[132] Østrup wanted to go to Copenhagen by way of Holland in order to seek justice, but he died in a hospital in Amsterdam.

Governor Suhm restored our nation to a respectable state again. During his term, when a case was being tried at Christiansborg they always had to have in court two Dutch soldiers as assessors. I have never been able to find out in our archives the reason for this, and I still cannot understand it. Undoubtedly copies of these records could be found at the office here [in Copenhagen] where the truth of that statement might be checked. Captain-Commander Suhm wrote the instructions for the Governor and the Secret Council at Christiansborg that still apply. He established stable conditions for all the officers, and then travelled to the West Indies, where he became a governor.[133] During Suhm's term of office the suzerainty the Dutch insisted they had over our territory was abolished. I do not know how, or when, this started, but it certainly appears to me to resemble [the privilege] of some noblemen in Germany who do not have *jus non appellandi* [no appeal allowed] when their *Cancellie* [Chancery] hands down a decision that the parties may at will appeal to a mediator. In the same manner do our Negroes run to Dutch Accra when we demand payment of a debt, or the settling of other affairs between them. /38/

In place of Suhm came his Merchant, by the name of Pahl, who was besieged by the Aqvambu because Mr. Suhm had taken the gold the king had deposited and delivered cowries instead. This cost the Company a good 10,000 *rixdaler*. Pahl died, and Willemsen was his successor.[134] Willemsen, in turn, was replaced by Werröe, and this Werröe has really been the Governor who did the most damage of any governor

---

[132] According to Nørregård, there were two successors: Niels Jensen Østrup, who died after a few months, and an Assistant, Christian A. Syndermann. The latter was relieved by Captain Henrik Suhm in December 1723 (Nørregård (1966) 74).

[133] Henrik Suhm, turning over the governorship to Frederik Pahl, a Merchant, sailed to the West Indies in 1727, where he became vice-governor of St Thomas.

[134] Andreas Willemsen took over in September 1727 and remained in office until December 1728. Although taken prisoner and investigated (for mismanagement?), he subsequently became a town judge on St Thomas in the West Indies (Nørregård 1966, 76).

the Company has had on the Coast.[135] He brought his wife and two daughters with him to the Coast. He had been the Company's ship-captain but was removed because of his dreadful behaviour and given a dishonourable discharge. At Christiansborg the story is told that, on one occasion, a soldier was to be discharged and chased out of the Fort, because of his repeated thefts. No one knew how to write such a discharge, so the Governor fetched his own discharge and ordered them simply to change the name. Werröe had lived here in Copenhagen very miserably for three or four years before the Directors granted him a pardon and sent him back to the Coast, accompanied by a Merchant who had married Werröe's eldest daughter.[136] I shall not describe their way of life because it shames all mankind, but I only heard this from others and never met any of them.[137]

The Dutch merchants exercised their authority among our Negroes as strongly as ever, and none of our Negroes dared to bring a slave to our fort unless he had the permission of the Dutch. The Dutch] did not want to buy old slaves, who then fell to our lot. It is true that Werröe and his Merchant, Sparre, once paid the Aqvamboes to besiege the Dutch fort, but it turned out badly, and you might say that the Dutch brought him and our Negroes back to a state of total obedience.[138] The Directors wanted to have him removed, but the new /39/ Governor, *Cammer-Raad* [Councillor] Jörgensen, died on the journey to the Coast, so Werröe remained for five or six years, until 1735. Then *Cancellie-Raad* [Chancellor] Schilderup was sent to the Coast, and if this man had lived longer he would have performed great services for the Company. He was decent, reasonable and a capable man. Although he lacked experience in trade, his understanding and care served him in its stead. The Negroes loved him, indeed they venerated him as a god. Our Negroes immediately threw off the Dutch yoke, and it is most remarkable that when the Dutch (the Dutch Director-General, de Bordes, was at Accra at that time) planned to use force they could not recruit one-third of their Negroes to attack us. But the Dutch Caboceer, Axania, who is mentioned in our Company books, came over to our side with all his people, so [Governor] Borris, later, had to use force to make them go back to the Dutch fort.[139] This was very damaging to us since we would have been the strongest at Accra had we retained them, but Borris feared the Directors would not accept the increase in costs which would incur. The Dutch were

---

[135] Werröe (Wærøe) is further discussed, and criticized, in Chapter 4, /145/–/147/, /149/–/151/, below. In calling him the most damaging governor, R. seems to have forgotten the governor against whom he himself rebelled (Appendix B).

[136] The merchant was H.H. Sparre.

[137] Although he says he will remain silent, R. cannot resist telling tales about them a little later.

[138] Cf. Chapter 4, /150/–/155/, below.

[139] For the successor to Schiellerup/Schilderup, Enevold Nielsen Boris, Governor from June 1736 to 1740, see Nørregård (1966) 99–103.

unable to succeed in any way against us because our Negroes came out of their fields and even set fire to the houses of the enemy. The Dutch Director-General was ashamed that he could do so little harm to us, and he returned to Elmina. He gave his factor [at the Dutch fort at Accra] orders to do us as much damage as he could. Shortly after the above crisis it became clear that the Dutch did not wish to obey their General.

Although there was war during the whole of Schilderup's stay—he was there only eight months—nevertheless he earned 14,000 *rixdaler* in gold for the Company and 6,000–7,000 *rixdaler* for himself. The Negroes came down from some 100 miles up-country, just in order to /**40**/ see him—which [much] moved him—and they were very comfortable in his presence. No Negro, other than his own [servants], visited him without bringing at least one *mark* of gold, that is, eight ounces, with which to purchase goods. If the Company had sent ten shiploads of goods during his term at Accra I have been assured he would have sold all. The kings in Akim sent a message asking if it were possible for him to come up to Rum because they wanted to meet him. They said that they would not ask this of him if they themselves had been able to come to see him without an entourage of some 1,000 subjects (which was against the kings' own wishes) and that they feared that these followers might do something to offend Schilderup. He answered that they should not come down, but at some future time he would travel up to them. (This was done, I think, only to keep them away from us, since it would have cost a us a great deal in gifts.) One of the kings, called Ursue, sent him a fine, grown-up daughter, accompanied by some slaves bearing a present of gold to him, and asked him to get her with child, but she was returned untouched.[140] I beg to be excused if I have over-reached the bounds of decency, but it really did happen and I only wish to show how much beloved in the land that man was. I do not know, nor have I heard from others, of any Englishman or Dutchman who has had the same good fortune. He died in 1736, of the stone, and never has any [Guinea European] been so mourned as he was. The Dutch held him in high esteem, and many of our Blacks would voluntarily have laid down their lives for him, their wives and children having their hands full [to prevent this].

The only thing you can say he did which has not brought honour, either to him or to the Company, was his cruel treatment of his predecessor. On several occasions he /**41**/ forced Werrøe and his daughters to submit to being called into court where they were searched, under the pretext of their having hidden gold on their persons. The searching extended to their private parts, the father in the presence of his daughters, the daughters in the presence of their father. I would not have believed this had I not heard it from many who were present. Never

---

[140] For the Akim kings, including 'Ursue', see Chapter 4, /159/, below.

mind that the daughters were prostitutes, serving both Blacks and Whites; never mind that their father kept them there for this purpose in order to earn money; still it was quite inhuman and can in no way be defended. I have heard Borris, who along with others did the searching, sigh about it on his deathbed. I have often wondered why this man [Schilderup] did not write full and just reports to the Directors about their affairs on the Coast. A busy pen, of which he was capable, could truly have accomplished much, but only a few of his letters have been entered in the Company's books. This was perhaps because of lack of copyists, since the letters lie bound together in our archives — so I have been informed -.in order that they be securely preserved. But I know that a Dane has no fear of a Hollander [anywhere] in Europe, why, then, should it have been in this instance the case in this country?

Borris was Schilderup's successor, and he was lucky to have such a great man as an example and model for eight months, since he had previously not seen much that was good. He arrived there very young and was appointed Governor at the age of twenty-five. Werrøe came home and began to present his case to the Directors. The gold Schilderup had left was also brought to Copenhagen. The Directors did not want to be hurt [financially], so they helped themselves to Schilderup's own money in order to pay for the court case (as we heard on the Guinea Coast) and his heirs received only some 100 *rixdaler*. Borris profited /**42**/ greatly because of the blessed Schilderup. He was a better trader than Schilderup, but not as fortunate. He was firm in respect of the Dutch, so they were no longer able to gain power over our Negroes. I arrived on the Coast in 1739 and Borris died in 1740.

I shall not describe the miserable time which followed, yet it was not quite so bad as long as the chaplain, Mr. Dorph, was there.[141] But after that, it became very bad. In 1744 the Directors sent Billsen to be governor, a man who thought Guinea and all the Danes were created just for his own sake. He was not ashamed to claim that one of his Secret Council would put things in order in the morning, and other such things. The Directors experienced this to their own injury and that of the Company, and I just wish to say that in my opinion it was a great loss to the Company that Mr. Major Lützow died so suddenly.[142] If I understand the Negroes correctly, they would have loved and honoured him just as much as they had Schilderup.

---

[141] Ole Dorph (1711–1777), newly ordained, was sent to Gold Coast in 1738, where he remained as chaplain for five years. He and R. were evidently good friends, and contact between them may have continued in Denmark, Dorph being perhaps one of those who helped R. by sharing memories.

[142] Major Magnus Christopher Lützow was appointed governor in March 1750 but, due to delays in departure, did not sail for the coast before the winter of 1751. He arrived at Christiansborg in March 1751 and died two days after his arrival (Nørregård (1966) 110).

My intention here is not to instruct the Directors on how they might run their affairs in such a way that instead of loss they make gains. That is not possible. Had conditions remained as they were in 1743, before the Akims were ruined, I would have said that sensible people must be sent to the Coast, along with a couple of shiploads of goods. These ships would not take the long route [via the West Indies] but sail directly back to Copenhagen as soon as the employees were provided with goods and had begun to trade. If the Directors forbid their employees to sell slaves to any other nation, they will say that they have to do that, since they have no provisions for their slaves, /**43**/ so the Company would then have to keep a sloop for them.[143] If the Directors were to send no goods apart from those requested, I have been assured that their ships would not leave the Coast empty. But that time is past, and I can assure you that when the Assiantees finally open the route to Elmina again, our Christiansborg will not buy 50 slaves or 100 *rixdaler* worth of gold a year, even with the finest goods and the most capable people.

I should also report on the obedience of our servants in following the instructions of the Company, and on how they live. If our Governor and Factor are to be compared to those of the English and Dutch, you can understand that both the Governor's 800 *rixdaler* and the Merchant's 300 *rixdaler* would have to be doubled. They must make this sum either by the trade carried on for the Company, or, when the opportunity arises, by trading privately. As regards the former, it is true that the price of slaves and goods must always be set so the factor makes a profit of 4–6 *rixdaler* on each slave he buys, otherwise he could not possibly cover the costs. And the traders must not be permitted to enter all their expenses on the Company's books, or they would exaggerate them. If it were true [that I did this] I would admit it here, but I take God as my witness that I have lost several hundred *rixdaler* in business with just as many ships as I have gained with others. But when the Directors send no ships, and a trader has goods to the value of three or four slaves, can you blame him for conducting business with those goods? And if he shows the slaves to the Dutch or English, where is the profit for the Company in this? Our earlier governors, returning home, have, like Sancho Pancha [*sic*], proved their honesty by their poverty and debt. I know /**44**/ that most of them have [only] themselves to blame, but the Directors should not begrudge a decent person, who really has done his duty, earning something to counter his losses. If the Coast belonged to us alone, such attitudes would be fine, since we could rest assured that what we do not receive with this ship we shall receive with the next.[144]

---

[143] This probably means that a sloop could be used to purchase provisions at other points on the coast (cf. CRA, V-gK 124, 30.3.1744).

[144] The remainder of 1756 deals almost entirely with the West Indies and forms Appendix A.

Chapter 3

About the Negroes' religion in general

Inasmuch as a people's nature and customs usually flow from their religion, I shall begin with that first, although it is difficult to write about the religion of a people which for them is not a precise system. For most of them never bother to think about such things, and the elderly among them who are meditative in most cases have opinions as distinct from one another as east is from west.[1]

What I write here is according to the statements of a chief priest, namely our Caboceer [headman], Putti [Okpoti] of Labode [Labadi].[2] Not only is Putti the greatest and most famous priest (fetish-maker) on Gold Coast, but the most important oracle (fetish) on the Gold Coast is also to be found in Labode.[3] I am careful to say that it is the most important, but it is not the most powerful, this being the one in Fante — as explained later.[4]

---

[1] In declaring that the 'Negroes' religion' being described here lacks a 'precise system', R. probably means, in part, that it possesses no sacred texts (p.c. Ivor Wilks). For past European attitudes towards African 'traditional' religions, see Eric O. Ayisi, *An Introduction to the Study of African Culture* (1980) 71–81; William Pietz, 'Bosman's Guinea', *Comparative Civilizations Review* 9 (1982) 3–22; Louis Brenner, 'Religious discourses in and about Africa', in Karin Barber and P.F. de Moraes, *Discourse and its Disguises* (1989) 87–103; and specifically for the discourse in the eighteenth century; William Pietz, 'The spirit of civilization: blood debt', in *RES Anthropology and Aesthetics*, 28 (1995) 23–5.

[2] Putti/Okpoti was notionally both the chief priest and the caboceer (headman) of Labode, but in practice the offices were separated. It is clear that Okpoti was so much involved in his secular duties, and his work with the Europeans and their trade, that he delegated religious duties to another priest (see Chapter 5, note 99, below). Labode (Labadi) was a Gã town and polity to the east of Accra. For earlier references to Labadi, see Jean Barbot, *Barbot on Guinea* (1992) 449, note 23.

[3] The oracle was *Lakpa*. For *Kpã* gods such as *La Kpã*, and the other gods of Labadi, see M.J. Field, *Religion and Medicine of the Gã People* (1937) 6, 39–41; A.K. Quarcoo, 'The La-Kpa. Principal deity of Labadi', *IAS Research Review*, 3 (1967) 2–43; A.A. Akrong, 'Sacrifice in Labadi (Ga) religion', MA thesis, University of Ghana, 1978, 7. For 'fetish', a term used by Europeans in relation to African religions, see Chapter 1, note 3. above. The term is here applied to both the oracular spirit and the physical object or objects associated with the shrine and representing the spirit.

[4] Fante was one of the polities of the central and western coast of Gold Coast, where the peoples were speakers of Akan languages and dialects. The Fante *obosom* ('god') was *Nananom Mpow*, whose shrine was at Mankassim (T.C. McCaskie, 'Nananom Mpow of Mankessim', in David Henige and T.C. McCaskie, eds, *West African Economic and Social History* (1990) 134–5).

What I write is also according to the claims of the old Caboceer of Tessing, Noyte, and some others. /50/

[Religious queries]

We have to be a long time on the Coast before a Black will give any answer to our questions about his religion. Furthermore, we must, in fact, have been there for several years without anyone seeing us laugh at their ceremonies, or, when they answered our questions, without a European ridiculing them. If we do this, and say 'it is nonsense', etc., they then answer, 'That may well be — believe what you will!' And they will even laugh with us. They do not usually answer us when we put to them more than one question at a time, or more than one question in the course of a single conversation we have with them.[5]

I can recall that, one afternoon, Caboceer Putti came to see me, bringing me greetings from the fetish (the oracle) which assured me of his [i.e. the fetish's] friendship and protection, and he added a request for a bottle of brandy.[6] However, since it had not been long before that I had given him some brandy, I objected, adding the challenge that his fetish, while not as great and powerful as the fetish of the Fante, was more thirsty for brandy than that one was. If, I said to Putti, your fetish can lift an ox or cow up into the air, as the Fante fetish can, I would be willing to wager our old ox to see it happen. Putti answered that the Labode fetish was unable to do this. I asked why not, and received as an answer that the ancestors of the Fantes were all with God, /51/ but their own (the Labodes') had died in war. Thereupon, when I asked if those who died in war did not also go to God, he fell silent, and sent away on an errand an old Negro who was with him. Then, when we were alone, he answered my question thus: 'Don't you know, master, that the Blacks cut each other's heads off in war, and do you think that God receives people without heads? Can he not get enough people who die in their homes and are buried with their heads on?' I had to be satisfied with that answer.[7]

All the Negroes know that there is a universal spirit who has created all things, and who directs, rules, and sustains the world. But some say that

---

[5] There could be several reasons for reluctance to answer such questions. (a) Questions may have been put in a manner revealing supercilious attitudes (cf. Pieter de Marees, *Description and Historical Account of the Gold Kingdom of Guinea (1602)* (1987) 37b 'we mock their monkey buffoonery'; Müller [1673] in Adam Jones, *German Sources for West African History* (1983) 156, 177; Johannes Rask, *En Kort og Sandferdig Rejse-Beskrivelse til og fra Guinea* (1754) 164–8); (b) The individual questioned may have been ignorant of the answers; (c) The individual questioned may have been in possession of secret, privileged information which he/she was not supposed to divulge. A Gã proverb warns about asking too much: 'If a chick digs too deeply it may expose its mother's bones' (p.c. I. Odotei).

[6] Note that here, and hereafter, R. follows the African usage and treats the oracle as a person.

[7] The body must be whole at death, as it was at birth. Even today many people in Ghana object to post-mortem examination (p.c. Irene Odotei).

there are subordinate gods, namely gods of heaven, earth, and the sea.[8] They [also] believe that there is a particular evil spirit and many other evil spirits subordinate to him, who have created all the evil in the world, and would visit all the injury possible on humans if God and the fetish did not prevent it.[9] In the Accra language, God is called *Niumboo*, and the devil *Sissa*.[10] I have seen no image of God but [I have seen one] of the devil, both wellfashioned and finely painted, made of clay or resin (gum), and for the most part as our painters have depicted him, with a pair of horns on his head /**52**/ and a tail.[11] They say that the devil is white, and paint him in the whitest colour. They picture the devil as usually a span tall and decorated with feathers and hair. When I asked if the fetish had ordered them to make such an image, I received the reply, no, it was an old woman who had fabricated them [*sic*], and she rented out the figure for eight days or longer to those people to whom the devil came at night, and who could get no rest because of him. For he, that is, the devil, was frightened of his own image when he had once seen it in a house, and never returned there.[12]

[A trickster spirit]

In addition the Negroes have traditions about a certain *Nanni*, particularly about his scheming and tricks. One might call *Nanni* the Negroes'

---

[8] That the African religions here treated were based on belief in a single Creator was understood by many early writers:(De Marees [1602] (1987) 36a-37a; Hemmersam [1663] and Müller [1673] in Jones (1983) 118, 158–60, 176, and note 156; Rask (1754) 86–7; Nicolas Villault, sieur de Bellefond, *Relation des Costes d'Afrique, appellées Guinée* (1669) 261; Jean Baptiste Labat, *Voyage du Chevalier des Marchais en Guinée* (1730) 336; H.C. Monrad, *Bidrag til en Skildring af Guinea-Kysten*.(1822) 34 ff).

[9] On 'fetish' intervention, see Max Assimeng, *Social Structure of Ghana* (1981) 34, which compares the practice of a divine intermediary with the practice of not approaching a chief directly; see also T.C. McCaskie, *State and Society in Pre-Colonial Asante* (1995) 105. On the need to placate evil spirits, see Monrad (1822) 21–2.

[10] The Gã name for God is *Nyɔnmɔ*, with the additional titles *Ataa* 'grandfather' or *Naa* 'grandmother' (K.A. Opoku, *West African Traditional Religion* (1978) 25). For variations in the attributes of the term, see J. Zimmermann, *A Grammatical Sketch and Vocabulary of the Akra or Gã Language* [1858] (1972) 243; Field (1937) 44. R. seems to have misunderstood the term *sissa/sisa* whose (modern) meaning is not 'devil' but 'ghost'. The spirit which can be evil and destructive is *gbeshi* (Field (1937) 94–99; R.S. Rattray, *Religion and Art in Ashanti* (1927) 153; Marion Kilson, *Kpele La la: Gã Religious Songs* (1971) 59–62; Akrong (1978) 11–14; Opoku (1978) 14; Assimeng (1981) 34–40).

[11] For an engraving from Zur Eich (1677), showing a creature with large pointed ears and animal claws for feet, purporting to be the Fetu *obossum* [spirit], see Jones (1983) 265; see also Müller [1673] in Jones, 159; Opoku (1978) 72–3. While the horns and tail may be mere coincidence, there must be a suspicion that a European picture had influenced the design of the figure described by R.

[12] For the 'devil' as central to one African religion, that of the Ewe, neighbours of the Gã, see Birgit Meyer, 'If you are a devil, you are a witch', *Journal of Religion in Africa* 22 (1992) 103–6. For this concept among the Gã, see Field (1937) Chapter 5.

Ulenspeyl.[13] The Negroes have nothing to do but sleep during the day, and assemble in moonlight, sitting out of doors, fifty in a circle, while the old people tell the young about this *Nanni*. The young find his scheming and swindling to their taste, and only wish to have any opportunity in the world to imitate this *Ulenspeyl*.

I must, however, say rather more about this tradition of theirs. A large black spider (Aranea) /**53**/, *Nanni* in the Negro language, on the orders of God created the first people (according to the idea of the Negroes, that is).[14] For this purpose, *Nanni* wove cloth (*materia*), and God created people out of the cloth. Being industrious, *Nanni* wove cloth for [the fashioning of] a multitude of people, until she could do no more. Naturally, *Nanni* expected gratitude from the people for her trouble. But they ran away from her, and [instead] the fetish instructed them how to behave. Out of the little cloth left over, *Nanni* created yet another being. This one was smaller in size than the earlier ones, and *Nanni* hatched [*sic*] him herself, giving him her own name. This is the hero to whom all their tales relate, being about how he was able to live in the world without working, namely by swindling others, and how he was able to dupe the fetish. When *Nanni* was about to sacrifice a chicken, his mother showed him how to eat the meat and stick the feathers and bones together again, [to look] like a [complete] chicken. When he was going to sacrifice an egg, she taught him how to make a hole in it, drink the contents, fill the egg with sand or earth, and paste the hole shut again—and even be given praise for having sacrificed so large and heavy an egg. And so on. /**54**/

When the Negroes tell this story about *Nanni*, they act it all out. If *Nanni* walked from one place to another, they also take a few steps. If he, that is *Nanni*, struck someone, the storyteller grabs hold of one of the party and strikes him. If *Nanni* ate something that tasted good, if he wept, laughed, danced, limped, and so on, the storyteller does the same. I have seen a Negro act out a *Nanni* [story], the one about the time *Nanni* had both hands chopped off. The storyteller did it so well that he had to repeat it several times, for me and for others. Moreover, he had to speak in Portuguese so that we could understand him better.[15] Five or six other

---

[13] *Ulenspeyl* is *Till Eulenspiegel*, the traditional trickster in German literature. *Nanni* is *Ananse kokuroko*, 'The Great Spider', a nickname for *Onyame* and *Onyankopon*, the Twi/Akan names for God (J.G. Christaller, *Dictionary of the Asante and Fante Language called Tshi* [1888] (1933) 330). The Gã name is *Anaani* 'Spider'. For *ananu* 'spiders', and more details, see Zimmermann [1858] (1972) 17. It is typical of *Ananse* stories that they frequently end with *Ananse* in disgrace and hiding in a corner, as spiders do. For African tricksters in general, see Robert Pelton, *The Trickster in West Africa* (1980) 1–4.

[14] For other local myths of origin, see Monrad (1822) 2–3; Opoku (1978) 19–24.

[15] The continued use of Portuguese by both Africans and non-Portuguese Europeans on Gold Coast at this date, the 1740s, is notable.

Blacks have to be present [when a story is told], since each one is given a role to play.[16]

To continue, here is the story [just mentioned]. There was once a poor harvest over the entire country, resulting in such a time of hunger that a bean (*faba*) cost an egg.[17] [The storyteller speaks.] *Nanni* has many wives and children, and his eldest and principal wife frequently reminds him to find food for them. *Nanni* knows that his neighbour still has a considerable supply of beans. The neighbour is a hunter, and when he goes out in the morning he orders his children to lay the beans out in the sun and move them around vigorously, /55/ so that the worms do not enter them. However, the children are not to eat the beans before he comes home, allowing him to share them out. When the hunter has gone, *Nanni* appears and greets the children, and they greet him in return. *Nanni* has smeared his whole body with tar and gum, and he asks permission to show the children a new dance that he has devised. The children say, Yes, willingly! *Nanni* begins to sing and dance, throwing himself about among the beans, many of which remain stuck to his body. When he finishes, he shows the children his hands, and says, 'You can clearly see that I am taking nothing with me'. 'No, certainly you are not!', say the children. Then he collects the beans from his body and gives them to his wife. When the hunter comes home, the children tell him that *Nanni* has been there, and they show him the dance he taught them. Then the hunter notices that his beans have decreased in number, and he suspects *Nanni*. One morning he goes out and hides in a bush close to his house. He sees that *Nanni* is stealing his beans in the manner described above. He catches hold of *Nanni*, chops off both of his hands, and lets him go his way.

Nanni comes home, hiding his hands under his sash, and begins to scold his wives for not having obtained food, and /56/ [he says that] in future he will no longer give [food] to his wives but will feed only his children. He then orders his children to come to his [own] house, where he will feed them.[18] The wives are satisfied with this and each wife brings her children to *Nanni*'s house. Eventually *Nanni* goes in to the children, closes the door,

---

[16] Traditional theatre is still popular in Ghana. Collectively the stories of *Anansi* are called *anansesɛm* and are an important element in the education and socialization of children. Audience participation is expected; individuals make comments and sing songs pertinent to the tale, all of which helps to keep the listeners awake and interested, as well as having a high entertainment value (R.A. Rattray, *Akan-Ashanti Folk Tales* (1930) xiii, 43, 55, 63–74; Peggy Appiah, *Tales of an Ashanti Father* (1967) and *The Pineapple Child and other Tales from Ashanti* (1969); Pelton (1980) 67–70; Assimeng (1981) 74, 78).

[17] The concept of hungry times was commonplace in West Africa. An annual 'hunger season' was (and to some extent still is) common among agricultural communities, being the time of year before the new food crops become available but the previous year's stores are approaching exhaustion. The Gã ceremony of *Hɔmɔwɔ*, literally meaning 'hooting at hunger', is later described. *Faba* represents Portuguese *fava* 'bean'.

[18] In a family compound, the husband and each wife has a separate hut.

pokes each child in the mouth with the stumps of his arms, and threatens that he will, in like manner, chop off their hands if they do not say that they have had their stomachs filled with food. The children promise this and stick to it for two days. On the third day they reveal all to their mothers, who sneak up on *Nanni* and see that he has no hands. All of them resolve to desert *Nanni* and look for other men, and with this aim in mind, they leave.

Nanni runs out and gets ahead of them, and he begins to cut firewood. The wives go past him and greet him, without seeing who it is.[19] *Nanni* disguises his voice and returns their greeting, asking them where they are going. The wives briefly tell him their story and intention, and they ask him if he does not need wives. *Nanni* answers them thus. 'My dears, if you would follow my advice you would return to your husband. I have had 20 wives /**57**/ but have shown 19 of them the door. In these expensive times I have more than enough with a single wife.' The wives take their leave and walk on. *Nanni* again runs ahead of them and [when questioned] pretends that he has had 50 wives and has chased 49 away. The same thing happens a third time, when he claims to have had 100 wives and rid himself of 99. *Nanni*'s wives take counsel among themselves and resolve to seek advice from the fetish. *Nanni* hears this and acts out the fetish from a bush where he had hidden himself. The end [of the story] is that the wives go back to the house of their husband *Nanni*. But he is there ahead of them and refuses to open [the door] to them before they had agree to many conditions favourable to himself.

Some Blacks can act out this fable all night and never let it come to an end.[20] To question how *Nanni* can chop wood when he has no hands — for the storyteller strikes with his fingers and makes sounds with his mouth almost as if someone is chopping wood, grunts at the effort, and copies *Nanni* in every way — that would spoil the whole play. /**58**/

[Other spirits: the Labade fetish]

All the Blacks are agreed on the existence of creatures (spirits) who are intermediaries for God and man (so says Putti). These spirits were created at the time God created the first humans, and they were created for the purpose of teaching humans to live piously and virtuously. With God's permission, they were to instruct people in [the difference between] good and evil. A number of [such] beings exist (if I have understood the Blacks correctly), since there are *Generis Masculini* & *Fæminini* [male and female individuals] who breed their like. And, in Putti's opinion, they die as well,

---

[19] Up to a point, plausible, because in West Africa it is often considered impolite to raise one eye's when facing a superior, and women may greet men with their heads lowered (p.c. P.E.H. Hair).

[20] Possibly the performance lasted so long that R. and his friends left before it was finished. The story may have ended with Ananse the loser. However, he is a creature characterized by ambiguity; sometimes the winner, sometimes the loser; sometimes the wily one, sometimes the fool. For a discussion of the complexities and functions of the trickster, see Pelton (1980) 25–60.

although they can live more than a thousand years. Thus, the spirit who lets himself be heard once every year in Labode is a man, the one in Dutch Accra is his wife, and their son and messenger (*Tie Tie*) is in our Ursu town.[21]

The oracle whom we shall first describe first calls himself *Giemawong* (God's messenger). His titles of honour, given him by the Blacks, are: *Bribi* (remarkable or inconceivable), *Adja* (fire), *Ursogrando* (a tiger of the largest variety).[22] A hut or house has been built for him in Labode town, three quarters of a mile from Christiansborg. It is round and, as usual, with a thatched roof over it, but has no ceiling. It stands in a pleasant /59/ place, planted round with palms and other tall trees.[23] A little distance away live the priests (fetish makers) and the women (female fetish makers) who keep his hut clean inside and out, put food and drink in the hut, and take care, when they are called by the spirit, to listen to his message.[24]

The New Year of the Blacks is at the beginning of August, and through his messenger *Giemawong* informs them of his wishes, and on what day he will appear, usually during the full moon.[25] This is immediately made known everywhere, and the evening before he is to appear the Negroes gather in great numbers outside the hut. All normally have gifts with them, consisting of a sheep, a goat, chickens, indeed, at times, a bull, and each one usually brings brandy along for the offering. (What I write here

---

[21] In recent times, the family structure of the Labadi spirit has been considered to be as follows: *Lakpa* is the god; *Korle* Lagoon is his wife; *Klote* Lagoon is their son; and *Kpeshi* Lagoon is the rival wife (p.c. I. Odotei). The names of the sacred drums, played only during *Hɔmɔwɔ*, correspond to the names of the god, his wife, and their son (Field (1937) 50). In Akan, *Tie Tie* is 'hear, listen', indicating a 'hear-ye!' or herald (Christaller (1933) 513). But the Gã have adopted the term for a similar function of *Klote*, as a messenger to his parents, and he is therefore referred to hereafter as *Tie Tie*.

[22] *Giemawong* (in modern orthography *Jemawɔng*) was the major or patron deity of a settlement. The term is derived from *je* 'place', *wɔng* 'deity' (p.c. Mary Esther Kropp Dakubu). In the form *dzemãwong*, see Zimmermann [1858] (1982) 51; and see also Field (1937) 4-5; Kilson (1971) 62; Akrong (1978) 14-6. *Bribi* is an Akan appellation, pointing out someone or something and invoking a characteristic of excellence, hence 'the excellent one'. (For *biribi*, 'something' in positive sentences, 'nothing' in negative sentences, see Christaller (1933) 22.) Akan *adja* 'father' is used as an honorific. *Ursogrande* resembles corrupt Portuguese, *urso grande* 'great (male) bear'. But alternatively *Ursu* may be Akan *osɔ* 'fox', or the whole term may be the Great Name of a particular Gã chief, Ursue/Owusu + Portuguese *grande*, meaning 'Ursu the Great' (for Owusu, see note 57 below). The term 'tiger' was used by early writers on West Africa, where there are no genuine tigers, to denote any large feline.

[23] For *gbatsu*, the house, or room, of the god, see Field (1937) 6-7. Her 1930s description is much like R.'s. For sacred groves, see Paul Erdmann Isert, *Letters on West Africa and the Slave Trade* [1788] (1992) 56, 105. Enclosures serve to maintain the mystery and power of the place.

[24] In recent times, two distinct groups of women have been attached to the shrine: *djranoyei*, who cook and take care of the physical environment, and *wɔyei*, the priestesses (Field (1937) 8-9).

[25] For the annual ceremony of *Hɔmɔwɔ* and rituals in preparation for it in the 1930s, see Field (1937) 41-6, 47-56. This remains the most important of the Gã festivals, being a confirmation of family ties, and a time for reconciliation and cleaning the slate for the coming year. Many of the customs and rituals which R. described are precisely the same as I have myself seen them performed in recent years.

is according to the statements of many old Negroes, and especially those of a man who was born there and has served in that country — this man is now here in Zeeland).[26]

Approaching 3 o'clock in the morning, *Giemawong* is heard in the air with a sound much like that of our wild geese when they fly over our heads in the spring. He then arrives at his house. The earth shakes, and the hut with it. /60/ The Blacks who are gathered there and are sitting in a large circle fall on their faces and give a greeting by clapping their hands slowly. They bid him welcome, and ask him to be good to them, calling him by his great or honorary names: *Adja, Bribi*, and so on. *Giemawong* starts by blessing them and then he begins an oration. First, he takes to task those who have committed evil [deeds]. Then he praises those who have lived piously that year, and commends them for their virtue. It is noteworthy that when he has spoken about one matter, he pauses before beginning another. His whole oration may last an hour and a half. He speaks in an out-of-date language, and mostly in parables, by which he also answers the Negroes' questions.[27]

Next, the fetish-maker (or priest) sitting nearest the door receives brandy from each of the Blacks in turn. He holds it out in front of the door, and it is taken in without anyone being able to see who has taken it. *Giemawong* drinks from the bottle so that the people who are nearest the door can hear the gurgle, and when the bottle is handed out again, each Black and his bottle are given a special blessing and an admonition [to behave well]. /61/ This fetish is remarkably desirous of brandy, and can consume more at one time than 200 Negroes. There are 2,000–3,000 people gathered there, and each one usually has a gift for him, although for most of them it is brandy. Towards daylight, at about 5 o'clock, he goes away again, with just as much shaking of the ground and howling as when he arrived. He leaves behind him a possessed fetish-maker, whom the Blacks place into the hut and to whom they give offerings in the same manner as [they did to] *Giemawong*.

The man mentioned above has assured me, by all that is holy, that he has heard that being, *Giemawong*, say, in his own language, this: 'You shall not follow the example of the *Blankes* [Whites] (Europeans), since, although they have God's pure word before them, as you (the Blacks) do

---

[26] Probably Frederik Svane, for whom see Chapter 2, note 130, above.

[27] In modern times, the ritual includes songs in 'the Bonni language' (Field (1937) 6, 41). It has been argued that the songs are not 'gibberish' but in recognizable Gã, apart from a few terms in an ancient, forgotten language (Quaye (1972) 26–7). The issue is discussed in M.E. Kropp Dakubu, *Korle Meets the Sea. A Sociolinguistic History of Accra,* New York (1997) 107–8. Oracles worldwide have, of course, always spoken in barely comprehensible language and ambiguous terms. By 'parables' R. probably means proverbs and other non-specific statements, such as that given below, /98/–/99/.

not, they are damned after death because of their evil ways'. *Relata refero* [I state only what I am told].[28] This individual is not the only person to have heard such [a statement]; so have many of those in the country who are born Christians. They have travelled to the east or west of our Fort and have heard [such] a being speak in many places, and mostly on the same subject, namely that it exhorts its listeners to be pious and virtuous.[29] These oracles have different /**62**/ names, and according to the statements of the Negroes, it is not *Giemawong* from Labode who annually visits the places on the Upper and Lower Coasts, but other spirits. Putti's brother, Qvassi,[30] told me that *Giemawong* once chased a prominent Negro out of this [annual] gathering, telling him, so that all present heard it, that he (*Giemawong*) accepted no sacrifices from one who had lain with his [own] daughter.[31] After that, that Negro was no longer highly respected among his peers, and shortly after that he killed himself.[32]

A Mulatto woman, a Christian, in the course of one year had had several persons at our Fort poisoned. When she brought forward her sacrifice (which was a bottle of brandy) *Giemawong* would not accept it, as he did the others. Instead, (it is strange, and I ask to be excused for writing it) he farted, and damned her with these words, 'Your memory shall be obliterated'. Many Blacks have told me this, and all of our servants at the Fort know it, so that the woman, the wife of a sergeant named Cornelius Petersen, dared not come to the Fort during an entire year, for

---

[28] The oracle is cited as saying that the Blacks lack 'true religion'; while the Whites, despite their having such religion, are thoroughly evil. Patently the sentiments are those of R. or of his informant — the latter a Christian African (though possibly a Mulatto) at the time living in Denmark. R.'s comment may indicate a measure of doubt on his part about the veracity of the anecdote.

[29] The 'born Christians' were mostly children of Europeans, therefore Mulattos. It is not clear whether R., by this terminology, is associating Svane with this group or otherwise distinguishing them from him. Svane may have been a convert rather than a born Christian. Further, R. loses the thread of his argument. The reader expects that what the others heard was a similar denunciation of the Whites for evil ways, but instead only a recommendation to the Blacks to be virtuous is mentioned.

[30] Qvassi/Kwasi is the Akan day-name for a man born on the day of the seven-day Akan week called Kwesida. Normally such names were (and are) only used by the Gã in a descriptive capacity and together with a Gã name (p.c. I. Odotei). But R. may have forgotten the full name of this individual. The Gã have a totally different naming system, based upon status in the family and family relationships (William F. Daniell, 'On the ethnography of Akkrah and Adampe', *Journal of the Ethnological Society* 4 (1856) 9–10; Field (1937) 174).

[31] I have not been able to trace detailed information on the concept of incest among the Gã, its application and punishments. But for Gã concepts of kinship, which determine what is incestuous, see Marion Kilson, *African Urban Kinsmen* (1974) 16–9, 28–9.

[32] Modern sources evidence that among the Gã, suicide is an accursed death, as is death by accident and during childbirth, the individual not being given a proper burial. For blasphemous deaths, see Field (1937) 58–9; and for 'premature death', Kilson (1974) 50.

fear of being railed at by our soldiers.³³ /**63**/ On that [festival] day, the Negroes enjoy themselves with the brandy which *Giemawong* has left them. Every other hour they receive a clay pot full of (pardon me) urine, into which they quite greedily dip their fingers and then suck them. They say that *Giemawong* has left it behind.

[A New Year ceremony]

We Europeans, that is, the Danes, the English, and the Dutch, willingly go to see the Negroes' peculiar ceremonies [at the New Year], which last for three days. We see nothing but three drums, each with its drummer, and these are old men.³⁴ One of the drums is respected as especially sacred, and it is never played other than on these three days every year. The drummer who beats it hangs it from a band around his neck, and behaves as if he is also possessed. He opens his eyes wide without blinking, and acts as if the drum has driven him involuntarily from one [spectator] to another who must dance for him. On all three drums they have fixed a sort of long beard of raffia, smeared with red earth.³⁵ The individual who has the honour of dancing with the drum, which is constantly being played, takes hold of this beard. No matter how old the Negro to whom the drum and the turn have come, you observe that, although he can hardly walk otherwise, yet he dances in /**64**/ a very respectful manner, and so rapidly, that you are amazed by it. With great respect he touches the beard of the drum, brushing his face and whole body against it, while performing his sacred capers.³⁶ All those standing in the ring, or circle, [also] perform movements, apparently accompanying the man dancing, but not moving from the spot. They sing what the possessed fetish inside the hut begins. It is in the ancient language, [sung] in such a sad and melancholy voice and tone, mostly nasal, with so much of *hui! ha.. ac..*,

---

³³ The woman in question was Anna Sophia, the Mulatto wife of Cornelius Petersen, a Danish Sergeant. The deaths of several Danes occurred during and after the rebellion at Christiansborg in 1744 (see Appendix B). R. reports the deaths as variously caused by illness or by excessive drinking. Petersen was imprisoned at Christiansborg for his role in the mutiny and the accusations against his wife were that she and her cohorts were killing persons in order to obtain her husband's release. After a series of deaths, including those of three governors who died in rapid succession, and out of fear that the rumours were based on fact, a new governor released Petersen (Per Hernæs, 'Den balstyrige bergenser på Guldkysten', *Norsk Sjøfartsmuseum Årsberetning* (1935) 135–7). As a Christian, Anna Sophia was hedging her bets by sacrificing to the fetish, although R. may have deliberately labelled her so to express disdain for Mulattos.

³⁴ For a description of the drums used during Hɔmɔwɔ, see below, /65/. For drums brought out in modern times on the particular Wednesday which is 'New Year's Day', ending a six-week period of their silence, see Field (1937) 52;2–43; Quarcoo (1967) 2–43.

³⁵ For explanations of the significance of the colours red and white in Gold Coast symbolism, see C.C. Reindorf, *History of the Gold Coast and Asante* [1895] (1966) 126/118; George P. Hagan, 'A note on Akan colour symbolism', *IAS Research Review* 7/2 (1970) 8–13; Kilson (1971) 73; McCaskie (1995) 203.

³⁶ For this (or a similar or equivalent) ceremony in the 1930s, see Field (1937) 53.

that it is impossible to describe or imagine what it sounds like. All the many Europeans among the ships' crews and those resident in the country whom I have taken there, have had to admit that they have never heard or seen such [things before]. It usually falls to us Danes to provide the treats at Labode, when so many strangers ask us to take them there to see something that they have never seen before but have certainly heard of. Their black servants remind them that no one should come to that sacred place with empty hands, but that they must bring as an offering an anker or half an anker of brandy. Once we are on our way with many ankers and bottles of brandy [carried] behind us, the /**65**/ possessed, or spellbound person in the hut knows — say the Negroes — that the Whites are coming with offerings for *Giemawong*. Then the fetish-maker starts to sing a special song, to which no one other than the highest priest, Putti, may dance. The words of the song are these: 'Whites! Children of Whites! Blessed may you be!' I know of no other translation of the words: *Blafonse biattum boo, etc.*[37] Stools are put out for us so that we can complete the circle. Putti then comes with the drum and dances the dance for each European individually. This drum is held to be particularly sacred, and no one but old and prominent people may turn capers to its accompaniment. For the ordinary, or younger, Negroes there are two other drums, similarly decorated with beards. The largest and most sacred is a good four feet high, the second one three, and the third one about two. The drummers have two dreadful [*sic*] sticks with which they beat the drums. The sticks are carved like crooks, or hooks, and strike [the drums] with such force that at times the thick elephant ear is snapped into pieces, and the players must stop their antics until it is repaired.

Toward evening of the first day, their [sacrificial] animals are slaughtered, not with knives but with a sharp /**66**/ stone.[38] The blood is brought to the fetish-maker in the hut, and he sprinkles some of it inside the hut and smears the forehead and breast of the bearer with some. The animals are left to lie in the sun with their hide and hair on, as well as with all the unclean innards. They are still there the following day, and have become so swollen by the heat of the sun that it is an easy job for the hide to be removed without a knife. On the third day they begin to smell foul, and then they are to the Negroes' taste. They usually treat all their meat and fish food in this way, and they accuse us of eating animals and fish while

---

[37] *Blafonse biattum boo* should possibly read *blafon sebi attumboo*, being based on the following phrases: *blɔfo* 'whiteman' (modern Gã *blofomei*), *shi bii* 'children under', *átù bo* 'may it be given to you'. This identification involves some guesswork, but is not far from R.'s translation (p.c. M.E. Kropp Dakubu).

[38] In certain African societies metal is tabu, either entirely, or at particular times or ceremonies (Field (1937) 46–7). For the ceremonial use of a stone knife in the Gã sacrifice of a bullock in the 1930s, when no one of any rank was allowed to wear gold jewelry during the celebration, see Field, 55, note 1.

still alive, asserting that it is the quantities of such unrotten food [we eat] that kills us.³⁹

A prominent Negro attends this feast on only one day, and he leaves the second and third days to those who are younger and of lesser rank. But if anything especially favourable has happened to these [prominent men] in the past year, they usually stay for all three days, and then there is a dreadful din. Nevertheless, we have never heard of any conflicts among them, which otherwise regularly occur when they drink too much. [Now] they lie down quite peaceably and sleep until waking up, having slept off their intoxication. And they begin [to drink] all over again. On the third or last day, toward evening, the festivities are completed with a ceremony I have often seen but whose meaning I was unable /67/ to understand until Putti gave me the following explanation.

Four Blacks, two at each end, carry a long tree trunk, or beam, straddled by a Negro who makes particularly ridiculous gestures. He climbs up on it at Caboceer Putti's house, and is carried through the town and on to the sacred place. All the little boys and girls follow him, and shriek, so that it pierces your ears. You are forced to retire a good distance from there to avoid being caught up in the crush. This is a ceremony that takes place in honour of Putti, because, in the time of one of his ancestors, his town (Labode) was suddenly attacked by enemies, and all the people, adults and children, were taken prisoner. The [enemy] did not dare lay hands on Putti's ancestor precisely because he was the chief priest. Being extremely wealthy, he redeemed all the people, his townsmen, and had gold weighed out for every single individual. The man who rides on the beam pretends to have a balance in one hand, and to be using it to weigh. With the other hand, he pretends to take hold of the person he has purchased, and to draw him behind himself. The young people run in front and alongside of him, calling out 'Buy me first! Buy me first!' And with that the great celebration comes to an end.⁴⁰ /68/

[The fetish oracle]

As for other rituals, when a Black wishes to ask the fetish (oracle) about something, either because his family, a friend, his children, or his wife are ill,⁴¹ or because he intends to embark on an important venture, he goes to the

---

³⁹ R. may have been unaware that, in Europe, meat, game birds, and animals were often 'hung' for tenderizing before cooking and eating.

⁴⁰ On the carrying of the representative of the king in the same manner in the 1930s, see Field (1937) 53. This was still being done in 1995. The ceremony occurs in the afternoon of *La Kpa* (Wednesday), and the man being carried (the *agbugbunte mantse*) is surrounded by a mixed group of both adults and children.

⁴¹ The order of persons given by R. may be intended to express common African familial attitudes, the family being those of the man's own lineage, for instance, his parents, therefore excluding his wife who comes last (p.c. P.E.H. Hair). Or it may just be R.'s style of writing.

fetish-maker — or the female fetish-maker; since our Ursue (the Negro town under Christiansborg) has only two miserable old crones who take care of *Tie Tie*. He asks if he may hear the fetish speak, to which she answers yes or no. But the sick person tries first to see if he can be helped with herbs or other [remedies] known to be effective in such an illness. [If the answer was yes,] the supplicant is ordered to attend the following day. He then brings his offering with him, which normally consists of a bottle of brandy and one or one half *rixdaler* in goods, or in *bossies* [cowries].[42] It should be noted that the fetish hut is always round, and inside you see a thousand kinds of worthless objects, hanging up or lying in it. A clay pot, standing in a corner, contains red earth in which there may be a feather from the tail of a cock. Sticks tied together with thread or raffia are placed on the wall or sides of the hut. Among the objects may be a red feather from a parrot's tail, or the hair of humans or animals. Indeed, you cannot count all the bric-à-brac they keep in those places — animal bones and other things. Under the roof, in the peak, hangs a bell resembling /**69**/ those our farmers hang around the neck of their cows or sheep when they go into the woods. A length of raffia reaching nearly to the ground is fastened near the bell. We must not forget the most prominent objects in the fetish hut, which are the fetish's stool, on which he sits, and the mat on which he rests. The mat is no larger than a man's hand, and the stool is in proportion. Always standing ready for him is also a little bottle of brandy.[43]

When, then, the supplicant arrives, he delivers his offering to the fetish crone, who sets it outside the hut. Then she crawls into the hut on her hands and knees, so that the length of raffia mentioned above lies along her neck or back. She then orders the supplicant to enter the hut, to close the door, sit on the ground, and bend his head down between his knees, keeping his hands in front of his face. This done, the crone performs her conjuring [up of spirits], urging the fetish to come to her. When the fetish is present, the bell rings. The crone becomes, or pretends to become, possessed. She stretches out her arms and legs, begins to giggle and foam at the mouth, and draws short breaths with a raised chest. /**70**/ The supplicant then knows that it is time to ask what he wants to know, for instance, 'Will my friend or brother recover from this illness? What should I give you so that you will take this illness from him? Why are you killing my brother? What has he done to

---

[42] For *Tie Tie*, see note 21 above. It is perhaps surprising that the shrine of such an important god as Tie Tie, alias Klote, was attended by only two old women, and not by a priest and priestesses (cf. Field (1937) 64). *Bossies* derives from Portuguese *buzio* 'cowry shell'. The particular variety used in West Africa as currency, *Cypraea moneta*, was imported from the Maldives (Marion Johnson, 'The cowrie currencies of West Africa', *Journal of African History* 11 (1970) 17–8; cf. Isert [1788] (1992) 85; Field (1937) 110–1).

[43] In recent times, bunches of sea shells are hung in a doorway, to sound when anyone enters (Field (1937) 7). A modern medicine-man's room may have a drum as its only small object (Field, 110).

you?', and so on. Whereupon the possessed fetish-crone, in a thin, squeaky voice (almost like a peeping chick), answers in their ancient language. The supplicant is nearly always given a good and comforting reply, with the condition that he kill, or tie it up tightly, alive, a white cock or chicken, and place it at a crossroads. Then he (that is, the fetish) will come and fetch it. At times the supplicant gets away with a better bargain, which consists of his placing only an egg at a crossroads, or alternatively he must take 10–12 wooden sticks and drive them into the ground, thereby driving his friend's illness out of his body and into the earth. There are over a thousand such types of offering.[44]

When the Negroes have told me such things, I have often asked them this: 'Why don't you lift your heads a little when you are sitting that way in the fetish hut, and open your eyes, in order to see who is ringing the bell? Couldn't it be the crone who is pulling the raffia?' /71/ Many of them have answered me, as follows. 'The first five or six times we had a call to the fetish, we were curious to see who and what it was that was up at the bell, and we saw something resembling a [blank], or a bird which appears to look like our owls, or else a [blank], a kind of small monkey, black with a white beard.'[45] Some of them have assured me that, every time they were there, they peeked through their fingers to see which of these two creatures was visible.

A rich Negro usually asks the fetish every month what condition he is in, even though he is hale and hearty. He receives the answer that his health is good; but in order that it should continue so, he is ordered to sacrifice a chicken or an egg. Instead, he slaughters a sheep or a *cabrit* (a goat), and the fetish is given not the meat but only a little of the entrails, and he brings the unclean part to the [cross]roads. He consumes the rest himself, in company with his friends. If, however, he falls ill, he does not hesitate to complain to the fetish that he has sacrificed so many animals during the year, and yet, despite the fetish's promise, he is being attacked by illness.[46] /72/

[Women possessed]

Some kings are found up-country who, when they make an offering in this way and their fetish is satisfied with it, asking only for a chicken or something else [of that sort], as is done at the coast, [nevertheless] in a barbaric manner they cut the heads off one or more slaves. It is often said that the fetish can *penjarte* (which in the Danish language can mean old crones possessed by

---

[44] Healing and divining were considered inseparable (William Bosman, *A New and Accurate Description of the Coast of Guinea* (1705) 151–3, 221–4; Kilson (1974) 89–95). For modern practices, see Opoku (1988) 148–51.

[45] The first blank stands for a bird whose local name R. appears to have forgotten. The term translated 'owls' is *Uler*, seemingly a misprint for *Ugler* 'owls'. By the description, the monkey whose local name R. has also forgotten is the Diana Monkey (*Cercopithecus diana*). In the highly emotional circumstances it is perhaps unlikely that there was, in fact, any 'peeking'.

[46] For medicines that fail to work, see Field (1937) 111–2; Akrong (1978) 87.

the devil) so that individuals go into convulsions, making such movements with their entire bodies which truly seem quite unnatural.⁴⁷ With staring eyes they foam at the mouth, gasping for breath. They usually enter this [state] suddenly and unconsciously, so that a crone can at times be walking with a water pot or something else on her head, talking to someone walking beside her, and in an instant she is possessed. I have seen some who have made all these contortions, and yet kept the water pot on their heads. One woman lay down on her back, turned her body rapidly three to four times on the ground, and yet maintained in balance on her head a pot full of water, without spilling a drop, even though the pot had a round bottom.⁴⁸ (Let our European acrobats try to copy these women.) Sometimes I have seen the pot broken when the subject carries on too long, [that is,] as the Blacks say, /73/ before the fetish can achieve the power to speak through her mouth. Then, when the first intensity is over, the old crone usually lies down on her back, and at times performs movements and contortions modesty forbids me to describe.⁴⁹

When this is over, she begins to speak. I have forgotten to mention that the Blacks, whenever they can, immediately form a circle around the old crone, and do not allow any European to enter it, out of fear that he will mock both the fetish and the woman. She usually begins—at least on as many occasions as I have witnessed it—with the words *'Haminse è bá'*, and she repeats these words a good ten times, whereupon those surrounding her answer *'è bá'*, and they clap their hands slowly. Translated literally, the old crone's pronouncement means 'May good come to you!', and those surrounding her answer, 'Let it come!' After this (according to what the Blacks say) she prophesies future events for them.⁵⁰ At Fredensborg I have often heard that the message of the fetish has not been anything other than these words, 'Be obedient to your Whites. Do what the Whites tell you to do.' /74/ You can well imagine how welcome such an oracular statement is

---

⁴⁷ *Penjarte* 'panyarring' is from the Portuguese *penhorar* 'to distrain, call in a debt'. Panyarring was the seizure of an individual as repayment for a long-standing debt. The individual was not necessarily the debtor himself (or herself, although debtors were normally men) but a member of his family or someone from his village, reflecting the collective ethos of African societies. If the debt was not then paid the individual panyarred was often sold as a slave. In the present context, the panyarring is a spiritual seizure, the god taking control of the woman's personality and behaviour. For panyarring, see Isert [1788] (1992) 134; Adam Jones, *Brandenburg Sources for West African History* (1985) 317.

⁴⁸ This perhaps means that the woman, half-sitting, half-lying, swivelled round several times—otherwise the feat is difficult to visualize.

⁴⁹ On spirit possession and for the *wɔyo* (medium) in possession and in private life, see Field (1937) 104–9; Kilson (1971) 19–20. Possessed mediums behave like the animal associated with their god, thus a medium whose god is a python may lie down and wriggle like a snake (p.c. I. Odotei). But, as R. notes, the wild and apparently uncontrollable behaviour of possession resembles that of sexual excitement.

⁵⁰ The phrases (in modern Gã orthography) are probably *hã mínsh ébá*, 'Let happiness come!', and *ébá* 'Let it come!' or *eébá* 'It will come' (p.c. M.E. Kropp Dakubu).

for us Europeans, who at all times suffer mischief from malicious and stupid Negroes, especially in that very place. I myself have often given a bottle of brandy to such a soothsayer and wished that she might be possessed every day, since this makes such a great impression on the Negroes.[51]

Some old crones continue their madness for several days, running from one town to another. When we meet such an old woman on the road, the Blacks usually carry us a bit out of the way, in order to let her follow her path alone. If a European is on foot, they ask him to step out of the way, so that the fetish-woman will not become angry with him; for it is better to be bitten by a mad dog in Europe than to have such an old crone pour out her gall over us with her curses. The Negroes would consider a European [who refused to move aside] an ill-fated person who would certainly suffer the accidents the possessed old crone wished on him. Other than fear of their curses, those who are subject to, or perform, such contortions, are held in honour and respect.[52]

In all the houses of the Negroes you see signs and evidence of the fetish, many in some homes, fewer in others. In the homes of most of them you see one or more poles /75/ leaning against a wall, two feet above ground, painted red and white. Tied to the ends with raffia are either feathers or hair, usually smeared with blood.[53]

[Sacred objects]

Once I unexpectedly came upon an old Negro's curio cabinet in which there were more than twenty thousand of such foolish trinkets (I do not know what else I can call them). This Negro was our Caboceer Noyte, in Tessing, two miles from Christiansborg.[54] I had come from Fredensborg and was on my way to Christiansborg, arriving in Tessing at 4.30 in the morning, after a difficult night, since we had had two travados [storms] in one night. I went there to put on dry clothing, and expected that the caboceer would have breakfast made for me. I dismounted at his house, as usual, and asked for the caboceer, but his people answered that he had not yet got up. I waited a while, and asked again, but received the same answer. I could not understand this, for I had often come in the middle of the night and Noyte had always arrived immediately to bid me welcome. Meanwhile the time

---

[51] The supposed admonition to be obedient to the Whites is implausible and was no doubt a polite and diplomatic piece of misinformation on the part of informants, designed to keep R. and the other Whites happy.

[52] According to present-day observations, women with this ability are honoured when they are possessed and are considered the mouthpiece of the god. Their status in the community depends on the relevance and success of their pronouncements, which are taken very seriously.

[53] On red and white stripes and their uses in various present-day connections, see Field (1937) 44, 180–1. For shrines in private homes in the seventeenth century, see Villault (1669) 263–4; Müller [1673] in Jones (1983) 161, 162–3.

[54] Tessing is the locality of Teshie. For more on Noyte, see Chapter 4, /115/ and note 25, below.

stretched out and in order not to freeze I walked into his extensive courtyard, which is surrounded by the houses of his family.[55] I saw an open door which, on earlier occasions, I had often seen closed with a /76/ padlock. I was curious, looked in and saw, to my greatest astonishment, my old friend Noyte [of] Tessing sitting among many thousand of knick-knacks, among which I saw the heads of elephants, oxen, sheep, and other animals. He did not see me before I had stuck my head and half my body in through the narrow door, thus casting a shadow inside. He stood up and asked me to leave. I did not wish to do this, but promised him that I would come no closer, if he would tell me what it all meant. He swore by his father — a great oath among the Negroes — that he did not know one hundredth part of the amount of good that had come [from the collection of sacred objects], but that all of it (perhaps with the exception of some one hundred items) had been collected by his forefathers, and each piece which I saw had helped his forefathers in some way, because of the help of God and the fetish. This discourse having left me as wise as I was before, I asked what he had done with all these things during the last war, which had taken place the previous year, when the entire town had been burnt down by the Assiantees.[56] He answered that he had buried them before he and his people left the town in order to flee to our fortress at Accra, and in his lifetime these sacred articles had been hidden in the earth more than ten times. /77/ And even more remarkably, on one occasion [hidden] for fifteen years. Near me I saw an ordinary stone the size of a hen's egg. I picked it up and said, 'Tell me, Caboceer, what do you do with this? You could in a very short time collect many of these.' As I could sense, Noyte became somewhat vexed at my impudence, but he told me this story. 'Did you not see how keen the Assiantees were to harm me after they had won a victory over the Akims, and how they made their way to us instead of to our neighbours? If I had not at that time had the friendship of the Danes, who protected and pleaded for me, how would I have fared? I anticipated this [state of affairs] after I heard that my friend Ursue (one of the Akim kings) had been killed and his people had taken flight.[57] I buried these objects and other things at night, and was on my way up to the Fort. At the first step I took across my threshold I stepped on the stone and it hurt me. I thought, 'Ha ha! Are you there?' I picked up this stone of mine, and it did not leave me until I returned to my town and my house was rebuilt. You yourself — he said to me — have seen me pleading my case for four days in the council. Did you not notice this stone in my

---

[55] For a description of a shrine in Teshie in the 1930s — but a public shrine of the god *Ayiku* —, see Field (1937) 75. The combination of secular and priestly authority was not unusual. Even today, the *Mantse* (Chief) of Teshie is also the Chief Priest.

[56] For the Asante campaign and conquest in 1742, see Chapter 4, /184/–/188/, below.

[57] 'Ursue' is Owusu, commander-in-chief of the Akyem Abuakwa forces, and administrator in Ningo after the Akwamu were defeated by the Akyem in 1730, who was killed during the war against Asante in 1742 (J.K. Fynn, *Asante and its Neighbours* (1971) 71, 73, 74).

hand? /**78**/ And that when I lacked words to respond to the speeches of my opponents, it helped me to acquit myself? Must you yourself not admit that God and the fetish sent it to help me? And ought I not to be grateful?' I did indeed then remember that during the time that he was pleading [his case] he had had something in his hand which he squeezed hard. His case had been one of importance. The Assiantees had demanded of us that we deliver him and his entire family to them, since he was the slave of the Akim king. Not until he explained did I understand [his holding the stone], although before that I had noticed — and have noticed since — that when a Black has an important matter to decide, he always has something in his hand which he squeezes, first in one [hand] and then in the other, and at times with both hands. This was also Noyte's way of celebrating morning prayers, by sitting for an hour among these knick-knacks and rummaging among them.

[The Fante fetish]

As mentioned above, the Fante fetish is the most powerful one. Above Annamaboe [Anomabu], two miles from the shore, several hills of considerable height and overgrown with thick brush and tall trees form a semi-circle. Between these hills the ground is quite flat. (I am writing here of a place which I have never seen, but /**79**/ I record it according to the testimony of many). The hills are considered to be so sacred that not even the priests dare approach them but must keep a certain distance.[58] This fetish appears three times a year. At other times, if someone wishes to ask about something, he answers through the mouth of one of his priests or priestesses, just as the other fetishes do, and mostly in the same way as it is done in other places. This fetish is not as clear [in his pronouncements] as the one in Labode, and is very bloodthirsty. At [the beginning of] every month the Negroes must sacrifice a human being, and after he has accepted the human being, as an extra gift they sacrifice to him a pair of oxen. The sacrifice must be performed in the following way. When he himself is to be present, on one of the three times in the year, he is accompanied by an earthquake, and all the tall trees bend to greet the fetish. Then a whirlwind blows up, and all the Blacks, forming a semicircle with the hills (thus making a complete circle) fall on their faces, just as at Labode, and the fetish makes an oration. It is to be noted that he speaks like a man quivering and trembling, [almost] hiccuping hoarsely, and stammering. I cannot claim to know all that the Blacks say about his voice, [but] am relating this /**80**/ according to the description of Corrantrin's son Bassi, who, as I mentioned before, was in France for several years.[59] I and several other [Whites] have often been entertained by Bassi imitating the voice of the fetish, and delivering speeches to us in the language employed by the fetish. He himself had visited the fetish on

---

[58] For the Fante fetish and shrine known as *Nananom Mpow*, see McCaskie (1990) 139–43.
[59] For Bassi and his stay in France, see Chapter 2, /46/ and notes 103, 105; also 1756, /30/–/31/.

only one occasion, when he arrived home from France and Corrantrin, his father, obliged him to accompany him, in order to observe the sacrifice he had offered the fetish in gratitude for his son's safe return. But Bassi, who was angry with his thievish father, told me that he had only offered a goat, [despite the need for gratitude] for the beautiful goods which his father, at that time, had already intended to steal from the poor French.[60]

We come, then to Bassi's description of how the fetish receives his offering. The person or animal which is to be sacrificed is brought forward by about fifty priests and priestesses, who advance singing — and the song is just as melancholy as the one sung in Labode. The Negroes, sitting ten, and at times twenty, men deep, open their circle on one of the sides between the hills and themselves. The sacrifice is dragged three /81/ times around the circle, and all the Negroes sing the same song. Finally they stand up, and the priests and priestesses form a smaller circle around the sacrifice, not far from the [sacred] grove from which there comes a whirlwind which lifts the sacrifice up into the air. As long as they can see it they hear it screaming and roaring, but [after that] it is never seen again. Bassi and the others have assured me that as soon as the sacrifice leaves the earth, it is both twisted around and turned over, in the same way as an Easterly known as a 'twister' (*Trompe de Mer*) draws water up out of the sea. The revolving is less noticeable and slower when the sacrifice is not far from the earth, but the higher into the air it goes, the more twisting and the more circles it makes.

The Negroes do not feel this [whirl]wind, but they remain very quiet. Just as the symbols (*signa*) of the Labode fetish are some old drums, so fire is the symbol of the Fante fetish. It is kept permanently [burning] at a certain place night and day, year in and year out, at which place the priests sing an ancient song, and dance, every morning and evening. And since no one in that country can dance without a drum, they also have several players /82/ or drumbeaters. But these drums are not sacred.[61]

According to what the Negroes claim, the Fante fetish, in one of his regular orations, delivered the following parable. A player or drummer lived in a place where there were many lovely fruit trees. When he had an appetite for eating, the drummer played some lively music under the tree, and the snake which lived in the tree threw down to him as many of all the varieties of fruit as he wished. Thus he lived, satisfied, for several years, and became comfortable and fat. But it happened that he fell ill. He could not then play the music for the snake as usual, and from his house he could barely walk to his position under the tree, where he asked the snake for a couple of [blank] (a fruit resembling our plums but very

---

[60] For this incident, see Chapter 2, /46/-/47/, above.
[61] R. is thinking here of the sacred drums used by the Gã only during *Hɔmɔwɔ*, as mentioned above.

mealy and healthy to eat). Although the sick man promised to repay him after he recovered, the snake showed no goodwill to our drummer by throwing fruit down to him. The sick drummer had to be grateful for the unripe fruit growing low down on the tree, and he finally recovered. As was his due, he wanted to take revenge on the merciless snake. With his drum, /83/ he placed himself under the tree where the snake lived and called up to her. As usual, she needed to stick her head down out of the tree, in order to hear the music better. Being pleased that her drummer was well again, she did so, as requested. But, instead of drumsticks the drummer carried two chopping knives, and he swiftly cut off the snake's head. By telling this story the fetish intended to warn his listeners not to be lukewarm in their worship, or what the drummer [had done] to the snake he would do to them.[62]

According to Bassi, the first words of the Fante fetish when he arrives at his grove are, 'I greet you all!' — this being a translation of Bassi's '*Je salue vous Autres!*'[63] He speaks these words clearly, but then he begins to tremble and quake. Another time the Fante fetish said, 'If you do not love Good and follow it, and if you do not hate Evil and shun it, I shall in person support your enemies, and I shall murder you, also all the relatives close to you. It is only for the sake of your pious forefathers that I have spared you until now.'[64] /84/ So much for the reports of Bassi and others about the Fante fetish.

A competent drawing-master and copper engraver could make his fortune if he were to travel through that land and supply us with copper engravings of a possessed old crone, of the interior of a fetish hut, of some fifty types of fetishes, of the Labode gathering after the fetish had been there the night before, of dancing Negroes, of Negroes going to war, of a battle between two parties of Blacks, of portraits of Putti and Noyte, and of other scenes and features.[65]

Otherwise, [when not inculcating piety,] the Fante fetish is fearfully bloodthirsty, there being killed on his orders not only human beings who are slaves, but even those who are the most prominent among the Fantees. In the course of three years, the Fantees at one time or another had [killed by the fetish] five *Brafoes* (generals), individuals who exercise the highest command over the

---

[62] That is, a god neglected seeks revenge.

[63] The phrase is in French because this was the European language spoken by Bassi after his long sojourn in France (Chapter 2, /47/, above).

[64] The sentiments are so close to those expressed at points in the Old Testament as to be suspect. Either Bassi or R. seems to have been adjusting African piety to Christian.

[65] In fact, a drawing, by Christian Lindholm Schmidt, portraying a Gold Coast warrior equipped for action was published in Copenhagen in 1761, immediately after R.'s book appeared. See Appendix C. Since R. makes no mention of the illustrations in de Marees, Dapper, or Barbot, he may not have seen these works. He certainly knew Bosman, but the illustrations in this work do not portray the scenes R. wished to be represented.

entire nation.⁶⁶ These *Brafoes* are chosen from a certain family who, for many hundreds of years, has been responsible for filling this high position. Today this family has become so short of men that in recent years no *Brafoe* could be chosen, there being only several little boys available. The fetish has often ordered that the Negroes gathered at his shrine should immediately cut off the head of this or that prominent Negro, and this is /85/ frequently the fate of a *Brafoe*. The fetish does not receive him as an offering but is satisfied with his blood, and his friends can bury his body.

[Propitious days: sacred animals]

The Negroes reckon time in 'good days' and 'bad days'. I have never really been able to fathom this system of reckoning. Our Negroes at the seashore do not understand it either, except when a learned person (I speak ironically) from Akim or Assiante, 200–300 miles up-country, comes down and sets them right again. I shall record here, to the best of my understanding, the Negroes' reckoning of time, and I leave it to sensible people on the Coast to correct it, so that if this book is published again in the future, it can then be more reliable. When on the Coast, I never expected that, once back in Europe, I would at any time be writing about these matters, otherwise I would have taken notes while there. The Negroes have 21 'great good days' (*Grande bonos Dies*) which begin with a certain month and last, it is said, for 21 days, after which there come 15 'bad days' (*Male Dies*). Thereafter /86/ come 13 'small good days' (*Pikanne bonos Dies*), and 9 'especially bad days'. Then, finally, their 21 'great good days' begin again at a new moon. But this [sequence of days] in no way follows the phases of the moon. So, I shall leave this to a sensible man on the Coast, to have himself instructed by a learned Akim fetish-maker.⁶⁷ Each week every Negro has his own sacred day, the day on which he was born. On that day they decorate

---

⁶⁶ *Obráfo/abráfo*, a term defined only as 'executioner/s' by the nineteenth-century authority on Twi/Akan (Christaller (1933) 47), undoubtedly had a number of other meanings in earlier centuries, particularly among the Fante section, where it referred to several public offices, such as those of an assistant or follower of a priest or god, a guard, a messenger, or an agent. The meaning in the text is patently that of military leader. For an explanation of the various aspects of this office, see McCaskie (1990) 136.

⁶⁷ By 'begin with a certain month', R. apparently means, as he later states, begins with a new moon. The 'good' and 'bad' days are lucky and unlucky days, as in many other calendrical systems. If R. is referring to the Gã, he is almost certainly mistaken in claiming that they received help in adjusting their calendar from Akyem or Asante, both Akan-speaking territories. In recent times, the Akan calendar has been based on a cycle of 42 days (Rattray (1923) 114–5; McCaskie (1995) 152–7); whereas the Gã calendar has instead been based on the lunar month of 28 days, the year having 12 months plus 3 weeks = 357 days (Daniell (1852) 22–3). But for the Akan calendar as a determinant in trade, see Kea (1982) 212. R.'s days add up to 58 each cycle, that is, two lunar months of 29 days, but it is not clear whether he was simply wrong or the calendar later changed. R. describes the days in Portuguese, but he writes very inaccurate Portuguese, suggesting that his knowledge of the language amounted to speaking it to some extent, but not reading in it.

themselves more than usual, paint their faces and bodies with white earth, and put on a more beautiful cloth than otherwise worn.[68]

When a prominent Negress in Accra wishes to dress up, this does not comprise just a beautiful cloth, together with small gold pendants and many types of beads, but chiefly the adornment of her head. On certain parts of their heads they let their hair, or wool, grow to finger length, and they form it into a roll at up to four places, and sometimes forming it into one or more square pyramids. Other women let it grow like a cock's comb, and this fashion has innumerable variations. The pyramids are powdered with charcoal so that they attain the gleam of a blackness deeper than that of the Negresses' skin.[69] When a prominent Negress is to be adorned for her birthday, which comes every week, /87/ serious consultations with other women are necessary. She slaughters a hen or chicken, then places its heart on a wooden stick on her forehead, as our women do with Italian flowers.[70] A Negress thus adorned feels herself just as fashionably well dressed as do our women who consult a barber and a hairdresser. Fully and properly dressed, a Negress will have eight or ten pieces of *daler* coins hanging from a silver chain on either side of her hips, so that they can rattle and tinkle when she walks. Likewise, she will have silver spurs on her feet, and many keys at her sides [*sic*], although she may own only one chest with a lock.[71] When a noble Negress is pregnant, and shortly before she comes to delivery, according to custom she must walk through all the streets of the town with a great following, totally naked and wearing no sash, beads, or fetish.[72]

In addition, every occupation has its own sacred day, for instance, the fisherman have Tuesday.[73] And since /88/ the Negroes see the Europeans dress up more on Sundays than otherwise, some then think that all the

---

[68] For the 'name-day' celebration (children being named on the day of birth), see Bosman (1705) 153; Isert [1788] (1992) 62. For the significance of white colour, see note 35 above.

[69] Many early writers on Gold Coast commented on the variety of women's coiffures (De Marees [1602] (1987) 18b; Brun [1624] and Müller [1673] in Jones (1983) 52–3, 205–6; Villault (1669) 224–5; Olfert Dapper, *Naukeurige Beschrijvinge der Afrikaensche Gewesten* (1676) 104; Jean Barbot, *Barbot on Guinea* (1992) 494, drawing opp. 495; Rask (1754) 136; Bosman (1705) 120).

[70] No other references to the use of a chicken heart as a head adornment have been traced. R. may be confusing it with a practice on a particular occasion, or the ritual of a particular shrine. But the significance of the chicken is inherent in the modern Gã greeting between people born on the same day, 'We eat chicken' (p.c. I. Odotei).

[71] For keys and other ornaments, see De Marees [1602] (1987) 19a, 19b; Müller [1673] in Jones (1983) 205; Villault (1669) 225–7; Dapper (1676) 104; Bosman (1705) 121; Barbot [1732] (1992) 495; Rask (1754) 137; Isert [1788] (1992) 117.

[72] For rituals in connection with pregnancy, see Isert [1788] (1992) 117–8; Rask (1754) 247; Field (1937) 166.

[73] In recent times, Tuesday has been the sacred day for *Nai*, the chief of all the sea gods, and fishing was prohibited on that day (Daniell (1852) 23).

children in Europe are born on a Sunday, and say, in their [polite] way, when a European greets them, 'Thank you, Sunday's child!' (*Jo aussi*).[74]

Moreover, each town has its own animals and fish which are not eaten. Thus, the inhabitants of the town called Ursue, under our Fort Christiansborg, do not eat elephant meat. Nevertheless, necessity breaks all laws. I once met a hunter who had shot a young elephant but dared not bring the flesh into the town, where there were difficult times and a famine. The hunter reported it to the caboceer and the great men, as well as to the fetish women. These last said that they must first to ask the fetish for permission. The others, however, were unanimous in their opinion that in times of need they did not have to ask the fetish. But, in order not to make him angry, the flesh would have to be skinned [there], or else the hunter and his people who were carrying it would have to skin it before it was brought into the town. This was done, and our garrison, as well as the Negroes in the town, had a treat with it for two days.[75]

[Circumcision: oaths and tests]

Throughout Accra, all male children are circumcised. In Judaism it is done on /89/ the eighth day after birth, but [in Accra] they can sometimes be more than eight years old before circumcision. No one is considered a man unless he has been circumcised. But those boys who are to become *Remedorer* (fishermen) are not circumcised. When asked who taught them this practice, the Negroes answer that their forefathers followed this custom and will say no more.[76]

They have a special way of swearing an oath. We Danes call it 'eating fetish', [that is, taking an oath] to do or not to do such and such.[77] According

---

[74] R. had forgotten his Gã. 'Aussi', correctly *awushi*, is an appellation for both male and female among the Gã and is an expression of approval. The day-name for a Sunday child is *Kwashi*, male, or *Akushia*, female. And *Jo*, in modern orthography *yoo*, does not mean 'thank you!', but is a positive response, i.e. 'yes, certainly, OK' (p.c. I. Odotei).

[75] The locality of Osu had a mixed ethnic population, probably because it was close to three European forts and such forts tended to attract strangers, and therefore the inhabitants had varying tabus. Perhaps those willing to break the traditional local taboo were of an immigrant ethnicity not bound by the prohibition on elephant meat.

[76] Circumcision was universally commented upon by early sources. Some claimed that it was performed on both sexes (De Marees [1602] (1987) 11b-12a, 23 note 3; Müller [1673] in Jones (1983) 218), while others describe only male circumcision (Rask (1754) 134; Isert [1788] (1992) 131). Modern sources only report male circumcision (Daniell (1852) 10–11; Field (1937) 176; Kilson (1974) 49). However, the '*Remedorer*' (Portuguese *remador* 'oarsman, boatman'), who were fishermen as well as boatmen, were Fante, that is Akan, an ethnicity that did not practice circumcision.

[77] 'Eating fetish' was a practice and a term known to all the Europeans on the Coast. It meant to swear an oath, as proof of innocence or guilt, or to confirm a contract. Since the practice was universal and Europeans often participated, it was commented on in all the early sources (De Marees [1602] (1987) 10a-b, 35a, 55a-b; Müller [1673] in Jones (1983) 174–6; Villault (1669) 279–81; Bosman (1705) 149–51; Barbot [1732] (1992) 572; Rask (1754) 180–3; Isert [1788] (1992) 129–30; and cf. Monrad (1822) 35–9; Reindorf (1895/1966) 124/117).

to the laws of the land, we can force a Negro who has swindled us or stolen from us to eat fetish [to prove that] he had not done it. We pay two *rixdaler* to [hire] the fetish of our broker Adoui.[78] Together with the fetish there usually come into the Fort a whole swarm of old Negroes, so that it costs us an additional two *rixdaler* to serve them brandy. This fetish is carried on a mat covered with an old cloth. The fetish consists of a stuffed snake skin, without head or tail, but in their stead, the hair from an elephant's tail, or a cow's or wolf's tail,[79] mingled with feathers from a cock, so that it looks horrible. By custom. it is made like a necklace, with threads at both ends, so that /**90**/ the individual who wishes to wear it can tie it at the back of his neck. This is placed at the feet of the Europeans who are accusing the Black, and after the case has been explained to all present, the old cloth is taken from the sausage-like fetish and a crumb of dough as large as a pea placed on it. The accused then comes forward, goes down on his knees, holding his hands behind his back, and utters this oath: 'If I have done that', or. 'If I have stolen this or that, then let the fetish kill me'. With his mouth he takes the dough from the snake skin, holds it on his tongue, and by opening his mouth, proves that he really has it there. Then he swallows it. He has thereby been freed of the accusation.

Instead of an oath, the Negroes have many types of method [of testing guilt] which they use, such as this. After putting a pot of oil on a fire until it boils, they throw into it a cowrie,[80] and the accused person must pick it out with his hand. If he is innocent, it does not injure him. The same [trial by ordeal] is done by piercing his tongue with an awl or a large sewing needle, or drawing a glowing knife over his arm, and there are many other such acts. /**91**/ We noticed that, in some cases, Negroes have taken such an oath [successfully], although we knew that they really had committed the piece of roguery of which they were accused. I revealed my thoughts to Putti, who admitted that, with some small gift, they could buy themselves free from such minor fetishes as Adoui's. But if we were to spend four *rixdaler* on the Labode fetish, then he would guarantee that he (the fetish) would really punish. on the spot, those who 'ate' and were guilty.[81]

---

[78] Adoui was the broker for the Danes at Christiansborg.

[79] The 'wolf's tail' was probably the tail of a hyena. Wolves are not found in Africa, but early sources often employed the term for hyenas (cf. Rask (1754) 158).

[80] For 'cowrie', R. employs the Danish term *snoge-pande* 'snake skull', a term used by Scandinavians and Germans to indicate cowry shells, presumably because they thought that cowries resembled, or actually were, the skulls of small snakes (Erik Tilleman, *A Short and Simple Account* [1697] (1994) 33; Rask (1754) 84–5; Isert [1788] (1992) 61).

[81] R. views this as bribery of the fetish. The Gã view is that a case or a judgement can be 'turned' by a more powerful god, who is invoked by a more valuable offering than that of the other party. The term for this form of counter-invocation is *dai*, literally 'to withdraw or revoke a curse' (p.c. M.E. Kropp Dakubu).

[The Labade fetish again: a fetish anecdote]

Putti told me something which he swears is true, and that no Negro who is not a priest knows, namely, that the Labode fetish, on which they swear an oath, is made of gold, and formed like a human head, but a little larger. In a period inconceivably long ago the head was found in this form in the earth. *Giemawong* had shown them the place where it lay. Putti said, further, that when there was [such] danger that the Blacks had to flee from their town, the fetish possessed two of his priests and two of his priestesses, the guardians at night of this lump of gold as well as the sacred drums, so that they themselves did not know [any longer] where it was [hidden and] located. When the danger was over and the Negroes had returned to their town, the fetish possessed four individuals /**92**/ other than those who had carried it away, to restore this sacred object to its place.[82]

On one occasion the Labode Negroes had been forced to leave their land and town for [a period of] four years, and those who had guarded these *curiosa* died before the Negroes returned. Yet it was no more than a month before the fetish possessed two other priests, who recovered the object. Since the fetish was of gold, no one in Labode town dared to wear or own gold, brass, and copper, and suchlike.[83]

A short time after this conversation I had the opportunity of visiting the Labode fetish. I imagined that the fetish could be seen just as the object was, but I was mistaken. They had now smeared 'him' all over with red earth, so that none of the gold was visible, yet it did have approximately the shape of a head. Moreover, they had placed the fetish in a large wooden basin containing water, and half of the lump was under water. For the person who was to eat fetish they had prepared, not dough, but a lump of red earth. Later a Negro from Ursue told me that I must cite no Labode Negro before this fetish, since any locals could buy themselves free. Thus /**93**/ there is nothing [sacred] among these evil people by which one can be assured of their fidelity.[84]

I must include an example of this. An Aqvamboe Negro who wished to buy some of my goods was brought by my black servants to see me. I opened up, and the Aqvamboe searched for more than half an hour among my goods without saying what kind he wished to have, or what he had for

---

[82] For instances of local conquerors digging for hidden treasure, see Isert [1788] (1992) 61.

[83] Among the Gã, on *La Kpa* day the wearing of gold in the presence of the god is still forbidden. R.'s statement that no one dared to wear or own metal objects is misleading. He should have limited the taboo to the wearing of metal objects or ornaments on this occasion. Certainly brass and copper utensils continued to be owned and used regularly.

[84] 'Free' presumably means free from the guilt of the crime of which they were accused. Slaves escaping from local masters could flee to important shrines where they threw themselves on the mercy of the god, but they did not become free, being considered thereafter a slave of that shrine (Isert [1788] (1992) 162). A number of locations labelled 'powerful Fetish, which protects runaway slaves', including one in Labadi, are shown on Peter Thonning's 1838 map (CRA, *Kortsamling* no. 337 XVIII).

payment. Finally I told him (and my servant interpreted for me) that I had beautiful goods, but it was a pity that he had nothing with which to pay. I gave my servant a reprimand for having brought me a fool. My servant took the Aqvamboe and set him outside the door. The Aqvamboe asked if he could come in again, saying that he had [with him] a young wife who was from Crepe (a region),[85] but her father had made him eat such a strong fetish against his selling her that he feared for his life if he acted against this. My servant knew immediately what he was after, and answered him: 'Is that all? I will bring a couple of comrades along and we will beat you up to such an extent that the fetish will be /94/ satisfied'. At that, the Aqvamboe was pleased, and asked only that, if he protected himself as well as he could, they would not be angry, and this was promised him. An hour later the rogue came back with his wife, who helped to choose the goods, not knowing that they were to be traded for herself. Our Aqvamboe left the goods lying and went outside, where some men, standing there, seized his wife and threw her, as usual, into shackles (irons). I cannot describe what an uproar he made in attempting to fight those who had taken his wife. But the four [attackers] were also prepared for a fight. He fought them for a good half-hour. My four threw him to the ground and beat him mercilessly, but only with their fists. Finally he warned them that it was enough, and my servants released him. He went off, dried off the blood and dirt, put on another cloth, and came back to fetch his goods. I heard my servants arguing with him, and I wished to know what the reason was. Their conversation could be translated approximately thus. My servants said, 'You show-off! You made too much of this game. Don't you know that a Crepe fetish is easy to pacify? If you had received a couple of /95/ slaps in the face (*kotte cou*), that would have been enough.[86] Give us a bottle of brandy for our trouble!' The Aqvamboe's head and body were quite swollen and he could scarcely see, but my servants pestered him, and he had to give them a bottle of brandy from his anker, and then it was over. Undoubtedly he has not thought of his wife since, or of her father's fetish.

[Prophecies]

If I am to give an opinion about the [operation of the] fetish. I must admit that I believe Satan is powerful among these unbelievers. I myself have never seen nor heard *Giemawong*, nor any of their other fetishes. I have been

---

[85] 'Crepe' was a term used by early writers to identify the Ewe living on the eastern bank of the delta of River Volta, but the Crepe are actually only one constituent group of the Ewe and their region is limited to an area much farther to the north, east of Akwamu. For 'Volta Krepe' and 'the true Krepe' in a later century, see Thonnings map (1838).

[86] This incident may indicate that there was an inherent danger in inter-ethnic marriages (which were probably uncommon), as the father had suspected. The term *kotte cou*, in modern orthography *akotokú*, denotes 'blows, punches' (p.c. M. E. Kropp Dakubu).

disgusted that some men of our nation have received trinkets from the fetish priest and have worn them on their bodies, underneath their clothing, as has been occasionally noticed by their room-mates. We have had such fools among our people, individuals who have gone there as young men, and their Negresses (their mistresses) have asked them to put on such things, supposed to be good for this and that.[87] Yet I myself have experienced events which I still cannot explain, other than that it must be true that Satan can take possession of the mouths and tongues of the Blacks. I cannot recall in which year this event [I now describe] occurred, because /**96**/ it is now ten years since I left the Coast. But I am certain that, upon inquiry, some of our nation still living [there] can confirm what follows, and more of the same, to be true.

We had an important case to decide between two of our most prominent Negroes at Christiansborg. They had been in the Fort with their case, but it was so unclear, and the evidence so poor that we had to order the parties to confer amicably with their witnesses on both sides, each in his own town. When this had been done, they were to report to us, and we would hand down a decision. As is the custom among them, when a caboceer who is knowledgeable in the customs of the land has come to town from another place, he is taken along to the court, which is held in the marketplace. It so happened that our 'Millie Caboceer', Aborre from Accron, was with us, and was one of the judges. He had with him at that time (as he had had at other times previously) one of his wives, who at times was possessed by the fetish. Our soldiers, when they are not on guard duty, like to go to such places and listen, because there is drink available, and I have [equally] heard about this event from many Blacks shortly after it happened. A tumult occurred, and I feared that our Negroes had come to blows. The /**97**/ prophetic old crone, Aborre's wife, began [to act] as if she were mad. She ran around with her hands on her head[88], and shouted, 'Aborre! There lies one of your people, who has been shot to death!' (She jumped around and made sounds imitating the firing of a musket.) 'And there lies another!', and shortly after that, 'There lies the third!' This happened at four o'clock in the afternoon, and was immediately reported, not just to me alone, but to all the Danes. Our Negroes presented their case, but Aborre came into the Fort and mournfully told me that an accident had occurred

---

[87] Given the frequency of illness and the high rate of mortality among the Europeans, as well as the non-efficacy of European medicines at that time, it would have been entirely natural for many Europeans to seek help from Africans in their practices of healing, practices inseparable from the local religion. For the diversity of clients and practitioners of healing among the modern Gã, see Kilson (1974) 89–95. For twentieth-century European and African viewpoints regarding African traditional medicine, see Field (1937) 133–4.

[88] This is a classic gesture signifying mourning, still seen today. It is also seen in the West Indies and is mentioned in a child's rhyme: 'Hands on your head, your mother's dead!' (p.c. Marcia Burrowes).

in his town and that he had sent one of his people to see if it was all over. I comforted him by [saying that] it was probably not true, but he, on the contrary, assured me that his prophetic wife had never lied. I gave him a bottle of brandy to allay his fear, and he left. I requested him to let me know as soon as his messenger came back. The town was only 4½ miles away, and early in the morning he learned that it was all too true. Yet it had not happened in his town but in another town a mile beyond his, where a score of his people had gone to fetch a bride and in [a state of] inebriation had become involved /98/ in a fight with the others. Three of Aborre's men had been shot to death, at the very hour the crone had been carrying on in our marketplace.[89]

Another example. An Akim king named Pobi and the Aqvamboe king, Oppoccu Chuma, were facing one another, on campaign, about 20 miles up-country. This resulted in our receiving neither Negroes nor provisions, the whole way from Accra to River Volta. All of us Europeans wished that they would have their battle so that our routes might be opened again, since both armies had been drawn up in that place for three months without attacking each other.[90] One forenoon Putti sent a message to me to the effect that a battle had been joined that morning, and that the Aqvamboes had lost. I requested Putti to come up to me so that he might explain to me in what way, and with what words, his fetish had presented this news. He told me that the fetish had barked in his hut, like a dog, and that one of the priests who lived not far from there had informed Putti. He (Putti) went to the hut immediately, and told the priest to creep into it, as usual, and the possessed priest had uttered these words. 'Two Aqvamboe elephants were swimming /99/ in the river. They thought that they would manage to get across, but their heads have fallen off.' Two days later we found out that the battle had been fought the same morning that the Labode fetish had said this, and that Oppoccu Chuma and Adjang, the most prominent men in Aqvamboe, had tried to swim across a river after their armies had taken flight, but both were shot to death while in the water. The Akims had drawn them up on land and cut their heads off. I could add more of such happenings, but these are not as well known to our whole staff as this one is.[91]

It is reasonable that I also include some of the prophecies of the Labode fetish which have not come as precisely true as the foregoing. I have also

---

[89] This woman clearly played an important role in relation to the caboceer since she accompanied him on this occasion. It is always women who become possessed, and in that state they wield more power than the male secular authority because their utterances are directly from the god. Their status can change dramatically from a low one to the highest possible, if and when they are successful in their prophecies.

[90] For King Pobi of Akyem and King Oppoccu Chuma of Akwamu, see Chapter 4, /188/, /215/, below.

[91] The reference is to the wars and skirmishes between Akyem and Akwamu in the 1740s (Chapter 4, /227/, below).

heard some of the answers to Putti which were so obscure that he himself could not really interpret or explain them, but he had, as did all the others, to await the outcome of the case. And this, even though Putti (according to his own testimony, and using an approximate reckoning) is more than 80 years old, and has spent his entire lifetime in this study (if I may call it that).

In 1739 our Negroes at Accra—the Ursue, Labode, and Tessing Negroes—were at war with the /**100**/ Dutch Negroes. The Dutch caboceer, Dacon, was the commander of the enemy army, and Okanie was the general of our army.[92] After several skirmishes of no great importance during the first half-year, they began [to fight] in earnest. The fetish at Labode told Dacon that he was in the wrong and that he should make an end to the war by a settlement, and should give his counterpart satisfaction. But Dacon refused. Because of this, *Giemawong* had his messenger tell our Negroes gathered [there] that Dacon would die within three months, or, in these words, 'Dacon shall not eat of the new corn (*millie*) which is now standing in the fields'. You can well imagine what joy this occasioned among our Negroes—and what fear among the enemies, when, moreover, the fetishes in the enemy's own town and in Ursue confirmed the judgement of the Labode fetish. Dacon was then looked upon as a man who was, so to speak, already dead, and no one wanted to have anything to do with him. Our Negroes, with only a few people, frequently drove a great number of the enemy to flight. Because of this and other circumstances, the Dutch had to make peace on our terms. But, /**101**/ despite everyone's expectations, Dacon lived for three years after that, and did not even die a natural death, as the prophecy seems to have been predicting. On the contrary, he helped the Akims against the Assiantes, and after the defeat of the Akims he sought refuge with another nation, who cut off his head and the heads of all his people. These Negroes came down later and wished to sell his head to our Negroes, but we Europeans would not allow it. However, we have since found out that Okanie bought two of Dacon's upper front teeth for eight *rixdaler*, had holes bored in them, and wears them around his neck on his sacred day, along with other objects of the same sort.[93]

I often confronted Putti with this [failing in the fetish]. His answer nearly always was as follows. 'Master! How can I know what the good God has found in Dacon since he determined the evil [that was to descend] on him? Perhaps Dacon asked him that it should not happen, and God for a long time spared him. But during the three years after the judgement had been proclaimed, you well know that he continued with new provocations

---

[92] Dacon, correctly Dako, was a caboceer of Dutch Accra. For Dako's lineage, and for conflicts between him and his brother-in-law Okanie, alias Okaidze, in which the Danes and the Dutch were involved on opposite sides, see Wilks (1959) 392, 394, 398–400; Albert van Dantzig, *Les Hollandais sur la Côte de Guinée* (1980a) 249; Nørregård (1966) 98–9.

[93] For the death of Dacon, see Chapter 4, /185/, below.

against us. God therefore planted in his heart the poor advice to go up with 50 men and help the Akims. How could that help the Akims who had 200,000 men in the field? And see, did he not /**102**/ [in the end] get a worse death than was prophesied?'

[Death beliefs]

They do not like to hear any mention of death, which, according to their beliefs, is the greatest evil they experience.[94] Out there, I once offended our broker, Adoui. He had not been well for several days and came to me at the Fort, complaining about it, and asking for a glass of brandy. While my servant was away fetching it, I asked him who would be the successor in his service [to us] when he died. He became quite upset at this, stood up and answered, 'God has sent me into the world with many years on my head. Do you think that I am like the Whites, who come and go?[95] But since you wish to know, don't you know my brother Atte?' He did not wait for his brandy, but went his way.

The Negroes display a kind of honour to the sun when it rises over the horizon in the morning. And they perform very laughable gestures for the new moon. They talk to it, and shake their limbs as if they wanted to throw /**103**/ off their arms and legs. They finally take a firebrand and hurl it, as if they wanted to throw it up to the moon, and with that the ceremony is over.[96]

They have many differing opinions on their condition after death. Putti says that God considers the pious worthy to be received to Himself, and especially those who die on their bed (mat) and are given an honourable funeral.[97] But he has a comment on death which [to me] is unintelligible. It is this, that the body, when separated from this world, is the greatest obstacle for the soul in the other life, since (he says) it is also separated. Putti becomes completely unintelligible when, to explain this, he tells of his revelations and dreams.[98] I have heard an old Negro sigh and wish that after his death he might become a rich European, and when asked the reason for this, he answered, 'I would

---

[94] Bosman cites a proverb, 'Death is never without a cause' (Bosman (1705) 221, 226). As generally elsewhere in West Africa, an untimely or premature death is considered to have been caused by witchcraft. Today among the Gã, various tabus surround death. During Hɔmɔwɔ, no one is supposed to die, and priests must not see or touch a dead body (Field (1937) 44).

[95] Many elderly Europeans would be upset by R.'s tactless question. Adoui responds by referring to the high rate of mortality of the Whites on Gold Coast, who did indeed 'come and go'.

[96] For celebrations in relation to the moon, see Müller [1673] in Jones (1983) 160; Monrad (1822) 2–3.

[97] In recent times, a peaceful death is identified with one spirit, *sissa* ('ghost'), but a violent death, in battle or in an accident, with another spirit, *otɔfɔ* (Field (1937) 94, 202–3). The *otɔfɔ* is a restless, savage spirit which threatens the living. (See also Christaller (1933) 525.)

[98] Undoubtedly R. and Okpoti were operating at different levels of understanding. For Gã concepts of body and soul, see Field (1937) 201–2; Kilson (1974) 50.

rather be a poor Black than a poor White, since a poor White must have the same superfluous things—shoes, stockings, and clothing—as the rich, and, therefore must at times starve'. It must be noted that this Negro, like others, believed in /**104**/ reincarnation, and was convinced that his soul [would] travel to Europe and he would be born [again] as a European. There are those who believe that their souls travel in animals, birds, or fish.[99]

Yet another belief is illustrated by the following example. One of our black mason apprentices, the company slave, Qvacu, kept working at 12 o'clock midday, although they were free from 11 o'clock to 2 o'clock. A European walking by said to him, 'Qvacu! Why are you working? It is 12 o'clock.' He answered (quite annoyed), 'Our Master is so mean to me today that he says I have not worked enough and therefore, before I may stop, I must finish this piece. But I know what I shall do.' *Question.* 'What will you do, then? *Reply.* 'When I die, I shall ask God not to send me back into the world as the slave of the Whites, and if that prayer does not help, I shall discuss it with him. *Question.* 'What do you want to be, then, when you come into the world again?' *Reply.* 'The slave of Frempung.' (Frempung was a great Akim king.) *Question.* 'Why do you not ask to be Frempung himself?' *Reply.* 'No, that is not /**105**/ possible, for I know that as often as I have been in the world I have been a slave, and as often as I come back, I must be a slave.'[100] When I pointed out to Putti that this statement, and other things, showed that his countrymen were of differing opinions, he answered, 'Sir (*Seignore*)! I have never been dead and come back to life, to enable me to debate with such certainty about the other life, as your holy man did in the time he was here'.[101] This holy man, whose name in the Negro [language] I cannot recall, is the priest, Mr. Elias Swane, here in Zeeland. He was the priest at Christiansborg for four or five years, being repatriated in 1726. I have never met him, but I cannot adequately describe the degree of veneration the Blacks have for him, even to this day.[102] And many years after his departure from there, our sailors have conveyed his

---

[99] Other early writers addressed the concept of life after death but did not refer to reincarnation. The modern Gã believe in reincarnation but not in animal form (Field (1937) 197). R. may have picked up the alleged desire to be born again as a White from earlier sources (e.g., Bosman (1705) 156; Rask (1754) 191).

[100] This anecdote is surprising and perhaps suspect, since reincarnation, as a concept in West Africa, is not generally considered to involve returning in the same status. Moreover, slaves in West African societies, though sometimes subject to being killed as sacrifices (see above), could in certain contexts improve their status, become a member of a family, acquire property, and rise to an official post. For slavery in Gold Coast societies, see Rattray (1955) 43–4. Frempung Manso was the ruler of Akyem Kotoku (Kwamena-Poh (1973) 36; Wilks (1975) 86, 706–9; McCaskie (1995) 98–101).

[101] Possibly Okpoti was being ironic, although alternatively he may have accepted the European claims to special knowledge of life after death.

[102] For Elias Svane, see Chapter 2, note 130, above.

greetings to this or that Negro, in order to get a couple of chickens, which they usually are given by each individual to whom they deliver his greeting.[103]

I thought it necessary thus to describe the Negroes' religion, as well as it /**106**/ could be done, and is known to me. For it is certain that from mankind's morals flow its activities and habits. So may the reader now be prepared to look at the history [of the inhabitants of Gold Coast] from 100 years ago to the present day, and at their extreme inhumanity in wars and undertakings, which otherwise would appear unbelievable, and thereby learn about their temperament, nature, customs, and more! /**107**/

---

[103] This indicates that there could exist a positive relationship between Europeans and Africans, since Svane's name could still generate respect. It also reveals the pragmatism of the sailors who capitalized on that respect.

Chapter 4

About the Negroes' history, customs, and way of life

Before I begin to narrate the history of the Negroes I must report certain things about the countries and nations known at Accra, so that what follows can be understood. [But] I must say beforehand that the information will be incomplete, since a reliable report cannot be given without [European] geographers being sent up into the country, who would be able to describe for us better than the Blacks can where these countries and kingdoms lie in relation to each other. The most well travelled Black can [only] show us with his hand where this or that kingdom lies. He knows approximately where the sun comes up and where it goes down, and that is all he knows about [the points of] the compass. We know that when our Accras travel inland to Akim or Assiante, they have to go most of the way along the banks of small fresh-water rivers, otherwise they could not possibly make their way through the bush. It is clear that they could save a journey of many miles /**108**/ if there were regular roads in Africa.[1] When you ask the Negroes at Accra who lives on the last high mountain which at times you can see from the coast, they answer 'No one!'; and [they claim] that no human being has ever climbed, or can climb, those mountains. Furthermore, the Negroes state that when they are going up to Akim it takes them fourteen days, after [passing] those high mountains where no one lives before they come to [the borders of] Akim, and they still have to walk for eight to ten days, going through both dry or otherwise [*sic*] regions, before they come to Akim inhabitants and towns.[2]

No doubt many such countries or places in Africa have until now been inaccessible to the other black inhabitants [of the continent]. Thus we can

---

[1] The establishment of permanent roads in West Africa at that time was difficult. Routes adapted to altered political situations (Ivor Wilks, *Asante in the Nineteenth Century* (1975) 24–5; *Forests of Gold* (1993) 191 ff). Further, permanent roads required the organization of constant clearing of brush, while maintenance of smaller roads or paths was affected by the changing conditions of the numerous streams, especially in the rainy season. For an attempt to depict the routes of the early eighteenth century, see K.B. Dickson, *A Historical Geography of Ghana* (1969) 109–12.

[2] The 'last high mountain' was probably *Nyanaoase* 'under Nyanao' (p.c. Ivor Wilks), an inselberg rising to a height of 1,618ft/493m. This was supposedly the home of the Akwamu before their defeat and was subsequently uninhabited.

understand, when we hear it later, that an entire nation of Africans, consisting of about a million people, has hidden itself away for an entire year, and neither its enemies nor any one else knew where they were. I am of the opinion that a nation could be hidden for an entire century or more, if its people knew of a way to cook their food without lighting a fire, since the smoke would betray them. They would not lack food because they could get sufficient roots, fruits, and other things. The Negroes say that adults could easily /**109**/ do without cooking, but that the children could not tolerate raw food, and the nights are not always dark enough to permit the cooking of food [without the smoke being seen]. All these mountains and regions are nameless, although they stretch as far as River Volta. The Negroes have had to follow these routes—either through a dry region or along the bank of a river—when they went to Akim from one kingdom to another, for instance, from Bang's country to Ursue's, etc.[3]

[Territories and peoples of Gold Coast]

The whole of Gold Coast runs WSW-ENE, or for the most part west to east, with many small promontories, [the forts at] Elmina, Cape Coast, and Christiansborg being built on small spurs of land. Accra lies at 51°N 211°[E].[4] Taking Accra as a starting point, I shall describe, as fully as possible, the location of the kingdoms and countries mentioned here.

On the coast west of Accra are these countries: Agona, Akron, and Fante. The inhabitants of these three countries are often identified by the name 'Fante'. Note that Agona must not be confused with a Negro town [also] called Agona, east of River Volta. We estimate that Fanteland extends fifty miles inland.[5] /**110**/ On the coast, lying east of Accra are the Adampi country and River Volta.[6] Inland from Accra, NE-by-North of Adampi,

---

[3] The 'mountains' seen from Accra are the Akwapim-Togo hills (E.A. Boateng, *A Geography of Ghana* (1970) 18–19). The territories R. calls 'Bang's country' and 'Ursue's country' were apparently parts of what was later known as Akyem Abuakwa. For recent 'traditions' relating to Owusu [Ursue], see J.B. Danquah, *Akan Laws and Customs* (1928) 242; J.K. Fynn, *Asante and its Neighbours* (1971) 71; and see also note 140, below.

[4] The stated location of Accra at 21°E is probably based on the meridian of Ferro Island in the Canaries, as was common at the time, but nevertheless is inaccurate; in modern measurements Accra lies at 0°15'W and 5°33'N.

[5] For descriptions of these territories c.1700, see W. Bosman, *A New and Accurate Description of the Coast of Guinea* (1705) 60–2 Akron [Accron], 62–4 Agona [Agonna], 55–59 Fante. The 'Agona' located east of River Volta is the place termed 'Augna/Awuna' by the Danes, that is, Anloga, where the inhabitants were the Anlo Ewe (cf. Paul Erdmann Isert, *Journey to Guinea and the Caribbean Islands* [1788] (1992) 31–58).

[6] Adampi is Adangbe/Adangme, an ethnicity whose language is closely related to Gã. According to recent writers, the Adangbe coastal polities were Kpone, Prampram, Ningo, and Ada, and the inland polities Manya Krobo, Yilo Krobo, Shai and Osudoku (M.J. Field, *Religion and Medicine of the Gã People* (1937) 677; E.N. Quarcoopome, 'Self-decoration and religious power in Dangme culture', *African Arts* 24 (1991) 56). For traditions about the founding of the early settlements, see Dickson (1969) 25–7.

three to four miles from the coast and scattered through the lower mountains, live the Mountain-Negroes. These are the survivors of the many millions of people who lived in the nearer mountains and higher up in the land about one hundred years ago.[7] Inland from Accra, five miles to the NE, lies Aqvamboe. This land is now deserted.[8] Akim begins NE of Aqvamboe, 160 to 200 miles inland. We call the people of this nation Akenists [Akims].[9] Akim is divided into three kingdoms.[10] Inland from Akim, possibly [sic] to the north, is Assiante. The people of this nation are called Assiantes and in 1749 their king was named Oppoccu. He died in 1751 and Qvassi is his successor.[11]

East of Fante is Akron, which for about twenty miles from the coast is inhabited, or I should say, more correctly, that you find Negro towns here and there. The rest of the thirty miles [of Fanteland inland] to the NE is uninhabited, and I think that there must be high mountains for a great distance, which are /111/ unclimbable and cannot be crossed. I conclude this from the following fact. In former times the Assiantes had [instead] to pass through the uninhabited land behind Fante and Akron when they wished to go to Elmina and other western forts to trade. It was on these paths, or in this uninhabited land, that the Fantes captured many Assiantes and sold them at the coast, and since 1745 they have absolutely refused to allow the Assiantes to use this route. The Akims have occupied that [? uninhabited] country since 1744.[12]

---

[7] The identity of the 'Mountain Negroes' is unclear but they may have been members of interior Adangme polities (see previous note). Alternatively, they may have been distinguished by language from the. the Gã/Adangme, by speaking Akan or Guan dialects (p.c. I. Wilks). Supposed early settlements of Guan and Akan groups are discussed in Dickson (1969) 15–25. R. does not explain how he knows about population 'about one hundred years ago' and his reference to 'millions' is mere rhetoric.

[8] For R's account of the defeat of the Akwamu and their relocation to the east bank of the Volta, see /154/–/158/ below.

[9] For R.'s use of 'Akenists', here translated 'Akims', see Chapter 2, note 13 above.

[10] It has been contended that there were not three 'Akim' kingdoms but only two, Akyem Abuakwa and Akyem Kotoko (Fynn (1971), 20; R. R. Atkinson, 'Old Akyem and the origins of Akyems Abuakwa and Kotoku', in B.K. Swartz Jr. and Raymond Dumett, eds., *West African Culture Dynamics* (1980) 361–3; Robert Addo-Fenning, 'The Akim or Achim in 17th century and 18th century historical contexts: who were they?' *IAS Research Review* 4 (1988) 1–11).

[11] The *Asantehene* ('ruler of Asante/Ashanti') Opoku Ware held office from c.1720 until his death in 1750, and was succeeded by Kusi ('Quassi') Obodom, who held office until 1764 (M. Priestley and Ivor Wilks, 'The Ashanti kings in the eighteenth century', *Journal of African History* 1 (1960), 92–3; Wilks (1975), 128–9; T.C. McCaskie, *State and Society in Pre-Colonial Asante* (1995) 175).

[12] For probable eighteenth-century trade routes from Kumasi to Elmina, see Dickson (1969) 109–11; Wilks (1975) 24–5. For Fante control of a section of the coastal trade, see James Sanders, 'The expansion of the Fante and the emergence of Asante in the eighteenth century', *Journal of African History*, 20 (1979) 356–7.

When you tell rational Negroes at Accra that you fear the Assiantes will discover another route to the western forts on the coast, and that they might, perhaps, find a route higher up in the land [*sc.* further to the east], so that they do not come closer to the Fantes' border than fifty miles, they answer, 'No! There are no routes higher up'. Assuming that River Volta runs from the up-country east-by-north, and that Akim, the land of the Mountain Negroes, and Assiante [all] border on River Volta, then this is understandable.[13]

[The history of wars: the Benin era]

The Blacks have no written languages which would have made it possible for scribes to record their history, therefore, as accurately as possible, we shall describe their wars — or the destruction of entire nations, since war and the total destruction of the losing party /112/ are almost the same thing on the Guinea Coast. And because there is always [another nation] more powerful than the victor, over a period of fifty years nations from the coast and up to 200 miles inland (the Fantes excepted) have been seen to wipe each other out, or as good as doing this. We cannot report on more nations than those known at Accra, and even that [information] is incomplete, since an old Black never tells the history as it really was, but you are told something at one time and something different at another.

Out of this disordered tale I shall describe, as far as I can remember it, the history of several nations. I will begin with the Negroes' golden era, which was under the Benin government, before any of the Europeans had arrived. Only a few of the old Negroes know about this era in their history; or, if they do know about it, it seems more like a fable to them, although the era cannot be more than 200 years ago.[14]

It is strange that during that period, when there were a thousand times more people in the land than there are now, they had no [specific rights of] ownership in respect of fields and land, but planted and harvested anywhere they wanted to, just as now.[15] /113/ [Today,] should a European wish to take possession of a piece of land of a square mile or more, I have been assured that no one would argue with him, even though a Negro had cultivated part of it

---

[13] The Danish sentence reads: *Naar man nu vill antage, at Rio Volta kommer Østen til Norden fra Landet, og at Bierg-Negernes Lande Akim, og Assiante grændser til Rio Volta: saa bliver følgende forstaaeligt.* The last phrase is difficult to understand. As translated above, R. may be trying to say that Asante did not extend far enough west to be able to find a route to the coast from that direction. For routes from Asante to the western forts, see Wilks (1993) 191.

[14] For the myth about Benin extending to Gold Coast, see Chapter 1, /16/–/20/, above. As R. should have known, the Europeans arrived on Gold Coast in the 1470s, nearly 300 years before he wrote rather than 'not more than 200 years ago'. R. goes on to describe the alleged Benin period in terms of the contemporary European myth of the 'Noble Savage'.

[15] R. is confused regarding land rights. Although land was normally not individually owned, collective ownership was general, hence individuals could not farm anywhere they pleased but only within land owned by a collective (e.g. the village or quarter). R's confusion may have been due to the rotation of cultivation, so that the same patch of land was not always in use.

for two years and intended to do the same for the third year. Indeed, I believe that even if the Negro had already begun to clear the land, I could still buy him off for a pot of brandy. He would relinquish the place on behalf of himself and his descendants; and would even be glad to have received a bottle of brandy into the bargain. He would begin to plant in another place. He would tell this to his friends and they would come and offer me more land for the same price. In that way I could acquire an entire principality, if that was of any use.[16]

A Negro's wealth consists only of his children and his slaves. If none of his ancestors is buried there, he would sell his hut for a few *rixdaler*, and with the help of one or more friends would fix up another hut for himself in another place. Some muskets and cartridge pouches, a couple of chests, some drinking basins, some calabashes, a couple of clay pots, and a mirror make up his entire household equipment and furniture; /114/ with, perhaps, a cat or a dog also [owned]. Anything else is unnecessary.[17] His children and slaves are really his wealth, his power, and his protection. Indeed, the more of them he has, the more he is held in esteem in their *Senatu Gentium* [Tribunal of the People], since in a land where *Jus Manus* [Might is Right] is still fully in operation, power must be driven out by power, or, as we say, one knife must keep the other one in its sheath. If there are fishermen among his slaves or children, then all that they catch is his. Some [of these] go to the fields at certain times of the year, to plant *millie* (Turkish corn), patatos [sweet potatoes], beans, and other crops. He uses others of them in trade. When necessary, he uses all of them in war, either for offence or defence.[18]

I cannot write much about the Benin period, since the Blacks had not waged war at that time. They still recognize the law that was in force then, which comprised *in Puncto Sexto* [the Sixth Commandment (forbidding adultery)].[19] This made a distinction in respect of whether the

---

[16] What the Europeans were being offered was the use of the land for a fixed period, on a rent. Europeans had to negotiate with chiefs, the custodians of the land, to be allowed to build, and then pay tribute for the usufruct (Pieter de Marees, *Description and Historical Account of the Gold Kingdom of Guinea* [1602] (1987) 56a–57a; Danquah (1928) 215; R.S. Rattray, *Ashanti Law and Constitution* (1929) 340 ff.; M.J. Field, *Social Organization of the Gã People* (1940) 202–3).

[17] On houses and fittings, see De Marees [1602] (1987) 38a–39a; W.J. Müller [1673] in A. Jones, *German Sources for West African History* (1983) 201–3; N. Villault, *Relation des Costes d'Afrique appellées Guinée* (1669) 241–4; J. Rask, *Rejse-Beskrivelse til og fra Guinea* (1754) 215; Isert [1788] (1992) 36.

[18] It is not clear whether the last sentences were intended to refer to children as well as to slaves, or perhaps to both. For early views on the division of labour in Gold Coast, see De Marees [1602] (1987) 89b and note 2; Bosman (1705) 199, 204; Isert [1788] (1992) 136. For recent views on the historical status of slaves in Gold Coast societies, see A.N. Klein, 'The two Asantes: competing interpretations of "slavery" in Akan-Asante culture and society' *IAS Research Review* (1980) 44–8; R.A. Kea, *Settlements, Trade and Polities in the Seventeenth.Century Gold Coast* (1982) 5–6, 197–99, 200, 290.

[19] Normally this is the Seventh Commandment, but R. is using the numerical order of the Lutheran 'Little Catechism' (p.c. E. Ytteborg).

[adulterous] wife was freeborn or of a slave family. If the former, for two or three successive mornings the transgressor had to carry a large piece of firewood on his head to the offended party [sc. the husband], place it before his door and ask for forgiveness on his knees. If the wife was of slave family once was enough.[20] For unmarried people there was no punishment in such cases.[21] There was /**115**/ no law about robbery since this never happened. No one had any need to steal foodstuffs from any one else because anyone in need was given as much as he wanted at his request. The Negroes still maintain this system.[22] They had neither treasures nor any other precious things, except for their aggreys and contreterées [sc. beads], which no one dared to wear, unless they were those so permitted by the emperor, as a mark of distinction.[23] They needed no clothing; since they went around quite naked — and they still wear only a cloth around the waist. Iron was much rarer than gold for them, and when they could not get iron they had to smith gold in order to have hoes and knives for cutting the bush and furrowing the earth for the seeds which they wished to plant.[24]

The old Blacks tell us about millions of people once living on the Accra coast alone, a stretch of [only] four miles. If you doubt this and ask where they got their food, they answer that they got it from both the sea and the land, there being greater blessings during that time than there are now. Noyte, the caboceer in Tessing [Teshie] (who is said to have known the Portuguese at Accra and thus must have been about 130 years old),[25] assured me that in earlier times the coast at Accra was /**116**/ covered with coconut and palm trees. He had seen entire forests of them in his younger days. But God had become angry with the inhabitants, so that now not a drop of water falls from the heavens, sometimes for as long as nine months, and this causes such drought that the trees wither away. It was not only the coast that was densely populated. One and one-half miles inland lay [Great] Accra, where the king and viceroy had their

---

[20] R. cannot be inferring this from what he had read about Benin practice in Bosman (1705) 442–3, which reported severe punishment of adultery (and no mention of firewood).

[21] Contrary to R's wording, sexual intercourse between unmarried parties is not adultery.

[22] R. may have been influenced by the assertion that robbery and murder were both very rare in Benin (Bosman (1705) 449–50).

[23] Perhaps R. was thinking of the reported importance of coral beads in Benin (Bosman 1705), 435–7). For *aggreys*, see Chapter 1, note 36, above.

[24] An unthinking statement. R. must have known that agricultural tools made of gold would be useless. For the relative value of gold and iron in pre-contact Gold Coast, see P.E.H. Hair, *The Founding of the Castelo de São Jorge da Mina* (1994) 2–3.

[25] Noyté was the Danes' broker at Christiansborg Castle in Accra (Chapter 3, /75/–/77/, above). The Portuguese held Christiansborg (renamed Fort Xavier) in 1679–1683 (Erick Tilleman, *A Short and Simple Account of the Country Guinea* [1697] (1994) 26), only some 60–65 years before R.'s time on the Coast, so Noyté could easily have remembered that period without being preternaturally aged.

residences, and two miles farther inland, where the mountains begin, [the district] was full of towns and people everywhere.[26]

[The rise of Aqvamboe]

The first conflict that the Negroes can tell us about during that period, their time of innocence, occurred in Assiante. Two prominent Blacks (the Negroes also know their names) became enamoured of a woman who was a member of a prominent family. These men agreed to put it to the woman which of the two she wished to have for a husband. She chose one, and the other pretended to be satisfied with that, but he came at night and took her by force to his dwelling. That same night he ran away with her, accompanied by all of his people, and after six weeks of a difficult and hurried journey they arrived in Accra. /117/ This Helena was the ancestress of all the Aqvamboe kings. The man who had kidnapped her, or she herself (I cannot recall which one), was named Aqvamboe; hence the entire nation is called Aqvamboe.[27] These people went to the king of the Accras and asked for his friendship, which they were given, and they settled a little farther inland, four miles from the sea. In half a century they became a great people. Aqvamboe had no more than one son and one daughter. The son, when somewhat young, was lodged with the king of the Accras to be given instruction, his father being dead. The Accras instructed the young king in their fetish worship, or religion, and in order for him to be worthy of being accepted in it, they had him circumcised. (All the other nations did not have this custom then, and they do not have it now.)[28]

The old Accra king died.[29] But before he died the Portuguese came to the Coast and brought brandy and swords, as well as gunpowder and muskets to

---

[26] R. is apparently referring to Great Accra, or Ayawaso, actually ten miles NE of Accra. For earlier Dutch views concerning Great Accra, the power of its king, the size of its population, and its trade practices, both at the coast and in the interior, see Olfert Dapper, *Naukeurige Beschrijvinge der Afrikaensche gewesten* (1676) 82–3. Although R., purportedly citing informants, makes wild rhetorical estimates of population sizes in the past, archeological evidence tends to suggest that the coastal area around Accra was already well populated at the time of the European arrival and probably for many centuries earlier (Boateng (1970), 150; M. Kilson, *African Urban Kinsmen* (1974) 5, 13 note 3). For plausible early Gã-Adangbe population patterns, see Dickson (1969) 25–7, 50.

[27] 'Helen' is, of course, Helen of Troy. For possible 'origins' of the Akwamu, see Ivor Wilks, 'The rise of the Akwamu empire', *Transactions of the Historical Society of Ghana* 3 (1957) 99–101; Ivor Wilks, 'Akwamu 1650–1750', MA thesis, University of Wales (1958), 3–6.

[28] R.'s story was embroidered in C.C. Reindorf, *History of the Gold Coast and Asante* (1895/1966) 13/25, 20/32–2, which claimed that the son was called 'Prince Odei', and that the circumcision was a ruse on the part of Gã chiefs to cause trouble for the King Okai Koi (cf. Irene Quaye, 'The Gã and Their Neighbours', PhD thesis, University of Ghana, 1972) 97–9). For the growth and expansion of Akwamu inland in the seventeenth century, see Tilleman [1697] (1994) 28–30; Wilks (1957), 105–7. 'All the other nations' means the Akan peoples, who do not, and apparently did not, practise male circumcision.

[29] The death of Okai Koi is elaborated in Reindorf (1895/1966) 22/34, where the date is given as 1660, which appears to be incorrect (note 35 below).

the Blacks. The Benin supremacy declined of itself, and the viceroys, who already held inherited positions, became sovereign kings, except that a successor had to receive confirmation from Benin.[30] The successor of the old Accra king did not emulate his predecessor's /**118**/ virtues but made himself hated among his nation because of the evil deeds which he committed while drunk.[31]

The Aqvamboe king could not assume power over his nation because he had lost his foreskin and was called Akotja (amputated) by his subjects.[32] After several years of dispute between the king and his subjects he had to promise, in a national assembly, that he would fetch or recover his foreskin from the Accras. He sent frequent messages to the Accras asking them to send it to him, along with the fetish priest who could put it in place again, but the Accras made excuses. Finally the Aqvamboes made threats, but the Accras only showed disdain. The Aqvamboes did not dare attack their enemies since there were twenty times as many Accras alone as there were Aqvamboes. In addition, the Mountain Negroes and the Adampes were subjects of the Accras, since the ancestors of each, having settled [either] at the coast to catch fish, or in the mountains to establish plantations in the fertile earth, had become slaves of the Accras. Both the Mountain Negroes and the Adampes had multiplied during all that time, so that there were (according to the Blacks) millions of them. The consolation of the Aqvamboes /**119**/ was that the king of the Accras was hated by his nation because of his cruelty and tyranny. Nevertheless, the Aqvamboes hired two other nations, namely the Agona and the Akron, [from] west of Accra, to help them to attack the Accras.[33] The Aqvamboes gave each of these nations a chest full of gold, [of a weight] which four men could scarcely lift and carry. However, to insure that those hired kept their word, these two chests of gold were to remain with the Aqvamboes until the war was over.[34]

---

[30] During a period of Benin over-rule of the Yoruba polity later known as Lagos the royal house and chiefs were required to obtain confirmation of their titles from the Oba of Benin, and also to pay customary tribute (A.F.C. Ryder, *Benin and the Europeans* (1969) 5, 8, 11–15). But it is unlikely that R. knew this. Confirmation of title from an overlord was a well-known European (and universal) political phenomenon.

[31] The old king may have been Mampong Okai (Reindorf (1895/1966) 15/28).

[32] *Akotja* is probably *kɔte* 'penis' + *twa* 'to cut' (J.G. Christaller, *Dictionary of the Asante and Fante Language called Tshi* (1881, rev. 1933) 259, 544). The Akwamu still speak of what they know of as the 'War of Akotia's Foreskin', and the *Akwamuhene* ('ruler of Akwamu'), Akotia, is well remembered (p.c. I. Wilks) — although their memories may have been strengthened by reading Reindorf.

[33] Relations between Agona and Akwamu in the 1680s, and the subsequent shifting of alliances, are discussed in Wilks, 'Akwamu 1650–1750', (1958), 22–4, which combines archive sources with R.'s account.

[34] For Akwamu's successful campaign against the Gã in 1677, see Tilleman [1697] (1994) 28; Jean Barbot, *Barbot on Guinea* [1732] (1992) 441–2 note 3; Wilks (1957) 106–07; Quaye (1972) 101–10.

[Accra under Aqvamboe]

The king of the Accras, who knew all this, regarded his enemies with disdain since he had many thousand of archers, throwers of assegais or spears, and swordsmen, and each of his eighty generals had a musket and ten rounds of powder and shot. He knew that the Aqvamboes with all their allies did not have a tenth of the number of people, and no muskets at all. However, the Accra generals had secretly agreed with the enemies of their king to desert him as soon as the battle began, in order to deliver him, as well as his children, into the enemy's hands. This was done, and the Accras thought that the Aqvamboes would be satisfied with the king's death; [but] instead they fell upon the Accras in their disorder and massacred a fearful number of them.[35] /120/ The sister of the Accra king escaped with her two children and several slaves, and fled sixty miles below [sc. east of] Accra to a place by the sea, called Little Popo. She is the ancestress of the Popo kings, who have by now become quite strong.[36]

The Accras, instead of now staying together in order to obstruct the further progress of the Aqvamboes, came to blows amongst themselves about who should be their king and leader, and a whole score of pretenders emerged. The Aqvamboes profited by this dissension and forced the Accras into three battles in one year, all of which fell out to the Aqvamboes' advantage. Such dreadful numbers of Accras were murdered [sic] that the rest had to give themselves up to the Aqvamboes. As a result the Adampes and all the Mountain Negroes became subjects of the Aqvamboes.[37]

The Aqvamboes now had control over a country stretching from the Accra lagoon to River Volta, a distance of twenty miles, and twenty-five miles inland from the coast, a district in which there were many millions of inhabitants.[38]

---

[35] For references to, and descriptions of this battle, see Tilleman [1697]) (1994) 28 (dating it to 1677) ; Wilks (1957) 106; Wilks (1958) 9–11; Quaye (1972) 100–09. According to Reindorf's reconstruction of the battle, the Akwamu were led by Ansa Sasraku, and the Accra king, Okai Koi, after the death of his eldest son in the battle, committed suicide (Reindorf (1895/1966) 21–2/33–40). In 1661 the king of the Gã signed a treaty with the Danish representative, Jost Cramer, ceding land in Osu to the Danes for the construction of a fort (CRA, V-gk 77, 18 8 1661). The king's signature reads *Kanckoy* (i.e., the ruler whom modern local writers, following Reindorf, term *Okai Koi*), therefore Reindorf's dating of his death to 1660 is wrong.

[36] On the flight and removal to Little Popo, see Barbot [1732] (1992) 441–2 note 3; Wilks (1957) 107; Quaye (1972) 110–12. For a discussion of the various versions of this exodus and the identities of the leaders, see N. Gayibor, 'Les Rois de Glidji', *History in Africa* 22 (1995) 198–204. Reindorf introduces in his account the story of the evil mother of Okai Koi, 'Dode Akabi, who ruled both the Akras and Obutus with a rod of iron' (Reindorf (1895/1966) 18–19/29–30).

[37] On the 'Mountain Negroes' as subject to Akwamu, see Wilks (1957) 106–07; Kwame Yeboa Daaku, *Trade and Politics on the Gold Coast* (1970) 154–5; Fynn (1971) 21.

[38] For the extent of Akwamu suzerainty, see Bosman (1705) 64; Rask (1754) 93; Wilks (1957) 108–11; Quaye (1972) 117–9. In contrast to R.'s absurd 'many millions of inhabitants', an earlier writer estimated that two villages close by the forts at Accra mustered respectively 60 and some 500 men with guns (Tilleman [1697] (1994) 25).

Aqvamboe, or the region where the true Aqvamboes lived, was no larger than an area in which their king could have called /121/ together his Big Men with a cannon shot when he wished to go into counsel with them.[39]

Now the war was over, the foreign auxiliary troops wanted to have their gold. Instead of the two chests filled with gold the Aqvamboes gave them two others that were filled with a variety of large, ordinary stones. The foreigners had a great deal of trouble in bringing the chests to their own country; and when they had succeeded, and all the elders and Big Men were gathered to divide the treasure, they discovered that they had been cheated. The Agona and Akron Negroes then resolved that, since the Aqvamboes had cheated them, they and their descendants would 'eat' all the Aqvamboes whom they could get hold of—that is to say, they would seize all the Aqvamboes they came across, sell them as slaves, and enjoy themselves with the goods received in exchange. In reprisal, the Aqvamboes made the same vow.[40]

At first the resolution only applied when an Aqvamboe entered the other area, or the Akron Negroes went to the Aqvamboe area. Thus, the catch was of no great significance. But when the other European nations, such as the Danes, the English and the Dutch, came to the Coast, these peoples practised to improve themselves in this business in order to receive greater profit from their /122/ slaves. The most ingenious young men of the Aqvamboe, as well as those of Agona and Akron, went to the enemy's land, sneaked into their plantations, lay down in the bushes not far from the paths which led from one town to another, and fell upon the passers-by. They bound their hands, put a gag over their mouths, and brought them back to their own town. From there the captives were taken to the forts and sold to the Europeans. This was the beginning of the great Accra trade, when a fort at Accra could certainly commit itself to load a ship every month with 500 to 600 slaves.[41]

From the time they became masters over the Accras up to 1734, when the Akims attacked and as good as wiped out the entire nation, there were fifteen kings in Aqvamboe. Since then the few survivors, numbering perhaps 500

---

[39] A 'Big Man' (Akan ɔbirɛmpɔn) was a man of high status, wealthy and powerful, but the term was also therefore a hereditary title for a territorial chief (McCaskie (1995) 275).

[40] I have not found the story of the chest and the betrayal in any other early source (but it was borrowed in Reindorf (1895/1966) 21/34).

[41] For the conflict between Akwamu and Agona, see Daaku (1970) 170–1, which argues that the Akwamu acquisition of control over the trade and trade routes to the coast was concomitant with the increasing demand for slaves by the Europeans. Be that as it may, with the Gã on the coast already familiar with, and expert in, the marine import/export trade, the growth of Accra as a slaving entrepôt followed (Tilleman [1697] (1994) 34; Barbot [1732] (1992) 39, 447 note 17; Bosman (1705) 70; John Atkins, *A Voyage to Guinea, Brasil and the West Indies* (1735) 176–80; Daaku (1970) 30–31; Albert van Dantzig, *Forts and Castles of Ghana* (1980b) 36–7, 43; K.Y. Daaku, 'Akan trade in the seventeenth and eighteenth centuries', in C. Meillassoux, *The Development of Indigenous Trade and Markets in West Africa* (1971) 169 ff).

families, have had to flee, first here, then there, and they still have no permanent residence.[42]

The regime of the first Aqvamboe kings was very mild for the Accras and all those subjugated. The Accras could no longer settle inland in their country one and one-half miles from the sea, but had to live under the European forts. Later this was /**123**/ somewhat advantageous for the Accras. They became brokers for the trade that the Aqvamboes brought to the Europeans, and the Accras were able to cheat and fool the Aqvamboes at every turn. Although the Aqvamboes knew this, they did not react very strongly since most of the time their goods cost them nothing.

[The Akims threaten Aqvamboe]

During the reign of one of these Aqvamboe kings a situation arose in which the Aqvamboes became indebted to the Akims in the following way. The latter had to pay an annual tax to a nation NE of them, namely the Assiantes. The Assiante king finally demanded more than they could raise, so the Akims resolved to desert their land and their gold mines in order that the king in Assiantes should have nothing at all.[43]

Like all these nations, the Akims had a certain family whose women produced male children as heirs to the Akim throne. (There are three kings or kingdoms in Akim). They sent six of these women to their neighbours, the Aqvamboes, and asked that they keep them until the Akims returned to their own land, or until they could come and fetch them. The Akims had resolved /**124**/ that they would not return home until the king of Assiante promised that he would never again demand tribute from them. Three years elapsed before the king of the Assiantes would agree to that, but he finally did. The Akims returned to their own land and sent a message to the Aqvamboes about [the return of] their noble women. But these women had married the king and [members of] the royal family in Aqvamboe, and had given birth to children. And the women did not wish to return to Akim, since the Aqvamboes had treated them better, giving them beautiful cloths and brandy, which they had never seen or tasted in Akim. Now in dire straits, Akim decided to go to war against the Aqvamboes in order to recover by force their six noble women, to kill the children the women had borne in

---

[42] The number of kings is probably exaggerated, in line with R.'s frequent practice with numbers. A modern historian counts only five Akwamu kings in the period between the conquest of Great Accra in 1677 and Small Accra in 1681,and the fall of Akwamu to the Akyem in 1730: Ansa Sasraku who died in 1680; Basua who shared the throne with the young Prince Ado 1680–1699; Ado alone 1699–1702; Akonnor 1702–1725; Ansa Kwao 1725–1730 (Quaye (1972) 122). R. discusses the destruction of Akwamu by Akyem in 154 ff, below. It appears that sections of the Akwamu then settled in various small enclaves among the inland peoples, with their chief new settlement on the east bank of River Volta.

[43] This may be a reference to the Akyem Kotoko abandoning their settlements and mines in the Oweri Valley, with the abandoned area, now under Asante control, becoming known as Asante Akyem (p.c. I. Wilks).

Aqvamboe, and [hence] to allow them to bring children into the world according to their own [Akim] custom. That is to say, these Negresses should not have to marry a particular man, since in no way should [these noble women] give the appearance of being at all humble.[44] The Aqvamboes feared the power of the Akims and offered to deliver the women back, but the Akims answered that they had waited too long, since all the arrangements for making war on them had been completed. The Aqvamboes would not only have to repay them for their trouble, but also give them an annual tribute. /125/ The Aqvamboes agreed, and the danger was over for the moment.[45]

The Aqvamboes had otherwise made it a policy never to allow the Akims to come to the coast, indeed not even to Aqvamboe. Instead, the Aqvamboe black merchants went to Akim with their goods.[46] They painted us Europeans as very frightening, saying that we were sea animals who not only were able to walk on the sea but who bought these lovely goods from sea gods who made them. They described the Europeans as being so repulsive and hideous that the poor Akims were not anxious to see us. During the regimes of the first three or four Aqvamboe kings the sale of gunpowder and muskets to the Akims was prohibited, under penalty of death.[47]

[The Accras as brokers for the Aqvamboe]

Time and time again, the Aqvamboes were rougher and harder on the Accras and others among their subjects [than they had formerly been]. Innocence and honour had, little by little, gone completely out of use, even among themselves. Their Siccadinger,[48] the crafty young men whom they

---

[44] The original reads *Disse Negerinder maa ikke gifte sig til en vis Mand, at det ingenlunde skal have anseelse, at de vare nogen underdanige*. The meaning is not transparent, but R. may be trying to say that these noblewomen were expected to select a man from their own clan to father their children (p.c. T.C. McCaskie).

[45] Views of this alleged resolution of a crisis can be found in a Copenhagen archive document (CRA, V-gK 122, 'Breve og documenter', 20 9 1725); and in print in Reindorf (1895/1966) 68/66; Wilks (1957) 123; Daaku (1970) 173–4; Fynn (1971) 68. Wilks later suggested a simpler explanation of the conflict than that preferred by R., basing it on Akwamu delinquency in repayment of gold borrowed from Akyem (Wilks (1958) 30–1).

[46] For the entrepreneurship of African middlemen, see Rask (1754) 151; Wilks (1958) 74; Lars Sundström, *The Exchange Economy of Pre-Colonial Tropical Africa* (1974) 54–7; Atkinson (1980) 355.

[47] Contrary to what R. implies, the Akwamu, fearing the growing strength of Asante, allowed the Akyem to trade at the coast for a short period in 1715, during which time they purchased guns and powder (Daaku (1970) 174).

[48] The term *siccading* appears to be a Danish version of a term not otherwise recorded, possibly being a corruption of Gold Coast Portuguese for raiding/raiders, from Portuguese *sacar* 'to drag out, derive gain, profit' (p.c. Mary Esther Kropp Dakubu), with the ending (-ing) of a Danish verbal noun to indicate the act. It has been suggested that the term stands for 'black gold', a metaphor for slaves, from Akan *sika* 'gold', *ding* 'black' (Quaye (1972) 162 note 3; M.A. Kwamena-Poh, *Government and Politics in the Akuapem State* (1973) 28, note 7; Albert van Dantzig, *Les Hollandais sur la Côte de Guinée* (1980a) 243 note 1; Kea (1982) 162). But since the term in context refers to slavers rather than to slaves, this seems implausible.

sent to the neighbour's land in order to steal people, often came back with empty hands, and often with bloody heads. Not wishing to have taken this trouble in vain, they therefore sometimes seized their own /**126**/ countrymen and [even] some from their own city, and sold them to the Accras, who would gladly have seen the entire Aqvamboe nation sold as slaves. In turn, the Accras sold the captives to the forts, where there were dungeons or secret prisons, so that no one could see these stolen Aqvamboes until a ship came into the road and they could be sent aboard at night. Often the Aqvamboe Siccadinger did not leave their own country, fearing injury in the country of strangers, so they stole their neighbours' children and their friends, and sold them, as stated above. They dared not seize the Accras since one Accra would not be a 'fence' when another was to be sold, but would be an informer instead. The Aqvamboes had to admit that the Akron Siccadinger, or crafty men, surpassed them by far in their expertise, and that the Akron received ten times the price the Aqvamboes received. The Akron Negroes brought their trade to the Accra road, which was rarely empty of ships.

When the Accras tell us about that period, they are very joyful and wish that they might live once more in such a delightful time. During that period (they say) we earned more /**127**/ in one day than we do now in an entire year. We could become as rich as we wished and had no need to work or to worry ourselves about anything. Our Whites profited so greatly that, unasked, they would give us entire ankers of brandy, while now we have to beg for a glassful, and they show us the door at times.[49]

In order to understand this, it is necessary to know how the Aqvamboe merchants carried on their trade. When it was a matter of stolen goods (Negroes) taken from among his friends or his nation, and whom no one should be allowed to see, an Aqvamboe would usually go, at night, to the home of his good friend, an Accra. In this house there was usually a dungeon in which these stolen Negroes were hidden until the Accra called on the sentries at a fort and asked for the gates to be unlocked, there being so many slaves whom the Blacks must not be allowed to see. The slaves were admitted into the fort, and kept in its dungeons. However, if they were from other nations [than the Aqvamboes], either bought or stolen, these precautions were not necessary. But the Aqvamboe still brought his goods to the home of his Accra friend, who negotiated the trade for him

---

[49] Inter-African warfare undoubtedly provided slaves, and both at the time by some slavers, and in later centuries by all abolitionists, was claimed to be the major provider of slave cargoes (cf. Barbot [1732] (1992) 550). Whether this was so is, however, doubtful. Warfare interrupted commercial land routes and inhibited in subsequent periods the more regular import-export exchange, including that involving slaves. Given that wars could produce immediate large cargoes (and hence the Accra brokers' 'delightful times'), the argument that overall the products of wars outweighed regular enslavements requires the assumption that wars were endemic — a belief fondly held by abolitionists (and leading to a negative view of Black Africa) but not likely to have been correct (p.c. P.E.H. Hair).

with the Europeans. The Accra was always prepared for this transaction with one or more bottles of brandy, and he /**128**/ treated the Aqvamboe and his people to as much as they wanted to drink. He had water brought so that the Aqvamboe could wash — since these were stolen goods, the Aqvamboe had not dared to use the ordinary path but had had to creep through the bushes, so his skin had been badly scratched by thorns. The Aqvamboes drank themselves into a stupor a couple of times [*sic*] and then slept it off. Meanwhile the Accra had sold the slaves, and, as was customary, had stolen [for himself from the payment] 12 to 16 *rixdaler* for each slave, a sum he asked the merchant at the fort to hide for him.[50] The Aqvamboe, wishing to set off for a new catch, asked the Accra for his goods, which were then delivered. The Aqvamboe might then have said, 'My friend! Have you received so many lovely goods for three or four poor slaves? Stop, stop, that's enough! Keep the rest, I have enough. They haven't cost me much', and so on.

Sometimes the Aqvamboe was not pleased with his catch and he would set out to cheat his friend, the Accra. He would come to see the Accra, who, as usual, would make a great occasion of the visit, serving brandy and food. The Aqvamboe might well say that his people were following him, with the slaves [for sale]. The Aqvamboe would then be on the lookout for /**129**/ the least cause of complaint he could find against the Accra in order to punish him to the value of a couple of slaves. Sometimes, when he arrived the Aqvamboe might say to the Accra, 'My friend! I'm freezing, let me have some hot water to wash myself with!' The water would be brought; the Aqvamboe would dip his whisk into the water and stroke it over his body. He would then jump up as if he had scalded himself [with boiling water], and would deliver an immediate judgement upon the Accra, who would then have to pay [as compensation] one or two hundred *rixdaler* in goods. Or, while the Aqvamboe was eating the food the Accra had served him, a sheep, a hen, a chicken, or a dog might come in and try to eat with him. The Aqvamboe would allow this, but afterwards the Accra would have to be punished for not having more polite dogs and cats. If the Accra had removed these [animals] before serving his friend the food, and the Aqvamboe could think up no other [immediate] excuse, then, if a rooster crowed or a dog barked and thus disturbed him in his sleep or his thoughts, or if the Aqvamboe felt unwell after [having eaten] the food which the Accra had given him [he would demand compensation]. He could invent countless such excuses to get back twofold what the Accra had stolen from him. /**130**/

But the Accra could play the same game. He knew that if he complained to the Aqvamboe king, the king would side with his countryman, and the Accra would receive twice as much punishment as he had suffered previously. If he

---

[50] In 1760, 16 *rixdaler* was the exchange equivalent of one ounce of gold, and in R.'s time, somewhat earlier, the price of a prime male slave was 96 *rixdaler* (cf. /318/–/319/, below).

accused his friend, the Aqvamboe, of having often stolen people from his own city and [from among] his own people, the Accra exposed himself as a 'fence', and therefore was just as liable to punishment as the thief. Furthermore, he would, perhaps, ruin the 'craft' (that is, of being a 'fence') for all the Accras.[51] In this case there was no solution other than to give the Aqvamboe all he demanded, and in addition one or more bottles of brandy, in order to make him and his men drunk. But in advance the Accra had alerted his neighbours to keep themselves in readiness on the evening or night that the Aqvamboe would be leaving. Then the Accras, ten or twenty men strong, went a short way ahead, captured all the Aqvamboes and their goods as well, and sold them secretly. In this way the Accras escaped not only without harm but with considerable profit.[52]

The King of Aqvamboe and his Big Men also wanted to live off the public, and they accomplished this in the following way. To every town they took some women, three or four, according to the size of the town, and settled them there. Then every year the men travelled around /131/ and [at each town] had these women eat fetish [*sc.* take an oath] to reveal who had touched them [sexually].[53] The women admitted this quite willingly, since they received part of the fine, and unless their friends ransomed them the gallants had to be sold as slaves.[54] These *maximer* [methods] were also employed by the Akim kings, and anyone who was on the Coast during that time knows what great numbers of merchants ran after Bang, the King of Akim, with their trade-goods when he made his annual tour.[55] In such circumstances, it can be seen that Accra was the best trading place on the entire Coast. It also follows that the Aqvamboes became weaker and the Accras stronger, which aroused hatred on the part of the Aqvamboes.

---

[51] R. (ironically?) uses the term *haandværk* 'craft', to describe the trade, implying skill.

[52] Anecdotes about individual Africans cheating each other, although no doubt correct, are turned into generalized statements which must be exaggerated, since the Africans concerned are presented in contradictory fashion, as both clever business men and yet very naïve.

[53] For 'eating fetish', see Chapter 3, note 77, above. Among the Akan, adultery was a serious crime, especially if the woman was the wife of an important man. Punishment was usually the payment of a fine, and those who were unable to pay were probably sold into slavery (Barbot [1732] (1992) 503–4; Bosman (1705) 200–1; Isert [1788] (19920 134).

[54] An Akan ruler could take as his wives women known as *ayete* ('substitute wife') from certain servile villages, and by locating them in different towns and villages could claim high adultery fees from all who had sexual relations with them (p.c. I. Wilks). In any case, the practice of acquiring multiple wives was a not uncommon means of obtaining cheap labour (p.c. Adam Jones). For multiple wives and the profit aspect of adultery, see Villault (1669) 228, 365–6, 368; Müller [1673] in Jones (1983) 189–90; Bosman (1705) 200–2, 211–15; Rask (1754) 129; Isert [1788] (1992) 134; H.C. Monrad, *Bidrag til en Skildring af Guinea-Kysten og den Indbyggere* (1822) 61–2.

[55] *Maximer* is a term R. uses in other places (e.g., 1756 in Chapter 2 above, /32/, /33/, /44/), in the sense of concepts, systems or methods. Here it seems to convey the sense of 'sharp methods, games, dirty tricks'.

[War customs]

All so far reported about the traditional enemies, Aqvamboe and Akron, indicates behaviour very close to the inhumane, yet it cannot be compared to what now follows. When an Aqvamboe has stolen some of his countrymen at night, in the dark, in order to sell them, it will sometimes happen that among them he discovers old or ill individuals, or infants. He knows that the Europeans would not buy these, so he drives them away from the path, kills them, and buries them. Should the Aqvamboes capture any of their traditional enemies, the Akron or Agona Negroes, and /**132**/ among the prisoners is an old man, or a member of one of the prominent families, they do not sell him but [instead] torture him dreadfully, finally cutting off his head, and boiling the flesh off in a pot so that the bones or skull are bare. Then the entire nation gathers in the Residence [*sic*]. Their king and prominent people make sport of the head, wipe their feet on the jawbone of the murdered [man], pound on the skull, spit on it, etc. The Agona and Akron Negroes do the same to any prominent Aqvamboes whom they take as prisoners. Finally, they tie the skulls to their drums, so that they may have a great many heads hanging on the town's drum. They believe that the spirit or soul of the murdered Black experiences very great pain from the sound and noise of the drum, and they are not satisfied with having tortured him in life but also want to torment him after death.[56] I do not believe that any stories [told] from the beginning of the world have described such inhumane and terrible things as you find here. When you think of it afterwards, you cannot but be sickened by it.[57]

The Negroes are of the opinion that these evil customs are not more than one hundred years old among them, and that the Aqvamboes and their neighbours were the first to start /**133**/ this [particular] practice. It is known that the Aqvamboes did not take the head of the Accra king 150 years ago. It is also known that about 130 years ago the Assiantes were at war with the Akims, but the Assiantes have on display no heads of the Akim kings or Big Men killed at that time. However, from the last two occasions [of war] (the last time being in 1742) the Assiantes have more

---

[56] On mocking and making sport of heads of enemies, and on skulls and jawbones as trophies on drums and horns, see Dapper (1676) 112; Barbot [1732] (1992) 566, 607; Isert [1788] (1992) 71, 73; Monrad (1822) 116–17; Jones (1983) 93, note 281; McCaskie (1995) 217–19. R.'s references are fully confirmed, and they represent a particularly strong European reaction to these practices and clearly influence his overall attitude to the African cultures and societies involved. In fact, such practices do not seem to have been general across West Africa, and the reason for their cultivation in Gold Coast is not clear (p.c. P.E.H. Hair). See also note 223 below.

[57] The well-evidenced public atrocities committed in inter-ethnic warfare on Gold Coast were frequently invoked by Europeans to justify the Atlantic slave trade, it being argued that war captives were thus rescued from torture and death (cf. Pontoppidan's Introduction above, 7). Such atrocities were, of course, not unknown in contemporary Europe (albeit arguably on a smaller scale) — or for that matter in twentieth-century global society (albeit less publicly).

than 4,000 Akim heads, as I shall report later.[58] It is thus probable that the Aqvamboes practised this custom first, and that other nations have acquired a taste for treating their enemies in the same manner, in order to make themselves more fearful and visit on their enemies more disdain, shame and humiliation.

I have often reflected on [the nature of] mankind in that land, and in general I wonder whether perhaps the great Creator was not in fact truly angry at that race [of Blacks], something which the old Blacks have, indeed, often stated to me in confidence, and in their simple way. Could not God use other means to eradicate them from this earthly paradise in which they live? — this people who, having God's law written in their hearts, as does all mankind, yet follow the devil's blind way which leads them to that /134/ unnatural and abominable evil Satan alone could conceive.[59] By such reflections, God's Word has become sweeter to me than it was before, and the universal Saviour's teaching of faith, love, hope, and patience have brought me greater encouragement to strive for the precious virtues which, the more they are practised in the Christian world, the more they promote the bliss of mankind.

No misery among Christians is comparable to the agony and pain that a Black experiences when the heads of his forefathers are in the hands of the enemy. It rankles and offends him as long as he exists on earth; and he bequeaths that rankling and pain to his descendants, who, in turn, during their lifetimes plot how they can retrieve the head and wreak revenge on the descendants of their ancestor's enemies. If they see the slightest glimmer of hope of achieving that goal, they risk their life, their head, and all those who are dear to them.[60] On the few occasions I have engaged in confidential conversations with such Blacks, I started by assuring them that the deceased felt not the least pain, no matter how much his enemies mistreated his dead

---

[58] The theory of the origin of decapitation, attributed to 'the Negroes', would appear to be R.'s personal speculative opinion. Far from the practice having been invented only '100 years ago', that is about 1650, among early references to the practice are those of De Marees [1602] (1987) 91 (the collection of heads in war as early as 1570); Brun [1624], Hemmersam [1663] and Müller in Jones (1983) 91–2, 117, 199 (a 1618 battle producing an alleged total of 40,000 heads; heads as trophies c.1630; sport with heads in the 1660s). As for the Assiantes not having heads from '150 years ago', it is generally held that Asante did not exist as a polity at that date. The 1742 Asante victory over the Akyem is discussed in /183/ ff below.

[59] R.'s complaint is in the tradition of earlier European writers on Gold Coast, who, although in many cases accepting that the Africans believed in a Supreme Being, still ascribed their religious practices to the worship of the devil. For similar attitudes, see De Marees [1602] (1987) 36a-37b; Brun [1624], Zur Eich [1659–69] (an engraving of the devil), Hemmersam [1663], Müller [1673], all in Jones (1983) 58, 65, 75–6, 119, 156–60; Barbot [1732] (1992) 577–78; Rask (1754) 194. On diabolatry, see P.E.H. Hair, 'Heretics, slaves, and witches — as seen by Guinea Jesuits c. 1610', *Journal of Religion in Africa* 26 (1998) 131–44.

[60] On the necessity of retaining or recovering the heads of ancestors, see Müller, who, although writing of the Akan polity of 'Fetu', evokes the same measure of intensity and gravity (Müller [1673] in Jones (1983) 199–200).

body or bones, and if I were in the individual's place I would laugh /135/ at it, and never think about it again. One of them asked me to say no more, and assured me that, meeting one of his friends or acquaintances, he did not dare to look [straight] at him. He felt that he could read in everyone's eyes that they were saying, 'Fetch back the heads of your king, your ancestors, your friends!' Another responded that as long as he could be sure that enemies would be satisfied with those heads of his ancestors they already had, he would willingly forget it; but he was certain that they also yearned for his, to hang it on their drum. He had therefore to struggle day and night to contrive a way of removing his enemies from the world. Both men assured me that they could not relax other than after they had drunk brandy, and as long as the intoxication lasted.[61] Do these people not carry a hell within themselves? Is not a Greenlander in his cold and barren land far happier than a wealthy African king or a prominent Negro?[62]

I condemn the English out there on the Guinea Coast, at Cape Coast [Castle], for having nearly thirty human heads lying in an iron chest with many locks on it. Fifty years ago the English were at war with /136/ the Dutch on the Coast. This war was not waged with Europeans, or with Europeans against Europeans, but each side hired Black nations who, for money, and by flattery, willingly go to war with each other, even though the opposing party had never done them any harm. On one occasion the English Black army was fortunate enough to force the Dutch Blacks to total flight, and the army took the heads of the most prominent of the enemy's leaders. Since it was the English who had paid the soldiers, the heads had to be delivered to the English chief agents, and the war was over.[63] The English had the heads boiled, as the Blacks do in such cases, and packed the skulls in an iron chest. However, they did not tie the heads to their drums, and they made an offer to the descendants of these murdered caboceers that if they would pay the costs of the war, which was many thousand pounds sterling, they could then recover their forefathers' heads. But it is known that the descendants of the murdered leaders recovered their forefathers' heads at a more advantageous price. This is how it happened. Less than ten years later, when these [particular English] Chief-Agents were dead, or had left the Coast, and there were others in their

---

[61] An unusual but probably sincere excuse for heavy drinking—to forget this onerous social obligation and the risks involved.
[62] In 1721, the Norwegian minister, Hans Poulsen Egede (1686-1758), settled in Greenland and established the first Christian mission to the local Inuit, becoming renowned throughout Scandinavia as 'Greenland's Apostle'.
[63] R. is probably referring to the 1664 altercations between the Dutch and the English at Cape Coast, in which the Fetu and Elmina were also involved (Müller [1673] in Jones (1983) 147; Tilleman [1697] (1994) 4, 22; Barbot [1732] (1992) 403, notes 3-4, 414 note 5; K.G. Davies, *The Royal African Company* (1957) 42; Daaku (1970) 16-7; Van Dantzig (1980a) 33-5). But none of these sources mentions skulls in a chest.

place, the new ones allowed themselves to be bribed (as they say) by the descendants, who offered twice as much gold as the skulls weighed. This [offer] was accepted, the descendants acquired the skulls, and the Chief-Agents /137/ had skulls of dead slaves [secretly] packed into the chest instead. I believe they are still there and at the installation of new Chief-Agents they are counted as the inventory of the fort just as if they were the same heads they received during the war.

I have to admit that all the Europeans — Danish, English, and Dutch — who have been factors, or who were sent to a station to trade, are, at times, forced to imitate the Blacks in their cruelty. Such a situation may occur when two black kings are at war with each other. Both parties have formerly been friends and traders, but one of them is the victor, winning the head of the other, as well as taking many of his subjects as slaves. The victor in person, or one of his generals, brings us his opponent's jaw bone, bound to a whip, and before he will promise to bring any of the captured slaves for trade the factor must place his foot on this bone and prove thereby that he does not grudge him his victory, congratulating him in this way.[64]

[How the Aqvamboe captured Accra]

Earlier it was said that the Aqvamboes became envious of the Accras, since while the latter increased in number noticeably, the former decreased. The Aqvamboes dared not attack for fear that the Accras would hire /138/ their arch-enemies, the Akion and the Agona, who would willingly help to destroy the Aqvamboes. About eighty years ago a war broke out between Fante, a republic and nation twenty miles above [sc. west of] Accra, and Agona and Akron. The Fantes were fortunate and conquered both nations. They ruined the Agona Negroes completely, and beat to death more than half of the Akron Negroes. They collected many heads as a sign of victory, and sold many thousand of their enemies.[65]

While the Fantes were in the process of wiping out the Agona and Akron Negroes, the fetish (so the Negroes at Accra say) appeared at an unusual time and ordered the priests to send immediately for his children (the Fante Negroes) who were engaged in exterminating their brethren, who were just as dear to him (the fetish) as was the Fante nation. For two days and two

---

[64] The Europeans had to adopt at least some African customs to allow trade to flourish. In some instances, it was even a matter of survival of the particular trading relationship, e.g., by acceptance of the practice of swearing an oath by 'eating fetish' (cf. 89–90 above; also Isert [1788] (1992) 130). For an explanation of the function of 'fetish oaths' between strangers, see W. Pietz, 'The spirit of civilization: blood debt', *RES Anthropology and Aesthetics* 28 (1995) 29. Note, however, that the concept of swearing on oath to fulfil an obligation was commonplace in contemporary Europe.

[65] At the turn of the century the Akron were living peacefully with the Fante, their protectors (Bosman (1705) 61). Bosman also describes the flourishing condition of Agona, but without mention of Fante (63–4). For Akwamu against Agona, see Wilks (1957) 118–9; Sanders (1979) 353–9.

nights he created a great disturbance in his sacred grove. Whirlwinds succeeded each other, pulling up trees and bushes by the roots, and hurling them a whole *fjerding* distance away. In order to placate him, the Fante caboceers came in great haste with many slaves for a sacrifice, but the fetish would not let himself /**139**/ be placated. The slaves had to be freed immediately, and the brafoes (generals) and twenty-four of the greatest and oldest caboceers had to be decapitated in order to placate him. The heads of the Akron and Agona caboceers were delivered back to their surviving relatives, and the Fantes themselves had to pay for them to be given an honourable funeral. They even had to be present at the funeral, and to bury them. Since then the Fantes and Akron Negroes have been good friends.[66]

Our Aqvamboes profited on that occasion. They knew that the Akron Negroes, although they continued to eat Aqvamboes (as they say), would not be able to wage another offensive war for fifty years, so they attacked Accra. The first place they attacked was Labode,[67] on which they made a surprise assault at night, killing [many] and taking anything they came across. (The fetish had evidently not warned [the Labodes] of this in advance, or they would have been on their guard). Putti has assured me that the number of people they took from him alone was over 2,000, namely his relatives, children, slaves, and children of slaves. Putti and all the Labode Negroes who saved themselves by running away fled some 200 to 300 miles to Crepe (the Blacks call the entire country which lies SE [*sic*] of /**140**/ River Volta, Crepe), where the inhabitants still live in a state of innocence. Once this had been done, the Aqvamboe king sent a message to all the other Accra towns and assured them of his friendship and protection. He told them that he had been forced to act thus for this or that reason (perhaps the sort of reasons which an Aqvamboe used against an Accra when he wished to insult him, for instance, that a chicken had eaten of his food, or a rooster had crowed). The other Accras had to be satisfied with this because the Danish, English, and Dutch fortresses would not stand by them. The Europeans acquired the trade [in slaves], although it was in their own Negro subjects.[68]

Another year the Aqvamboes assaulted a town situated below the Dutch castle, in the same way as they had done at Labode. The Dutch factor wished to defend the town but could not, because at night he did not know the difference between friend and foe, therefore he could not assist his Negroes with his cannon, which the Europeans usually load with grapeshot. The Dutch

[66] On the powerful Fante 'fetish', see Chapter 3, note 4, above.
[67] At the time 'Accra' seems to have comprised seven units, perhaps distinct polities: James Town (British Accra), Kinka or Ussher town (Dutch Accra), Osu or Christiansborg (Danish Accra), Labadi, Teshi, Little Ningo, Tema (Reindorf (1895)/1966) 12/24).
[68] For the Akwamu take-over, see Tilleman [1697] (1994) 28–9; Barbot [1732] (1992) 430, 435–6; Wilks (1957) 110–11; Daaku (1970) 153–4; Quaye (1972) 125–6; Kwamena-Poh (1976) 21–2.

Negroes had to go the same way as the Labode Negroes. Thereafter the Aqvamboes remained /**141**/ quiet for a couple of years, and then it was the turn of the Mountain Negroes and Adampes.[69]

[Aqvamboe policies]

All this happened under an Aqvamboe king named Acondo, who ruled from approximately 1702 to 1720. Finally, he pretended to regret these enterprises of his. Without a doubt he was frightened of the Akims, to whom he paid an annual tax — without allowing his subjects to notice this, since they had made it a condition of his investiture that he should no longer pay the tax to the Akims, as so many of his predecessors had done. Then Acondo had a clever idea. When the Akim messenger came to receive the tax, [his arrival] could not be hidden from the people. Therefore Acondo assembled all his Big Men, and the messenger had to state his errand [in their presence]. Acondo acted as if he were angry and threatened to kill the messenger. But at night he had him come to his residence, he weighed up as much gold as was required for the tax, and he let him go the same night. His servants were made to spread the word among their friends that the Akim messenger had been killed that night.[70] /**142**/

It has already been stated that the Aqvamboe king, Acondo, appeared to regret the evil he had done to the Accras. This conclusion can be reached because he had them called back [to their homeland], and all the Europeans at Accra had to be his guarantors [sic: ? witnesses] that he meant them well and would absolutely not attack or assault them any more. They returned, and as a sign of his friendship he delivered their forefathers' heads back to them, and, in addition, he gave one of the Aqvamboe noble women to each of the two most prominent Accra caboceers. Putti received one of the women, and Dacon, a caboceer under the Dutch fort, received the other.[71]

Acondo's scheme was very clever. He intended to make one nation out of the Accras and the Aqvamboes, which would indeed have been accomplished had the Accras given the Aqvamboe some of their nobles. Yet, scarcely a

---

[69] By mentioning the Mountain Negroes at this point, R. is apparently referring to the fall of Kwahu, an Akan polity in the hills inland, after a campaign which took three years (Wilks (1957) 129–30; Wilks (1958) 38; G. Nørregård, *Danish Settlements in West Africa* (1966) 67; Van Dantzig (1980a) 197–8). Rask gives the date of the fall of Kwahu to Akwamu as May 1710, while he himself was on the Coast (Rask (1754) 152). The process by which another polity, Akwapim, eventually fell under the sway of Akwamu is discussed in Kwamena-Poh (1976) 22–5.

[70] For the Akwamu king Acondo (Aconno/Akwonno) and some confusion of names, see note 72 below. For his career, see Wilks (1958) 36–9. The payment of tribute to Akyem was recorded in Rask (1754) 150–1 (cf. Reindorf (1895/1966) 70/66; Van Dantzig (1980a) 196–8).

[71] For Dako (Dacon), see Chapter 3, note 92, above. R.'s story reappears in Reindorf (1895/1966) 72/69 (cf. Quaye (1972) 125–6).

hundred years [passed] before his descendants ruined everything.[72] No doubt the Supreme Being was weary of that nation, which had now become thoroughly evil and an abomination to God.

Acondo died in about 1726 and Aqvando succeeded him.[73] Like his predecessor, he had to promise the Aqvamboe nation /**143**/ that he would pay no tax to Akim. The Big Men in Aqvamboe knew that the deceased Acondo, despite his own promise, had done this. We have recounted earlier the scheme Acondo used with the Akim messenger to keep his nation happy. [But] the Akims had learned about this, and, to torment Acondo, for several years in a row they had sent to him the very same individual to collect the tax whom Acondo had declared that he had killed one night. Aqvando made the same promise to his Aqvamboes, and he, indeed, kept that promise. The first time the Akim messengers came to collect the tax he had all of them, except one, decapitated — and this was done in the presence of all the Big Men. Then, packing the heads in a sack, he gave it to the single survivor to carry on his head, and had him accompanied to the border. The Aqvamboe gathering applauded their king vigorously for this deed, and promised that in the event the Akims made war, they would fight for him as long as there was life and blood in them.

Aqvando knew very well, as his predecessor had done, what acts of roguery were perpetrated in his land, namely, that individuals stole each other and sold the captives secretly. Acondo himself had maintained /**144**/ a thousand Siccadings (crafty men), in order to capture Akron Negroes. He had lived on [the profit of] this and on the [rents from] the three Accra fortresses, each of which paid a tax of 32 *rixdaler* monthly, as well as on what his wives earned.[74] Aqvando, when he inherited the throne, did not wish to send his people into the land of the enemy, from which they sometimes returned with their heads bloodied and having left behind fully a score of their

---

[72] The Akan marriage system made such integration possible (Ivor Wilks, 'Akwamu and Otublohum: an eighteenth-century Akan marriage arrangement', *Africa* 29 (1959) 391–4).

[73] There appears to be a confusion of names at this point, Acondo and Aquando seeming to be only variants of the same name, in modern form Akwonno/Akonno. It has been suggested that when Acondo/Aquando died in 1725 and was succeeded by Ansa Kwao, the latter adopted and continued what was perhaps a stool name (that is, a title), Akonno (Wilks (1958) 86, note 1). A counter view, that the successor's stool name was Ansa Sasraku IV, is claimed to be based on Akwapim traditions (Kwamena-Poh (1973) 23, note 3). For the family relationship between the two rulers and the succession, see Wilks (1959) 392, 395–6).

[74] The forts paid precisely the same amount monthly to the Akwamu in the 1690s as in R.'s time (Tilleman [1697] (1994) 28). Later, the Dutch paid Akyem the same as they had paid the king of Accra and Akwamu (Van Dantzig (1980a) 248–9). After 1742 and up to the end of the century, the forts at Accra still paid the same amount monthly, 32 *rixdaler*, but now to the Asante, although with the addition of a considerable annual gift (A.R. Bjørn, 'Bjørn's Beretning 1788 om de Danske Forter of Negerier', *Thaarup's Archiv* 3 (1797–1798) 201–2). For this and other sources of revenue for the African polities, including tribute from property owners and agriculture, see Tilleman [1697] (1994) 29; Reindorf (1895/1966) 73/70–1; Quaye (1972) 122–4, 128–9; Kea (1982) 165, 314.

comrades [killed]. Instead he felt that he and his own thieves were just as good [at stealing] as the poorer Aqvamboes,[75] so he stole and robbed people of his own nation, of the Mountain Negroes, and of the Adámpes. But he seized no Accras, since they had to help him to obtain goods in exchange for the slaves, goods consisting mostly of brandy. Thus, you might say that Aqvando and his crafty men drank up a couple of thousand of their own people each year — in addition to the number their neighbours, the Akrons, Fantes and Accras, stole from the Aqvamboes annually. There were also those who were killed when the stolen Negroes were [found to be] old or sick, as well as those whom the Big Men in Aqvamboe stole.[76]

Up to this point in time Accra's agreeable slave trade continued, and in Europe they could not fathom where all the black people came from. It was thought that the Blacks in Africa produced children only in /**145**/ order to sell them to the Europeans. Or, again, that in Africa, as had actually happened in East India, in many places where frequent famine occurred, individuals sold themselves so as not to die of hunger. I believe that all those who now read this will no longer accuse the Africans of selling their children.[77]

[A Danish governor]

We come now to the well-deserved total destruction of the Aqvamboes. Before it can be understood, we must describe the Europeans who were at that time the leading persons at Accra, and particularly their expertise in trade. I have forgotten their names.[78] We [*sc.* the Danes] had a governor who had been a ship's captain in the Company's service. He had been previously dismissed because of his poor management and declared incompetent to serve in any post in the future. This, however, did not prevent his being chosen to be governor on the Guinea Coast. At that time there were not many of our captains who could write more than a ship's log. You could reasonably expect a man who from his youth had travelled in ships to be able to guide a vessel safely and securely through the sea, to be able to judge if a cable could hold out one more trip, and so on. But reasonable folk would never expect a skipper, and [a man who was] only a skipper, /**146**/ to be able to understand public affairs in such a difficult and

---

[75] The Danish reads: *Han mente da, at han og hans Tyve vare ligesaa gode, som de ringere Aqvamboer.* The final phrase is obscure.

[76] On the oppressive rule of 'Aquando' and the Mountain Negroes turning against him, see Wilks (1958) 92-3; Quaye (1972) 162, 175, 191; Kwamena-Poh (1973) 30. But these modern accounts draw heavily on R.

[77] R.'s argument that enslavement of Africans by Africans was not out of necessity but only out of normal human cupidity is curious. Was it meant to be ironic? (p.c. P.E.H. Hair).

[78] This is not strictly true. R. knew the name at least of the Danish governor about to be mentioned, A.P. Wærøe (see the next note, also 1756 in Chapter 2 above, 35, 38). The Dutch factor in 1730, the year of the Akyem victory over Akwamu, was J. de la Planque, and the English factor was probably William Knight (CRA, V-gK 122, 15.5.1730, letter from Wærøe).

important post.[79] It is true that at that time [nautical knowledge] was of no importance to our nation, since we sent a ship there only every second or third year — yet the planters in the West Indies bought our slaves from the Dutch and English, who had probably purchased them at Christiansborg.[80]

This good man spent his time just as he had been used to do on board, by taking sights. It is amusing [to note] that although he never sailed with his fort, yet he made his observations every day and imparted this information to others, keeping a daily log of the weather, etc. He was a fairly accomplished mechanic, so he bought old watches, repaired them, and sold them. He had a marked tendency to lose his temper, and he expressed his vehemence both to the Directors in his reports and to the English and Dutch in letters, in the manner of a sailor. He showed Negroes the door when they came to trade because they interrupted him in important business. The Negroes, who very much wished to make a profit by trading, were not well served by such a man, since he did not want to trade, and yet would not allow those who could have done it for him to do so. The Governor accused /**147**/ the Negroes of being schemers and a pack of thieves. And our Negroes did not act any better than what he called them.

Excellent sailor as our Governor was, just as skilled and shrewd a Coast Man was the Dutch commander at Accra, a man of dissolute conscience, who had been in service with the Dutch on the Coast since he was a boy.[81] He was not content [to live as a neighbour to] our peaceable Governor but sought to insult him and all the Danes on the Coast. First he enticed our free Negroes to move from our town to his.[82] This the Negroes did willingly since they could earn a little in his service but nothing under us. Then he enticed our Company slaves to join him, leaving us with very few. Finally he incited our own Negroes and slaves to hide in their empty huts with loaded muskets, and when they saw a Dane through the crenellations on the battlements, to shoot to kill him, which they did on several occasions. Our people bombarded

---

[79] The Danish Commandant at the time of the defeat of Akwamu was Anders Pedersen Wærøe, 1728–35, whose role has recently been interpreted more sympathetically (Nørregård (1966) 76, 82–3). Reindorf, embroidering R., refers to the 'sailor Governor' as illiterate, but a man who had captained ships for years cannot have been so (Reindorf (1895/1966) 78/75). The Copenhagen archives contain an example of a complaint sent to Elmina in Dutch, together with the response from Governor Pranger (CRA, V-gK 881, 6.12 1732).

[80] The infrequency of ships from Denmark to Christiansborg was a constant cause of complaint. Between 1698 and 1733 there was generally only one ship per year (Nørregård (1966) 82–3, 86–7, 90; P. Hernæs, *Slaves, Danes, and African Coast Society* (1995a) 198, table 251). For trade with foreign ships in the Danish West Indies during this period, see P.E. Olsen, *Toldvæsenet i Dansk Vestindien* (1988) 25–29. For instance, an English captain was advised to take his ship and slaves to 'the Island of St. Thomas in the West Indies, a Freeport belonging to the Danes, and sell them there' (William Snelgrave, *A New Account of some Parts of Guinea* (1734) 241).

[81] The reference is to Jacob de la Planque, and what follows is also described in a letter from Governor Wærøe (CRA, V-gK 123, 28.12.1733).

[82] They moved from 'our town', that is, Osu, to 'his', that is, Little or Dutch Accra (now known as Usshertown).

the huts close to the fort, but the Dutch lent the Negroes half a score of rifles, and when all the houses and huts were shot to pieces, the Blacks lay down between the fallen clay walls and the roofs and killed a few more [Danes]. /**148**/ If any of our staff went outside the fort our own Negroes took him prisoner and carried him to the Dutch commander, who pretended to be angry with the Negroes. But since the seizure involved a Christian man (as he said), he would buy him. He paid the Negroes two *rixdaler* apiece for five or six of those whom our Negroes had seized in that manner, set them free, and sent them back.

On one occasion they took prisoner the chief merchant at Christiansborg. The Dutchman wanted to thoroughly humiliate him. He gave orders that the Blacks should remove all his clothes until he was naked, bind his hands behind his back, put a sack over his head, and take him, in that condition, to the Dutch fort. The Dutch commander stood at the gate and received him, and then followed the Danish merchant through the courtyard of the fort where the garrison was drawn up and presented arms to the naked Dane. After that, I believe the least honourable Dane, [acting] in place of our [weak] Governor, would have shot in the head the first Dutchman he encountered, no matter where. He would have hired Black nations to defend him and risked life and blood to take revenge /**149**/ for such a national insult, which only a Dutchman without a conscience could perpetrate.[83] The English factor at Accra remained neutral.[84]

Our Governor wrote to the Directors frequently and complained about the Dutch in general in vulgar terms of abuse, but reported no facts. The Directors answered the Governor ironically and mocked him with each letter. I think both actions were wrong. All the [Governor's] reports, together with the responses from the Directors, are in the archives at Christiansborg.[85] I recall that one of the numbered points in a report of the Governor said, 'I and my people, as well as the entire garrison, are in the process of starving to death. Therefore I have gone in the Company's ship to the Upper Coast, etc.' The response to this was that the Directors had previously received reports from the Guinea Coast that people had starved to death there; that he and his people, together with the garrison, were worth no more than his [and their] predecessors, and that he (the Governor) should have stayed in his place and accepted his fate, and not run away out of fear, etc. A real

---

[83] Given the tropical climate and the nakedness of some of the Africans, the extreme reluctance of Europeans to be seen naked (as here and in a later episode) was probably due less to innate modesty — even in front of women — than to the belief that clothes, and indeed an excessive number of heavy garments, were a hallmark of European prestige and cultural difference, and hence that to be seen naked was humiliating (p.c. P.E.H. Hair).

[84] The factor was following express orders from the Royal African Company headquarters at Cape Coast (Fynn (1971) 66).

[85] The English letters and reports are now in the Royal Archives in Copenhagen (e.g., CRA, V-gK 122, 16.5.1730, 30.8.1730, 24.12.1730; 123, 28.12.1733).

comfort [this letter]! It is known that the Dutch general and his council were sent weekly reports from Accra [including reports about the Danes], and such /150/ stories were most welcome for passing the time over a glass of wine, providing material for hilarity.[86]

For an entire year our Governor spent his time making wax images, especially a portrait of himself formed in relief in wax, clad in his wig and clothing and with a stick in his hand. He held this over the parapet on the batteries of the fort, and immediately fifty muskets were fired at the image by the Negroes. He had [beforehand] had a cannon loaded with grapeshot or small stones, and [now] fired it towards the places where the gunfire had come from.[87] With such childish activities he amused himself, until King Aqvando of the Aqvamboe offered to be a mediator [between the Danes and the Dutch]. Although the king took bribes from both sides, no compromise between us and the Dutch was achieved. The Governor had the priest at our fort write a letter in Latin, in humble terms, to the general and council at Elmina, but they sent it back and asked to have it translated before we could expect an answer.

Finally our Governor began to point out to Aqvando that he ought to protect us; that being our reason for paying tax. The Governor pointed out to him what a /151/ catch he could make in the Dutch town which was full of black people; that the Dutch fort was replete with trade-goods; and that the Dutch fort could not accommodate as many as a quarter of all those people, and much less protect them. Thus, three-quarters of the people would immediately fall into his hands. The governor also informed him that our fort contained gunpowder and muskets and other lovely goods, with ships [standing by] in the road, etc. Then, [in response], and for a very small sum which we paid him, the Aqvamboe king promised that he would attack the Dutch Negroes, besiege the fort, and so on. He retired to his land to prepare himself, but he stayed overlong and the wait became too protracted for us. Our Governor then went up to meet him in his town, under an escort of 1,000 armed Aqvamboes. [Seeing this], the Dutch commander and the Dutch Blacks were able to draw their own conclusions about our intentions and those of the Aqvamboes. The Dutch commander [promptly] made ready for a siege.[88] From Elmina he received garrisons thrice the size of his own, with proper gunners,[89] provisions, ammunition,

---

[86] The Dutch Directors General during Wærøe's term of office were Robert Norre (1727–1730), Jan Pranger (1730–1734), and Anthony van Overbeke (1734–1738) (Harvey M. Feinberg, *Africans and Europeans in West Africa* (1989), 163).

[87] This is, of course, a sensible military strategy — to draw enemy fire without damage to one's self while locating the source of that fire.

[88] The relevant reports from De la Planque are in A. van Dantzig, *The Dutch and the Guinea Coast, 1674–1742* (1978) 229–30.

[89] R.'s term here is *rette Constable*, which implies that the original gunners at Crevecoeur were inexperienced, inexpert, or inept.

etc. The Dutch Blacks sent all the people for whom there was no room in the fort to the Lower Coast or to Crepe, to await the outcome of the war. To a Dutch caboceer they sent costly presents and several resolute young Negroes to find out if it was possible /**152**/ to reach Akim on secret routes through the bush, in order to persuade the Akims to attack the Aqvamboes while they were besieging the Dutch fort.

A month later the Aqvamboe king arrived in Accra with his army and did in fact begin a siege. The English commander at Accra, wishing to be a mediator in this conflict, wrote to our Governor several times, but in vain. The siege occurred near the beginning of the year 1733, and lasted for four months.[90] Many Dutch Negroes starved to death, but only a few on each side were killed by gunshots.

[Aqvamboe conquered by the Akim]

The Dutch caboceer who had been sent to Akim reached there only after having made a journey lasting two months. He found the Akims willing to comply with the Dutch request, but they were afraid that the Assiantes, a more powerful nation north of them, would invade their land and take their wives and children prisoners — just as they (the Akims) intended to do with the Aqvamboes. It was scarcely thirty years since the Akims had fought a war with the Assiantes, [a war] in which they had been unfortunate and had had to wander for two years outside their own land.[91] Therefore the Akims resolved /**153**/ to send a message to the Assiante king promising him 500 slaves if he would assure them that he would not invade their land while they were warring with the Aqvamboes, a nation which for many years had been tributary to them but had, for a few years, refused to pay tribute any longer. The Assiante King Oppoccu answered that, for 500 slaves, he would give them five months' permission to fight the Aqvamboes, but when the five months were over they had to be in their land again, whether they had achieved their purpose with the Aqvamboes or not. Either way they had to give him the 500 slaves, even if they had not captured any from among the Aqvamboes. The Akims accepted this proposal. Oppoccu (the king of the Assiantes) believed that it was impossible for the total [forces of] Akim to destroy so powerful and impressive a nation as the Aqvamboes, and he thought that the Akims would come back with their business unfinished and still pay him the 500 slaves. He did not know that Aqvando was a scoundrel and was secretly hated in the hearts of his people because he was the greatest thief among them;

---

[90] The date is wrong. A somewhat different report, with the siege dated as from 14 February 1730 to 21 or 22 March 1730, is given in Wilks (1958) 100–2. R.'s material reappears in Reindorf (1895/1966) 79/76–78. The 1730 episode is noted in Fynn (1971) 70–71; Quaye (1972) 185–88; Kwamena-Poh (1973) 46 note 3; Van Dantzig (1980a) 246. The Danish Governor at that time was Wærøe.

[91] R. has described this in /123/–/124/ above.

that no clan or family in Aqvamboe [existed] from whom he had not stolen [individuals].[92] /**154**/

As soon as Aqvando heard that the Akims intended to go to war against him, and that Oppoccu had given them permission, he lifted the siege of the Dutch fort and returned to his country in order to prepare himself [for a war], as he did. The frenzied Aqvando refused to wait until his enemies came to him, as his Big Men advised him to do, but went out to meet them in territory that was unfamiliar to the Aqvamboes. In the first battle, and in a single day, the Akims overwhelmed the Aqvamboes and took many thousand prisoners — and the heads of Aqvando and all the Big Men. The wives and children of the Aqvamboes ran away from their country, trying to save themselves by flight. They had made no prior agreement with each other about where to hide should the battle go against them. So they fled, each in a different direction, since no one had imagined that the Akims would make such a speedy end to the Aqvamboes. The Adampes, the Mountain Negroes, and the Accras seized as many [captives] as they themselves cared to, and since it was the rainy season, many thousands of the Aqvamboes came out of the forest of their own accord and surrendered to the Accras. You can well imagine what they did with them, as long as they could get a *pott* [liquid measure] of brandy for an Aqvamboe.[93] /**155**/

We anticipated that no good could come [to us] of such an outcome, and we had reason.[94] The Accras recalled those [men] whom they had sent away, and they threatened us with a siege. The Akims later sent two messengers to inform us of the war and of their enmity. It was truly the most extreme situation for us. We had the fort full of slaves, but neither provisions nor ammunition. But note in what a remarkable manner we were saved!

When I think about it, how the honourable Putti and the other old Negroes tell this story still strikes me as amusing. All being ready and the Akims having all agreed to destroy us Danes on the Guinea Coast, our messenger, whom the Governor had sent up to the Akims with gifts, was taken prisoner, [with the intention that] as soon as they had come close enough to the shore to be able to see the ocean and the European forts he was to be beheaded as a

---

[92] For a report on the hatred the Akwamu harboured for Ansa Kwao/Aquando, see Wilks (1958) 104; Fynn (1971) 69. The breakdown of law and order is stressed in Kwamena-Poh (1973) 27–8.

[93] Discussing this war, in which Akyem and their allies routed Akwamu, Reindorf merely paraphrased R. (Reindorf (1895/1966) 79–82/76–8); and recent accounts of the war employ R. in varying degrees (Wilks (1958) 107–10; Nørregård (1966) 79–80; Fynn (1971) 69–70; Quaye (1972) 202–5; Kwamena-Poh (1973) 30–8; Van Dantzig (1980a) 245–7). For archival materials relating to this period, see O. Justesen, 'Aspects of eighteenth century Ghanaian history', *Ghana Notes and Queries* 12 (1972) 10–11.

[94] Because they had supported the Akwamu, the Danes' position was precarious. Governor Wærøe described the situation in letters sent to Copenhagen on 30.3.1732, 19.2.1733, and 28.12.1733 (CRA, V-gK 123, Generalbrev). The state of affairs is noted in Nørregård (1966) 76–80; Quaye (1972) 211–3; Kwamena-Poh (1973) 33. The 'we' used by R. is rhetorical, because he himself was not on the Coast in 1730.

sacrifice to the sea god. But lo! just in time [the fetish] Giemawong arrived, most conveniently—I really do not know if Putti had arranged for him to arrive—and [the oracle] made this pronouncement, that the Danish Whites were God's dearest children, in preference to the other Whites, and if anyone murdered them God would take even more blessings away from the country and the sea, etc. The same pronouncement was /156/ made by the fetish in the enemy (Dutch) town. Putti and all the Labodes promptly came to our fort, which was [now] considered impregnable. The Accras were aghast. They had endured so many miseries, and now the fetish was going to send them more misfortune. They did not think they could bear it. The Akims heard this, and being altogether too superstitious to do anything against the orders of a fetish, they released our messenger and declared themselves our friends, etc.[95] A decision of our Governor at that time helped, [a decision] which cannot be repeated here since it would be insulting to his descendants, but we know that Putti suggested it to him.[96] However, the Akims seized some forty Blacks who had remained too long in Labode before coming into our Fort where Putti and the others were.

I have often teased Putti when he has boasted about what a great service he and his fetish had done us Danes, and asked him if it was a counterfeit Giemawong who had arrived at that time, and if the Dutch fetish priest had not been ordered by him to have his fetish repeat that oracle? He insisted that it was not so, but thought, rather, that Giemawong /157/ had taken the trouble largely for his (Putti's) sake. Be that as it may, the Labode fetish saved our lives that day. The Danes had not all been killed, which in all probability would have happened if Putti or his fetish had cared less for us. That good fetish has served the Danes both before and after this happened, and can, perhaps, still be of service to us. A reasonable man who understands how to govern at Christiansborg will not deny the fetish a bottle of brandy at times.

In 1748 a disagreement arose between our Negroes and those of the Dutch. The Labode fetish stated that the Dutch Negroes were in the wrong. Skirmishes finally resulted, since our enemies did not concern themselves about the threats of the fetish. But the Dutch fetish ran straight [to Labode], taking her chair, her mat (bed), and a brandy bottle with her, if I remember correctly, and these furnishings were found in the sacred place at Labode. The Dutch female fetish had [thus] retired to her husband at Labode. And so ended this war, since a Negro does not willingly place

---

[95] Recent historians suggest that another explanation of the cessation of hostilities between the Gã (Accra) and the Danes was the intervention of the Dutch Governor, Pranger, who travelled to Accra in order to mediate (Quaye (1972) 211–13; Van Dantzig (1980a) 249).For comment on the priest's supposed intervention, see Reindorf (1895/1966) 82/78.

[96] I have been unable to find any other reference to this mysterious decision. Since it was on the suggestion of Putti, the chief priest, it presumably involved some form of behaviour intended to express gratitude to the fetish.

himself in danger without the fetish promising him that he will come out of it successfully. /**158**/

[Accra under Akim]

We now had the Akims as defenders of Accra and all that belonged to it, just as the Aqvamboes had been before. Of the Aqvamboes there were scarcely 500 families left, and they can still [today] muster barely 1,000 men with muskets. But what they considered to be their greatest misfortune was that no heirs to the throne survived, other than a child who was the son of the noble woman whom Acondo had given to the Dutch caboceer Dacon. All the others had been killed or taken prisoner. This small number of Aqvamboes fled to Crepe and stayed there. They had to take Acondo's son by a slave woman, who was the eldest man among them, and install him as leader. His name was Acondo Chuma (Little Acondo), and he was to be their leader until they could recover one of the true heirs to the throne, or until the young Dacon became a grown man.[97]

The three kings who ruled at that time in Akim were called Bang, Frempung and Ursue.[98] Bang was given the Dutch and English forts to rule; Frempung was Christiansborg's protector; and Ursue was given Adampi and the Mountain Negroes to rule, and then Fredensborg, which was built in his time.[99] All Ursue's hair, cut from him on a Bon Die (a Good Day [*sc.* an auspicious day]), /**159**/ together with eight ounces of gold, was sent [to Fredensborg] and laid under the first stone. This cost us something when the Assiantes became our masters in the year 1742, since they demanded that we should tear down the fort in order to retrieve for them their enemy's hair, which should not be lying in such a prominent place.[100]

The Aqvamboes, the Accras, and all the nations known to us, were surly and malicious. In the course of twenty years an old Negro might never have laughed or shown a kind visage, and the muscles in their faces had become so accustomed to this fierce [expression] that during their conversations they closely resembled a couple of wild animals or wolves baring their teeth at one another. The Akims, on the other hand, were mild, friendly, and honest, as far as one can say this about a black heathen.

The Akims had completed their affairs in less time than the five months that the Assiantes had allowed them. They now returned to their land and

---

[97] On the issues of succession, see Wilks (1959) 394, 397–8. Dacon (for whom see Chapter 3, note 92, above) is termed Dako Panyin in Reindorf (1895/1966) 84–5/80.

[98] According to Reindorf and later writers, the 'three kings' were Frempung Manso of Kotoko, Owusu ('Ursue') Akyem, and Ba Kwante ('Bang') of Abuakwa (Reindorf (1895/1966) 82–5/78–81; Fynn (1971) 74; Kwamena-Poh (1973) 36 37, 76–8; Atkinson (1980) 357–9, 363).

[99] Fort Fredensborg was built in 1736 (Nørregård (1966) 96–7; Van Dantzig (1980b) xii, 55, with an illustration of the fort). R. included an engraving of this fort (reproduced in this edition as Plate 4).

[100] The 1742 conquest by Asante is described in /173/ ff below.

paid Oppoccu his 500 slaves. They had profited greatly and increased in number, wholly because of the many prisoners they had taken from the Aqvamboes. All the other African nations had [always] sold their catch, and (according to the Negroes' way of speaking) had eaten them, but these Akims were wiser. They kept the slaves in their land and /**160**/ married their native slaves to these strangers. They treated them so kindly that the Aqvamboes quickly forgot their fatherland and king, and became, in the space of five years, as good as native-born Akims.[101] As a result, this nation was especially welcomed by all the Europeans at Accra and on the entire Coast. They knew it was now the only nation on the Coast which owned gold mines, or, it may be said, understood how to dig for gold — albeit in an inadequate manner (as will be shown later) — because the [goldmining] nation called Dinkero [Denkyira] had been destroyed by the Assiantes eighty years earlier.[102]

The Europeans now thought they had access to the source of all the gold which, hitherto, they had only seen at third or fourth hand, but from now on would come directly from Akim into their pockets.[103] They were not mistaken in this [assumption]. But they had to do with a thrifty and humble people who did not consume a hundredth part of their annual income, and did not bring it to the ale-house keepers at the coast (whom one might call the real chiefs of all the nations on the entire Gold Coast, if not worse). When the Europeans received the Akim gold directly from Akim and sent it /**161**/ to Europe, it had a weight of 22–23 carats, whereas the gold supplied earlier only weighed 17–18 carats, presumably because of what was added to the gold by those through whose hands it was traded.

At that time, everything was decided between the Akims and us through our emissary, the decision being that we Danes would belong to Frempung, and that he would be paid our monthly tribute of 21 *rixdaler*. In return, Frempung would procure trade for us. But he wanted to see one of his Whites (a Dane) before he returned to his land. He had heard earlier that all the Europeans were fearful sea animals, but our emissary had assured him that the Whites were formed just like the Blacks. In order to see if

---

[101] On the claimed integration of captives into Akan society, see Kwamena-Poh (1973) 48. For other forms of integration, especially among the Asante, see Wilks (1975) 80–2; McCaskie (1995) 95–101. R.'s reference may throw light on the history of those parts of Akyem-Abuakwa (especially the Asamankese region) that still consider themselves Akwamu in origin (p.c. I. Wilks).

[102] Before its destruction by Asante in 1701, Denkyira was reputed to be the leading producer of gold (Bosman (1705) 72–4; Daaku (1970) 158–9). Gold mining methods are described at /177/–/180/ below.

[103] Routes by which gold reached the coast were noted in Villault (1669) 387–9 (cf. Dickson (1969) 89). For trade via Abonse, the famous market town in Akwapim, see T.F. Garrard, *Akan Weights and the Gold Trade* (1980) 58.

that was true, he asked our foremost emissary, Jancon (the fort's drummer), to return home with a request that one of the most prominent Danes should come to visit him in his own country, about forty miles from the coast. This was done, and our bookkeeper, Niels Kamp, went up-country to visit him.

This audience was particularly amusing and worth recording. In the morning, while he was among a couple of hundred of his wives, King Frempung was given the report that the prominent Dane had arrived. He requested /**162**/ that Mr. Kamp come to him immediately. Frempung was sitting, as do all the Negroes, on a low stool a span high. When our bookkeeper realized that it was the king who was sitting there, he greeted him in the European manner. He took his hat off, bowed very deeply and scraped his foot [along the ground behind him]. Frempung, never having seen such compliments before, thought Kamp was only bowing in order to spring at his head, like any wild monkey, and he hastily threw himself flat on the ground so that Kamp would spring over him and not injure him, and he called on his wives for help. The wives came and formed a circle around their king. Our emissary, Jancon, by shouting and calling to the king, assured him that his White had no evil intentions but that this was the Whites' expression of honour. Frempung, scarcely believing this, called to Jancon to tell his White to stop acting in that way, but he assured him of his friendship. Instructing Kamp to remain where he was, Frempung ordered a score of his wives to stand between himself and Kamp. He perused Kamp's upper torso, and at times his wives had to step aside so that he could also see Kamp's lower torso. Thinking that Kamp's clothes, or most of them, were parts of his body, Frempung /**163**/ called Jancon to him and reproached him for having given him an incorrect description of the Whites. Particularly did Kamp's pig-tailed wig strike him as suspicious. He thought that the pigtail was the Whiteman's tail, and that while the tails of other animals were in other places, the Whites had them on their necks. Our Jancon did his level best to explain to Frempung that it was cloth the White had drawn over his body and that it was by no means [a hide] grown on the body, while the tail he saw on the neck of the White was only an imitation.

This lasted for a good two hours since Frempung also wanted to see if the White was able to eat. He had food brought in and this suited Kamp nicely. [Next,] Frempung gradually approached Kamp, and finally he asked our messenger to persuade his master to take his clothes off and let himself be seen naked. Jancon did his best to persuade Kamp to submit to the king in this, but Kamp said he would not do it unless Frempung would go aside with him, alone, so that none of the women could see him. Frempung could not fathom why the White did /**164**/ not want to be seen by his wives, but he agreed to this, after having asked several old men for advice. Our bookkeeper undressed himself and Frempung came very close to him, touched his limbs, and burst out in wonder with these words: 'You really are a human, but as white as the devil!' Frempung gave Kamp two slaves and several ounces of gold as a gift, and the following day the king granted our bookkeeper a fine farewell audience.[104]

When they came to the coast to trade the Akims usually numbered 1,000–2,000 at a time. They brought mostly gold and very few slaves, and most of the goods they bought consisted of gunpowder, muskets, shot, and flints. When they arrived at the fort they sent the most prominent among them inside to haggle over the goods, a process which might last three days. When the terms of purchase were agreed upon, this was made known among them, and they purchased. This was very different from the way things were done with the Aqvamboes.[105]

Our Danish muskets had particular appeal for the Akims, and they paid us 32 *rixdaler*, or two ounces of gold for seven muskets, when for the same price they could get ten from the Dutch and twelve from the English. /**165**/ Our musket barrels [however] were all provided with double loading and did not explode. In contrast, nearly half of the Dutch and English muskets exploded to pieces, the buyer thus suffering injury not only in respect of [the loss of] his musket, but in respect that the shooter of the musket was usually injured in addition, sometimes losing his hand.[106]

The ordinary Akims did not drink brandy except when it was served to them. The most prominent among them did indeed buy it, but [they bought] not a hundredth part of what the Aqvamboes purchased. The greatest brandy drinker among them was Bang [when accompanied by] about one hundred followers, or his Big Men. He willingly paid us money each week for a score of ankers of Flensborg corn-brandy, having developed such a taste for it that he could tell if it was Flensborg or not. We often tested him by sending him Dantzig Aqvavit, etc., or French brandy, but he told us it made him ill, and we had always to have enough of our Flensborg brandy for him among our supplies. A governor at our fort was once annoyed by the complaints Bang was giving him when he did not have the right sort, and the governor said to the Akim emissary that his King /**166**/ was a proper

---

[104] Reindorf repeats this entire story, but identifies the locus as Dà, the capital of the Kotokos, and those accompanying Kamp as Adam Malm, the drummer, and Noi Afadi, the government interpreter (Reindorf 1895/1966, 82–3/78–9). Reindorf does not state his additional sources, but probably they were archive documents, since a traced archive source mentions Noi as at one time an emissary to the Dutch (CRA, V-gK 122, Generalbrev, 16.5.1730).

[105] R. is referring to what he described earlier (/125/ above), the Akwamu stopping the Akyem from going to the coast to trade.

[106] However, twenty to thirty years later, another observer wrote of Danish guns exploding in the hands (Isert [1788] (1992) 66). In later centuries, the term 'Dane gun' was used in West Africa to describe a very cheap and simple gun which was also dangerous to use. On faulty firearms in general, see R.A. Kea, 'Firearms and warfare', *Journal of African History* 12 (1971) 203–5 (and cf. note 184 below).

drunken K...e.[107] Our interpreter stupidly translated this for the emissary. [As a result], Bang threatened to declare war on us, but he let himself be placated with a score of ankers of the right sort. When Bang and his good friends drank brandy, corn-brandy was the best sort for him since Bang would nightly have an entire anker with the bottom knocked out set on end in front of himself and his friends, and smaller containers having been laid out, each man could serve himself. If the gathering was large, or if it became very lively, three to four ankers were easily drunk up in this way. To reach Accra, those Akims had to walk for thirty days, from which I conclude that their land was about 200 miles from the coast.[108]

[Akim and Asante]

The Assiantes were very jealous of the good fortune of their neighbours, the Akims, who were increasing rapidly in number. Because of the populations over which these three kings ruled, they could muster 200,000 men in arms. They seldom sold slaves unless they were men who had taken liberties with Bang's wives. Yet it was rarely that such men were brought to the coast, since their friends usually bought them back from the merchant to whom their king had sold them. /**167**/ [Otherwise, a slave] might be someone who had committed robbery or another crime several times. On the other hand, the Akims themselves bought slaves for gold, thus increasing the size of their families.[109] The Assiantes, watching with unease the growth of the Akims, began to arm themselves. They had opened a route from their land to Elmina, Cape Coast, and the forts which lay west of Elmina,[110] and, in the course of six to eight years, they bought a tremendous quantity of muskets and gunpowder.

Oppoccu, the Assiante king, termed Bang, the greatest king in Akim, his slave. The reason was that, during the time of Bang's predecessor, and in the war last fought between the Assiantes and the Akims, during which Oppoccu's predecessor had been shot, Bang, as a very young man, had been captured by the Assiantes. Oppoccu had released him for a very good

---

[107] The incomplete word 'Ke' probably stands for *kanalje* 'rascal', from French *canaille* 'rabble, scum'.

[108] The distance, 200 Danish miles or 1,500 km (one eighteenth-century Danish mile = 7.5 km), would put Akyem near River Niger and is therefore a gross exaggeration, the true distance being about 95 km (58 English miles). R.'s estimate of an average day's journey as one of about 50 km (30 miles) was almost certainly also an exaggeration. Even if the journey actually took as long as thirty days, the route may not have been direct and no doubt the length of a day's march varied according to the conditions and was sometimes reduced to a few miles.

[109] On keeping slaves to increase the size of the family unit, see Kwamena-Poh (1973) 48; J.M. Postma, *The Dutch in the Atlantic Slave trade* (1990) 6.

[110] For the nineteenth-century routes that Wilks has identified and labelled Great Roads V, VI, VII, and VIII, linking Kumase, the capital of Ashanti with the coast, see Wilks (1975) 11, 24–5, 191.

price, namely for 1,000 ounces of gold, since Oppoccu had noticed that there was nothing outstanding about him.[111]

Frempung, whose land was closest to Assiante, was by that time a weak old man. He had once presented Oppoccu with a young tame elephant, and Oppoccu had received this gift very well, swearing that as long as Frempung was alive he would not attack the Akims. /168/ Frempung ruled his subjects quite mildly and he was much beloved. As [was the custom among] the other Akim kings, he, too, had a thousand wives spread around in the land, but during the preceding twenty years he had never forced them to reveal their secrets. He, too, travelled around the land every year, but it was only in order to acknowledge the children these wives had borne him in the meantime, and to count them as his own, since each of his wives had to give him a millie grain for each child she had, and in this way he made his overall account of his children.[112]

The land of Ursue lay closest to the coast, immediately behind Fredensborg [? and extending] twenty days' journey up-country. He was heir to Bang's throne, and it was to the detriment of that finest nation on the Coast that the wanton Bang did not drink himself to death before the Assiantes went to war against Akim. Ursue would then have been the greatest king in Akim, and master over two-thirds of the entire Akim dominion. Everyone was certain that he would have been able to withstand the Assiantes. He was more than a little hard on his slaves during the first two years [of his reign], at times cutting their throats for only a slight reason. One of his slaves had stolen a hen from a free Negro, so Ursue cut his jawbone from his face while he was still alive, and /169/ forced him to stand in the market place until he died. Every year he sent one of his generals to Crepe with 2,000–3,000 men to catch slaves, and at times he joined them himself. He sold only a few of them and distributed [the rest] throughout his land. Certainly, if that hero, Ursue, had been master of that two-thirds of Akim, the Assiantes would not have dared to attack the Akims. Oppoccu admitted as much himself in a speech he made over the dead Ursue, a speech which might be called a funeral oration and which I shall describe later.[113]

Ursue wearied of tyranny in a few years and after he was told how the Europeans punished their thieves, etc., he followed their example. He no

---

[111] For this war, in 1717, in which Opoku Ware's predecessor, Osei Tutu, by tradition the first Asantehene, was killed, see Reindorf (1895/1966) 83–4/79–80; W.E.F. Ward, *A History of Ghana* (1969) 123; Daaku (1970) 176; Kwamena-Poh (1973) 36; Wilks (1993) 253–4.

[112] For Frempung and (next paragraph) Ursue, see note 98 above. Frampung's was not an entirely unusual marital and paternity situation, since in many African marriage systems a man 'buys' the womb of a wife and its usufruct, and can legally claim as his the children of the womb by whomever begotten. This naturally applies particularly to old (and/or impotent) men with multiple wives (p.c. P.E.H. Hair).

[113] The funeral oration is given in /187/–/188/ below.

longer sent his people out to catch slaves, but sent them [instead] with gold to buy them in Crepe. Since the Akims carried on their trade in that way, we Europeans at Accra could, up to a point, be called 'traders', and with quite a clear conscience could carry out our commission, whereas in earlier times we could be called 'fences', and accomplices to murder and robbery. /170/

Little by little the Akims became displeased with the Dutch who were selling quantities of powder and muskets to the Assiantes, their enemies.[114] We Danes then became their favourite European nation. They bought no goods from the other nations as long as they could get them from us, even buying English and Dutch goods, whenever we had them. Our Company could have sold a cargo worth 25,000–30,000 *rixdaler* every month, but at that time it had only one ship — which had to sail the great triangle between Africa, America, and Europe before returning to us with goods. I and several others know that our Governor loaded 2,000–3,000 *rixdaler* worth of gold in one day (that is to say, for as long as the Company had goods) and he kept the books in the following way. A cargo load which he had sold during a period of two months or less was entered in the commercial journal as an entire year's trade, since he knew that we would receive no ship before that [length of] time was out, because the Directors had none.[115]

The Akim nation had a very good opinion of us, and we Danes no less of them, although all the [European] nations wished the Akims well. Indeed, there were none among the Europeans who were at all acquainted with the character of the land who were not intensely /171/ saddened over the news that they were now ruined, and only a few among us Danes received the message without tears in our eyes.

For many years Ursue did not practice that ugly, abominable, habit of marrying women and letting them go their way in order to seduce young men. He had only 400–500 wives and he kept them in a building similar to the Turks' seraglio as described — surrounded by high walls and full of guards at night.

The crafty Dutch on the Coast wanted to cut us out by telling the Akims many things not to our credit. They especially claimed that there was a fetish on our muskets, and those who used them against their enemies were bound to lose. You can well imagine we did not spare the Hollanders' name and reputation. We cannot say that the English have at any time attacked us in such a low and sly manner. However, the Danes and the Dutch were good

---

[114] As often, the European traders found themselves caught up in African rivalries (Van Dantzig (1980a) 144, 176 ff, 248ff; Sandra Green, 'The Anlo-Ewe: their economy, society and external relations in the eighteenth-century', PhD thesis, Northwestern University, 1981, 136). The Dutch factor at Crevecoeur, Van Kuyl, sent requests to Elmina to provide arms for the Akyem (Van Dantzig (1978) 354, doc. 422).

[115] During the second quarter of the eighteenth century, goods were being sold in great quantities to both Dutch interlopers and French ships (Nørregård (1966) 86–7, 90). The Governor in question may have been Anders Petersen Wærøe (1728–1735).

friends among themselves, although you can also well imagine that they came to know what we said about them, just as we came to know what they said about us.[116] Furthermore, it was quite advisable for the Dutch to be our friends at that time, because the Akims often offered to do whatever we wanted them to do, against whomever that might be. In /172/ a little war we had with the Dutch, lasting twelve to eighteen months, their fate at Accra really was in our hands, as long as the Akims were in power. But [their help] was not necessary at that time because our good friend, the fetish at Labode, was able to keep the Dutch in check.[117] This is the way matters stood at Accra from 1733 to 1742.

It is our own fault that we Danes did not profit by the opportunity to trade. During those years we could have made such great profits that [for the next] fifty years we could have covered losses. We did not have to buy our goods on credit then, as we have had to do since. During that period a factor did not have to keep thirty to forty servants up-country in order to be on the lookout for trade to be brought to the fort; or have to buy slaves thirty to forty miles up in the land when he did not wish to rely on his Blacks. During that time we could most certainly have stored our goods in the fort's magazines, keeping them there until a Bon Die, and then they would assuredly have been sold. The Akims did not betray one another, as the Aqvamboes did. An Accra had permission from us to steal only two *rixdaler* per slave, deserving as he was to make some profit /173/ since he was acting as a broker. For gold the Accras received nothing.[118]

We now come to the point in time (*periodus*) when that beautiful, friendly and honest nation was ruined. I must admit that I still cannot write about that matter without being moved. Yet, as a comfort to myself, and perhaps others, I must report we heard that, seven years later, in 1749, when they had been beaten at the coast, Ursue's successor (Pobbi) took a census of his men and found he himself could muster 40,000 men in arms. Now, if you consider that the other two kings had each the same number, Akim is still one of the most prestigious nations in Africa, although, as is their custom, they count [as fighting] men [all individuals] between the ages of 16–60.[119]

---

[116] It would have been unnatural if the handful of Europeans living and working in the same region, although commercial rivals, had had no social intercourse. Furthermore, many of the staff serving the Danish company were actually Dutch (Van Dantzig (1978) 239). The Europeans also did one another favours by storing goods for each other (CRA, V-gK, 10.3.1739).

[117] The reference is to the Danes having been saved by a pronouncement of the Labadi fetish, /156/–/157/ above.

[118] This odd remark may mean that the Gã did not function as middlemen in the gold trade, but that the gold was purchased directly from the inland merchants who brought it to the coast.

[119] For Pobi, the *Okyenhene* (chief of Akyem Abuakwa) (1742–1765), see Fynn (1971) 75; and for continuity in the Akyem government, Kwamena-Poh (1973) 74, 78, 79.

[Gold mines]

First, however, we must say something about their gold mines and how they find gold in the earth. A Dutch author by the name of Bosman, who wrote most dependably about the Guinea Coast in 1686, states that the Blacks find it in three ways. The first is by taking ordinary soil or sand, washing it in water or the sea, and finding gold on the bottom after all the earth and impurities are rinsed away. The second way is carried out /**174**/ after the rainy season, when all the rivers and brooks flood, running over their banks because of the tremendous amounts of water which fall during the travados. At that time the Blacks search at the foot of the mountains and in the ravines which the water has cut into the earth, and as the gold is heavy it remains lying there. [The last way] is when they dig holes in the ground and find it there.

But the good Bosman has never seen any of the nations who dig for gold.[120] As far as we know, only two nations on the entire Coast dig for gold, or, more correctly, have dug for gold. Beyond a doubt gold is mined in all the countries on the Guinea Coast, just as it is in Akim, and if European mining experts and workers were to come here they might find [another] Peru and [another] Mexico in a few mountains in Africa not far from the seacoast.[121]

It is true, as Bosman writes, that the Blacks sometimes find small lumps of gold of one *lod*, more or less, in the gutters the rain has formed in the earth.[122] But if more gold was not found by the Blacks than what they find in this way, or than what /**175**/ is washed out by the old crones at the seashore, there would be little or nothing for the Europeans on the Coast to acquire. The gold washing at the seashore is normally done by female slaves who were born in Akim, and I have seen many such. They do not take all types of soil or sand but collect the sweepings which are thrown away at the fort, where we have the habit of strewing sand in our rooms. That gold would have been spilled [to any extent] is not to be expected, since each person takes great care [in handling gold]. Moreover, at times we have not weighed gold in the fort for an entire month, but our rooms are swept every day and strewn with sea or beach sand. Yet sometimes you can see half a score of old crones saving those sweepings, and at low tide they put three or four handfuls into a round wooden basin, they walk knee-deep into the water, and they flush some sea water around in the container,

---

[120] What Bosman actually said was that the Africans kept the mines secret and the Europeans away from them (a true statement of the position since the European arrival) (Bosman (1705) 80–1; cf. Rask (1754) 82).

[121] For European attempts at mining gold in Gold Coast, all unsuccessful, see A. Van Dantzig, 'The Ankobra gold interest', *Transactions of the Historical Society of Ghana* 14 (1973) 169–85. On the various Gold Coast 'nations' which produced gold, see Bosman (1705) 72–80. For mining methods, see note 128 below.

[122] One *lod* = 15.6 grams.

always turning the container so that the water and sweepings swirl around in it. In this way the lightest sweepings are rinsed out with the water, and the gold, which is the heaviest, remains lying in the basin. It should be noted that these female slaves are not willing to let it be seen how much they get, so that they will not be forced by their husbands to do this work for them. They themselves do it only for their own sustenance.[123] /**176**/

That gold should lie loose within the sand is not possible, either, since the sand washed up by the sea, being the lighter material, would then be on top, and the gold, as the heavier material would not be on top of the beach, in the [surface] white sand which is used in sprinkling our rooms. I think, then, and a microscope has confirmed this, that the gold has stuck to the grains of sand, and the Europeans, frequently walking across [the beach] with their shoes on, have rubbed the gold loose in the contact between their shoes and the pebbles. It is this that the old crones finally obtain in their wooden basins.

A man of our nation, once out walking with a Portuguese priest, came to a point a half-mile from the coast where the land formed a rise, or bank, made of the red clay used by the Blacks for colouring. Many wild plants growing there produce the so-called red *taqver* (small red beans), twelve of these beans being normally considered equal to two *rixdaler* worth of gold or one-eighth *lod*.[124] The Portuguese priest [suddenly] stood still and crossed himself. The Dane, a young man and a Protestant, said, 'Mr. Pater! There is no sacred image here! Why are you crossing yourself?' The priest replied that he was amazed at the riches /**177**/ which were hidden in the earth [here], and wished that he owned a little piece of [such earth] in Brazil. In order to test it he took a pocketful to the fort and asked for three chemicals: mercurium, sal amoniacum and aqva regia.[125] We searched in the fort's pharmacy but could not find them. He assured [us] that all the gold in Brazil was prepared or proved from such soil, and that [the miners there] had to fetch from far down in the earth what lies on top of the earth here.

As our Accras and Akims themselves tell it, they dig holes in the ground at whatever place they wish to. They only see to it that the hole is a good distance away from their roads and not too near the paths to prevent their children and animals falling into the holes. At half a man's depth a landing is constructed, so that they can hand to each other the basin or container holding the soil

---

[123] Other contemporary sources noted women panning for gold (Dapper (1676) 94; Bosman (1705) 80–1; Rask (1754) 83; Isert [1788] (1992) 143). For modern comment, see Birgitte Menzel, *Goldgewichte aus Ghana* (1968) 16–7; Garrard (1980) 129–31, 135.

[124] In the early eighteenth century, one *taqver* (Akan *taku*) bean counted as the equivalent of 80 cowries (Rask (1754) 85). For the Gold Coast cowrie currency in general, see Barbot (1732) (1992) 548, 555 note 14; Bosman (1705) 86; Isert [1788] (1992) 85, note 16; M. Johnson, 'The cowrie currencies of West Africa', *Journal of African History* 11 (1970) 347–8; Garrard (1980) 173–4; Robin Law, *The Slave Coast of West Africa 1550–1750* (1991) 49–50).

[125] R. appears to be mistaken here, since *aqua regia* is a mixture of nitric and hydrochloric acids and this liquifies gold. To assay gold, *aqua fortis*, that is, nitric acid alone, was used (Bosman (1705) 84; Isert [1788] (1992) 87; Garrard (1980) 87.

taken from down in the ground. While the Europeans [in their mines] make entire streets underground and support them (as I seem to have heard or read), and use winches with which to hoist their ore up, etc., the Akims only make a hole which goes at a slant into the ground, and looks like a stairway, each step being one and one-half *alen* high.[126] If it is not rich, the earth taken out of the hole in the first six to ten *alen* is thrown away, and they dig at another /178/ place. At intervals they carry a full basin [of earth] to the water and prove it. If they do not find rich earth when they have dug more than ten *alen* down — that is, at the height of four men or eight steps — then at that place their labour has been in vain and they go and dig in the same way in another place. Yet they seldom make a mistake in finding the rich earth when they have dug from four to six *alen* underground. Normally it is so rich that each of the workers is able to deliver eight ounces of gold a day, which is the least their masters will accept. The Blacks have assured us that Frempung has had mines from which each of his people who worked in them could deliver a half-*potte* container of pure gold dust a day.[127] In such rich mines the Blacks work both deep downwards and [also] out to the sides, and it happens, not rarely, that fifty or even a hundred people are buried in them [when they collapse].[128]

As soon as one of the two rainy seasons comes, the mines become filled with water and the miners must wait until that season is over. They cannot use the same mines again since they are full of water at the bottom. Then, to prevent /179/ their being drowned in the new mine, they must dig it a good distance away from the old one. Many men are required to work a mine. If I recall correctly, the smallest number is forty men. Sometimes a mine has 50–60 steps,[129] and then more men are needed. Some must work underground to dig the earth loose with a wooden or iron pick; some must fill the basins; and there must be one on each step in order to pass the full basins farther up and the empty ones down again. This earth is then either dumped above ground close to the hole, or is carried directly to a river or stream. It is first pressed or groped through to [discover and] remove pieces of rock (and small lumps of gold) found in it. Then they do the same as our old female slaves do with their sweepings at the coast. They wash it, but with this difference, that up-country they normally collect 16–20 *rixdaler* worth of gold and more from each basin of earth, while our old crones can

---

[126] One *alen* = 62.8 cm.
[127] One *potte* = 0.97 of a litre.
[128] For mining methods, see De Marees [1602] (1987) 95a-b; Dapper (1676) 94–5; Isert [1788] (1992) 142–3; Garrard (1980) 131–5, 140–1; Wilks (1993) 77. The remains of these mines, to be seen today in the Oweri Valley around Konongo, point to workings of an impressive size (p.c. I. Wilks).
[129] Each step was therefore 94.2cm, and with R's minimum of fifty steps the total depth would be 47.1m. Mines up to 80 feet or 24m deep have been reported (Garrard (1989) 133). R. perhaps again exaggerates.

stand for three to four hours, as long as it is low (ebb) tide, and each of them might perhaps collect one or at the most two *rixdaler* worth.

The stupidity and superstition of the Akims hinder them from taking more gold out of the ground. (Yet we must also admit that if they took more than enough for themselves, perhaps we Europeans /**180**/ would say *Plus ultra* [too much]).[130] In my opinion, their ignorance consists in not building houses or sheds over the holes in their richest mines, to prevent water from running into them, etc. And their superstition harms them in the following way. When they find a nugget of gold weighing close to two ounces they have to take a chicken or hen down into the mine, kill it near the place where the nugget was lying, and, as the Akims say, placate the god of the earth with its blood. If it is a larger nugget they have to sacrifice a sheep, an ox, or (what is most abominable) a person.[131]

It is claimed as a fact that Frempung's people once found in a mine an entire rockface of gold. They reported this to the king, and asked if they should take chisels and hack off as much as was possible, since the travado season would soon be upon them. Frempung went into council with his Big Men and they decided that, since the cliff must be the mother or father of the small gold, no one should touch it, and the men should leave the mine alone and begin in another place. /**181**/

[Akim conquered by Asante]
Frempung died in the beginning of 1741 and his successor was Appau, a decent Negro, who, before he became king, normally came to our fort every other year with the trade of his mother, his brother, and himself.[132] Frempung and Bang had never seen the sea, and Ursue had seen it once only. Oppoccu, the Assiante king, sent a message to Bang telling him that his promise had been fulfilled, Frempung being now dead, and Oppoccu could wait no longer in fetching their heads, otherwise they would become too strong for him.[133] Bang, in his usual state of drunkenness, answered just as coarsely, namely that he intended, in a short time, to put the heads of Oppoccu and several [other] Assiantes on his drum. The [more] reasonable Ursue was of the opinion that they should [now] leave their land and flee to Crepe, in order to take to safety their wives and children, as their forefathers had once done, thus [also] saving themselves. If Oppoccu did not want to give them permission to continue to live in their land as a free people, the young

---

[130] Presumably R. means that over-supply of gold would reduce its rarity value and hence price, or simply that there would be too little for the Europeans.

[131] For the local belief in a spirit of the earth associated with gold, see Garrard (1980) 136–40.

[132] Frempung's death and the succession by 'his sister's son Apau' is noted in a letter from Governor Jørgensen (CRA, V-gK, Generalbrev, 2.4.1742). This was while R. was himself in Gold Coast.

[133] According to R. (/167/ above), Opoku had promised that, as long as Frempung was alive, he would not attack Akyem.

men among the Akims should become robbers and plague the Assiantes for so long that Oppoccu would make peace with them. They could summon more than 100,000 young men for this strategy, and the Assiantes' weak neighbours could not /**182**/ resist an army one-tenth that size. The Akims could then hope to weaken the Assiantes little by little by attacking one city [of the neighbours] after another, until, finally, if Oppoccu would not agree to a settlement, they would be able to attack the Assiantes themselves with their entire force.[134] So Ursue [argued], citing the example of an Assiante rebel, one Antufi, who, with 2,000 men had played the brigand for twenty years and plagued the Assiantes so much that Oppoccu had frequently offered to give him whatever he desired if he would cease stealing from his subjects.[135] Had the Akims agreed to this proposal, in all probability they would have [been able to return] to their land before two years had passed. However, Bang rejected the proposal, and overruled Ursue, saying that the latter was [unduly] frightened.

The [two nations] then resolved to meet at a halfway point where, at Oppoccu's suggestion, both parties would provide 10,000 men to cut down the bush and trees for a distance of a couple of miles, after which the battle would take place. The Akims wished to have [the support of] our Accras, Mountain Negroes, Adampis, and Ada Negroes, since they were their allies and subjects, but they did not arrive, with the exception of a Dutch /**183**/ caboceer named Dacon [who joined them] with about fifty men and several Mountain Negroes. All the Negroes thought the war would last at least two years, but it ended in six or seven months.[136]

We might have guessed beforehand that the Akims would lose, on the presumption of the overriding fear they felt for the Assiantes. The Akims often stated that their life-span would soon come to an end, and when asked why they doubted that they would grow old, they answered that the Assiantes' envy would not permit it. They themselves admitted that the very thought of coming events brought a distress so great that [for instance,] an Akim Negro who had [just] taken a young wife [simply] thought about the Assiantes and forgot to see her for eight days. Or, if one of them had a delicious dish before him and the thought of the Assiantes [crossed his

---

[134] R.'s account of this episode is repeated in Reindorf (1895/1966) 84/80 and Fynn (1971) 72, which place it in the context of growing conflict between Akyem Kotoko and Akyem Abuakwa.
[135] For purportedly wide-spread and socially significant brigandage and banditry, see R. Kea, '"I am here to plunder on the general road": bandits and banditry in the pre-nineteenth century Gold Coast', in D. Crummey, ed., *Banditry, Rebellion and Social Protest in Africa* (1986) 110–11.
[136] R.'s statement about Dacon and fifty men joining the Akyem (repeated in Fynn (1971) 74) conflicts with a Dutch report that no one from the Dutch town had gone 'except Makelaar Dakon; but he was already in Akim' (CRA, V-gK 123, 1.7.1743; BLL, Furley N44, 9.12.1741, letter from Van Kuyl, the Dutch factor at Crevecoeur, to Elmina). Reindorf, repeating R.'s material, refers, without explanation of the addition, to Chief Dācō Panyin of Otu-street in Dutch Accra (Reindorf (1895/1966) 84/80). For the relationships, both familial and political, between Dacon/Dako, his fellow Akwamu, and the Akyem, see Wilks (1959) 397–9.

mind], the food became rank and bitter in his mouth, and his appetite disappeared.[137]

At the end of 1741 the war began with skirmishes, and in early 1742 [there occurred] great battles in the field. The Assiantes were not more powerful than the Akims, but they had hired a nation which waged war with bows and arrows, and these people accomplished a great deal when travados came and the Akims could not use their guns.[138] /**184**/ In the battles the Assiantes lost just as many men as the Akims, if not more. [But], in the third great battle they fought, after receiving twenty-five fatal wounds Ursue fell. It is probable that if he had not risked his person in this way, the victory would have been indecisive. Instead of Ursue's men taking his body aside so that his head would not fall into the hands of the enemy, the Akims themselves killed all the old and Big Men, and lay down at Ursue's feet. Then they killed themselves by holding their own muskets to their throats and firing with their toes, so that the entire shot went through their heads. They killed not only the old men of Ursue's land but even those of the lands of Frempung and Bang. When the Assiantes saw this, they rushed in and seized Ursue's body, as well as close to 4,000 other dead bodies. After this Frempung's followers fell in nearly the same way. The cowardly Bang, who had no injury but saw that it would not go well for him, killed himself in the same manner at night. All of his drinking comrades and other old men followed his example. And where these kings lay dead, you could see several thousand others who had killed themselves, piled up on top of /**185**/ each other, at the feet [of the kings].[139]

Relations and friends had tried to keep the old men from killing themselves, telling them that for the sake of their relatives they should preserve their lives and flee with them to where their wives and children were. But the old men asked, very disdainfully, whether the relatives could [possibly] imagine that they wanted to live as comrades with such young people as the relatives were. And indeed, two years later, when the Akims came to the coast again, the eldest among them did not appear to be forty years old, the elders having killed themselves. Where the others had hidden

---

[137] Yet, in a letter to Elmina, van Kuyl cites a report, given him personally by the Akyem, 'that they were busy, daily, in order to fight the Ashantees; as the Akims were very desperate, and had no fear for King Pockoe [Opoku Ware]' (BLL, Furley N44, 7.12.1741). Cf. Fynn (1971) 73–4; Kwamena-Poh (1973) 76.

[138] The reference may be to Gonja, but there were any of a number of peoples in the northern Asante hinterland who had not yet acquired guns (p.c. I. Wilks).

[139] In his history of this battle, Reindorf adds to R.'s account the names of individuals and places, material he presumably drew from oral traditions (Reindorf (1895/1966) 85/81). For another instance of mass suicide following the death of a local leader, see Isert [1788] (1992) 173–4. Generals in battle, upon recognising their imminent defeat, did commit suicide, preferably destroying their heads in the process (in the manner described at 184 above), lest the head be taken by the enemy and subjected to soul-damaging treatment. Suicide was acceptable in Asante and appears to have been so among the Akyem, another Akan people (Wilks (1993) 230).

themselves, no one knows, and the Assiantes did not seize many of them. I do not believe they caught and sold more than 10,000 of them.

We Danes had descending on our necks a force of about 20,000 Assiantes led by an Assiante caboceer named Ursue Afrié. He plagued us until he received from us a great many goods.[140] The Dutch also received their share of trouble because of their caboceer, Dacon, who had helped the Akims and was killed with all his men.[141] We had neither military provisions nor food in our fort, so in a few days the price of foodstuffs rose so much that if a man bought bread /**186**/ it cost him three marks and he did not have enough money left for either dinner or the evening meal, indeed for absolutely anything for several days.[142]

We then had to deal with the Assiantes, who in no way resembled our good Akims but were an immodest and coarse nation. For a time we Europeans believed that the Assiantes were now the greatest nation [of Gold Coast], and [yet] we had nothing to fear from them. However, several years later we heard that there were two nations beyond Assiante,[143] each of [whose leaders] speaks to Oppoccu and the Assiantes in just as arrogant a tone as the Assiantes speak to the Akims and the Akims in turn speak to the Aqvamboes. One of these nations, which lies SE of Assiante (if I remember correctly) is called Cassianté, and the other lies NE. The latter is ruled by a woman and is very densely populated.[144] Two years after the Akims were

---

[140] Owusu Afriye (Ursue Afrié), the *Akyempemhene* and son of Osei Tutu (Wilks (1975) 330), may also have been eager to avenge the death of his father which had occurred during the 1717 Akyem defeat of Asante.

[141] On the caboceer Dako (Dacon), see Chapter 3, note 92 above. Asante claims on Dako's possessions and family members and Dutch attempts to protect his family and possessions are documented in BLL, Furley N45, 4.5.1742, 25.4.1742; CRA, V-gK 123, 11.7.1743. See also Van Dantzig (1978) 355–6.

[142] Presumably the local Africans seized the chance to inflate the prices of the foods they sold to the Danes. A letter was sent to Copenhagen by Governor Dorph complaining of lack of provisions due to short-sightedness on the part of the former Governor, P.N. Jørgensen (CRA, V-gK 123 Generalbrev, 11.7.1743); cf. Nørregård (1966) 102–3.

[143] The term here translated as 'beyond', but elsewhere translated as 'above', was used by R. as a geographical indicator. It was generally applied to the coast, when it meant to the west (that is, 'above', towards 'Upper Guinea'). Here, however, it is applied to inland areas and used even more loosely, since it apparently refers to territories both NE and SE of Ashanti. It is therefore translated 'beyond'.

[144] According to an eighteenth-century report, based on information obtained from slaves in America, the 'Kassenti' were neighbours of the 'Amina' (presumably the Akan); they lived a six-month's journey from the coast, and their true name was Tjemba but they were called Kassenti because of a phrase they used repeatedly; their neighbours included the Attem or Tem, whose neighbours in turn included Amina and who were four days distant from 'Akkran' [Accra] (C.G.A. Oldendorp, *Geschichte der Mission der evangelischen Brüder* (Barby, 1777), 279–81 (in translation, S-D. Brown, 'From the tongues of Africa', *Plantation Society* 2/1 (1983), 47–8). The brief vocabulary of 'Tembu' supplied in this source probably represents Tem, and that of 'Kassenti' Gurma (perhaps in the Kasele dialect), both languages of the Gur family and spoken today NE of Ashanti (and modern Ghana) (P.E.H. Hair, 'A further note on Oldendorp's interviews', *Plantation Society* 2/3 (1989), 343, and the earlier publications

beaten, Oppoccu wanted to wage war against those people, who are said to live in a land where there is no forest. But he considered himself lucky to have returned, head over heels, to his forest again, where that nation could not pursue him with their cavalry, as will be shown later.[145] It has since become known that Oppoccu ordered a couple of hundred rifles from Holland and before he went to war had some of his people practice with them /**187**/, and with these guns he had killed the Akim kings. But against this nation they did no good.

The Assiantes collected the heads from the Akim corpses, but Ursue's entire body was ordered to be brought to Oppoccu. [However] the people who fetched the body cut the head off on the way. This angered Oppoccu and he, in turn, had the heads of the perpetrators cut off. Our emissary tells us that Oppoccu ordered all of his generals to sit in a circle around the dead body of Ursue. Oppoccu then stood and delivered a speech about him, using approximately these words (according to the report of our emissary): 'Here lies a great man whose like cannot be found. After God and myself he was certainly the third [greatest]. How you would run (he said to his generals) if he could rise up to his feet! And what fear you would have felt if you had aimed at him during this war! It was only I who [by rights] could kill him. But, Brother (he called the dead man), what was the reason you did not wish to be less than I? You spared your people and thought you would kill me some day. You thought there could only be one great /**188**/ man to rule the entire world, and you thought correctly, as all Big Men do', and so he went on. At that time Oppoccu was certainly not bearing in mind the two nations beyond his land. It is known [in fact] that he first had to have permission from the Cassiantes before he dared to begin the Akim war, and he had to pay more for this permission than his booty amounted to.

The Assiantes returned to their country again. They had taken two of the Akim heirs to the throne as prisoners, namely Brunni, who belonged to Frempung's land, and Ascharri, who belonged to Bang's throne.[146] They took none of the royal family from Ursue's land, and Pobbi succeeded Ursue.[147]

---

cited). The polities NE of Asante conquered in campaigns in 1744–1745 could have been any of a number which had not yet acquired guns (p.c. I. Wilks). They may have included Gonja and Dagomba (Reindorf (1895/1966) 88/83-4; Fynn (1971) 77–8; Wilks (1975) 20–3; Van Dantzig (1980a) 91 note 35). The reference to a woman ruler may be R. confusing Dagomba with Dahomey, hence with stories of the Dahomey Amazons (p.c. I. Wilks).

[145] See /218/–/222/ below. R.'s report has been described as 'the first contemporary account of Asante's thrust to northern Ghana from written sources' (Fynn (1971) 77–8).

[146] The odd switch from 'land' to 'throne' perhaps reflects some uncertainty on R.'s part about the local concept of sovereignty. Or it may be simply a careless slip.

[147] Broni (Brunni) was from Akyem Kotoku, the land of Frempong Menso (see note 98 above), while Asare (Ascharri) was from Akyem Abuakwa, the land of Ba Kwante (Wilks (1975) 24). According to one historian (Kwamena-Poh (1973) 78–9), Pobi (alias Pobi Asõmanin: Reindorf (1895/1966) 86/82) became the chief of Akyem Abuabkwa upon the death of Ba Kwante ('Bang').

Oppoccu sent a message to the Akims stating that if they would install these two, namely Brunni and Ascharri, on their hereditary thrones, he would return them gratis. The Akims could send deputies to testify that he ate fetish, promising that as long as he lived he would not attack them, provided that they (the Akims) gave him no cause. He desired no tribute from them, but he did want customs from the European forts, as well as a free route for his people and traders through the Akim land to Accra, because it was closer to him than Elmina.[148] /189/

Although, among those not taken prisoner were older and thus closer heirs to Bang's and Frempung's thrones than these two, the Akims accepted Opoccu's offer, and the closest heirs had to relinquish their claims to the thrones. It was Oppoccu's ambition to be able to say that the two kings in Akim were his slaves. Ascharri and Brunni had to eat fetish with him, swearing that when Oppoccu went to war, and [provided that] he informed them two months in advance, they and all their people would accompany him. Thus the Akims returned to their land, after having been in hiding for an entire year, but they did not come to the coast for two years. The Assiantes then came to Accra to collect their tax, but all the Europeans had agreed to make it clear to Opoccu that we paid the tax for the sake of trade, and when he sent us good trade, he would receive the tax — otherwise not. He agreed to this, and when he had it sent us considerable trade. The Assiante gold was a good ten per cent poorer than the Akim [gold]. We thought they had falsified it but we found out later it was obtained like this from the mines in Cassiante, a land two months' journey SE of Assiante.[149]

The /190/ young Akims now had their forefathers' great treasures at their disposal, but still used them as poorly as their forefathers had done. It was said that Frempung's successor, for one, using fifty slaves, had been busy for many nights burying his gold in various places before going to war, and that no one except the royal wives was allowed to see where it was hidden. The wives were immediately sent to the place where it was agreed the survivors were to assemble in the event of the war turning out badly for the Akims. The fifty slaves who had helped to bury the gold were killed, because if they had been taken prisoner in the war they might have revealed the hiding place.

Our messenger described Oppoccu's appearance as being almost that of a monster. He was taller than any of his own people, [his colour] quite red instead of black, and this the Negroes consider to be the most beautiful

---

[148] For the controversial issue of the payment of rent to Asante, see Nørregård (1966) 102–3; Fynn (1971) 71, 75–6; Quaye (1972) 235–7, 239–40; and especially L.W. Yarak, *Asante and the Dutch* (1990) 152–6. On Fante expansion and Asante attempts to circumvent this and establish a route through Akyem to the coast, see Wilks (1975) 24–5; Sanders (1979) 356–8.

[149] It is difficult to know why R. describes Cassiante as SE of Asante, since if it was in fact as distant as 'two months' journey' this would surely put it at least on the coast (if not in the sea), whereas it was patently in the interior. If he over-estimated the interior penetration of Asante, perhaps he meant 'south of east' (p.c. P.E.H. Hair).

colour. His body was very thin, almost like a Black with consumption. In proportion to his body, his hands and feet were twice as long as they should have been.[150] Our messenger assured us they could not look at him without fear, and this was considered by the Blacks to be [evidence of] something great and awe-inspiring. /**191**/ We could not make many of our Accras go up to Assiante although they had previously gone to Akim willingly. Indeed, many had run off to Akim with our emissaries, even when they had no business there. When we asked our people why they were so unwilling to go to Oppoccu they told us about Oppoccu's tyranny, that he had people's heads cut off almost every hour of the day, and sometimes of the night [too]. One of them assured me that he [once] counted 73 people who had been murdered in twelve hours, or from sunrise to sunset, and this [goes on] every day, more or less. [I was told] that they (our Accras) were not used to seeing such frequent murders. They assured me that no food tasted good to them in that land, and they longed for the day when they would be dismissed from there. All these heads were thrown down not far from his palace or residence, resulting in such a quantity of skulls that no one could see it all at a glance.[151]

Oppoccu holds audience outside his house under a large tree with many branches and leaves on it, a tree [entirely] made of gold. His throne is a lump of gold with rope bound around it and poles through the rope, requiring the use of eight men to carry it in and out. Together with the throne they bring out a gold /**192**/ basin into which he places his feet. His servants anoint his entire body twice a day with tallow, and then strew fine gold dust on it, as well as in his hair, and in this guise he holds audience.[152] If a copper engraver were to draw Oppoccu's portrait he would have to portray Oppoccu on his throne with his Big Men around him, his whole body shining with the gold dust sticking to his tallow-smeared skin. He would be wearing a hat with *Point d'Espagne* [lace] and a white feather on it; many rows of aggrey [beads] around his neck, arms, legs and waist; and a scarf of gold brocade lined with taffeta around his waist.[153] There would be one hundred plaintiffs and defendants lying prone before him, twenty executioners with swords [standing

---

[150] As described, the appearance of Opoku Ware is identical with that given in other contemporary reports (p.c. T.C. McCaskie). His unusual appearance may have been due to a medical condition (Wilks (1975) 330–1).

[151] The locality may have been the one known as *apetesɛneɛ*, this being the place where criminals were executed (McCaskie (1995) 304–5).

[152] For the assembly place, *dwaberem*, see McCaskie (1995), 280. Ostentatious display of gold and regalia signalled power and prestige (T.C. McCaskie, 'Accumulation of wealth and belief in Asante history', *Africa* 53 (1983) 26–9; Wilks (1993) 127 ff).

[153] A large-brimmed or three-cornered hat trimmed with Spanish lace and ostrich feathers was popular in eighteenth-century Europe. For nineteenth-century descriptions of chiefs and regalia, see McCaskie (1995) 45–6. For colour photographs of twentieth-century Asante chiefs dressed in some of their regalia, see A.A.Y. Kyerematen, *Panoply of Ghana* (1964) 3; H.M. Cole and D.H. Ross, *The Arts of Ghana* (1977) 24.

by], in the process of executing several miscreants, with others awaiting their turn to be beheaded, as soon as the executioners have finished beheading those with whom they were occupied. And the engraver would have to give us a view of the place where the miscreants' heads were thrown. You may protest that with [as many as] one hundred accusers and accused [awaiting trial and judgement], twenty executioners could not possibly be doing their job all the time. But you need to understand that this Assiante enemy of mankind has the innocent killed together with the guilty.[154] It is not /**193**/ the parties in conflict who personally bring their cases to his throne, but Oppoccu has them brought in from everywhere in his land. He listens to their Pro and Contra, and both parties receive the same punishment, namely to lose their heads.[155]

[Asante and the Europeans]

When Oppoccu has any messengers from the Europeans at his residence, they [are ordered to] be present to watch his judicial system, since he feels his greatness consists precisely in his being capable of destroying a portion of the African human race. Furthermore, when the messengers take their leave, he urges them not to forget to tell their masters what they had heard and seen of his greatness. No one dares speak his name, under penalty of death, but one must say: 'The Highest', 'The Flame-coloured', and so on.[156]

Now follows a [report of a] leave-taking audience and conversation between Oppoccu, King of Assiante, and Noy, an emissary of the Danish Company. The titles of honour which they [actually] gave each other in this conversation, and at other times, are terms in the Negro language, and Noy, who related this to us Danes in Portuguese, used [in his translation] these terms: /**194**/ 'Seignore el Re' and 'Seignore Moss', that is, 'Mr. King' and 'Mr. Boy'.[157]

---

[154] R. actually writes (in translation) 'the guilty together with the innocent', but this is obviously a slip. He means that time was not wasted in hearing cases, and that both accusers and accused were executed (which takes some believing, if a habitual practice).

[155] On judicial execution, see Wilks (1993) 215–17; McCaskie (1995) 202.

[156] For other descriptive names, see /204/ below.

[157] The Portuguese is corrupt, but it is difficult to say whether this is due to the broken-Portuguese spoken on Gold Coast, or to errors by Noy or R. The forms presented stand for '*Senhor el-Rei*' and '*Senhor Moço*' (Portuguese *moço* 'young man, servant'). In Gold Coast Portuguese the latter term may have meant 'representative, steward, etc.', especially when an important person was addressing an inferior (p.c. M.E. Kropp Dakubu). The term was already in use in the seventeenth century (Jones (1983) 187; Adam Jones, *Brandenburg Sources for West African History 1680–1700* (1985) 147). The term 'boy' was in general use in the colonial period to describe an African domestic servant; being used most obviously by Europeans, it was therefore eventually regarded as demeaning and 'colonialist', but it may well have been borrowed from African usage (p.c. P.E.H. Hair). This conversation, though seemingly exaggerated, follows a recognizable traditional form used on such occasions (p.c. T.C. McCaskie). For 'royal speech', see McCaskie (1995) 178–9, 279, note on *adehyeɛ kasa*). It should, however, be recognized that, as we have it, this rodomontade—also mentioned by Governor Billsen (CRA,V-gK, 21.7.1744)—was filtered through three languages, Twi/Akan (Opoku Ware to Noy via his linguist), Coast Portuguese (Noy to the Danes), and Danish (R. writing it down ten to fifteen years later).

Noy asked one of the *okras* (life-slaves)[158] of Oppoccu to tell the king that he would very much like to return home to his Whites, lest they be angry with him for staying too long in Assiante, and if it were convenient, he would like to take his leave the following morning. Oppoccu sent him the message that he could come to take his leave. On the specified morning, at seven o'clock, after Noy had been shown in to the innermost court in Oppoccu's residence, he saw the king, already decorated with several pounds of fine gold dust plastered or strewn over his skin and hair, which had been smeared with tallow. Oppoccu spoke to Noy as follows.

Oppoccu: Mr. Boy! Have you been well treated at the home of the caboceer whom I ordered to receive you and your people in his house?

Noy: Oh yes, Mr. King! My people and I have lacked nothing.

Oppoccu: Mr. Boy! You have only been here for six weeks and I like you and wish you could stay here longer in order to see more of my greatness, which you /**195**/ could then report to your white masters. Have you seen my equal?

Noy: Never, Mr. King! And your equal does not exist in the world!

Oppoccu: No, you are right in that, and God in heaven is only a little greater than I.

(No one should take offence at a black African king swollen with pride.)

Noy: I have seen many kings in the world, but your equal would not exist even if they all were combined!

Oppoccu: Mr. Boy, I wish to offer you a drink. Do you realise that I have just as much wine and beer as your white masters?

Noy: Mr. King, everything in the world belongs to you, and you can take anything.

Oppoccu orders a servant to bring a bottle of English ale. This is done, but the servant who brings it forgets to remove the steel thread with which the bottle was bound. Oppoccu starts to put it to his mouth to drink, but pricks himself on the steel thread. He looks very angrily at the servant who brought it, and gives /**196**/ it back to him.[159] The servant removes the steel thread from the bottle, and Oppoccu drinks to Noy's health. Noy is given a stool. He sits down, takes the bottle from Oppoccu's hand, and drinks to his health. Oppoccu takes it back again, and holds it up, saying :

Oppoccu: Mr. Boy, you drank only a little.

Noy: Mr. King, I dare not [drink more]. I already feel it going to my head.

Oppoccu: Mr. Boy, it is not by the ale you have become inebriated, but by my face, which makes all the people who see it become inebriated.

---

[158] The Akan term ɔkra/kra signifies the essence or 'soul' of a human being, one of a person's four essential components. Those whom R. calls 'life slaves' were servants or slaves recruited especially for the service ('washing') of the *kra* of the *Asantehene*, hence *nkradwarefo* 'washers of the *kra*' (McCaskie (1995) 67–8, 292–3). For an interpretation of the relevant general concepts, see J.B. Danquah, *The Akan Doctrine of God* (1968) 86–7.

[159] Given the character of the king as described, one might have expected that the servant would have been instantly executed.

Noy: Mr. King, you are right, because when I am in the warehouse of my Whites and have drunk a whole *pott* of brandy, I have not been as happy as during these days when I have seen your face.

This was untrue flattery, since it was Noy, with other Accras, who complained that they had no appetite when they were in Oppoccu's residence, and indeed they had been thin and wasted when they came back again. /197/

Oppoccu: Mr. Boy, do not forget to tell your white masters this and other things, and say to them that at Elmina, and at six lesser forts, I have emptied (by purchase) all their warehouses three times a year. In the same way your Whites' warehouses will be emptied three times a year. My people will not be like the mean Akims who walk around for a couple of days and have discussions before they buy anything. Be a friend to the people whom I shall send to the coast. Show them the places where the sea-devils come ashore, so that they can take care when going there, and so that I may not lose too many.

N.B. The Elmina Negroes and others at the coast steal Assiantes too, pretending that sea-devils come ashore and carry people away with them. With this, the audience came to an end and Noy had permission to go home.

A half year later the same Noy was sent to Assiante again, and in a conversation he /198/ had with Oppoccu, the king persuaded him to promise that when he went to war, Noy would accompany him and observe more of his greatness. Noy went along [with Oppoccu] in the famous campaign that Oppoccu launched against a nation NE of Assiante; and our good Noy, together with others, starved to death (as the fetish at Labode had prophesied to him before he left Accra). Even if he had returned alive, Noy would not have been able to tell us anything other than that Oppoccu and the Assiantes could also show their backs to their enemies.[160]

It is strange that although Noy and several others (when they spoke to us) admitted they felt loathing and disgust for Oppoccu and his tyranny, yet our Accras would in no way deny that Oppoccu was indeed the greatest in the world, until that campaign during which they became acquainted with several Assiantes. They then discovered that the king SE of Assiante held Oppoccu and the Assiantes to be his vassals and tradesmen, and it was with them [*sic*] that the Assiantes exchanged all their gold for iron and salt, etc.[161] [However,] the Assiantes who later came to the coast absolutely

---

[160] The reference must be to the campaign against Dagomba in 1744, which ended in deadlock (Wilks (1975) 21-2).

[161] A possible source of iron for Asante would have been farther east, rather than allegedly SE, in the iron smelting localities in the Togo hills, possibly in the Bassari area. The archers there were much feared, and the Asante would have been very hesitant to deploy military force against such groups ensconced in their hills (p.c. I. Wilks). The acquisition of salt at an inland point, if not indicating a trade route from the coast, suggests a contact with some polity that was itself in contact with traders from the north, part of the commercial network that brought salt across the Sahara (p.c. P.E.H. Hair).

denied this, in the conviction that Oppoccu would certainly demand the head of anyone who /**199**/ had dared to say such things, etc. It was the same with the Akims. We did not learn their secrets until they had been defeated and some Danes obtained slave boys from among them, whom they then used as servants for several years, teaching them to speak Portuguese and Danish.

Oppoccu had a house built in his residence for each of the heads of the Akim kings. The skulls were decorated with the gold and jewels (aggreys [sic]) which the deceased had been wearing at the time the Assiantes took their bodies. Several of the heads of their most prominent friends were set around the head of each king. Five slaves were kept in each house to keep it clean, and to put out food and drink for each head.[162]

Despite all his tyranny, Oppoccu still tries to establish factories in his land, and since the distilling of brandy was the most prominent and profitable industry [on the coast] during the period when he had routes open to Elmina, he approached four Dutch soldiers who promised to teach this business to some of his subjects. Oppoccu having agreed to pay them a great sum in gold, these four soldiers arrived safely in Assiante. They had already constructed all the equipment needed, using clay pots instead of copper ones, /**200**/ bamboo for tubing, etc., and they would actually have started distilling had not the Government at Elmina, using pleas and threats, and many marks of gold as presents to Oppoccu's Big Men, had these soldiers delivered back to the coast, where they were immediately hanged.[163]

Oppoccu then began to form another kind of industry. Some of his subjects were able to spin cotton and weave it into strips three fingers wide. Then, when ten to twelve of these strips, each three *alen* long, are sewn together they make a *pantjes* or scarf [sic]. One strip may be white, another blue, and sometimes a red one is included. Such a scarf can cost 50 *rixdaler* or more. Oppoccu had his traders buy silk taffeta cloths in all colours. The artisans unravelled these so that, instead of red, blue, green, etc. cloth and taffeta, they had many thousand *alen* of woollen and silk thread. These threads were woven in among their cotton [fibres], producing [a cloth of] many colours, and such a scarf could cost up to 500, or even 1,000 *rixdaler*.[164]

---

[162] R.'s description is that of skulls of vanquished enemies placed, at certain times, beside the stool of the *Asantehene* who had defeated them (p.c. I. Wilks). Perhaps, therefore, R. is referring to the royal stool rooms, *nkonnwafieso* (Kyerematen (1964) 15–6; Wilks (1993) 234).

[163] The Europeans at the forts would certainly not have welcomed a local distillery competing with them in the sale of European-style spirits (cf. Wilks (1975) 26).

[164] R.'s contention that large-scale production of cloths was attempted may be correct, but weaving of cloth was, of course, not new. For the early history of weaving in Asante, see R.S. Rattray, *Religion and Art in Ashanti* (1927) 220. Archeological evidence shows the use of strip weaving in the sixteenth century (Cole and Ross (1977) 16) The weaving of cotton cloth on the Gold Coast at the end of the seventeenth century was noted (Barbot [1732] (1992) 101), and it has been suggested that the use of silk thread obtained by unravelling imported cloth was the practice 'probably since the seventeenth century' (J. Picton and J. Mack, *African Textiles* (1979) 28). For weaving techniques, see Isert [1788] (1992) 91–2; Rattray (1927), chapter 24.

[Gold Coast products]

I dare state, as a certainty, that on the Guinea Coast coffee beans grow wild. Cotton, indigo and sugar cane grow there without the least trouble for the inhabitants; and perhaps cloves and nutmeg too. /**201**/ Until a few years ago I had never seen cloves and nutmeg in their shells, then, on one occasion, I received several preserved nutmegs and cloves in their shells.[165] Almost every afternoon when on the Coast, I went into the fields with a musket, looking for a water hole. You conceal yourself in the bush, and only rarely does it happen that game birds, such as pheasants, partridges, wild pigeons, etc., fail to come to the water within a short time. Meanwhile you pass the time in looking around or picking berries, or fruits, from these bushes. It is not recommended that you taste them, except for those varieties the Blacks eat. [But] I think I have seen fruits resembling cloves and nutmegs in their shells.

To produce the colour blue, the Blacks do not use indigo but instead the roots of a type of tree. It would be worth the trouble to bring some of these to Europe, since their blue colour is faster than ours, although their red colour is quite poor. They have absolutely no green or yellow.[166]

Up-country there are trees from which the Blacks collect tallow. I have never seen the tree, but have often seen the tallow. It does not become as hard as ours but smells the same and is astringent to the taste. The Blacks could obtain enough /**202**/ of this tallow to smear their bodies, but since ours comes from a long way off and is ten times as expensive, they prefer to buy the European tallow for this use. According to what they tell me, they collect the tallow in the same way as they collect the sweet palm wine from the palm trees. They break some leaves or small branches off the tree, hang a container under that spot, and the fat drips into the container. They might collect three or four *potter* from one tree in a single day, depending on the size of the tree.[167]

The honey available on the Coast is a variety in which Africa, without a doubt, excels over the other parts of the world. It is good for health, has an

---

[165] Cotton (*Gossypium* sp.), indigo (*Lonchocarpus cyanescens*), sugar cane, cloves (*Eugenia caryophyllata*); and nutmeg (*Myristica fragrans*) are indeed found today in Ghana (D.K. Abbiw, *Useful Plants of Ghana* (1990) 52, 69–71, 74, 224). But nutmeg appears to have been introduced from Indonesia, and it has been suggested that R. may have confused the Asian spice with one of two species of African nutmeg (S.B. Alpern, 'The European introduction of crops into West Africa in precolonial times', *History in Africa* 19 (1992), 38 note 128).

[166] For plants used in dyeing, see F.R. Irvine, *Woody Plants of Ghana* (1961) 384–5 (*Indigofera arrecta*), 390 (*Indigofera tinctoria*); Abbiw (1990) 223; 225. Green obtained by mixing yellow and indigo, purportedly 'a secret trade of certain Hausa families' (Abbiw, 225), may not have been known on the coast in R.'s day.

[167] The bark of the Tallow Tree (*Allanblackia floribunda*) is pounded and used on the body to relieve pain (Irvine (1961) 143–4; Abbiw (1990) 287). Describing an ointment in more universal use, R. must have been mistaken in naming tallow, and actually have observed instead the use of oil from the shea butter tree (*Butyrospermum parkii*), which was (and is) used as a pomade, as well as in soap making (Abbiw (1990) 587–8).

excellent flavour, and is aromatic and nicely scented. It often serves us Europeans as a substitute for sugar in our tea and punch, and on our food, and sometimes as a spread on our bread. It is very thin, almost like water, and clear, when there have not been young bees in the honeycomb. The African bees store it in honeycombs in hollow trees, just as ours do in a bee hive. During and after the rainy season, when it is available in great quantities, we Europeans — as many as us who have households — buy a little, or a lot, and have it boiled, skimmed, and poured into bottles. If the cork is not set too tightly into the bottle it can be preserved in this way for several years, and it then becomes as thick as syrup. /203/

Trees [can be found] whose bark can be prepared like sheep- or lamb-skin. The Blacks strip the bark from the tree, dry it, pound it, and wear it like a cloth. It is just as soft and as slow to wear out as a prepared sheepskin.[168]

[African-European relations on Gold Coast]

See what a delightful land these black people own! And a thousand times as many people could, with a little work, live better than the few people who are now there. There is no risk for many centuries of there being too many people in the land, whereas, unless they are trained in morality, together with God's Word, one would prefer to be in cold Greenland or Iceland than in that blessed land.[169]

The Blacks sometimes poison Europeans. To do this they use the gall of a caiman or crocodile. Or, when they shoot a sea cow that has a calf with her, they use the impurities found in the intestines of the calf to make an even stronger poison. Thus these black heathens seek to revenge themselves when they think they have been treated unjustly. This [resort to poisoning] has not occurred among us Danes — God be praised! — although on the Guinea Coast we are especially jealous of each other.[170] /204/

Those Europeans whom the Blacks especially like are known most of the time by black [sic] names. It is a common practice that, when new Europeans arrive in that country they are each given a name during their first eight days, and it is amusing that the names they are given are rather well suited to their temperaments and the condition of their bodies. Names are changed, too,

---

[168] The Bark Cloth Tree, *Antiaris toxicaria*, produces a cloth which is strong, white, and easy to wash, and it was also formerly used by the Krobo for hammocks and sandals (Abbiw (1990) 113).

[169] The Danish is crabbed and somewhat obscure, but the sense seems to be that Greenland with its natural disadvantages is a better place than Guinea because of the heathenism of the latter's natives. As earlier, R. links Greenland with the recent Christian mission there, but now adds, less relevantly, Iceland.

[170] However, upon the sudden deaths of three successive Danish governors during R.'s time on the Coast, rumours of poisoning as the cause were rife (Nørregård (1966) 105–6; Per Hernæs, 'Den balstyrige bergenser på Guldkysten', *Norsk Sjøfartsmuseums Årsberetning* (1996) 136). On poisons from plants, see Abbiw (1990) 206–12.

when the European changes his behaviour. For instance, an Assistant at Christiansborg who spoke French and had to manage all the trade with the French captains carried on at our fort was called 'Frenchman' by the Blacks. Some time later, on a number of occasions, he revealed that he did not lack courage. The Blacks then unanimously gave him one of the 'great names' of Oppoccu, *Tentjen Koko* (the Fire-coloured).[171] In nearly all the towns there are children who are called 'Frenchman', and when you ask them why they do not call their children by that man's [new] 'great name', since they have named their sons after him, they answer that the son must first prove his virtue before he can receive the man's 'great name'. Little girls are sometimes called 'Madame', after a European woman. It happens that the Blacks give both bad and good names to the Europeans, such as 'a rotten citron', 'a beautiful bird', 'a horse', 'a false animal' or 'a true animal', etc. /205/

For fifteen years the two greatest and most prominent families in our Ursue town, under Christiansborg, have been in conflict, namely the families of our caboceer Ursa and our broker Adoui. These two could not agree on which of them was of the oldest noble family. Each claimed the higher rank, and since it is the practice that one of the most prominent men in every town has a flag on his house to show which [European] nation he is linked to, we gave our flag to Adoui. But Ursa threatened to shoot Adoui to death the next time they met, and people on both sides began to arm themselves. We loaded all our cannons with grapeshot and the people were told we would send it all straight into the houses of the first side to begin shooting. But all our threats were to no avail. They would certainly have murdered each other had we not sent out soldiers to cut down the flag-pole at Adoui's house. In spite of a cease-fire the argument, or conflict, continued. Each party hunted for old crones who, when they were assembled, could reckon back many centuries, and who had known the party's grandmothers and to which noble family they had belonged.[172] We became tired of hearing about the issue practically every month, and of serving an entire anker of brandy to nearly one hundred old men and /206/ women as they disputed Pro & Contra. Finally, this really important issue was settled, and you might call it a national judgement, [the agreement being] that Ursa should present to Adoui a personal article of great value and Adoui should present to Ursa a personal article of lower value. Such was the judgement delivered, according to the statements in the Negroes' language. I think it is just as short and pithy as our High Court judgements. It meant that they were both of old nobility, but Adoui had rank and custom over Ursa.

---

[171] Among Opoku's praise names was *Tenten* 'the tall one' and *Korkor* 'the bright/white one', but R. seems to have misunderstood the latter name (p.c. I. Wilks). For Opoku Ware's appearance, see note 150 above.

[172] It appears that old women were custodians of genealogy.

Adoui then had the flag raised [again] over his house and both parties were satisfied.[173]

Among themselves the Negroes have strict laws in respect of cases of debt and *in puncto sexto* [adultery]. In debt cases the rule is an annual *centum pro centum* [*sc.* 100% interest], so that a debt of one male slave has at the end of one year become that of two.[174] However, when they borrow from the Europeans, they do not pay even a low interest on the principal, but we have to feed the security they give, which usually means their own or slave children, sometimes feeding them for several years. Should we wish to sell the security, the debtor's friends and any caboceers and fetish priests with whom they are acquainted come and plague us, begging us to have patience for yet a few more months — so [sometimes] we have fed their children until they became fully grown.[175] /207/

Most of their cases and disagreements concern *in Puncto sexti*. The Europeans certainly cannot allow those Blacks who live along the coast to decide their cases themselves, since the Negroes would undoubtedly come to blows and murder one another. We take both parties into the fort and arrange for the case to be decided in the easiest and best manner, so that each party can be satisfied, to a degree. If the dispute goes so far that the Negroes *penjarer* [seize one another] in their *palabres* [discussions, arguments], it rarely ends otherwise than by their shooting at one another.[176]

The staff on the Coast often use such forms of expression (namely to *penjare* during a *palabre*) and other Negro-Portuguese terms in their reports to their superiors here, as well as to those in England and Holland.

---

[173] The extent to which the dispute between Ursa and Adoui can be attributed to a disruptive effect of the European presence on the balance of power in the Gã towns is difficult to judge. Quarrels between Big Men no doubt had occurred in earlier times for other reasons. Nevertheless, those leaders who were brokers for the Europeans [*megler/makelaar*] gained economic advantages which must have enhanced their political power and strengthened them vis-à-vis the other local power-brokers claiming dependence on 'traditional' authority. Yet African political structures were often sufficiently flexible for individuals to combine both the 'traditional' and the contemporary sources of authority in their communally acknowledged status. It is notable that the settlement of the dispute turns on a 'traditional' form of assessment (p.c. P.E.H. Hair).

[174] For *in puncto sexto*, see note 19 above. Among the Gã in modern times, a man found guilty of adultery pays a fine called *ayifale* and the woman's husband may divorce her (Field (1940) 111).

[175] The children are pawns. However, non-slave children may sometimes also have been placed with Europeans for fostering. Whether the children (normally boys) were pawns or being fostered, some parents may have been in no hurry to retrieve a child because of the training it was receiving from the Europeans, even if merely by contact with them. This form of domestic out-housing of children was once not uncommon in Europe and is still practised by African parents under certain limited circumstances (p.c. P.E.H. Hair).

[176] R.'s statement that Africans were unable to settle their own cases without coming to blows was erroneous and partial. He must have seen many cases of 'palavers' (arguments, negotiations, disputes) being settled by discussion and consensus among the Africans themselves, without any help from the Europeans (see /209/ below). For a good description of the palaver process, see Monrad (1822) 75–84.

I do not know if the English and Dutch directors understand their staff on the Coast, but I know that we here ought to compile a dictionary of Negro-Portuguese and Danish in order to make the reports which come from the Guinea Coast comprehensible. To *penjare* means to seize an individual. For example, a creditor lives in one town and the debtor in another. The creditor has often in vain demanded repayment of the debt. He then promises six or seven good friends that he will treat them to drink if they will be /**208**/ of help to him, to *penjare* for the debt owed to him. Then either the creditor sets off to [the debtor's] town with his friends in order to seize some Negroes from among the debtor's townsmen; or [perhaps some of] the debtor's townsmen are found in the town where the creditor lives — however [? unfair] that may be. The creditor then seizes two or three individuals, depending on the size of the debt, puts them into shackles (irons) in his house, or brings them into the fort. The creditor then informs the caboceer and the Big Men in the town where the debtor lives that one of the townsmen owes him a certain amount, and if he does not come and pay the debt, he (the creditor) will then sell the Negroes he has seized and recover the debt himself. Then, according to the Coast's manner of speaking about this type of issue or conflict, that Negro, town, land or province has *palaber* with the [other] Negro town, etc.

The word *palaber* ['palaver'] does not always denote a conflict and a court case. On the Coast you also say a Negro 'makes *palaber*' [*sc.* talk, negotiate] for you to lend him something; you make *palaber* in order to buy or sell a slave; you make *palaber* in order to *callisiare* (to marry).[177] A European not acquainted with these ways of speaking might hear two of his own countrymen speaking in his mother tongue and yet not understand them. We come here as young men. On the Coast we see, /**209**/ from Copy-Letter Books, that our predecessor has used the Guinean way of speaking, and we think the Director here [in Copenhagen] is just as well acquainted with [those terms] as we are in that country. On the Coast I have seen an old Letter Book in which a certain governor reported to the directors here that the Dutch Negroes had penjaret in a palaber with our Negroes who long ago had been hûjra accusæ..æ. In order to understand this, you must know that when a case among the Blacks is decided, it is established custom that the plaintiff says '*hûjra*', to which the defendant and all those present answer '*accusæ..æ*', and they repeat these words alternately several times. The entire case is then at an end, and each one goes his way.[178] In

---

[177] This can be understood as — 'you enter into negotiations (with her parents) to enable you to marry (the girl of your choice)'. The coastal term *callisiare* was apparently derived from Portuguese *casar* 'to marry, set up house' (cf. Isert [1788] (1992) 141, and note 65).

[178] *Hújra*... *Accusæ* is perhaps Gã *hiao, owura* 'amen, sir' + *àkù see* 'it has returned/been returned', the whole in this context meaning, 'so be it, sir, it has been adjourned' (p.c. M.E. Kropp Dakubu). Cf. *me cusa, me cusa* 'may things go well for me', said after a sacrifice, although purportedly in an Akan area (J.B. Labat, *Voyage du Chevalier des Marchais* (1730) 343).

the same way the Negroes bid farewell when a score of them, or fewer, have drunk one-half anker of brandy, or several ankers of palm wine. They finish the party with '*hûjra accusæ..æ*'.

[Gold Coast warfare]

It is a very comical sight when the Negroes go to war or to a campaign in the field. Their uniforms and arms are in no way comparable to those of warriors in Europe. If a Black finds out that another has an outfit like his in which to go to war, he will most certainly change /**210**/ his, in order not to be mistaken for the other one.[179] A Negro keeps his war equipment quite secret, and no one is permitted to see it before the very moment in which he is to go to battle. Most of them have a cap made of a piece of animal hide, the skin of a monkey, tiger or wolf. Sometimes it is a piece of the hide of a roe deer or tiger with the tail attached. The hide is drawn over a board, in the same way as a stocking weaver [does with his material], and since the raw skin or hide of an animal before it dries is easy to shape to suit any taste, the Blacks can fashion it as they themselves wish. Then they put the hat on so that the tail waves in front of their face. When they wish to appear differently, they soften the old hat in water and draw it over a new form.

A number of them use the skin from the head of a tiger, buffalo, or hart, and look out through the same holes where the tiger, etc., had its eyes, so they will appear really gruesome and fierce when their enemies see them. They have a strange form of cartridge pouch which I cannot describe, and which holds ten to twelve small boxes containing powder, a small bag for shot, and a calabash (a wooden container)[180] [with a reserve of powder]. The whole pouch is covered with hide sewn around it, and it holds altogether three or four pounds of powder /**211**/ from which [*sc.* the container] they can provide themselves when their boxes are empty. They paint their faces and bodies with white earth.[181] Moreover, each prominent Negro normally has his own particular emblem. For example, Putti has a horse tail which he fastens to his body at about the same place where the horse had it. Soja takes a live red cock, tears it apart into many small pieces, removes the fat, and smears his body with it. Then he ties the tail feathers together, and attaches them, sometimes, similarly, to the place on his body where the cock wore them, sometimes to other places. In that way all of them have their particular marks.[182]

---

[179] Total lack of uniformity was also reported by Isert [1788] (1992) 38–9; whereas only a degree of uniformity among the Akwamu is claimed in Kea (1982) 163.

[180] Strictly, a calabash is not a wooden container but the hard shell of a variety of gourd.

[181] On the use and significance of white earth, see Isert [1788] (1992) 50, 63–4; Reindorf (1895/1966) 126/118; Feinberg (1989) 116; McCaskie (1995) 203, 282, 287–8. For a much earlier reference to soldiers whitening faces, see Hair (1994) 39 and note 220.

[182] For local military attire in the period, see Barbot [1732] (1992) 605; Rask (1754) 90; Isert [1788] (1992) 38–9. For a 1760 drawing and description of a Gold Coast warrior in full attire, see Plate 5 and Appendix C.

For the space of an hour beforehand, a Black lets his musket lie on his fetish, to ensure that it will not fail him, then he takes it and goes into battle. A Big Man wears a sword at his side, or behind him. He uses it, whenever an enemy falls, to cut off his head, in order to hang it on his drum as a sign of victory. When a young Negro, thus equipped, appears before the enemy, he gambols and capers so high and so artfully that I doubt if our Como and Pescarollo could imitate him. [183] A Negro thus entices an enemy to fire /212/ his gun at him. He [then] pretends he has been shot, in order to lure the enemy to come after his head. He lies hidden in the tall grass, or bush, with his musket loaded, so that he can shoot the other man and kill him, and perhaps take his head.

The Negro loads the first shot in the same way as the Europeans, with powder, wad and shot, but when their shot in the small boxes is used up and they need to take some from their reserve container (the calabash), they normally take an entire handful and put it into the barrel of the gun, which has not been cleaned. [The powder] remains stuck to the pipe or barrel, together with a couple of balls of shot. This normally happens an hour after the battle has begun, when they have become excited. You can then see them standing scarcely ten paces from each other, and firing so that they burn each other's skin and faces [with the powder flash], but the shot, most of the time, does not even emerge from the musket.[184]

The Assiantes do not dig for gold. They say they have no gold mines, but [in fact] they have never tried mining. Yet there is more gold among the Assiantes than among the Akims. They acquire it from Cassiante, where (according to the statements of the Blacks) the Assiantes exchange it for its equivalent in iron.[185] They /213/ describe the route to that land (Cassiante) as particularly dangerous, unless the company of travellers is made up of 3,000–4,000 armed Negroes. The danger is supposed to be [of attack] from a species of large bird which can seize a person with his carpet bag and all, and fly away with him, as a hawk does with a

---

[183] '*Pescarollo*' must be a mis-spelling of *Pesquariello*, a classic character in the Comedia d'el Arte, figuring as an acrobat, and usually dressed in black velvet, which may have been another reason for R.'s reference, since he was seeing dark-skinned people perform. The '*Como*' is puzzling since there is no character with that name. Conceivably R. is using a familiar, short, term for the Comedia d'el Arte. (I am indebted to Britt Ingrid Wang for this information.) On pantomime before battle, see Isert [1788] (1992) 53.

[184] On loading and overloading of muskets, see Isert [1788] (1992) 66. Flash-firing could be because the musket was defective or the gunpowder had too high a percentage of saltpetre (Kea (1971) 204–5 and note 131. See also /213/–/214 /below.

[185] Gold mines in Akan country, reported when the Portuguese reached Gold Coast in the 1470s, had no doubt existed long before; and it is implausible that by R.'s day none existed in Asante. R. noted earlier (/198/ above) the exchange of gold by the Asante for iron from their interior neighbours, a plausible commerce (note 161 above). But now he has the Asante exchanging iron for gold, a slip on his part.

chicken.[186] This country and kingdom lies SE of Assiante, and we have often had slaves from that nation. They are especially tall and strong of limb.

The surviving Akims blamed our Danish muskets for their having lost the war. They felt the Dutch had not lied in telling their forefathers there was a fetish on them. We on the Coast hastened to inform the Directors that our muskets had fallen out of fashion among the Akims, and that they should have them altered a little, above all by making them one and one-half handbreadths longer, which would help.[187] Since then our muskets have been just as saleable as before. The English on the Coast noted that as long as we had muskets that helped us to sell all the other types of goods, they had little trade. The chief [English] agents sent one of our [old] muskets to England to have it copied a year before they went out of use, and nearly all the English shipowners distributed these muskets to their captains as part of their cargoes. /214/ The English Company did the same, and sent several thousand to their forts on the Coast. Indeed, [even] the French ordered them from England, and sent them to the Coast. But just at the time when this great quantity came to the Coast through the hands of the English and French, the fault in our good muskets became known, and they could not be sold. The English then became weary of copying our muskets, and we [now] had another type, on which, we assured the Blacks, there was no fetish.[188]

We Danes, although absolutely blameless, have received a bad reputation because of the so-called 'Dane guns'. A certain person had responsibility to the Directors for the delivery [of guns], and they were unaware that the deliverer had not ordered these approved muskets from other cities, but had had the locks, shafts, and the rest of the fittings made here, in this city. However, since then they have found out that the completely finished muskets were ordered from Zelle [Celle] in Hanover, which is still the case

---

[186] This is a common myth appearing in folk literature in other cultures as well (p.c. Alan Tye). Known to eighteenth-century Europeans through the tale of Sindbad the Sailor in the Arabian Nights, it had already appeared in the account of Marco Polo. R.'s reference to the myth fails to explain the relationship between the threat and the need for a very large number of armed men.
[187] On the gun length, see Kea 'Firearms' (1971) 199.
[188] Assertions about the poor quality of the goods of rival European nations were naturally common. Thus, an Englishman asked an African in Dahomey to report to the king that French muskets were poor imitations of the English variety, and that they 'split in firing, and hurt the soldiers' (Snelgrave (1734) 90). Nevertheless, there may well have been differences in the quality of the guns supplied. De la Palma, the Dutch governor, reporting that the Africans would pay two ounces of gold for a dozen muskets, suggested that the English muskets were superior to the Dutch ones (Van Dantzig (1980a) 144). On English and Dutch types of gun expressly for the African trade, see Kea (1971) 198–200. While R. begins by considering the Danes 'absolutely blameless', his later comments seem to accept that some of the Danish guns were inferior. Another problem of certain Danish guns, reported by Governor Erich Ligaard in 1707, was that their barrels were too narrow for ordinary bullets (CRA, V-gK, *Generalbrev*, 12.4.1707).

with some of them. [So] if they had fetish on them they certainly brought it from there. The Dutch purchase theirs from Liège.[189]

[Aqvamboe survivors]

The few remaining Aqvamboes unexpectedly placed a king on their throne again, and this happened in the following way. A genuine heir to the Aqvamboe throne was among the captured Aqvamboes. /215/ He had not been recognised, and it was his lot to be in the hands of an ordinary Akim, for whom he had to work. He did not reveal his status, otherwise he would have been killed. Nine years later, during the war of the Akims with the Assiantes, he was captured and revealed his secret to several of the Assiante Big Men. They brought him to Oppoccu, who, being a friend of the Aqvamboes, was pleased that there existed an heir old enough for the Aqvamboe throne. [The Aqvamboe] was freed and Oppoccu gave him the name Oppaqva, or Oppoccuaqva (meaning Oppoccu's slave). The regent [sic] then arrived among his own people, who received him willingly and with joy. He did not tell them what name he had been given, and [instead] called himself Oppoccu Chuma (Little Oppoccu).[190]

One year later, Oppoccu, in Assiante, heard of the Aqvamboe king's presumptuousness in having himself called Little Oppoccu. He threatened Oppoccu Chuma, ordering him to lay aside that title and use Oppaqva. Oppoccu Chuma excused himself by saying he would not be able to have any authority over his nation if he used such a poor title. After much mediation between them the case was decided thus: the Aqvamboe king should buy the [new] title from Oppoccu for 100 slaves, etc. Oppoccu /216/ Chuma demanded of his people that each one should contribute to the sum he had to pay, but they did not want to [do this]. Oppoccu Chuma then resolved to do something which was typically Aqvamboe, and quite like [the mindset of both] him and his predecessor. One day he provided many ankers of brandy at a feast [he gave] for 300–400 Aqvamboe young men, and had them eat fetish [as a promise] to follow him. The following night they attacked an Aqvamboe town, killed the caboceer, and seized his children and slaves; and by this means the king paid off his debt to Oppoccu. The Negroes expected great things of this young king. If he had had control over such populous nations as his predecessors had enjoyed, he would certainly have brought the Accra slave trade to life again. But it was his misfortune that, had he frequently performed such heroic deeds [of enslaving his own people], before too long he would have run out of Aqvamboes [because of the limited population]. From this you can observe the devilish

---

[189] R. does not explain what precisely was wrong with the guns from Celle. Liège was an important centre for the manufacture of firearms (Kea (1971) 198–9; S. Alpern, 'What Africans got for their slaves', *History in Africa* 22 (1995) 21).

[190] For Opoku Kuma, see Wilks (1958) 136–7; Fynn (1971) 76.

temperament of the Aqvamboes, since even though they would have been weakened by [more of] this [royal exploitation], and even though those remaining might expect the same fate, yet they praised their king for this deed. When a European reprimanded them, they answered: 'What should our king have done otherwise?' /217/

[Asante wars]

The Assiantes had a mortal hatred of the Fantes, a nation west of Akron. That country is only six or seven miles wide along the coast, but extends a good fifty miles up into the country, and the higher up-country, the wider it becomes. Fante is the only known coastal nation on the entire Coast that has never been unlucky in war. That is to say, their enemies have never gained power over them in a violent manner.[191]

Fante is especially populous. They trade, fish, and cultivate the land, and in general they can be considered richer and more powerful than any other coastal nation. But 'it requires strong legs to bear good days', especially in that land. For many years the Fantes had seized Assiantes when they went to Elmina and other western forts to trade. At times they seized up to one hundred Assiantes, with their goods and all, and sold them. Oppoccu could not tolerate such a small nation insulting him. He would have liked to attack the Fantes if he had not feared the Akims would, in the meantime, fall upon his land. He had no choice but to reduce the Akims first. Then, after Oppoccu was /218/ successful against the Akims, everyone presumed the same fate would befall the Fantes. All the Europeans and the Blacks under them felt the Fantes deserved it, since they were a thieving and haughty nation. Perhaps the Europeans would have been more kindly disposed towards the Fantes if they had brought the goods they stole to them, as trade, but [instead] they sold their goods directly to ships at Anomabu, concerning themselves only little with the Europeans based on land.[192]

Oppoccu armed himself again and ordered the Akims, together with the Aqvamboes, to come up to him with all their people. The three Akim kings came, each with 10,000 men, and the Aqvamboes with 300 men. Everyone thought they were about to attack the Fantes. Instead, in the beginning of 1744, Oppoccu broke camp with his men, with the intention of going to

---

[191] On Fante and its main trading places, see Barbot ([1732](1992)416; Bosman (1705) 55–9. Fante rose in power and influence dramatically between 1700 and 1720 (Daaku (1970) 166–70; Sanders (1979) 350–5).

[192] That is, the Fante had established their trade very strategically by buying goods from interlopers at Anomabu cheaply and then selling them to the interior—or so it was alleged (M. Priestley, *West African Trade and Coast Society* (1969) 10–14; Daaku (1970) 41, 167–8; Fynn (1971) 86–7; Sanders (1979) 358–9). A documented example of Fante trade with interlopers is that of goods purchased over a period of years from a Captain Hamilton at Anomabu (BLL, Furley N45, 30.6.1742, despatch from Elmina to the Netherlands).

war against the powerful nation lying NE of Assiante. Some of our Accras, who were with Oppoccu at that time as Danish emissaries, also travelled with him, and this was recorded in their reports to us. I cannot recall the name of the nation.[193]

Oppoccu planned to surprise [the northerners] by coming upon them suddenly, and none of those in his army knew where they were going. They made their way for twenty-one days, at times hindered by bush and rivers. /**219**/ After this they arrived at a desert where there was not a blade of grass to be seen. They walked for fourteen days in quicksands, and on occasion the army was without water for two days. As long as they were in the bush they ate fruits and roots along with game meat, and suffered no want, but in this desert many starved to death. Finally they came to a flat land where they saw many well-populated cities. (Oppoccu was accompanied by many of his people who had travelled and traded in that land.) The Assiantes fell upon the inhabitants and took them prisoner. Advancing still farther, they came to a large city where Oppoccu and his 300,000 men made camp, since the inhabitants of the city had deserted it. Since Oppoccu's army filled only a small portion of the city, they concluded that in that one town more people had resided than lived in the whole of Assiante.[194] The Assiante traders assured their king that he would go through many such towns before he came to the [capital] Residence. Provisions were found in abundance, cows, sheep, goats, hens, horses; and Oppoccu acquired horses for some one thousand of his men who [then] served as cavalry.

He sent out these riders to collect information about the enemy but saw nothing more of /**220**/ them. Several prisoners taken from that people said all of the riders had been beaten to death, and that many hundreds of thousands of horse-riders had attacked the Assiantes in order to kill them. These people were of the Turkish religion, and at Accra we have seen many Arabian [*sic*: Arabic] books found by the Assiantes when plundering the city mentioned above. They also took as prisoners several Moors who had undoubtedly come from Barbary to that country to trade. Two of these Moors still live in Assiante.[195]

The Assiantes stayed in that city for an entire month because Oppoccu was afraid to advance farther. Finally Oppoccu's enemies came and surrounded the entire city with a numberless army. The Assiantes then had to fight their way through the enemy ranks, which they did, suffering great

---

[193] The campaign is thought to have been through Gonja and Dagomba, north of the middle stretch of River Volta and in the north of modern Ghana (Wilks (1975) 20, 21 note 109); Ivor Wilks, N. Levtzion, and B.M. Haight, eds., *Chronicles from Gonja* (1986) 130).

[194] The invading Asante, passing through Gonga, would have encamped in the city of Yendi (p.c. I. Wilks).

[195] For Muslims in Asante later in the eighteenth century and apparently arriving mainly as war captives, see D.J.E. Maier, 'Military acquisition of slaves in Asante', in D. Henige and T.C. McCaskie, *West African Economic and Social History* (1990) 122).

losses. The enemies' horses were frightened by the [sound of] shooting, since these riders had no guns but used lances or spears, and swords.[196] Wherever the Assiante army marched the enemy surrounded them, and this continued through the desert, right back to the Assiante forest. Thus ended the war for Oppoccu, who had considered himself to be the greatest king in the entire world. He had captured several hundred prisoners and horses, etc., but /**221**/ he and his allies had lost 40,000 men in the desert, where one of our messengers also starved to death.[197] This campaign lasted for eight months. Each of the allies went back to their own country, and on Oppoccu's orders they were to arm themselves for a new war to be waged against the Fantes.

Oppoccu became ill, and all the fetishes were consulted for advice, but he was given only meagre comfort. The Assiante fetish reminded him that he (that is, the fetish) had often warned him not to spill the blood of so many people. Now all that blood was transformed into fire in his body. It would burn him, and within a few years he would die, etc. All the fetishes of the other nations confirmed this judgement. Oppoccu then asked the Dutch general to send him a coffin of glass and a throne, and after a short time these arrived at Elmina from Holland. However, Oppoccu has not yet received them because the Fantes have threatened to lay siege to all the Dutch forts in Fante and murder all the Dutch they can get hold of.[198] The Fantes went on to form an alliance with all the nations lying between the coast /**222**/ and Assiante, to stop Oppoccu's people from coming to the coast in to buy gunpowder and muskets. All the nations west of Fante joined this alliance.[199]

The Fantes were afraid it was now their turn, and they had reason for this. Fear of all their neighbours was well-grounded, because after the Aqvamboes — who were enemies of the Fantes — and the Akron Negroes had been ruined, the Fantes began to seize Akims travelling to Accra to trade. Similarly they lay in wait for the Accras when they went to fetch provisions from the interior, captured them, and sold them. The Akims and the Accras asked the Fantes why they did these things, and received as an answer that the Akims and Accras had ruined Aqvamboe which had been their larder. Formerly, when they became hungry they could go to Aqvamboe, seize

---

[196] On cavalry and guns in local warfare, see J. Goody, *Technology, Tradition and the State in Africa* (1971) 55–6; R. Law, *The Horse in West African History* (1980) 139–44.

[197] Some historians accept R.'s account of this war as credible, quoting it at length, and providing confirmation from archive sources (Wilks (1958) 136–40; Fynn (1971) 76–8), Wilks adding information from the Akwamu point of view. 'One of our messengers' refers to Noy, the same envoy who had had the long conversation with Opoku Ware (/198/ above).

[198] I have been unable to trace evidence that the coffin of glass was actually delivered.

[199] For the background to, and establishment of, the Fante alliance, see Priestley (1969) 11, 12, 16, 23; Fynn (1971) 80; J.K. Fynn, 'Asante and Akyem relations', *IAS Research Review* (1973) 73; Sanders (1979) 357; Fage (1995) 278.

some people, sell them, and enjoy themselves. But since the Aqvamboes were no more, they had to make recourse to them, namely, the Akims and Accras. [However,] the Akims proved that they, too, could be cunning people when they wanted to, and on several occasions they seized entire gangs of Fantes who had placed themselves in their way in order to steal. But the Accras /223/ had to suffer continuous brigandage by the Fantes for many years.

In spite of these occurrences the Fantes, in fact, made friends with the Akims and Accras in 1745. Oppoccu tried to open the route to Elmina, but his people were beaten and taken prisoner by the Fantes and the surrounding nations. The Dutch general and Council at Elmina paid great sums to the enemies of the Assiantes, [in an attempt] to persuade them to allow the Assiantes free passage to the coast, but in vain. The Assiantes considered a route to the coast through Crepe, east of River Volta, [and then] to Fredensborg at Ningo, to the English fort at Prampram, and to the Dutch lodge at Ponni. They dared not go to Accra because it was too close to Fante.[200]

The Aqvamboes who for several years had been living forty miles up River Volta were helpful to their friends, the Assiantes, and became brokers of their trade. [But] they cheat them at every turn, and since the Adampes also wish to make a living, they too take their profit. We have often intended to treat the Assiantes just like the Akims, and not allow anyone to cheat them in their trade, but we have been obstructed in /224/ this, because the Assiantes always entrust the Aqvamboes with their trade, and the Aquamboes can take it to whichever nation they themselves wish. If we do not allow the Aqvamboes to rob their friends, they will not bring their trade to us, but to the Dutch or English, for whom it is no matter if an Aqvamboe steals half of the trade or less [sic]. To tell the truth, we wish that wicked nation no good.[201]

It is amusing to see how the Assiante Kottoko ('Great Assiantes', as they call themselves) are fooled by the poor Aqvamboes, and not only in trade.[202] An Aqvamboe caboceer might come to us with fifty Assiante traders, and will normally sell half a score of them before he leaves. He convinces them that the place where they reach the sea is a particularly dangerous place in respect of the sea-devil who, at times, comes up on land and drags people with him into the sea. The Aqvamboes and Adampes, who receive their share, watch to see

---

[200] On the Asante route to the coast via River Volta, see Wilks (1958) 140–1; S. Tenkorang, 'The importance of firearms in the struggle between Ashanti and the coastal states', *Transactions of the Historical Society of Ghana* 9 (1968) 5–6,16; Fynn (1971) 80; Wilks (1975) 24, 25; Green (1981) 130, 131–7.

[201] Letters were sent from Accra reporting that the Akwamu were preventing Asante from free passage to the coast, that trade was being obstructed, and that slaves were being smuggled to the ships at night (BLL, Furley N47 (1749), letters 21, 22, 30). On the situation, see Wilks (1958) 141; Fynn (1971) 80–1; Kwamena-Poh (1973) 74; Green (1981) 127, 221 note 25.

[202] Akan kɔtɔkɔ 'porcupine' (Christaller (1881/1933) 260. The porcupine is the animal symbol of Asante still in use today.

when young Assiantes have 'necessary business' outside the city. They usually go into the bush or the tall grass, where several Aqvamboes and Adampes fall upon them and lead /225/ them to a secure place. When there had been a ship in the Fredensborg road, or only a boat, it has been observed that the Aqvamboes, with the help of the Adampis, have taken two or three Assiantes away before the eyes of the others, and led them, carried them, or thrust them to the edge of the sea, shouting at the top of their voices. A boat would be lying ready to transport them further, and far from the other Assiantes reacting to this swindle, chasing after the robbers, and rescuing their countrymen, they run away and hide so that the sea-devil will not take them with him. Then, when the Adampis and the Aqvamboes return to the Assiantes, they express regret at not having been able to overpower the sea-devils, who were so strong that even though they fought them all the way to the edge of the sea, nevertheless several Aqvamboes and Assiantes were seized.

These circumstances continued until 1746 when there arose a conflict between Oppoccu and Brunni, Frempung's successor. This was because of a slave, a native Akim, who had been captured in war and since that time had been an Assiante slave. He had fled from Assiante to Akim, and Oppoccu demanded his return. Brunni sent five ounces of gold as ransom /226/ money for this slave, but Oppoccu sent it back with many threats. Brunni and his neighbour, [King] Ascharri, became frightened and fled from their country to the border of Fanteland, where they were made welcome.

Pobbi [the Chief of Akyem Abuakwa] remained in his country a long time after that, and Oppoccu sent him an Assiante heir to the throne, as an assurance that no evil would befall him and he would not he be attacked. Pobbi kept the noble child and pretended to be satisfied. He promised that he would remain in his country, but realized that Oppoccu only wanted to make him feel safe in this way, and would suddenly attack him. Therefore he retired to the others, where the Akims are still said to be, but none comes to the coast. The Fantes take goods, etc. to them, fifty miles up-country.[203]

Great disorder arose at times among the small nations, such as the Mountain Negroes. Some sided with the Akims, some sided with Aqvamboes, or with the Assiantes. They made war on, or more correctly, sneaked up on, one another, and killed each other. So the matter stood until 1749, when Oppoccu died. He had chosen his successor himself, and had made his people promise they would make him king. But there was a /227/ closer heir to the throne who, after Oppoccu's death, killed the chosen one and all his people.[204]

---

[203] For Brunni, Ascharri, and Pobbi, see note 147 above. The Akyems left their country and became allies of Fante (Fynn (1971) 80).

[204] R.'s statement is only partially correct since it was the elders of Kumasi who chose the successor on the basis of blood-line and ability. The leading candidates were Kusi Obodom (an elderly man) and either of two brothers, Dako Panin and Dako Kuma. There are several versions of what happened to the brothers — either they left after being defeated or they were killed in battle — and Kusi Obodom was installed as the third *Asantehene* (king of Asante) (McCaskie (1995) 175–7).

Before Oppoccu died, his chosen heir to the throne had to promise to make an effort to acquire from Elmina the coffin and throne mentioned earlier. He was then to put Oppoccu's body into the coffin, declare war on Fante, and take the body with him to the war. Once Fante had been destroyed, the body was to be carried everywhere in Fanteland, so that Oppoccu could look around. After that was done, they were to bury him, accompanied by the throne, etc., [items] of which Oppoccu would avail himself in the other world.[205]

Ever since the Akims fled from their country, small wars have almost regularly been fought between the Akims and the Aqvamboes. In one of these wars Pobbi killed two Aqvamboe Big Men, namely their king, Oppoccu Chuma, and Adjang. The Akims took their heads, an occurrence which our Labode fetish had announced at Labode at the same moment as when it happened, twenty to thirty miles away.[206] At the time he was installed on the throne Oppoccu Chuma resembled his forefathers in every way. He took from Acondo Chuma almost everything he had, and the other Aqvamboes helped him in this.[207] It can thus be seen that the same temperament still /228/ exists among these people as [was evident] in former times, although they can reckon only 4,000 souls among them, while our Accras are more than twice as strong [? numerous].

[Future conditions?]

The reader can [now] see what conditions prevail in the very famous Guinea slave trade. As things go in Accra, so do things above and below Accra, along the entire Coast. How they will go in the days hereafter can be concluded from the past experience. Had the Europeans, when they first came to that land, divided the Guinea Coast among themselves, they would have had more authority over the Blacks than they do now. They could have prevented many inhuman deeds and much destruction by refusing to sell to a tyrant gunpowder, muskets, etc. But it cannot be done now. If one party does not want to, another does. As said earlier, in commerce it is profit and interest which make us Europeans accomplices of murderers and thieves. It is clear in the nature of things that if the Assiantes destroy the Akims and Fantes, together with their allies, and if the Assiantes are then destroyed by a nation beyond them, then the land will be quite empty of /229/ inhabitants for a distance of two hundred miles along the coast, and three hundred miles up into the land. The Europeans could then establish colonies there, and perhaps acquire gold at a price equivalent to that of

---

[205] On the carrying around of a corpse, see Rattray (1927) 167; Field (1961) 200. Even today, the coffin bearing a deceased is carried through a town, so that leave can be taken of the dead individual's family and friends; and the coffin 'directs' the bearers, forcing them to lurch and move in directions desired by the deceased.

[206] For the prophesy, see /98/–/99/ above.

[207] For a critique of R.'s report, see Wilks (1958) 135–7.

iron. Furthermore, in order that the Europeans should not lack slaves for the West Indies, they would have to set up new establishments above [? west of] Gold Coast. Within a few years, cunning Aqvamboes would also be found among the most devout Blacks in Africa, unless the Europeans became as mixed on the new Coast as on the old. Anyone can see that this is written ironically.[208]

We Danes could, perhaps, hold out the longest in respect of slave trade on Guinea provided that we retain [exclusive rights to] River Volta, as we have done thus far, and will continue to do as long as we have reasonable people in the government there. It is our property, as will be shown later, and no nation has a stronger legal right to establishments from which they can exclude others, than we have to River Volta.[209]

[Some cunning Africans]

Before I end this chapter I must tell [the reader] about some of the cunning and pranks of the Blacks on the Guinea Coast. For several years King Assiamboe of Little Popo had swindled so many ship's captains that finally no one would /230/ anymore go ashore to trade with him. He once saw two large ships sailing past. He sent a messenger to say that if they would come ashore with goods and trade with him both of them could purchase their [cargo of] slaves, since he had a thousand young, fine slaves. They sent the Blacks from the Gold Coast they had aboard as sailors, to see if this was true.[210] The Blacks could not report anything other than what they had seen, which was, that in the king's residence a great number of shackled slaves were sitting. The captains still did not want to believe their sailors, but anchored and sent an officer ashore. He reported the same

---

[208] The exact point R. is making is less than transparent, partly because of his claim of writing 'ironically'. He is perhaps saying that European colonies would bring (a) missionaries and conversion to Christianity, thus improving even the Akwambu, and (b) order and morality to the existing trade, rendering it more profitable. But it is unclear how far back the 'irony' extends. Perhaps he recognized that the idea of European colonies was, at the time, utopian, and he perhaps hints that there would always be 'cunning Aqvamboes', or their equivalent, eager to make a quick profit. It is also unclear what kind of 'mixture' R. is referring to, a mixture of European nationals, or an admixture with Africans, commercially and/or biologically.

[209] The Danes' first attempt at gaining a foothold in the River Volta area was in 1710 (Nørregård (1966) 95). Their interest continued sporadically, but by R.'s time other Europeans were competing with the Danes. R. later speaks of River Volta as 'indisputably our property' and of 'our exclusive right' to the river awarded by the Ada after the Danes had saved them from an attack by the Akwamu (278–81 below). This claim to commercial monopoly (but not territorial acquisition) was repeated in 1781 to justify Danish attempts to control the marine export/import trade of the area (Green (1981) 160–1). A renewed thrust under Governor Kiøge resulted in Danish participation in a local war on the side of the Ada, and the construction of two forts (Isert [1788] (1992) 37–8, 74).

[210] The employment of Africans as ocean sailors being uncommon in this period (although professional canoemen existed on Gold Coast), R.'s reference, if correct, is of interest.

thing, and the captains were pleased that they would be able to purchase their slaves so quickly. They came ashore themselves, and in a few days each fetched his cargo [of trade-goods] ashore, and was ready to begin buying slaves and transporting them on board. But at night all those slaves ran away (according to [the explanation offered by] Assiamboe). In fact, they were all young, free Negroes, to each of whom their king had promised a present of a bottle of brandy if they would sit in chains for a few days. In this way Assiamboe enticed the captains ashore with their goods, and they could not leave until the king himself was able collect slaves to give them, for which the captains had to pay a much higher price than they had contracted. /231/ They had to stay there for nine or ten months, taking both young and old [as slaves].[211]

During the time I lodged with Assiamboe at Little Popo, I was bothered once a week by two score of Assiamboe's musicians who, on the [week]day of his birth, paid their respects outside his residence, not far from where my house was. They began at 12 o'clock at night and continued until the next midday. The most remarkable person among these musicians was, in my opinion, an old, blind singer. He often groped his way forward along the walls to reach the courtyard. His head and body were hung about with bells. The bells tinkled when he moved, and when he had arrived in the courtyard he always sang the same song. When that was over, he leapt, and at every leap he shouted one of Assiamboe's great names, and he also recited almost a complete threescore of names of Big Men, men whose bane Assiamboe had been.[212] My servant translated the words of this song for me and it goes like this. 'A little boy lives in this house, but when he grows up, what will become of the entire world?' This is as if to say that Assiamboe would be fortunate enough not only /232/ to wipe out his enemies, but also the whole human race, and would turn the entire world upside down.[213] The Negroes also take titles of honour from those they have killed, which we come to hear when they are drinking or are drunk. Those present make it a point to please a Big Man, and in order to do so even more, (the drinker) reminds a Big Man of his great deeds by calling and shouting out, '[You

---

[211] This anecdote is not very convincing. If trade at Aneho [Little Popo] was already languishing because of the swindling of Ashangmo (Assiambo), why would he perpetrate yet another swindle? Painting a picture of Ashangmo as totally untrustworthy does not fit with R.'s later encounters with him, and the trust placed in him in regard to the Danish establishment at Keta (see Appendix B). In fact R. maintained contact with Ashangmo long after he had returned to Denmark. In 1767 he wrote in warm terms of friendship to 'my friend, the King of Popo', wishing him well and sending him gifts (*Herrnhut, Archiv der Brüder-Unität*, R1 5 N5/13 dd, 27.11.1767 — I am indebted to Adam Jones for providing me with this document).

[212] On this type of 'verbal art', consisting of reminiscences and memorized speech, see J. Vansina, *Oral Tradition as History* (1988) 11–17.

[213] R.'s explanation of the laconic words may or may not have been correct. This type of 'birthday' celebration was certainly performed only by wealthy men and perhaps women. For descriptions of similar occasions, see Rask (1754) 177; Isert [1788] (1992) 62.

have been] N.N.'s nemesis!', etc. For instance, when Oppoccu drinks, those around him shout, 'Nemesis of Bang! Nemesis of Ursue!', and so on.[214]

Corrantryn at Anomabu, whom the French have often called the Emperor of the Guinea Coast, frequently takes pleasure in entertaining Europeans in his house and treating them sumptuously, whether they are those who live on the Coast or are officers from the ships. He willingly gives them lodging for the night, and usually brings to each one a black woman, inviting him to pass the night with her. But this evil Black has had an infected women brought in, and when the Europeans leave him the next day, to return to either their forts or their ships, he [later] asks about them eagerly. And when he hears that these good friends are ill, or /233/ are lying in the steam cabinet, he is tremendously pleased by it.[215]

Corrantryn was once discovered to have seized, or to have had seized, two of his townsmen, and to have sold them to a ship whose captain was to sail that same night to the Lower Coast. The friends of the two who were seized sent a boat (a canoe) after the ship and ransomed them from the captain by a payment of four slaves. They then returned to Anomabu. Now here was clear evidence that Corrantryn had seized them. The two Negroes who had been ransomed and had returned explained the manner in which they had been seized; in which of Corrantryn's slave dungeons they had sat for eight days; which of Corrantryn's people had stolen them; and which other [of his] men had taken them aboard the ship at night. They said that Corrantryn himself was on board and had received goods [for the slaves], and had asked the captain to be sure to hide these stolen slaves, etc. But the captain, contrary to his promise, had anchored at Accra, where the friends came after him and ransomed the slaves. Everyone on the Coast now thought that Corrantryn was finished, that he now had to take responsibility for all the robberies which had taken place over a score of years in Anomabu city, because /234/ people had gone missing every week, just as in other places, and no one had known what had become of them. The insulted caboceer, to whose family belonged the Negroes who had been seized and who returned, was ten times as strong as Corrantryn. Everyone thought if the insulted caboceer did not kill Corrantryn, he would at least take from him everything he had in the world. But, note [as follows] how [Corrantryn] saved himself and escaped [punishment].

---

[214] R. chooses to use the present tense, but by the time he wrote Oppoccu (Opoku Ware) was dead.

[215] The steam cabinet was a standard treatment for syphilis at the time. The man described so colourfully and in such demeaning terms was Eno Baisie Kurentsi, alias John Currantee, the influential Fante leader and merchant, and founder of a dynasty of powerful chiefs. See Chapter 2 above, note 104. For his manoeuvring between the French and the English during their rivalry for influence at Anomabu, a main centre for the slave trade, see Priestley (1969) 39–42, 45–6, 50–1. R.'s disapproval of the man was no doubt related to his frustration at seeing the extent of the trade at Anomabu compared with that at Christiansborg.

The insulted caboceer, Corrantryn's enemy, sent a messenger bearing gifts to all the Big Men in Fante, inviting them to come to Anomabu on a certain day to hear and judge this case. They all arrived on the appointed day. The caboceer at Anomabu and the witnesses presented their case against Corrantryn, in his presence and absolutely clearly. This happened on the first day. It was decided that Corrantryn should defend himself legally on the second day, or suffer the punishment. Corrantryn was present the following day, and all the Fante Grandees sat to hear his counter-evidence. Corrantryn stepped forward and said that everything his enemy had presented was false, and as proof of this he would cut the throat of his dearest son. Corrantryn took hold of a child about /235/ twelve years old, took out his dagger, and [moved as if he] was about to kill him. All the judges and those present jumped up to stop him. Since that time this case is neither thought of nor spoken of any more.

In the event of the case being taken up again the child's mother feared for his life, so she sent the little boy to me at Accra, since I already had his brother, Bassi. I supported these children, and others, in order to retain Corrantryn's friendship with the Danes, not only for the sake of the trading ships but also for the safety of our Company slaves, who, at that time, had to fetch provisions for us from Fante.[216] I have never met Corrantryn or any of his wives, but I have heard him spoken of nearly every day. Another point should be noted. Corrantryn has in this instance imitated Nanni, with this difference, Nanni would really have murdered four of his children, and thereby moved all the judges to [condemn and] take the lives of his accusers, even if they had proved Nanni's commission of a number of pranks.[217]

The Negroes have certain degrees in their ranks, and [in relation to this] they use the expression 'to make custom [*Coustyme*]'.[218] The first custom is (in Danish) the *Smørball Coustyme* ['butterball ritual']. When a Negro is about sixteen years old, he must /236/ build himself a hut. When it is finished he announces to his comrades (little boys) the exact day on which he will make custom, that is to say, he will no longer be in their guild [*sc*. age-set] but will now count himself among those who are considered to be young men. He will have spoken to the young men previously, and they will have declared him worthy to be included in their number.

---

[216] Bassi was the son of Kurentsi who had been in France (/80/, /83/, /84/ above). This is an example of the system of fostering the children of leaders with Europeans, for their training. This practice, together with that of providing education in Europe for the sons of caboceers, was an important component in African-European trading relations (J.J. Crooks, *Records relating to the Gold Coast Settlements* [1923] (1973) 26–7, 28–30; Priestley (1969) 20–1, 39–40).

[217] The reference here is to *Ananse*, the trickster described at length earlier (Chapter 3, /52/–/57/).

[218] R. is referring to a social system of age groups (age sets) and the consequent *rites de passage* between sets, rites known as 'making custom' (Isert [1788] (1992) 132; Field (1937) 191–5).

The candidate will have prepared a great portion of a [particular] dish (*smørballer*, which is actually a porridge containing palm oil). He has many small clay pots filled with *smørballer* for the little boys who have been invited to be his guests. The candidate sits himself down in his new hut with this dish in front of him. His guests arrive and form two lines in front of the candidate's door, as if he were going to run the gauntlet [through them]. Each guest picks up a small pot containing *Smørball* and pretends to be eating. When there are several score gathered outside the hut, the candidate waits no longer but comes running out of the hut and runs between the rows of his comrades. Each of them takes the pot of the food described above, and [with it] strikes the head or body of the candidate. He runs to the first water he can reach, washes himself, and thus he has become a man. Slave children can also perform this custom, but it has no significance [for them].[219] /**237**/

When a Negro or Negress has been married and a child has been born, or he has acquired several slaves, etc., then they perform the Tiger Custom. A hunter kills a tiger, and the Negro making the custom, and his friends, eat the meat. He carries the hide of the tiger around for a few days, with a great following, singing and dancing. Then follows their Buffalo Custom, when they act in the same way as they do in the Tiger Custom.[220] Finally they have the Barbaric Custom, when they cut off the head of a slave, take out the jawbone, and carry it around with a similar following, drinking, dancing, and shouting.[221]

They have yet another custom that is rarely seen. It is celebrated when they are building a house, and the clay for the walls must be moistened with brandy, or, which is less desirable, with palm wine. The king at Little Popo, Assiamboe, has not only had his entire residence, which is of great size, built with brandy, but, at every half-span of the walls he has stuck on all manner of European goods, such as cotton [cloth], Silesian linen, etc. This widely renowned residence, in which I lodged for six weeks, looks dreadful. Rain has washed some of the clay walls away from the exterior, exposing /**238**/ the [textile] fibres. It much resembles a great heap of sweepings. The patches hanging exposed there are so bleached that one

---

[219] R.'s *smørball* is his analogous identification of a ritual dish called *fotoli* made of cooked corn dough and palm oil. The male puberty rite, today known as *butrumwoo* or *kromotsunwoo*, appears to have been practised in a similar fashion for at least two centuries (Isert [1788] (1992) 132; Monrad (1815) 55–6; Field (1937) 191–5).

[220] For 'tigers' in Africa, see Chapter 3, note 22.

[221] It is implied, although not stated, that all these 'Customs' are also age-set initiation rites, occurring when a man achieves a particular age. For the rites of 'buffalo custom' and 'tiger custom', see the description of a feast in which a caboceer honoured his senior wife with the the hide of a buffalo or 'tiger', i.e. leopard ('Inboorlingenrecht van de kust van Guinea 1851', *Bijdragen tot de Taal-, Land- en Volkenkunde van Nederlandsch-Indie* 88 (1931), 311–12). I owe this reference to René Baesjou.

cannot see what colour they originally were.[222] The Negroes at Popo called this residence a fortress, and I believe it has cost easily as much as a fort. Assiamboe has four cannons without their gun carriages. Shortly before I arrived there, he had caught four of his enemies (Dahomet Negroes), whose heads he had cut into small pieces, placed them in the cannons, and shot them away. He told me his enemies would have to hunt for a long time before they could recover their heads.[223]

At the Dutch fort at Accra a Negro named Qvaté was in conflict with a fetish priest in the same town. He took his revenge as follows. The fetish priest had been out fishing so late that it was dark when he was returning to his home in town. Qvaté, together with some of his sons, waylaid the priest on the path and killed him. Qvaté cut off the head of his enemy and buried the body. The alarm was immediately raised. What had become of the fetish priest? But no one knew. They asked the fetish himself about his priest and received the answer (according to the Blacks) that Qvaté had killed him, and /239/ the head was in his house. Qvaté appealed to greater fetishes, but they all said the same thing. The friends of the fetish priest and all the townsfolk attacked Qvaté in his house, and after ransacking it they found the head of the missing priest, as well as the heads of some thirty other people, all of whom had been his enemies. This devilish Qvaté had diverted himself every night with these skulls. He had had a large hole or cellar dug and had covered it with boards upon which he laid his mat, or bed, and there he slept. You might say that he brooded over these heads. He picked them up at night, pounded on the skulls with an iron stick, and derided them in other ways. The only punishment he received was that his eldest son had to shoot him to death, and each of the families of the dead was able to retrieve the head belonging to that family.

Many Negroes have such a strong desire to gamble that sometimes they gamble away all they have and hold, and finally gamble away their own body, which is sold by the player who has won it.[224]

At times we Europeans are swindled by the Negroes who sell female slaves. When they are young we buy them. At times the [sellers] keep back

---

[222] On wall decoration, see L.E. Jefferson, *The Decorative Arts of Africa* (1974) 180ff.; Cole and Ross (1977) 86ff. Since this was a royal residence, brandy may indeed have been used to moisten the wall surfaces to assure adherence of a finish rendering coat, but it is more likely that it was used to pour libations rather than as a component in construction. The use of imported cotton or linen cloth (a use not mentioned in other sources) may have been because this was regarded as more sumptuous than the use of prosaic materials such as straw or chaff (p.c. LaBelle Prussin).
[223] On the conflict between Ashangmo and Dahomey in which Dahomey was defeated in 1737, see Law (1991) 316–7. On veneration of heads, especially those of royalty, see R. Law, 'Between the sea and the lagoons', *Cahiers d'Études Africaines* 29 (1989) 404, 405, 407, 413. Given the importance of heads for display, a deliberate destruction of heads was the ultimate insult. In West African ideology, the deceased whose body/head had been mutilated, would not be able to take up a position as an ancestor in the world after death.
[224] On love of gambling, see Isert [1788] (1992) 137; Monrad (1822) 248; Law (1991) 69.

in town an unweaned child belonging to a female slave, and after they have received their goods /**240**/ they produce the child, asking us if they should throw it away, or if the mother should have it. The European sees that he has been swindled, and the child is given to the female slave. When a French captain buys a slave from us he, too, must not be allowed to see the children, otherwise he thrusts aside the slave woman who has the child. The factor does the same thing to the captain as the Negroes had done to him. When he delivers the slaves and the ship's officers are waiting to receive them at the coast, each mother carries her child on her back. Then I have seen most of the French take the child from the mother's back and throw it onto the beach, pushing the mother into the boat, and sailing away with her. I have never seen the English ship's officers do this. The French say, and this is true, that a female slave with a child takes up thrice as much room as a single slave. We Danes have then [rescued] these abandoned children and delivered them to be brought up by the female company slaves who cook food for the purchased slaves, but I have seen none who have reached adulthood: At other places I have seen these discarded children where they were left, lying like a kitten, until, at night, a wolf may have dragged them off.[225] Those slaves who come from far north in the land /**241**/ think we Europeans have bought them to be fattened like swine, and that we eat them when they become fat. I cannot describe to what degree of desperation this fear drives them, so they seek to kill us.[226]

[Gold Coast ceremonies]

For the Negroes' enjoyment, and for funerals, there must be music. Their most important music is the [sound of] hornblowing. The horns are small, hollowed-out elephant's tusks, and at a breadth of one or two fingers from the pointed end there is a hole into which to blow. Both high and low sounds are produced by large and small horns.[227] Among the [other] instruments are to be found large and small drums, which are accompanied by the vocal music of the dancers. This is the most pleasurable music for the Blacks,

---

[225] These remarks are typical of R.'s attitude to the various European nations on the Coast: the French are totally heartless, the British are paragons of virtue, the Danes are pragmatic (and the Dutch are treacherous). An English source mentions the taking of women and children, with no indication that this was undesirable (Snelgrave (1734) 120). For the French export of children (aged up to 11 or 12) calculated at 26.6% of all slaves in 1715–1792, see D. Geggus 'Sex ratio, age and ethnicity in the Atlantic slave trade' *Journal of African History* 30 (1989) 26–27, 28 table 2, 39–40.

[226] Other contemporary sources also report this fear (Barbot [1732] (1992) 550; Isert [1788] (1992) 175; Snelgrave (1734) 163; Monrad (1822) 297). The particular fear of being killed to be eaten seems to have related to the belief that the eater acquires the vital power, the 'soul', of the eaten, and so removes the latter's other-world prospects (p.c. P.E.H. Hair).

[227] On horns, see Bosman (1705) 138; Isert [1788] (1992) 40; Reindorf (1895/1966) 122/114; Kyerematen (1964) 56–61; Cole and Ross (1977) 168.

but the most abominable for a European.²²⁸ Next comes the so-called kitt, a flute as long as a medium-sized Spanish cane. The [players] blow through the thickest end, and toward the thin end they have [cut] three holes. This means that they can produce three notes on them, and their octave is six notes in all. Then they have the drums and the klink klink, or hollow iron, on which the rhythm is beaten with an iron rod. The flutes are actually hollowed out Spanish cane. The cane grows in the north interior in low-lying places where there are entire forests of cane. An Englishman /242/ who has visited the places in China where the cane grows, told me that the Chinese put a varnish on it; and if it were cultivated on the Coast, they could produce more Spanish cane in Africa than in Asia. The flute music is somewhat more pleasant to listen to, provided the drum and clinking are not playing.²²⁹ Apart from this, the Blacks can easily provide their own music, by simply tapping their hands on a board, to a certain rhythm to which they dance. As soon as a child can stand on its feet, the mother claps her hands and clicks her tongue, [providing rhythms] to which the young one performs his movements.

A marriage is usually decided with the bride's father, who is given a couple of bottles of brandy as earnest money, and then the bridegroom can let the bride wait for several years, if it is not convenient for him to make his custom immediately. The father does not dare give his daughter to another, since he has taken earnest money, as stated.²³⁰ When the wedding is to be held, or, in the Negro language, custom is to be made, the bridegroom gives to the bride's father and mother, and perhaps to some of her brothers and sisters, a cloth (a *pantjes*),²³¹ which is made up of a *favn* of cotton, /243/ chintz, silk taffeta, or whatever type of cloth they wish.²³² The bride is normally given three or four *pantjes*. Then their friends gather and consume one or two ankers of brandy in toasting the bridegroom. They usually borrow kitt players (or musicians) and dance throughout the entire day, and then the ceremony is over. The eldest wife has rank above every

---

²²⁸ On drums, see Rask (1754) 217–9; Bosman (1705) 139–40; Monrad (1822) 244; and for modern descriptions, Rattray (1923), chapter 22; J.H.K. Nketia, *Drumming in Akan Communities of Ghana* (1963) 11–2, 14–5, 110–111, 196–7; Kyerematen (1964) 60–6.

²²⁹ On the 'kitt' (Akan *kete*) ensemble, see Isert [1788] (1992) 137–8; Monrad (1822) 245–6; Rattray (1927) 143, 193, 196, 199, 201, 281–2; Nketia (1963) 128–33, 149, 182; Kyerematen (1964) 57, 61.

²³⁰ Earnest money' is known in Gã as *agbo im* 'door/gate-knocking drink'. Although the cost, value and contents of Gã marriage gifts have changed over the years, the basic components of the gifts remain the same today: for the bride, cloth, together with scarves, jewellery, etc.; for the mother and father of the bride and for her brothers, money; for the guests, drinks and money (p.c. I. Odotei).

²³¹ Dutch *pantjes* 'waist-cloth, loin-cloth' (Isert [1788] (1992) 38–9). Variants of this term, related to the French *pagne* or Portuguese *pano*, are found in other eighteenth century sources: *paan* (Bosman (1705) 121); *pankis* (Rask (1754) 215).

²³² A *favn* (etymologically related to the English 'fathom') is a unit of length of about 2m.

other wife, and everything a Negro gives to his wives is shared out among them by her.[233]

Their funerals are held in nearly the same way. They weep during the first day, but then they play and dance for eight days. The corpse is normally buried in the house where the person has lived, but no one, except for the closest friends, knows the [exact] place.[234] Afterwards each person who has been a friend of the deceased arrives, bringing an anker, or a half anker, of brandy to be contributed to the enjoyment of the whole party. If the deceased was a caboceer or a Big Man, in addition to an anker of brandy there must be given forty to fifty pounds of gunpowder, which is fired off. On the last day they all paint themselves white and carry large staves in their hands, as if they were going on a long journey. Each one normally has a book in his hand. The young and the old pretend to sing from the books, and this is to signify that the deceased, who can now read a book, is as wise as a European. /244/ They steal books from the Europeans for this purpose. I have seen books printed in Latin and other languages that the Blacks have stolen from the Europeans and saved to be employed in this way.[235]

Up-country, when an important king dies a large and deep trench is dug in the ground, into which the corpse is placed. All the limbs of [each of] the favourite wives of the deceased are first broken and then the wives are flung into the grave (336 wives were treated thus at the burial of the Akim King Frempung).[236] Thereafter the *okraer* (life-slaves) of the deceased, who in Frempung's case numbered more than 3,000, are maimed in the same

---

[233] On marriages and gifts, see Bosman (1705) 197–9; Barbot [1732] (1992) 502–3; Labat (1730) 325; Isert [1788] (1992) 140; Monrad (1822) 46–8. For modern descriptions, see W.F. Daniell, 'On the ethnography of Akkrah and Adampe', *Journal of the Ethnological Society* 4 (1856) 12; J.M.B. Meyers, 'The connubial institutions of the Gãs', *Journal of the African Society* 30 (1931) 399–409; Field (1940) 37–40; D.G. Azu, *The Gã Family and Social Change* (1974) 25–6; Kilson, (1974) 50, 53.

[234] In 1842, Wulff Joseph Wulff, following his last will and testament, was buried in his own house (C. Behrens, *Da Guinea var Dansk* (1917) 294), and his grave can still be seen in the basement, together with that of his daughter. For home burial, see Bosman (1705) 232; Isert [1788] (1992) 132; A. Adjei. 'Mortuary usages of the Gã people', *American Anthropologist* (1943) 87, 92.

[235] For the use of white clay (*ayilo*), see Reindorf (1895/1966) 126/118; McCaskie (1995) 282. The concept of a long journey still holds (Adjei (1943) 91). The carrying of books may have symbolized the individual's employment by Europeans, or possibly a belief in the inherent power of the written word to ward off evil. But R. may have been generalizing from a single incident he had witnessed. However, for funerals which include aspects of European influence, see Monrad (1822) 11–21.

[236] I have been unable to trace any confirmatory reports of such details as R. describes. On 'human sacrifice' among the Akan of the time, see De Marees [1602] (1987) 72; Barbot [1732] (1992) 595–6; Bosman (1705) 228–32; and more particularly among the Asante, Wilks (1993) 215 ff. Wholesale immolation may have been to some extent voluntary: cf. 'if some of his wives wish to follow him', they are killed and buried with him (Villault (1669) 345). This practice, noted in western Guinea from an earlier period, drew particular European attention and came to be regarded as an outstanding mark of barbarity, as differing not merely in degree from European customs (as was the case, for instance, with public executions) but in kind. So R. was sending an especially powerful signal. Rask stated that the dead were buried in a standing position (Rask (1754) 191).

way. Down in the trench, these people can live for as long as eight days; and the king's subjects, one family after another, gather around the trench, shouting, dancing, shooting, drinking, and weeping. The Blacks have assured me that this noise and alarum can be heard for a mile away, which is indeed credible. The *okraer* of important kings are actually Blacks who have made an agreement with their king to die when the king dies, in the manner described above, therefore each of the other subjects must show them respect and give them everything they want. The king himself has /245/ no servants other than his *okraer* to wait on him, cook his food, etc.

I stated above, when writing about the marriage arrangements of the Black, that once a bridegroom has given his father-in-law a bottle of brandy as earnest money he can wait a few years [before completing the marriage] without anyone coming ahead of him to take his place. But there are no rules without exceptions, and so it is in this case. For instance, if a European appears and wishes to take the bride [for himself], the contract is no longer valid, but to satisfy the first suitor he must be given back his earnest money. It may be only a European soldier, yet he is given the bride, even if an important caboceer paid the earnest money. The Europeans call this manner of marrying to *callischare*.[237] There are Europeans who *callischarer* with more than one Negress, and under our fort, as well at as the forts of the other nations, we have many children begotten of such a [form of] marriage. They are neither white nor black, but yellow, and are called Mulattos. Bishop Worm has granted a dispensation allowing all the Danes at Christiansborg to take to themselves a black woman, yet N.B. (*nota bene*), not more than one, and on the following conditions: (1) the husband must promise to see his heathen wife converted to Christianity; /246/ (2) when the husband returns to Europe, he will take her with him, N.B. if she wishes to go. On these conditions each man of our nation has his mistress. Among other nations such ceremonies are not used.[238]

---

[237] An African family might be prepared to give a European precedence over a woman already promised as a wife to an African if this gained them practical advantages in terms of closer business connections with the Europeans. Marriage alliances as forms of business strategy were as well understood in West Africa as in Europe, in the former for instance, allowing itinerant African merchants to have a wife in each of several commercial centres. An African woman promised when young might be noted by a European and asked for, but given the small number of Europeans, the reservoir of nubile African women, and Gold Coast social and sexual ethics (with limited concern about pre-marital sex), it seems unlikely that the circumstance R. cites was more than very uncommon.

[238] Christen Worm, Bishop of Sjælland 1711–1737, was a reformer noted for his success in effecting changes in the Danish educational system, in the system of criminal punishment (abolition of the pillory); and, within the church and family, in strict Sabbatarian practice. I have been unable to find the document to which R. refers, but its substance is in keeping with the attitudes of Bishop Worm. Note that R. does not exempt himself in the penultimate sentence. Although 'others'—presumably men at the other forts—did not have precisely the same arrangements, at Elmina several marriages took place according to Dutch law (Feinberg (1989) 89). On the Danish marriages and the 'mulatto treasury' which assured a degree of financial support for the wife and children, see Isert [1788] (1992) 157.

The Negroes firmly believe that it is a great blessing to have a white child in their families, and a family, no matter how poor it is, will contribute to support the little Mulatto, supplying shirts, etc. We have seen instances of black royal women destined to bring into the world only heirs to the throne, who have married a soldier.[239] Although Mulattos cannot inherit the throne, they can inherit their mother's brother's wealth.[240] Christian Prott, who has studied here in Copenhagen, is actually heir to the wealth of Assiamboe at Little Popo, and, had he been black, would have been heir to his throne as well.[241] Indeed, according to the law of the Blacks, Christian Prott ought to have the kingdom of Afolli, who was Assiamboe's predecessor and Prott's mother's brother, but Prott was not present in the country when Afolli died, and Assiamboe took everything.[242] It is known that Christian Prott's father was a soldier at our Christiansborg.

Both good and evil come of these marriages (if they can be called that). What is good is that /**247**/ a wanton European [243] has a black crone, since

---

[239] Having a mulatto child as a family member had obvious advantages in terms of participation in the European establishment, as the important positions attained by many families involved in mixed marriages bears witness. This may have extended to mixed sexual unions (not always on the European side considered marriages): 'if a Negress is so fortunate as to give birth to a Mulatto child, she is entitled to support from this [Mulatto] treasury until the child is grown. The most usual amount given her is two *rixdaler* each month' (Monrad (1822) 378–9). Similar arrangements may well have existed in R.'s day. In general, on familial relations in mixed marriages between Europeans and non-Europeans in earlier times, and on the care of the children resulting, see N. Everts. 'Cherchez la femme' *Itinerario* (1996) 48–54.

[240] There seems to be some confusion here regarding laws of inheritance. What R. states resembles the Akan laws based on the matriline, whereas all the individuals under discussion are Gã, whose laws of inheritance are based on the patriline (for the law of succession among the Gã, see Quaye (1972) 251–3). However, the Otublohum quarter of Accra was mixed, and perhaps inheritance was based on the filiation that was most advantageous (p.c. I. Wilks).

[241] 'Prott' is Christian Protten (born Christiansborg 1715, died there 1769), whose mother was Gã and father Danish. For the education of Protten in Copenhagen, his involvement with the Moravian Brethren and his unsuccessful attempts to become a missionary on Gold Coast, see Reindorf (1895/1966) 221–2/214–6. What Reindorf neglected to report was that Christian Protten made his mark in the field of linguistics, having published a pioneering work on local languages, especially on the grammar of Gã, his mother tongue (*En nyttig Grammaticalsk Indledelse til Tvende hidindtil gandske ubekiendte Sprog, Fanteisk og Acraisk* (1764); translated as *Introduction to the Fante and Ga languages* (1971)), this activity making him the earliest West African and Ghanaian grammarian (p.c. M.E. Kropp Dakubu).

[242] 'Afolli' is probably Foli Bebe, otherwise Ofori Bembeneen (1694–1722), father of Assiongbon Dandjin (Gayibor (1995) 203–5).

[243] There is a problem in translation here. The original text has *en liderlig Europæer*, which translates as 'a lecherous/lewd/ wanton European'. But an adjective resembling *liderlig* in spelling, *lidende*, means 'suffering, in need, in dire straits'. If R. really meant 'wanton', the adjective was being applied to a group from which he did not exclude himself. It has, in fact, been stated (although without adequate evidence) that R. was married to an Akwamu princess (Nørregård (1966) 106). R. may well have wished to moralize when writing as a leading citizen of Copenhagen and an established paterfamilias. Nevertheless, the context, and the apparently sympathetic reference to Bishop Worm's dispensation, suggests that he meant to indicate that the European was *lidende*, that is, suffering/in need.

she will not let him starve to death. It is possible for her to obtain food for her husband from her parents or friends, and to take care, when the husband receives his salary, that they are repaid, although not very much, and at a lower price than a foreigner could purchase the food. She knows she would suffer greatly should her white husband die, since she will [then] be hated by her friends. Indeed, she could be sometimes severely beaten, because the Negroes believe that no young person dies a natural death but instead dies as a result of witchcraft, and the deceased's wife must not have felt enough love for her husband or she would have paid the fetish to save him.[244] But that Negress is truly unfortunate who has lost two white men due to death. The Negroes would consider a man mad who would [risk being] the third.

The evil [aspect] is when such a woman has relationships with other black men at the same time [as she is married to the European]. She knows that if she brings a black child into the world, the European will sell her and her lover — unless her parents ransom them. In order to escape accusation she [therefore] poisons her husband before she gives birth, after his death she goes into confinement and the baby is killed, /**248**/ while she claims that it was stillborn. The other young Negresses in town, who also would willingly be as fortunate as she had been, curse her soundly for several days, and then it is over. If we wished to prevent this evil, we would have to make it known that no Negress who is married to a European will be sold or punished if she misbehaves in such a manner [*sc.* by having relations with Blacks], but her husband can show her the door and take another woman. However, it would be shameful for the Danes to suffer a Black to get the better of them with impunity. Moreover, it might be the case that the knowledge of the shame and mockery such a woman would suffer at the hands of the other Blacks [when sent away by her European] would bring her to commit the same desperate deed [of poisoning him and killing the baby] as described above.[245] /**249**/

---

[244] R. presents a consideration of the advantages of a sexual and domestic partnership between a European man and a non-European woman not common in his time, by stressing the local circumstances. That the African woman was in a position to purchase food more cheaply and that such an alliance helped to lessen the European's home sickness was later stated by Isert [1788] (1992) 157. R. adds the advantage of nursing in sickness and therefore of life-preservation, a consideration of primary importance, given the high rate of European mortality on the Coast. Regarding unnatural death, that is, death other than that caused by old age, and the local concept of 'poisoning' (whether physical or supernatural), see Adjei (1943) 85–6; and further on 'witchcraft' and death due to melancholy, R.H. Debrunner, *Witchcraft in Ghana* (1961) 46–8. On the life of Europeans at Elmina, which was comparable to that at Christiansborg, see Feinberg (1989) 86–88.

[245] On miscegenation at Elmina, and attempts to hinder unfaithfulness on the part of the African wives or mistresses, see Feinberg (1989) 89.

Chapter 5

About the trade of the Danes, as well as about their forts and establishments on the Guinea Coast

Everyone knows that our trade to the Guinea Coast and the West Indies was not of the greatest importance in former times, and exceedingly little in contrast to what it could have been, considering the extent to which the English, French, and Dutch have carried on this trade.

Our islands in the West Indies have existed only for [the benefit of] other nations, especially the Dutch.[1] It is still a mystery to me why the trade from here to the Coast and the West Indies in former times was not better managed, since it was known that other nations had their maritime trade to thank for their wealth and their power at sea. To these nations we have been of service by virtue of the many thousands of Norwegian, Danish, and Holsteiner sailors and officers who have left their homes in order to earn a living from foreigners, because we had nothing to offer them.[2] /250/

[Monopolies and forts as trade hindrances]

Trading monopolies are the most damaging brutes a country can have, and a plague for a land having many such. We Danes can claim this from our experience and our losses. Had we opened our eyes twenty-four years ago, we would have advanced further by now than we have done. Thank God, the monopolies have been abolished! Therefore our great king's name

---

[1] For the 1747 reorganisation of the Company's monopoly of trade in the West Indies and its effect on the Danish trade, now restricted, in contrast to the trade conveyed in ships from other countries, see Waldemar Westergaard, *The Danish West Indies under Company Rule* (1917) 230 ff. See also O. Feldbæk and O. Justesen, *Kolonierne i Asien og Afrika* (1980) 368–9; Johannes Postma, *The Dutch in the Atlantic Slave Trade* (1990) 13–17, 195–200.

[2] In fact, service across national lines was fairly universal. A classic example is that of Henrik Carlof, a German, who worked first for the Dutch Company, then the Swedes, then the Danes, then as an interloper working variously for several nations, especially the Dutch and French. See Erik Tilleman, *En Kort og Enfoldig Beretning* [1697] (1994) 2–3. For 'so-called Danes', meaning Dutch in Danish service, see Albert van Dantzig, *The Dutch and the Guinea Coast* (1978) 239; *Les Hollandais sur la Côte de Guinée* (1980a) 2; K.Y. Daaku, *Trade and Politics on the Gold Coast* (1970) 15; Postma, *The Dutch* (1990) 152–3. This applied not only to personnel but to shipping as well. For Danish ships sent out from Amsterdam, see Erik Gøbel, 'Danish trade to the West Indies and Guinea', *Scandinavian Economic History Review*, 1 (1983) 24–5.

will be blessed by his successors.[3] We cannot praise the Dutch for having abolished this monopoly on the grounds that it would serve the nation, for [they did it] instead because Dutch interlopers often became involved in skirmishes when they met Company ships on the Guinea Coast and in the West Indies. Yet the [? Dutch] government has greatly restricted those private shippers who send their ships there.[4]

By sound reasoning the English have abolished the trading monopolies of their African and West Indian Companies, profiting greatly by it. We know of privateers in London who have more [goods] in circulation between Europe, Africa, and America, than our entire West Indies Company had in stock.[5] We already have businesses /**251**/ here in Copenhagen (thank God) which have had more ships returning home in one year than the entire former West Indian Company had in two or indeed three years. Such an advantageous change has occurred in this country during a period of [only] six years. It can, and should get better, with the help of God.[6]

It is a known fact that a ship on the Guinea Coast can trade at less cost than a fortress can. If a ship's captain finds there is no trade for him at one place, or it is too slow, he sails to another. Contrariwise, a fort must suffer its fate, and await better conditions for trade in the country where it lies. On the other hand, if a nation (such as the French) has no factor on the Coast, the captain finds it more difficult [to trade] on Gold Coast. The

---

[3] The Danish West India and Guinea Company was established in 1671 and dissolved in 1754. R. is probably referring to 1734, when the Company was reorganized so that it now held a monopoly on the sugar trade but private merchants were allowed a share in the slave trade. The reorganization was due to the purchase of St. Croix in 1733 and the subsequent need for more slaves. See Georg Nørregård, *Danish Settlements in West Africa* (1966) 90–3; Feldbæk and Justesen, *Kolonierne* (1980) 362–4; Ole Feldbæk, 'The organization and structure of the Danish East India, West India and Guinea Companies in the seventeenth and eighteenth centuries', in Leonard Blussé and Femme Gaastra', eds., *Companies and Trade* (1981) 153–6; Gøbel (1983) 24. For company monopoly vs. private trade in the period, see K.G. Davies, *The Royal African Company* (1957) 312–15.

[4] For the Dutch treatment of private shippers and interlopers, see Van Dantzig (1980a) 17, 24; Postma (1990) 78–83, 201–7, 210. It should be noted that interlopers were not pirates, nor was their activity criminal in any way. The Companies could, and did, seize ships, but the captains and crews were not liable to criminal prosecution. Cf. Davies (1957) 113–8.

[5] For private trade among the English, and English Company problems, see John Atkins, *A Voyage to Guinea, Brasil and the West-Indies* (1735) 156–7; Daaku (1970) 10.

[6] R. is referring to the period after 1754, the year in which the West India and Guinea Company was dissolved, the Government took over, and trade was open to all (Nørregård (1966) 113 ff.; Feldbæk (1981) 156; Gøbel (1983) 22. For a painting recording this event, see Poul Olsen, *Toldvæsenet i Dansk Vestindien* (1988) 38. However, R. makes no distinction between vessels sailing in the triangular trade (that is, carrying slaves) and vessels sailing directly, either Denmark-Guinea and back, or Denmark-West Indies and back. For companies not in the slave trade, see Gøbel (1983) 25, 27–30. Proof of many direct sailings to the West Indies is afforded by the general use in the Danish islands, in the construction of buildings, of yellow bricks brought in as ballast from Denmark. Such ballast was not used by ships sailing to Guinea, their holds carrying a weight of goods to be traded for slaves, this cargo in turn filling the holds rebuilt for the Atlantic crossing.

Negroes, as well as the Europeans on the Coast, consider that the French, as a nation, do not belong there, and they must pay more for what they wish to buy than others do. Let anyone ask a Guinean factor why he keeps the price of his slaves 24 to 32 *rixdaler* higher *per capita* when a French trader wishes to buy them than the price he demands from an English captain, he will answer, 'Because that one is a Frenchman and this one is an Englishman.' He can offer no other reason.[7] /**252**/

The Dutch have less than half the West Indian products on their islands we have on ours, but they receive at least 300 ships annually from the West Indies and Guinea. The English receive more than 4,000 from their temperate and tropical Americas.[8] The West Indian, and especially the Guinean trade, are in fact subject to many difficulties in themselves, and the difficulties become most damaging when obstacles are created here, whether as a result of personal gain, jealousy, or whatever the cause. I cannot write very much about our West Indian affairs, but I leave it to those who are there, or to patriots returned home, to explain to us how it is possible that our Company's ships must nearly always wait until the Dutch and English ships have taken on their cargo at our own islands; and the cargo we finally get is sometimes made up of the worst products available at our islands.[9]

[Trade from ships]

I shall confine myself to the Guinea Coast and report on the real difficulties in respect of the trade from ships. The most experienced ships' merchant cannot say with certainty which /**253**/ goods in his cargo will be most desired, and which will be those called 'commanding goods' on the Coast. A merchant might arrive at a place where there is, or is expected to be, a war farther inland. The Black merchant would then prefer to have payment for his slaves in gunpowder, muskets, and brandy. It follows that the trader has little to earn unless he knows of another place where he can buy the rest of his slaves without the articles mentioned above. Thus, his cargo was poorly selected.

---

[7] On the advantages/disadvantages of forts, see Atkins (1735) 156; Davies (1957) 263–4; Feldbæk (1981) 156; Gøbel (1983) 45. Jealous of the amount of trading between the French and Africans, particularly at Anomabu, R. is simplifying the situation. Interloper prices had little or nothing to do with nationality. On high prices because of the increase of French interloper trading, especially after the French had achieved a permanent settlement at Whydah in 1704, see Davies (1957) 270, 313–5. See also Chapter 2 above, note 102.

[8] For the Danish share of the trade, see Gøbel (1983) 48. For the volume of Dutch Company and private shipping, see Postma (1990), appendices 1 and 2. The number of English vessels, 4,000, seems exaggerated — could it possibly be a slip for 400?

[9] Company ships had fixed prices (and sources) but plantation owners, acting in their own interest, preferred to deal with ships that could sell at lower prices, these in turn depending on demand. See Gøbel (1983) 39; Olsen (1988) 19–20, 28–33. On foreign ships at St. Thomas, see Westergaard (1917) 151 and appendix J. Although R. says that he 'cannot write' about Danish affairs in the West Indies, in fact he had already done so, at some length, in his 1756 booklet; see Appendix A below.

Sometimes the Blacks do not care for these particular goods but would rather have the entire purchase sum in dry goods, such as cottons, gingham, *salempuris* [cloth], *calavap* [cloth], etc. A sensible ship's captain knows, at whatever place on the Coast he is, which of his goods are in demand. But he does not know which goods will be in demand when he goes fifty miles further along the Coast. There exist only a few things in the world for which one can cite certain rules, but in the Guinea trade one cannot cite any rules at all. At times, even an experienced tradesman can make mistakes on the Coast in such matters.[10] I beg to be permitted to include an incident which I myself experienced. /254/ At the time when the following happened I had already, for five years, been a copyist, overassistant, and bookkeeper at Christiansborg, and felt I was one of the most experienced tradesmen on the Coast. I observed that with every ship we received a thousand *slaplagen*, ordered by the Directors from Holland, at a price of 18–20 Lübeck shillings apiece. These *slaplagen* were nothing but old, worn linen pieces, 2½ *alen* long and 5 quarters wide. I had seen people in Europe use better cloth to burn as tinder. My conclusion was that we should order home-made *lærred* from Copenhagen at 10 shillings per *alen*, tear it into pieces of 2½ *alen*, and it would be even more desirable than the Dutch *slaplagen*—which you could almost blow to shreds, as you might a spider's web. We received several thousand *alen*, but to my complete surprise, the Negroes preferred the Dutch *slaplagen* to the Danish. It was incomprehensible to me, until I asked the advice of an old Negro, who explained the matter to me thus: the Negroes' wives wore a piece of *slaplagen* when they had their *menses*, and when that finished they buried the *slaplagen*, in its unclean state. It was of great benefit to them [they believed, since] as soon as it began to rot, the woman /255/ who had worn it became pregnant. The new and strong *lærreder* we had as *slaplagener* did not rot as quickly in the earth as did the Dutch [cloth].[11] This was a business in which I would have staked my earthly fortune, but I had made

---

[10] The selection of goods to be brought from Europe was a constant source of worry for the traders. For example, Danes on one occasion were left with brandy that the Akyem refused to buy (CRA, V-gK 886, letter of 17.2.1733, Wærøe to Copenhagen); Gøbel (1983) 29–30. Hence, the traders at the various forts occasionally stored goods for traders of other nations as well as their own (e.g., a statement and guaranty of storage of goods at Christiansborg in respect of an English Captain Bruce: CRA, V-gK 881, 10.3.1739). Five rules for selecting goods for the Coast were suggested (Atkins, (1735) 158–66). A Dutchman allegedly sailed for nine months along the coast without being able to sell all his goods (Thomas Phillips, *A Journal of a Voyage to Africa* (1732) 199). On this difficulty, see also Tilleman [1697] (1994) 34; P.E. Isert, *Letters on West Africa* [1788] (1992) 83–4. On reasons for fluctuations in trade on the African side affecting the choice of goods purchased, see Harvey Feinberg, *Africans and Europeans in West Africa* (1989) 61–2. The slave ship *Henrietta Marie* which went down off the coast of Florida in 1700 carried a large supply of pewterware, evidently unsaleable and being taken back to England (D.D. Moore, 'Henrietta Marie', *Seafarers*, I (1987) 201).

[11] This cloth is obviously gauze-like, therefore more absorbent than a more tightly woven variety would be, and more useful for bandaging, for example. The burial of soiled cloth as an aid to fertility may have been a special case, perhaps on instruction from a priest. Alternatively, it may simply have been done to keep living areas clean (p.c. I. Odotei).

a mistake. At any rate, the affair did not turn out nearly as well as all the sensible folk at Christiansborg had anticipated, since we had to treat our newly bleached canvases quite differently before we could manage to sell them.

A Black merchant makes many protestations when engaged in bargaining. Sometimes he wants most of it in brandy; sometimes he does not want that at all; and at other times he wants to have only iron rods, beads, etc.[12]

Among the difficulties on the Coast, we must take into account the strong surf along the entire coast, which sometimes breaks a half *fierding* from land, so that you are in mortal danger when you wish to go out to a ship in the road, or when you come from a ship and wish to land. You cannot come ashore using shallops or boats, but the Negroes have special craft, both small and large. Some are as small as kneading troughs and one man can row them; some are /**256**/ large, requiring 15, 21, or 25 black boatmen. It looks dangerous when you are sitting or lying in these Negro vessels (canoes) among those breakers. The waves come rolling as high as bell towers. You can see when the wave will break, and the black boatmen (*remadorer*) must then see to it that the canoes ride on top of the wave before it breaks, or, in all haste, row their vessel back, letting the wave break first. Should it happen that a wave breaks over the canoe, the vessel will be broken into small pieces, the goods will be lost, and the people, if they cannot swim, will be drowned.[13]

We make difficulties for ourselves on board the ships, since there is disagreement among the officers most of the time. How hateful the sailors are to the landlubbers, who are called 'Ravens', etc. At times we had to exercise all the authority we had at Christiansborg to prevent the newly-arrived landlubbers from sending each of the ship's crew back on board with bloodied heads, such bitterness was there among them. The ship's officers and sailors had treated the landlubbers very badly during the journey, cheated them of their clothing, and played many unreasonable and inhuman tricks on them. /**257**/ Here we must describe the unchristian and more than heathen performance in respect of the so-called Man of the Line, in which the sailors copy the Dutch, since other nations have no such practice among them. This is what happens.

---

[12] On haggling, see Pieter de Marees, *Description and Historical Account of the Gold Kingdom of Guinea* [1602] (1987) 55–6; Wilhelm Müller [1673] in Adam Jones, *German Sources for West African History* (1983) 248–9; Isert [1788] (1992) 84; Daaku (1970) 40, 44. It should be noted, however, that the African merchant was also dependent, in terms of the goods in demand at any one time at his own markets, often some distance inland, and this demand was in turn subject to changing political and other conditions, particularly whether there was war under way, or pending, or general peace. Given the length of time it took for information to reach Europe and for ships to arrive on the Coast, the problems for European traders in this respect must have been the rule rather than the exception. But they were not, as several early writers implied, merely the inevitable consequence of frivolity and constantly changing tastes on the part of the African consumers.

[13] On canoes and the dangers of passing through the surf, see Jean Barbot, *Barbot on Guinea* [1732] (1992) 528–33; Isert [1788] (1992) 28, 88; Robert Smith, 'The canoe in West African history', *Journal of African History* 11 (1970) 517, 522, 524, 532.

[The Man of the Line]

When our West Indies and Guinea ships (and, as I understand, also our China and East India ships) have passed the Tropic of Cancer, and the weather is good, the ship's crew, who have sailed in these waters before, decide among themselves on which day the Man of the Line will come [aboard]. For a full fourteen days those of them who are in the plot have stood around saying to each other when one or several of the newcomers was close by, 'Dear me! Isn't it a pity that the Devil will take this handsome man? But, you know the Man of the Line is always the same. He particularly dislikes a Seeland sailor, anyone from Fyn, anyone from Jutland, a Norwegian, etc., and I fear he will take all of our newcomers this time, since he forbade us the last time to bring more new people aboard, and we had, indeed, promised not to', and so on. The newcomers laugh at such talk when it is only the sailors who say these things, but they do not know what to think when the captain himself, or the officers, over several days, quite seriously ask them to prepare themselves for a great danger, which /**258**/ might cost them all their lives. And this is said with such mournful faces, [referring] to the Man of the Line as the one who will injure them.

The night before the morning when the Man of the Line is to appear, the sailors chose a person amongst them who is best suited to act out this character. They sew him into a couple of shaggy goat skins, or a sheep skin, paint his face black with a red ring around his eyes, and attach a tail, so that the individual in no way resembles a human being. This transformation takes place below deck in order that none of the newcomers will see it, and if any of the newcomers is present he is sent away on an errand, while the Man of the Line, completely made-up, climbs the main mast. There he stays until morning, and he has several buckets of water for his use.

In the morning, when it is daylight and everyone is either in the cabin or on the quarterdeck, all are called to prayer by a bell. A prayer is said, then a psalm is sung. As they begin the last verse, the Man of the Line begins to shout. Everyone is aghast, or pretends to be so. They close their books and ask what is going on. One of them answers that it is, without doubt, /**259**/ the Man of the Line. Another one says he cannot believe that because the Man does not normally come so early. The Man of the Line shouts once more from up on the mast, and then no one doubts any longer that it is indeed he. The officers and ordinary sailors then come forward. The captain takes off his cap as a sign of great respect and asks the Man of the Line to come down. He comes down and asks how many new people the captain has with him. The captain lies and says, 'None at all'. But the Man of the Line points at each of the newcomers. He also knows if any of them have hidden themselves, and they are fetched.

This madness can continue as long as a whole hour. The Man of the Line wants to take all the newcomers away with him. They promise to buy their freedom. The Man of the Line says that he must, at any rate, have half of them. The captain pleads for them, etc. Finally the Man of the Line goes up the mast again and the newcomers are placed so that he, from up in the mast, can pour out the water which was carried up during the night, and it strikes the heads of the newcomers. The whole ceremony ends with each of the newcomers being bound by a rope around their waists, hoisted up under the mainyard and dipped into the sea three times.[14] /**260**/ A Dutch captain who had sailed more than thirty years on the Guinea Coast told me that as long as he has commanded a ship he has performed that comedy only twice, because the second time he decided to perform it, it became a tragedy, in the following way. Among his crew the captain had a particularly naive Norwegian. (*N.B.* The captain was himself Norwegian).[15] His officers and crew had played silly tricks on this particular sailor, and thought to divert themselves even more when the Man of the Line arrived. Our Norwegian became dismayed at this strange figure (the Man of the Line) and eventually, after a long discussion [with the Man of the Line], the captain and officers agreed he could seize the Norwegian. The Man of the Line tried to get hold of him and pretended that he intended to take him away. Our Norwegian tore himself loose, rushed to the gun chest on the quarterdeck, seized a cutlass and split the head of the Man of the Line, who died on the spot. This was done so swiftly that none of the other members of the ship's crew could prevent his doing it. The captain of the Dutchman had to allow the Norwegian to go his own way, as soon as possible, since, had he delivered the delinquent into the hands of the authorities, without a doubt the officers would have received the same punishment as the Norwegian. /**261**/ I think there is as little humanity in this leisure activity as there is in the fetish practice of the Negroes. In that practice, Satan himself appears in strange shapes; in this activity, he is imitated.

[Discipline in ships and forts]

I will not claim that we Danes sin more than the Blacks in these practices, but it is indeed barbaric and murderous to plague and tease foolish and innocent persons, who, for most of the time, are willing and would like to be instructed. By experience we know for certain that grief, injury, etc. remove more people from the world in that hot climate than a widespread pestilence does in Europe. In this respect we ought to look to the English, especially to the English warships, as a model [for behaviour aboard]. As soon as they arrive in the hot climate all reprimands, cursing, the use of the

---

[14] For initiation rituals when crossing the Line, see Barbot [1732] (1992) 755, 758 note 14; Isert [1788] (1992) 24–5; Harry M. Lydenberg, *Crossing the Line: Tales of the Ceremony during Four Centuries* (1957) 3–38; Henning Henningsen, 'Linje- og vendekredsdåb på norske og danske skibe op til 1814', in *Vestfold-Minne* (1961) 237–9.

[15] R. has just remarked that the captain was Dutch, but he must have meant a Norwegian captain of a Dutch ship. See note 2 above.

cat-o'-nine-tails, and thrashing are abolished, except for the most grave offences. And the shame [an Englishman] feels at not being able to do his duty is punishment enough for him. We do not hear of such high mortality among them as there is among us. On an English warship, when [as many as] eight men out of one hundred have died in a period of eighteen months, it is most unusual (sea battles excepted). It can also happen when disagreements arise among the officers, and each one has his supporters on board who bait /**262**/ one another. At such times they can throw overboard one-half or two-thirds of them, as we do.[16] [But] we also have had captains who have rarely had any deaths on board. These have taken care, as said before, to treat their officers and ordinary crew in a friendly and humane way, and to keep the ordinary man from wanton behaviour in the West Indies.[17] Our sailors thought that they could tolerate just as strong doses of West Indian brandy as they could of Danish brandy, but one can see that it is poison for them. I have heard an objection made to this — that fear makes the ordinary man fulfil his duty. But, my dear man, you must admit that you can more easily rely on your subjects when they feel affection for you than when they look upon you as a devil, plaguing the very life out of them. And rest assured that on the occasions when the officers do their duty, the ordinary man does his as well.

All the rational arrangements I have seen on ships, as well as in the small governments on the Coast, have the second in command — the Chief Merchant (*Ober-Kiøbmand*) or the Chief Officer (*Ober-Styremand*) — acting the part of a bugbear to all the other employees. /**263**/ His deportment must always be strict, so that the Commander [in contrast] can show mercy, and ameliorate or entirely cancel the punishment. It is a poor arrangement if the [individual in] highest authority has himself to impose punishment on an offender. Should the officers, or only one of them, feel sorry for those being punished, they might raise protests and cause unrest. Conditions on board, or at the Fort, would then [so deteriorate] that it would be preferable to spend the period in slavery rather than spend it among such people. No one except those who have tried it can imagine what it is like when some thirty to forty persons in a small area feel bitterness

---

[16] That English and Danish ships, apparently on more than one occasion, had crew troubles which led to them (? the officers) throwing overboard half or two-thirds of the crew is one of R.'s most bizarre notions, but curiously similar to his later claim that, when in difficulties, ships poisoned (and threw overboard) 'one hundred or more' slaves (/320/ below). Perhaps by 'throw overboard' R. simply meant that those who had died during the trouble or been killed were buried at sea, but this only slightly reduces the oddity of his statement.

[17] There is no evidence of particularly 'friendly and humane' treatment of crews on English ships. Again, R. is romanticizing in favour of his good friends, the English staff of the Royal African Company — good friends indeed, since they tried repeatedly to entice R. to come and work for them. As for treatment of the staff at the English forts on the Gold Coast, see Atkins (1735) 90–103, which presents a picture very different from the glowing report given by R.

towards each other, yet must still be in constant contact, eating together and addressing each other.[18]

In the West Indies, as well as in Guinea, in former times we also had the Dutch habit of bullying newcomers, and calling them *baar* ('bears').[19] The old hands shared the newcomers' clothing amongst themselves (if the ships' crews had not already seized it) and decided among themselves who would buy, at [the post-mortem] auction, the suits, hats, vests, etc. of the newcomers, who were still quite alive and standing there, listening to such talk. If the newcomers complained about this and other things to the authorities, they laughed at them, saying that they themselves had had to put up with the same [treatment]. /**264**/

[Foodstuffs]

Our way of life on the Coast is subject to great changes. Game meat and fish are our food. Sometimes we have none at all, sometimes a surplus, and the price of *millie* [grain] can rise and fall swiftly, according to conditions inland. You may at one time be unable to finish eating [the amount of] bread (*bolle*) purchased for 10 *bos* (one Danish shilling), and perhaps a month later a [single cake/loaf of] bread or *boller*, costing 20 *bos* (two shillings) might be as small as a dove's egg, or even smaller.[20] After the rainy season game meat is available at Accra in great quantities. Hares, partridges, pheasants, etc. are daily fare for our soldiers at such times. Then the normal fare of buffalo, hart, or roe deer is much too poor to be served at their table. Fish is also a good buy. A *sardin* (herring) costs one *bos* (one-tenth of a shilling). [But] sometimes our hunters dare not go into the countryside when it is insecure. The sea can be so rough for an entire month that the Blacks cannot go out to fish, and our Accra, which just previously was the land of milk and honey, becomes a land of hunger. Our soldiers must then buy a dry herring from the Blacks and fry it in a little palm oil, but the bread to accompany it is so dear that a meal might in one month cost one-half *rixdaler,* while four weeks earlier they could have had a better meal for two shillings. Most of us Europeans buy a great quantity of fish when it is a good buy, /**265**/ skin the large fishes, sprinkle salt on them, and put them in the sun to dry.

---

[18] R. may be referring to the period of Billsen's governorship (Nørregård (1966) 104–5; see also Appendix B below). On the behaviour of Danish officers at Frederiksborg, see Barbot [1732] (1992) 401–2. Later in the century, Isert commented, with a degree of distaste, on life in close quarters at the forts (Isert [1788] (1992) 156–9). In the next century, Monrad, although ridiculed as a chaplain opposed to the slave trade, exhibited a more tolerant attitude to aspects of life at the forts (H.C. Monrad, *Bidrag til en Skildring af Guinea-Kysten* (1822) 363–7). On living conditions at the forts in general, see A.W. Lawrence, *Trade Castles and Forts of West Africa* (1963) chapter 4.

[19] The Dutch term *baar*, here given its primary meaning of 'bear', also means 'inexperienced sailor, newcomer'.

[20] The Danish *courant daler* of the eighteenth century was divided into six marks of 16 shillings each; that is, in all 96 shillings or *rixdaler*. Each mark of 16 shillings represented one ounce of gold.

Within eight days these fish are dried out, and as for taste, are like our 'old cheese'. A piece of that dried fish, fried with Spanish pepper (*piment*) in palm oil and accompanied by bread, is a tasty ragout for the Europeans living in that land. You can well imagine that those newly arrived in the land have to be there for several months before this and other dishes taste good to them. But, when you have become accustomed to it, all the Negro food is not only most healthy but tasty — Europeans at times have left standing the best pâtés made by a French cook and chosen to eat the Negro dish.[21] Certain persons here in Copenhagen, who have been in that land, sometimes wish that they could be served a Negro dish. The Negroes use palm oil in all their dishes. When it is fresh it has a pleasant flavour, like that of olive oil.

It will appear strange to many to learn that the Europeans experience periods of hunger in that land, given that you have read about domestic chickens, sheep, goats, and cows, whose keep costs nothing, consequently [you think that] there must be great numbers of them. To this I have to reply — certainly these animals would be there in great numbers, if we had peaceful times for ten years in a row. /266/ But if instead we experience three or four months of war in our vicinity, it would again be just as empty of animals. An eight-day-old lamb, a six-weeks-old calf in that land would then cost just as much as a sheep, a cow, or a grown bull. At times we have had up to fifty cows, several hundred sheep, goats, pigs, etc. A year later we might have no more than ten cows, and no other animals. Whenever we have them, we slaughter our domestic animals. Most of the cows belong to the Company. A Christian commander [*opperhoved*] cannot see his garrison starve to death as long as he can prevent it, [but] we must keep some eight or ten cows alive in order to preserve the species. They are too wild for us to milk them, so we keep them purely for slaughter.[22]

Close to Fort Fredensborg, at Ningo, lies a lagoon that is salty but rich in fish.[23] For a pipe of tobacco a Negro will fetch a fish dish for a soldier, and, when the countryside is not unsafe, a black hunter will willingly take it upon himself to deliver two roe deer a day. When a soldier at Christiansborg is in debt, he is usually pleased to /267/ be moved to Fredensborg, where he can earn enough to pay his debt. Half a *fierding* east of Fredensborg is a reef of rocks, these being the last rocks on the whole Lower Coast.[24] A great number of turtles are found there, and you can order them from a Negro —

---

[21] On African food and European appreciation, see Isert [1788] (1992) 125–7; Monrad (1822) 239–41.
[22] On cattle used only for meat, see William Bosman, *A New and Accurate Description of the Coast of Guinea*, (1705) 235–6; Johannes Rask, *En Kort og Sandferdig Rejse-Beskrivelse*, (1754) 95.
[23] Today the lagoon is known locally as *Djani*, and the people there are Adangme. A current tradition states that the Ningo people came out of the lagoon and that the ancestor emerged eating raw fish (p.c. I. Odotei).
[24] At Ningo there is a fishing bank known locally (in Adangme) as *tɛ kpaago* 'Seven Rocks' (p.c. Isaac Djangmah). This may be the reef to which R. is referring. The coast eastward of Ningo is 'fringed by a broad ledge of rocks... These rocks are the last seen upon this coast when proceeding eastward' (*Africa Pilot* (1967) 466).

so fish for food is almost never lacking at Fredensborg. But *millie* can be just as rare there as at Christiansborg. More will be said about this later.

The local bread is made of Turkish corn, called 'Portuguese *millie*' here. *Millie* is found in two varieties, small and large. The latter sort is the more common, and is eaten daily by both the Europeans and the Blacks at the Coast. The large *millie* is also found in two varieties, white and red.[25] We rarely have the latter sort at Accra. This type of bread is much healthier to eat in the hot climate than rye or wheat bread, since the latter [types] are not digested as easily as *millie* bread. Most of the time the Negroes eat bread that is cooked [*sc*. steamed], and not baked bread as we Europeans do.[26] The Akims, and other nations living in the interior, cannot bear to eat the *millie* bread, either cooked or baked, but they eat roots and *patatos* instead of bread.[27] This corn or *millie* /**268**/ is not ground, as is our rye and wheat, but the black women grate it on a flat stone two and one-half feet long and one and one-half feet wide. They put a couple of handfuls of *millie* on it, sprinkle water on it, and using an elongated, smaller stone, they grate it until it becomes a dough.[28] In this way a Black woman can rub and bake — or cook — bread for fifty persons in half a day.

The sorts of fish available on the Guinea Coast are not the same as those in Europe. I know of only two sorts whose like I have seen in Europe: bream and herring. I have never seen the remaining sorts in Europe. A variety is found here which we Danes call 'Old Crones'. I have been told they are not found either in the East or West Indies. The fish itself looks horrible but tastes good. Further inland there are fresh lagoon fish, but all the types I have seen are extremely horrible in appearance. Our sea scorpions here, near the Customs House, are beautiful creatures as compared to those monstrosities. He must have been a truly brave man who was the first who dared to lay a hand on these African fish, and eat them.[29]

---

[25] *Millie* is a problematic term. 'Turkish corn' normally at this period meant maize, while *millie* probably indicates in general 'millet' (*Pennisetum* spp.), of which there are many varieties native to West Africa. However, large red or white *millie* suggests sorghum. For maize, sorghum and millet, see S.B. Alpern, 'European crops in precolonial Africa', *History in Africa* 19 (1992) 24–5.

[26] The 'bread' is probably *kenkey*, a cake made of maize, ground or grated, and then steamed.

[27] R.'s 'roots' doubtless included yams, the indigenous root crop of the region, but may also have included taro and cassava (a Portuguese import from the Americas and by the mid eighteenth century probably spreading through eastern Guinea). The 'patatos' were *batatas* 'sweet potatoes' (p.c. Stanley Alpern). For yams and *batatas*, see also D.W. Abbiw, *Useful Plants of Ghana* (1990) 27–9.

[28] The same method is used today for grinding pepper and herbs (p.c. I. Odotei).

[29] The variety of bream referred to here is *Dentex macrophthalmus*, known in Ga as *tfile* (F.R. Irvine, *The Fishes and Fisheries of the Gold Coast* (1947) 164; for herrings, see *ibid.*, 109–10. In fact, there were many varieties of Guinea fish which were recognizable to eighteenth century Europeans, for instance, mackerel and flounder. For a list of fish, see Müller [1673] in Jones (1983) 295–7; and for references to local fish and fishing, see also Barbot [1732] (1992) 521–6; Bosman (1705) 277–80; Rask (1754) 15–26; Isert [1788] (1992) 23, 27, 33–4, 126, 136. For 'Old Wives', described as being a scaly, flat fish with a face thought to resemble 'that of a Nun', and probably a variety of plaice (*Pleuronectidae*), see Atkins (1735) 47; and for a drawing of this fish, Barbot [1732] (1992) 217, note 57 (plate 6 in 1732 text).

As slave provisions on our ships we always send yellow peas, which we know by experience provide an unhealthy diet at sea. Instead /269/ of peas, we ought to send beans.³⁰ Once or twice a week our slaves should be given prunes in their diet, and rice [should be given] to the Upper Coast slaves, as the French do. No one should dare to strike a slave, or look angrily at one, so as not to upset him or her. Some of our surgeons have removed the skeletons from dead slaves, and truly, this makes the slaves desperate and weary of life. When, in an unavoidable emergency, a surgeon has to bleed a slave, he should be sensible enough to do it, preferably in such a way that none of the other [slaves] see it. Indeed, if possible, not even the ill one himself should see it, because the Blacks do not understand that this is done for their benefit, and they think we are going to kill them. A ship's medicine chest should only contain anti-scorbutics and anti-venerics. Should the slaves fall victim to the [endemic] illnesses of the land, such as worms, etc., a couple of the female slaves can be allowed to take over, after we have supplied them with *mallaget* and *piment*, palm oil, and citrons, from which they can prepare [African] medicines, and the sick will feel well afterward.³¹

[Future dispositions on Gold Coast]

If the Assiantes open the routes to the western forts again, it will be the end of our trade at Accra and Adampi. Yet, as long as the union between the Akims and the Fantees is in existence the Assiantees cannot go to Elmina, etc.³² It is not to be expected that these people will attack the /270/ Assiantes in their country. Instead, the Assiantes will attack them, and if they get the upper hand they will without doubt totally destroy both

---

³⁰ R.'s recommendation of including beans in the slaves' diet is mystifying, considering that that was precisely what they were given. For instance, a rations list dated 22.11.1749 shows the following: Sunday — pork, beans, porridge, tobacco; Monday — beans, porridge, tobacco, brandy; Tuesday — beans, porridge, tobacco; Wednesday — beans, porridge, brandy; Thursday — pork, beans, porridge, brandy; Friday — beans, porridge, tobacco; Saturday — *millie* (twice), brandy (CRA, V-gK 62, 239). Beans were in fact a regular part of the slave diet on the ships of all nations.

³¹ The medicines noted were probably the standard ones aboard ships, for treating white sailors. It is uncertain whether the major venereal diseases of gonorrhoea and syphilis were common among Africans at this date, but yaws, which was common in Guinea, might be mistaken for either. Scurvy was common among sailors on long voyages but was probably less likely to affect slaves shipped and landed within a reasonable time. Citrons are *Citrus medica*. The use of citrus fruits to prevent or ameliorate scurvy was fairly well known by the mid-eighteenth century. Nevertheless, lemons or oranges were sometimes carried on slave ships, allegedly to aid the health of the slaves (Barbot [1732] (1992) 461; Isert [1788] (1992) 105). Slave women clearly played an important role in medical treatment because of their expertise in the preparation of the foods to which the slaves were accustomed.

³² For the alliance between Akyem and Fante against Asante, see Chapter 4 above, /223/ and note 199.

nations. The King of Assiante can then be called the Emperor of the Guinea Coast, as long as others north of them leave the Assiantes in peace. It is unlikely that these nations NE of Assiante will attack the Assiantes, because they would not be able to get through the forest with their horses. However, the nation to the SE of Assiante is also a forest nation, and can also advance on foot by paths which a tiger, or a wolf, etc. has made for them.[33]

When here in Denmark we speak of the Guinean forest, people think that it is woodland, but you never see woodland here [in Denmark] that a traveller on foot cannot walk through. The forest on the Guinea Coast is quite different. There, a great number of young trees twenty to thirty feet tall grow so closely together that in most places you cannot stick your head between them — sometimes not even a hand. In some places you can walk as if in a vault, and on the footpaths the Negroes have cut through the thick bush you might not see the sun. You also come upon forest in some places, but only a few. /271/

A restlessness has appeared in the temperament of the Blacks, with the result that these people, who could live in security, cannot remain peaceful, and if they are not insulted by others, they themselves insult others. Hence no nation is without enemies; indeed no nation is without [conflicting] factions. You find no [single] family in a town which does not desire the ruin and complete destruction of another [family], if it could be accomplished without their own ruin. They only allow one another to go on living because, in the event of their town, or land, etc., being attacked by a more powerful neighbour, for as long as that lasts they could stand together.

It is known that the Aqvamboes, although they are only few, still do not spare one another when in the field fighting their enemies, but they steal from one another within their ranks. From this you can conclude that conditions on the Guinea Coast will not always be as they are now. The whole world, even more so its parts where reasonable law prevails, is subject to change, but most of all in Africa. Considering all the circumstances, it can be prophesied that as soon as they see the opportunity the Assiantes will ruin the Fantes and the Akims.[34] Should the same thing be done to the Assiantes by the nation lying SE of them, /272/ it cannot be expected that Cassiantes would come to the coast often, because it is an eight- to nine-month journey out and back home. And if Assiante should remain as it is now, that single nation would not suffice to supply all the Europeans with trade in slaves and gold, since the small nations would soon destroy one another.

---

[33] For the nations NE and SE of Asante, see Chapter 4 above, notes 138, 144, 160.

[34] Throughout the eighteenth century there were rumours of imminent attack by Asante on Fante, but the attack eventuated only in the next century (Ivor Wilks, *Asante in the Nineteenth Century* (1975) 209 ff).

The Assiantes will without doubt fall upon their enemies as soon as the disagreement existing among them since the death of Oppoccu has been resolved.[35] That they will achieve victory can be concluded by the fact that Fante is a republic where each free Negro is his own absolute master. They have no leader.[36] If they had had a competent general (*brafoes*) they would have killed him, on the orders of the fetish.[37] Among themselves the Fantes hate one another and desire each other's ruin. The Akims cannot hear the Assiantes spoken of without losing all their courage. It is certain that the Fantes and their allies can muster more people in the field than the Assiantes. But Oppoccu was a source of fear and punishment for all the nations, and if Assiante gets his like on the throne, it will not even experience the opposition from the Fantes and their allies together that they experienced from the Akims in 1742. /273/ When this happens, we shall have delightful times on the Coast for six months and longer, since we can expect to buy a slave for a bottle of brandy, as was the case in 1733 [*sic*], the year the Aqvamboes were beaten.[38] But after that no people were to be found [? in the contested area], consequently they could not sell one another.

These nations — Assiante, Akim, Fante, and Aqvamboe — are, or have been, the largest nations known between Axim and River Volta. We know that 60–80 years ago populous nations existed above/beyond Axim, and farther down-coast, such as Dinkera, Fetu, etc. But they are now of no more importance than our Mountain Negroes at Accra, who also often wage war against each other.[39] The same has occurred on the Lower Coast at Whydah, Jakin, Patakai, and so on.[40] For instance, the Whydah nation, described by Bosman as being so populous, and its land so fertile, has been destroyed by a nation north of them called Dahomey. The Dahomeys have

---

[35] For the conflict in Asante following the death of Opoku Ware in 1750, see Ivor Wilks, *Forests of Gold* (1993) 258; T.C. McCaskie, *State and Society in Pre-colonial Asante* (1995) 175–7.

[36] On Fante fragmentation and the beginnings of federation, see Margaret Priestley, *West African Trade and Coast Society* (1969) 10–11; James Sanders, 'The expansion of the Fante and the emergence of Asante in the eighteenth century', *Journal of African History* 20 (1979) 352–5; T.C. McCaskie, 'Nananom Mpow of Mankessim', in D. Henige and T.C. McCaskie, eds, *West African Economic and Social History* (1990) 137.

[37] For the definition of '*Brafoes*' (*obrafo*, pl. *abrafoo*), see McCaskie (1990) 136. For the Fante 'fetish', see Chapter 3 above, /78/–/84/.

[38] For the defeat and conquest of Akwamu by Akyem in 1730, see Chapter 4 above, /154/–/158/. The traders lived in a constant state of self-contradiction, complaining, on the one hand, that frequent wars disrupted trade and acquisition of provisions, while rejoicing, on the other hand, that war produced 'delightful times', when slaves were plentiful and cheap.

[39] Denkyira was defeated by Asante in 1698–1701 (J.D. Fage, *A History of Africa* (1995) 176–8). Fetu was steadily weakened by wars against Fante from 1679 to the mid-eighteenth century, when it was absorbed by Fante (Sanders (1979) 352–3; Jones (1983) 137). For 'Mountain Negroes', see Chapter 4 above, note 7.

[40] 'Patakai' is presumably Badagry, which was founded in the 1730s by refugees from the expansion of Dahomey (p.c. Robin Law). 'Jakin' was a coastal settlement near Whydah corresponding to modern Godomey (Barbot [1732] (1992) 631). R. referred to it in 1756 as 'Chaqvin' (1756, /16/, within Chapter 2 above).

been beaten and driven away by a nation called Oyo, revealing then that the power of the Dahomeys was so limited that Assiamboe at Popo could wage war against them, and sometimes come out the victor. The reason Assiamboe did not completely destroy the Dahomeys is that his free Negroes, or subjects, /274/ refused to follow up their victory in the land of the Dahomeys, fearing that if Assiamboe became more powerful he, like all the other great African kings, would become a tyrant — and they were certainly right. I have neither asked nor heard whether the nation of Oyo has an even more powerful nation north of it, but I do not doubt it, because the Negroes' disposition is not at all to sit still when they can destroy a lesser neighbour.[41] Even if they acted as other victors do, making the conquered nation their subjects and allowing them to remain in their land, it would normally make little difference, for the conquered do not trust the conquerors, and they have extremely good reasons for this attitude.

When such circumstances come to pass in Guinea, which is sure to happen sooner or later, certainly the Europeans will have only expenses and no trade. This will result in their losing interest in maintaining any longer forts or establishments on the Coast. What they will decide to do after that is not clear, but each one could acquire much land and plant colonies.[42] We must hope that the Europeans would then be better reconciled to each other in Africa than they are in America, and better reconciled to each other than the black nations /275/ who owned this magnificent land before them were [to each other]. As indicated earlier, we Danes could last longest because of [our ownership of] River Volta, and, if we were to trade 200–300 miles up-river, we might be able to supply our own and other colonies in the West Indies with slaves from there for an entire century and longer, since other European nations would have to go to other places in Africa in order to obtain slaves for their own West Indian plantations.[43]

It is not to be expected that in the great heat in the West Indies the Europeans will reproduce in sufficient numbers to enable them to cultivate their plantations, because we know that if they did not [now] receive reinforcements annually they would die out in twenty years and the islands would soon be deserted. And even if they did reproduce, it is known that those born there are of a particularly weak nature, and throughout the hot West Indies we have seen no instance of a native-born reaching the age of fifty.[44]

---

[41] Dahomey, an interior polity of the Fon ethnicity, warred regularly with Oyo, the neighbouring interior polity of the Yoruba ethnicity. For these campaigns, see Robin Law, *The Slave Coast of West Africa* (1991): that is, for the Dahomey conquest of Whydah in 1727, 282–87; for the defeat of Dahomey by Oyo in 1728–1732, 287–95; for Assiambo, Chief of Little Popo, and his conquest of Dahomey in 1737, 317–18. On Assiambo (Assiongbon Dandjin), see also N.L. Gayibor, 'Les Rois de Glidji', *History in Africa* 22 (1995) 205.
[42] For a later Danish attempt at establishing a plantation, a possible start of a colony, see Isert [1788] (1992) 190 and appendix 3.
[43] For the Danish position on River Volta, see /282/ ff. below.
[44] Later, Isert was to contradict this statement (Isert [1788] (1992) 200–01).

It is rare for one to reach forty years old. But we could be more optimistic and say, with a degree more certainty, that if the Black Negroes whom our planters [now] have, or [subsequently] acquire, could reproduce, the planters could almost do without [fresh] Guinean slaves. In that case the planters would /276/ have to treat them quite differently from the way they do now.[45] You might say that it is probable that the agricultural nations in America could do without Guinean slaves, but certainly not the gold and silver mining nations — never.

I suppose that, hereafter and always, Negro slaves will be just as unavoidably necessary for gold and silver mining as they have heretofore been for agricultural nations in the West Indies. Furthermore, I reckon that [in time] none will be available on the Gold Coast, or not enough, so the Europeans must prepare for themselves another Gold Coast on the western shore of Africa (Madagascar or the eastern shore of Africa cannot serve, as experience has taught us).[46] We must then, of necessity, occupy the coast of *Males Gentes* [the Bad People], since [the inhabitants there] most closely resemble the nations of Gold Coast.[47] Some thirty or forty fortresses established there, manned by Europeans, would give the same encouragement and produce the same notable effect on the coast of *Males Gentes* as they have done among the Blacks on the Gold Coast. These fortresses would result in more trade than from several hundred ships sailing past.[48] We can state as a certainty that the gold and silver mining nations in America will always be short of people. In Africa the situation is the opposite. /277/ Therefore, I cannot come to any other conclusion than that we ought to establish four or five forts over a distance of one hundred miles, and defend ourselves only on the coast of *Males Gentes*. The nation of Europeans which acquires

---

[45] The argument that slaves could be bred in sufficient numbers in the West Indies rather than imported there was a paramount factor when the Royal Ordinance of 1792 was issued in Copenhagen, ordering the end of the Danish trans-Atlantic slave trade on New Year's Day, 1803. During that ten-year period,, encouragement was to be given to the import of slave women to the West Indian islands, implicitly in the hope of breeding slaves there. See Nørregård (1966) 175–6.

[46] Presumably R. is referring to the geographical and nautical problems that slave-trading from East Africa to the West Indies would involve. He may, however, have been aware that there was a considerable slave-trade across the Indian Ocean, from East Africa to Arabia and India, but that this was in the hands of 'Arabs'. The export of East African slaves around the Cape of Good Hope was at times attempted by the Portuguese and other European nations, but was very limited in extent.

[47] For 'the coast of *Males Gentes* [the Bad People]', that is, western Côte d'Ivoire, see Chapter 2 above, notes 11, 12.

[48] The 'notable effect' of the strong European presence would be the greater inclination of the local Africans to participate in the marine export trade, including the trans-Atlantic slave trade, they having a reputation for being uninterested in coastal trade and hostile to Europeans. However, the reputation may have been undeserved: a general lack of harbours had led to trade being merely conducted in the circumstances of canoes contacting ships sailing along the coast, R.'s 'passing ships'. But R. does not suggest how forts would create harbours and the particular coast was in fact to remain somewhat isolated from pre-colonial world trade.

Cape Lahou, Grand Jack, and River Sassandra will certainly be better off than [trading] on the entire Gold Coast, considering what will come about within fifty years, according to all estimates.

[The Danes on River Volta]

If we Danes do not greatly wish to be the first to resolve to do this — although here you might say that 'he who comes first to the mill, grinds first' — and if this project also presents difficulties, nonetheless we ought even now to try to go higher up River Volta. It is indisputably our property. Both the English and the Dutch have often tried to establish themselves there, but by our opposition and threats, etc., we have defended it until now. As a result, they have had to recognize that, according to our rights there, in all fairness they could not settle there without our permission. However, the English, as well as the Dutch, have built lodges (houses) beyond Fredensborg, the Dutch being at Okko, two miles from River Volta, although no Negro towns exist at either place. But two Europeans with ten /**278**/ to twelve Black servants live at each place, and they interrupt our trade, even though we have goods at Ada on River Volta.

Our exclusive right consists in this: River Volta has been our property since we acquired Christiansborg at Accra. Our fort stands at the only place, and the first one, where the Portuguese established themselves, after [founding] Elmina. The Swedes, and then we Danes, have for a long time been alone at Accra, according to the statements of the old Negroes, and we have had our lodges at Ponni [Kpone], Tuberkue [Tubreku], Ada, and Qvitta [Keta].[49] The English came later, and the Dutch the very last, building their fort Creve-Coeur between the English and Danish forts, and only a cannon-shot from the English. This could not happen without the English and we Danes trying to stop it, but the Aqvamboe king at that time favoured the Dutch, and the more fortresses he had in his land, the more custom he would receive.[50]

---

[49] On the Dutch lodges at *Ponny* [Kpone], *Tuberkue* [Tubreku], Ada, and *Qvitta* [Keta], see Albert van Dantzig, *Forts and Castles of Ghana* (1980b) xii, 55, 57. On the Dutch at Kpone in 1706, well received at Keta, and building near the Danes at Tubreku, see Van Dantzig, (1980a) 197, 219–20, 249. Today there is no trace of the Danish lodge at Tubreku or the later Danish fort, Fort Kongensten, built in 1783 at Ada (Isert [1788] (1992) 37–8; Van Dantzig (1980b) xii, 55). At Keta, the Danish lodge (succeeding a Dutch one) later became the Danish Fort Prinsensten (built 1784), which was a prison in 1980, but most of it has since fallen into the ocean (for a recent photograph and drawing, see Leif Svalesen, *Slaveskipet Fredensborg* (1996) 225).

[50] R. is wrong about the chronology of the forts at Accra. The Danes built a lodge at Osu in 1661 but their headquarters were at Fort Frederiksborg at Amanful, in Fetu country, until 1685 when they moved to Christiansborg Castle, built on the site of the lodge at Osu. The English built Fort James in 1673. But the Dutch built Fort Crevecoeur in 1649 (Van Dantzig, *Forts* (1980b) 24). The support of the Akwamu king, mentioned in the next sentence, appears to relate to eighteenth-century events rather than to the fort-building of the previous century. For European competition, see ibid., chapter 3; Nørregård (1966) 95–6; Sandra Green, 'The Anlo-Ewe: their economy, society and external relations in the eighteenth century', PhD thesis, Northwestern University (1981), 131–7.

We alone held River Volta, apart from when we had no goods. Then, both the English and the Dutch were able to send their black servants with goods and buy the slaves available there—until 1730. At that date, when the Dutch factor had /279/ induced our free Negroes and Company slaves to run away from our town to his, the Dutch had a lodge built at Ada not far from ours.[51] We could scarcely defend our main fortress, and had to tolerate this [situation] for one and a half years, until the Aqvamboes had been defeated and wanted to flee to the island called Ada, in River Volta. All the smaller nations from the islands in River Volta, such as Mlefi, Tuffi, Graffi [Agrafi], etc. had gathered at Ada. Before the Aqvamboes arrived, our factor at Ada was so [cautious and] careful that he had a rampart thrown up around the lodge, and he distributed among the Blacks the gunpowder and muskets which the company kept there. Our factor and the Negroes urged the Dutch factor to do the same, but he declared to all the old Blacks who were present, and to our factor, that River Volta belonged to the Danes and if they wished to retain it they alone had to make the [defensive] arrangements. The Dutch packed their goods, intending to travel away from there. The Negroes had intended to murder the Dutch and plunder their goods, but our factor helped the Dutch so that they escaped from River Volta without the least injury or loss.

Three days before the Aqvamboes /280/ reached the island, our Chief Merchant at Christiansborg (Sparre) arrived there very conveniently, with a sloop loaded with gunpowder and muskets. He had intended to surprise all the Lagoon Negroes, beat some of them to death, and sell the rest. Sparre and all the other Danes [instead] brought all the Negroes and their families into the fortified area. On land they had [built] a deep trench and embankment. In the lagoon, [to cover] as far as the fortification extended, they had an armed sloop and a score of armed Negro boats. The River Volta Negroes now saw to what trouble and expense the Danes had gone to save them, and as a result they invited the Danes to come and see what they would do to show their gratitude. The Danes were shown to a place where all the old Negroes were gathered, with the Ada fetish in front of them. They swore an oath on behalf of themselves and their descendants, [swearing] that the entire River Volta would belong to the Danes alone. Further, if Whites of any other nation came to one of the islands, or even into the lagoon in a Negro boat without our permission, they were united in swearing they would bind their hands and feet and throw them into the lagoon. This oath was confirmed by both sides, and we

---

[51] This was a period when opposition to Akwamu suzerainty was crystallizing. The Danes refused to take sides against Akwamu, probably believing that the Akyem and their allies were not strong enough to oust them. Cf. /151/-/153/ above.

Danes promised to assist them also, if such circumstances were to arise again thereafter — which we have indeed done, twice since.[52] /**281**/

The Aqvamboes arrived on the island the next day with a hundred Negro boats. They kept our fortification surrounded for four days, and since they could not, or dared not, storm it, they agreed that we Danes, for the [exemption from Aqvamboe attack on the] River Volta Negroes, could pay in goods to the value of seventeen male slaves. After receipt of that sum, the Aqvamboes left the island for Crepe, and all the Lagoon Negroes were saved. The Ada Negroes are still registered as indebted for the sum in our Company's Debt Book. If I remember correctly, there was [also] a sum lent to them before this happened, and twice since. Furthermore, Sparre distributed 2,000–3,000 pounds of gunpowder, for which the Negroes promised to pay; therefore Wærøe and Sparre are still in debt to the Company. None of the other Europeans established on the Coast have such legal access to places where they can exclude others as we Danes have to River Volta. The Dutch at Accra once wished to strike a bargain with us and offered to pay for half of the seventeen slaves, and when we Danes refused this, they offered us seventeen male slaves *in natura* if we would allow them to establish a lodge on Ada or at other places on River Volta. Since we did not accept that either, they used threats. /**282**/ We, on the other hand, took to boasting. We assured them that we would follow the orders of the directors in Copenhagen, to bind hand and foot the first Dutchman who came to the lagoon, and throw him into it.

In 1740–1742 we transferred the lodge to Tuberku, which was on the mainland, close to the mouth of the lagoon. Nonetheless, no other nation has had the cheek to come to Ada or any other places on the lagoon. We have saved the River Volta Negroes [again] since then, in 1750, when they were at war with the Agona Negroes. The [Agonas] had surrounded Ada and, had we Danes waited one month longer before sending them help from Accra, the Volta Negroes would either have had to starve to death on their island, or surrender to their enemies. This, too, was not accomplished without expense.[53] And since we propose, at this point, to write a description of our forts and establishments on the Coast, we shall begin with River Volta — not that it is the most prominent or profitable place we Danes have on the Coast, but because it could be the most profitable, and should be the most prominent.

---

[52] For the reciprocal oath-taking, achieved through the efforts of the trader H.H. Sparre, see Nørregård (1966) 132–3.

[53] For Tubreku lodge, see Nørregård (1966) 96. For the war in 1750, termed the Nonobewa War, see Greene (1981) 134–6. A similar situation, the Sagbadre War, occurred in 1783 (Isert [1788] (1992) 31–7).

[River Volta described]

River Volta is one of the largest rivers in Africa. It is not known how far inland it extends, /283/ but it is known that many smaller rivers run into the Volta. It extends so far inland that at its source the country must have other [patterns of] rainy seasons than those along the whole west coast of Africa. May and September are the two rainy seasons on the entire Coast, even, as I have heard, somewhat south of the Line, and during these months all the rivers run more swiftly into the sea. At those periods [of rains on the coast], you do not see the River Volta increasing greatly, but [instead] it has its strongest flow to the sea before, during, and after the rainy season [on the coast]. The lagoon water and the sea crash against each other with such force that, for two to three miles out to sea, you can see what looks like a high mountain covered with snow rising into the air and falling down the next moment. Probably because of this the river has been given its name, namely 'Volta', that is, 'leaping'.[54]

At times during the year the sea may rise as high as, and higher than, the river. Sloops, boats, and perhaps larger ships can then be taken through the mouth and up the river.[55] It is most remarkable that the river, in the middle of November (which is the driest season in the entire country), swells and overruns all its banks. Often the Ada Negroes and all the [other] inhabitants on the island must retire to the mainland, or creep into trees and bushes, and /284/ stay there for fourteen days to three weeks, until the river falls. You can see small islets, with bushes and many large trees on them, which this great current has undoubtedly torn loose and carried with it. You cannot say that the water floods over the land, but the earth becomes so soft that you sink to your knees if you try to walk on it. That has kept us Danes from building small forts on the bank of the river, since every second or third year we too would have to move [further] to the mainland with all our goods when [the situation] became too difficult. At times the lagoon, or the current, takes part of the island away, and in ten years we have had to move our lodge on Ada three times because the current had washed away the ground.[56] Every

---

[54] For the geography of the River Volta, see Boateng (1970) 40–1. The Black Volta rises in the modern state of Burkina Faso and is joined by the Red Volta and the White Volta within the northern areas of Ghana. For the different seasonalities of interior rainfall, see ibid., 32–4. 'Volta', a name given by the early Portuguese, means in that language 'turn, return', the river being the point at which a particular exploration turned back. R. suggests that the name means 'leaping' probably because there existed a lively contemporary dance called a 'volta'.

[55] In 1756 R. claimed that he himself had travelled up River Volta, but without specifying how far (1756, 33, in Chapter 2 above). The geographical report which follows may have been given him by African informants. In 1788 Isert travelled up-river as far as Mlefi (Isert [1788] (1992) 241); and in 1827–1828 Lind explored the river as far as 'Asjotbale' [?Asuchuari], on the southern border of Akwamu (H.G. Lind, 'Undersøgelser, foretagne op ad floden Votal i 1827 og 1828', *Archiv for Søvæsenet* 7 (1834) 1–16). For early navigation by canoe, and detailed exploration, see K.B. Dickson, *A Historical Geography of Ghana* (1969) 109, 235–6.

[56] For seasonality of flooding, see J.M. Grove and A.M. Johansen, 'The historical geography of the Volta Delta', *Bulletin de l'IFAN*, 30 (1968) 1383.

year Ada loses part of its western shore. On the other hand, the current west of Ada has formed a fine island a musket shot from Ada, having a diameter of a quarter of a mile. A good engineer would know how to handle this, by driving piles into the lagoon so that the current can be turned away by them. A fortress built like a Norwegian house, purely of timbers, would be just as impregnable as others of stone. Enough logs can be found at River Volta. If we had six such fortresses up the river, a large fort at the seashore, ten armed boats, 100,000 *rixdaler* worth of goods, /285/ and sensible and able servants, we would have no need to fear the roads being closed to us, or that circumstances might arise on the Coast causing us to suffer loss.[57]

The mouth of River Volta is scarcely half a mile wide, with sandbanks both outside and inside. One mile up-river, and half a mile from the mainland, lies Ada, one of the largest islands, where we have our lodge. East of Ada, River Volta forms a large lake fifteen miles long and seven to eight miles wide. In this lake can be found a good one hundred uninhabited islands covered with bushes and forest. Thus, this land, seen east of River Volta by ships sailing by, is only a narrow strip of land, at some places three-quarters of a mile wide, at others not two musket shots wide. The towns of Agona, Qvitta, and Agojo lie here, as do many smaller Negro towns. From Ada you can approach on this lake to within two miles of Popo.[58]

Five miles up-river lies the island Mlefi, and higher up lie Tuffi and Agave. At present, the Aqvamboes are living on some islands 50–60 miles up-river from Ada. The Negroes use the name 'Crepe' for all the land lying east of River Volta and north of this lake, as well as several /286/ hundred miles up-river. West of River Volta are found, first, the Mountain Negroes, then Qvahu, Akim, and Assiante.

The Mountain Negroes, who border on River Volta, carry on a considerable trade in red earth. They come to Agona and Qvitta with these goods loaded in a Negro boat, sailing on this lake. I have been astonished to see how dearly they sell their earth. The Qvitta Negroes, and others, use it in their hair, like powder. The elderly among them rub their bodies daily with palm oil and red earth. A single portion, with which an old woman at Qvitta or Agona can powder herself, may have cost 20 *boss* (two shillings). The Mountain Negroes buy dried fish from the Qvitta Negroes, who have it in great quantities, and sell it at a good price, so the Mountain Negroes have their canoes (boats) just as heavily loaded with fish and dried shrimp as they are when they arrive with earth. When the river becomes unsafe for the Mountain Negroes and they cannot reach the appointed places with

---

[57] A generation later, Isert intended to establish his plantation up-river, at Mlefi, but found the area too unhealthy (Isert [1788] (1992) 229). A later source also concluded that despite the many possiblities for work and trade, the climate was too unhealthy for Europeans (Lind (1834) 16).
[58] For details of the River Volta delta, see Boateng (1970) 159–60. For the system of lagoons running parallel to the coast eastward from the mouth of River Volta, see Law (1991) 20–1.

their red earth, it is impossible to describe how anxious our Qvitta Negroes become. They are quite depressed and ill, since they cannot make fetish except when they are powdered.[59] /287/

[Qvitta]

In 1743 I was at Qvitta to install our factor, since we Danes had not had a lodge there for sixteen years.[60] Meanwhile the Dutch had established themselves there and had sent a native Dane, named From, to be factor there. After From had been there for three years and had built a defensive lodge, he and his garrison were killed by the Dahomey Negroes. It would take too long to tell the tale, but it was his own fault.[61]

I was at Qvitta for six months before I could come to an agreement with Assiamboe at Popo, and with others, and receive their assurance that Qvitta would hereafter belong to the Danes alone.[62] My assistant and black servants had to stay at the lodge and I took a pleasure trip to Crepe, since at that time no European ship was expected to come to the Coast, and we did not care to buy slaves since we could not sell them. From Qvitta my party and I sailed in a canoe at five o'clock in the morning, and arrived at the mainland north of Qvitta at two o'clock in the afternoon. The caboceer at the place where we arrived had visited me several times, and he had been well treated, so now wishing to repay the courtesy, he was particularly polite. During our five-day stay we visited four places /288/ in Crepe, and were, in the same

---

[59] The 'red earth' is probably camwood or barwood, a dyewood, which since it was imported from elsewhere in West Africa was costly. Red earth or laterite, on the other hand, was everywhere available, free. Camwood (*Baphia nitida*) is powdered, mixed with shea butter, and rubbed on the body for various purposes, medicinal and cosmetic (F.R. Irvine, *Woody Plants of Ghana* (1961) 365–7). Camwood also features prominently in modern Gã religious ritual, its employment perhaps representing a cleansing process (M.J. Field, *Religion and Medicine of the Gã People* (1937) 52,126). For the similar uses of red ochre, see McCaskie (1995) 290.

[60] R. and a colleague were sent to Keta to bring the lodge into operation (CRA, V-gK 123, letter of 21.7.1744).

[61] For the capture and death of From in 1737, see Van Dantzig (1978) 327–32. The Dutch lodge was Fort Singelenburgh (Van Dantzig (1980b) 55–56, and (1980a) 240–1).

[62] R. had close personal contact with Assiambo and evidently established good relations (for details, see Appendix B below). Assiambo has been identified as Assiongbon Dandjin (Gayibor (1995) 205). The Keta lodge was first established in 1710, under Governor Lygaard. Due to vacillations in trade and occasional threats of war during the first two decades of the eighteenth century, several times factors were placed there, then withdrawn. R. and a colleague, Klein, were sent there in 1744 to reactivate the lodge but were soon recalled and suspended from service. The lodge continued in Danish hands, however, and in 1769 during one of the many periods of unrest in the area, one Assiongbon, King of Little Popo, acted as peacemaker (Nørregaard (1966) 124). This was Amah/Assiongbon, the successor to R.'s Assiambo. Throughout the last half of the eighteenth century the Danes had contact with the rulers of Little Popo and Glidzi, evidently to the advantage of both parties (Gayibor (1995) 206). On the later history of the Keta lodge and the kings of Little Popo, see also Isert [1788] (1992) 71; A.R. Bjørn, 'Bjørn's Beretning 1788', *Thaarup's Archiv* (1797–8) 216–7.

manner, given a polite and friendly reception. The only thing I found strange, and which I had not seen before at Qvitta, or at any other places, was this: all the women, young and old, had completely smeared the hair on their heads with a crust of red earth and palm oil, making [their heads] appear to be twice as large as usual. You could smell these monsters before you could see them. Here I saw the freshwater fishes mentioned above, which were smoked. I would liked to have seen them alive but none were available there just then. A certain Latin author, whom I can recall reading in my youth, says, 'Africa is full of monsters'. Clearly, he had not seen these Crepe black women, or the African freshwater fish. Otherwise I know of no monsters in Africa whose like cannot be found in Asia, such as crocodiles, large turtles, etc. As they have been described, the fish mentioned above quite closely resemble a dragon, yet they are only one span long. You also find another species with two feet, like a mole. I think they are amphibians. Many doubt that dragons have ever existed, but I can almost believe it since their like exists in African fresh water. /289/ At Berekuso, a Negro town four miles inland, above Christiansborg, I have also seen freshwater fish which were fearful and gruesome, but in Crepe they were far more monstrous.

Normally the Negroes at Ada, Qvitta, etc. are not as shameless as are our Accras. An Accra and an Adampi can stand and nag and pester when you refuse to give him a loan. The Accra may try again later, begging and plaguing a factor to lend or give him something. The [Adas and Qvittas], on the contrary, as soon as they have been given an answer, go their way very politely.

The inhabitants of Qvitta and Agona experience great inconvenience because of mosquitoes, or *mouchetter*,[63] for three months of the year. It is thought that the great quantities of these vermin reproduce in the stagnant lake after the rainy season, when the water is fresh. These vermin are worse at night than in the daytime, and all the city people, adults and children, leave their towns and go to the shore. There they bury themselves in the sand, leaving no more than a bit of their faces uncovered.[64]

The caboceer at Qvitta, called Alovi, is a decent old Negro. Nor is there anything negative to say about the Ada caboceer, /290/ Acrofi, except that he could be a bit more abstemious. Tey, the fetish-maker at Ada, is a very decent Negro who serves us Danes in every way he can.

It is worth mentioning the small islands in River Volta, not far from Ada, where, at certain times of the year, many birds nest and hatch their young. Here you could collect a whole shipload of young and old birds, and eggs

---

[63] French *mouchette* 'little fly'.

[64] The claim of an exodus of an entire population to the beach each night, to bury themselves in the sand, is one of R.'s more bizarre statements. That some did do this at times may be correct, but with their knowledge of plant properties the Africans would have been able to utilise an insect repellent; e.g., the burned seeds of *Detarium senegalense*. the Tallow Tree, or burned gum resin of *Boswellia dalzielii*, the Frankincense Tree (Abbiw (1990) 165).

as well, if you so wished. The river itself is particularly rich in fish, although crocodiles are found there in great numbers. [Also seen there are] numbers of a bird larger than a swan, whose craw could hold two sacks [*skiepper*] of corn. You also see great numbers of sea cows, called sea elephants by the Blacks.[65]

[Fort Christiansborg and Accra]

From here we proceed to our chief castle, Christiansborg, at Accra. It is a massive, very strong building. All the warehouses are vaults with walls four *alen* thick. It was [at one time] a quite regularly shaped fort with four bastions, sixty *alen* square, if I recall correctly. The batteries are eighteen to twenty *alen* high and twelve *alen* wide, with some forty cannons.[66] Yet we did not have room for many goods, especially when we received 30,000–40,000 *potter* of brandy with every ship. Since room was lacking in the warehouses, we had to /291/ store kegs of brandy in the rooms of the servants. This caused great leakage, or, rather, 'drinkage'. There were too few rooms for the Europeans as well, so sometimes they had to live four to six in a single small room. At that time one of the governors took over the entire west battery, had another storey built on it, and three rooms furnished for himself. Under these he furnished quarters for his Corps de Garde of the soldiers, thus locating the soldiers' night quarters farthest away from the entry [to the fort], where they should have been. Another governor wished to build more warehouses, and had the so-called New Point built. This is a large bastion at the NW corner of the fort, more than half as large as the entire structure. Under this we now had three large, vaulted warehouses, and since that time we have not found it necessary to store our brandy in the rooms of the servants.[67] If we had a similar bastion at the NE corner of the Fort, it would be fairly regular again, but now it is the most irregular fort on the Coast, as can be seen in the copper engravings that follow, Numbers 1 and 2.[68]

The wall built around forts is the so-called 'outwork'. It is between this wall and the fort that our Negroes are placed when enemies threaten to attack them in the town. In the walls, as well as on the fort's parapet, are elongated /292/ arrow loopholes, wide on the inner side and narrow on the outside, so if the enemy should come close enough the Negroes can fire their muskets at them, and yet remain safe from gunshot themselves. At a cannon-shot NW of the fort, and two musket-shots from Ursue town, we

---

[65] For 'Bird Island' and hippopotamus, see Isert [1788] (1992) 80 and note h. The bird with a large craw was probably a pelican.

[66] In the 1730s Christiansborg was in poor shape (Atkins (1735) 153), but earlier its strength was noted (Bosman (1705) 68). For further comment on the fort, see Isert [1788] (1992) 28–30; Van Dantzig (1980b) 29–32.

[67] This reference is probably to Governor Henrick von Suhm (April 1724-March 1727) who made major repairs and added new buildings to Christiansborg.

[68] For views of Christiansborg, see Plates 2 and 3.

have a watchtower on which there are, or should be, eight cannon. This is called Prøve-Steen.[69] As long as we have food and provisions for war, 30 cannons, and 300 Negroes as manpower, these fortifications, as described and as shown in the accompanying copper engravings, are invincible and impregnable against all the forces of the Africans so far known on Gold Coast — even if the Africans were united.

In the middle of our fort is an underground cistern, built with walls of cement. It is 22 feet square, but is only watertight up to six feet, at which point the water leaks out. These six feet can hold 400 barrels of rain water, which, when it falls on the batteries and bastions, runs into the cistern through pipes, with the result that, at times, after a good travado we have our cistern full. In 1750 a worthy man built a larger cistern outside the fort, with a pipeline from the old one to the new. This is certainly very useful, and we can now also supply /293/ our ships with water of the best quality on the Coast.[70] Otherwise, when our cisterns were empty, the Europeans had to drink and cook their food in the salty so-called beach water, as the Negroes did. This beach water is actually sea water that collects in hollows six to seven *alen* deep in the sand, ten to twelve *alen* from the edge of the sea. Thus the sea water is filtered through the sand and becomes fresh, or [at least] brackish.[71] When we Europeans have to drink this water, many among us become ill because of worms and other forms of the country's illnesses.

These worms are hatched in part of the human body, in the arm, hand, thigh, leg, back, waist, head, etc. The infected individual experiences a high fever twice or thrice, one of his limbs becomes swollen, and he then finds the worm in the swollen limb. If [the worm] moves this causes indescribable pain. If it takes too long for the worm to eat its way out, the infected individual cuts a hole at the place where he thinks the head may be. But he must be careful about drawing the worm out. If it breaks in two, it causes a chancre. We have seen worms one and one-half spans long, and they are truly alive, since they move when they have come out as far as one half of a finger's length. Some individuals may walk around for eight days with a worm /294/ hanging out of part of their body. Some wind it on to a wooden stick, if they are afraid the worm will crawl back in again. The thickest worm I have seen has been as thick as a pen quill, but I have [also] seen them as thin as a sewing thread. The best advice is for the infected individual to keep the limb containing the worm in sea water for as long as he can stand

---

[69] *Prøve-steen* means 'touchstone'. For the tower, see Lawrence (1963) 206, 209.

[70] The cistern was built by Carl Engmann and can still be seen in the courtyard of Christiansborg Castle. According to the legend on the cistern itself, it was begun on 25 March 1753 and completed on 31 May the same year. The measurements there given are 28 ft. deep, 32 ft. wide. Carl Engmann, who was sent out as a surgeon, was governor in 1752–1757 (Lawrence (1963) 209–10; Nørregård (1966) 112; J. Reindorf, *Scandinavians in Africa* (1980) 136). Engmann composed the poem at the beginning of R.'s book.

[71] For water filtered through sand, see Isert [1788] (1992) 76.

it, and the worm often comes out by itself. The Blacks frequently make the mistake of cutting a hole in the body of the worm itself, and this then causes a long-lasting and dangerous [condition].[72]

The most remarkable thing at Christiansborg, and which no other fortress possesses, is a green [leafy] tree in the middle of the courtyard of the fort, where for three or four months of the year, a great number of small birds take up their stay. We Danes call them travado-birds because they arrive around travado time and leave when it is over. All the branches of the tree are full of the nests these birds weave out of blades of grass, in such an artful way that a Nürnberger artist could scarcely emulate them.[73] They are no larger than our sparrows. The males are yellow with a black head and tail, and red eyes. The females are greyish and smaller. Many Europeans among the English and Dutch have tried /295/ planting the same variety of tree in their forts. The trees have indeed grown, but these Europeans have not been so fortunate that birds come to them. At times we would like to be rid of some of these birds, since the tree is nearly hidden under the nests and the birds, and the birds twitter and sing from morning to evening, so you can scarcely hear yourself speak.

These small birds are surely the most thieving creatures in the world, resembling the Negroes in many ways. The males arrive first and build their nests. Some of them are industrious, flying to the fields, fetching long blades of grass, winding and binding them around a branch, flying off again straight away to fetch more grass, and weaving it into the nest. Such an industrious bird can have his nest finished in five or six days. Then the females come and examine the work of the males, and the male who has completed his nest usually wins a female. The latter does nothing apart from lining the interior of the nest with soft feathers, hair, etc. On the other hand, some males never, or rarely, leave the tree. They steal straw from the others' nests when they are out collecting more grass, and sometimes they complete their nests before the industrious ones do. They seduce one another's females. On the occasions when /296/ they are discovered doing this, the rivals begin to fight with such fury that they fall down into the courtyard, where we can capture them by hand.[74]

---

[72] Guinea worm (*Dracunculus medinensis*) attacks individuals who drink water containing small crustaceans infected by the worm. Understandably this phenomenon was widely discussed in the early European sources, all of them giving very similar descriptions of both the symptoms and the treatment but often varying in guesses as to the source of infection (De Marees [1602] (1987) 98b-101a; Olfert Dapper, *Naukeurige Beschrijvinge der Afrikaensche gewesten* (1676) 95–6; Bosman (1705) 108–9; Isert [1788] (1992) 144–5 and note hh).

[73] The 'Nürnberger artist' may be a reference to Albrecht Dürer (1471–1528).

[74] The bird is the Village Weaver (*Ploceus cucullatus*). These birds are abundant in towns and villages, breed in colonies of hundreds of pairs, and have noisy, chattering voices (W. Serle and G.J. Morel, *A Field Guide to the Birds of West Africa* (1977) 242–3. Their nest sites are traditional, hence planting the same variety of tree elsewhere would not necessarily attract them. R.'s detailed descriptions of nest-building, competition and thieving are correct—and they do often fall to the ground grappling (p.c. A. Tye).

In that same tree at Fort Christiansborg we nearly always have chameleons, so that anyone who wishes to observe them can do so. Our writers report that a chameleon can shift colour at will, [imitating] whatever colour it is placed on. Or that you can hold a colour up to its eyes and it will become that colour. I, and many others, can bear witness that this is not so. My observations are thus. A chameleon's skin is made up of small scales, and as it contracts its skin the day (light) falls on it and it reflects [the light], with the result that it is green in one place, at another blue, or reddish. A chameleon changes colour along its back when it is angry. The small scales on its back rise, just like a pig's bristles, and this immediately gives it another colour, yet it is the same one which we had seen earlier and later, when it was irritated. If it is afraid and wants to run away, it becomes another colour and in this way a chameleon can often change its colour. This animal is also one of the African /297/ monsters because of its ugly appearance, but as for changing of colour, I find the head of a turkey cock more remarkable than a chameleon.[75] You also find fish on the Coast which change colour, such as the *dorades*, and, if I have observed correctly, our herring also change colour.[76]

We have a small salty lagoon close to the eastern side of Christiansborg, which is scarcely one quarter of a mile long and a musket-shot wide.[77] From this water, which is saltier than sea water, the Negroes make salt. They collect the water in a container, pour it out on the ground close to the lagoon, and within two hours it is salt. It is very unclean when they first collect it from the ground, but when it is boiled and the scum removed, it becomes excellent salt. Some fifty years ago our Negroes had a profitable salt trade, but now, with no people in the interior any longer, as compared to former times there is but little consumption.[78]

This lagoon is called *Tié Tié*, like the fetish in Ursue town.[79] It is not known whether the fetish was named after the lagoon or the lagoon after the fetish. We built an embankment above the salty lagoon, behind which

---

[75] R. is right in saying that they cannot shift colour at will. The colour changes are limited and have as much to do with mood as background. But his explanation of the mechanism is wrong. It is not due to contraction of the skin but rather by the contraction or expansion of small sacs of pigment (p.c. A. Tye).

[76] For the dorado, identified as either the mammalian dolphin (*Delphinus delphis*) or the dolphin-fish (*Coryphaena hippurus* or *euqisetis*), see Barbot [1732] (1992) 757, note 5.

[77] This is the Klɔte Lagoon. See Chapter 3 above, /58/, and note 21.

[78] On salt making on the coast of Gold Coast, see De Marees [1602] (1987) 201; Bosman (1705) 308–9; Isert [1788] (1992) 60; Dickson (1969) 86–7. R.'s comment on the dwindling of the salt trade probably referred specifically to the trade of the area around Osu. To state that there were no longer inhabitants in the interior is another one of his exaggerations. The immediate interior was populated by the Aburi, Larteh, Akyem, and Akwapim, but trading routes had moved eastward, in response to changing conditions of political and economic power; for instance, Asante trade now went via Akwamu, hence down River Volta, and to Ningo.

[79] See note 77 above.

we intended to collect fresh /**298**/ water — which we have, in fact, done. In some years we had fresh water in this little brook for two or three months after the rainy season.]But] in other years we had such strong travado*s* that the dikes were washed away. Our efforts and cost had been in vain, and we had to begin anew. As long as we have water there, neither the Dutch nor the English can engage in any trade with ships without their having to count us in, for the sake of the water, because they have no fresh water to deliver to ships.

One thing I must remark, to the discredit of our nation on the Coast, is that we do not [generally] establish gardens, and when they are established, we let them go to ruin.[80] What a joy it is [to see] at Cape Coast and the other English forts, that each European resident can be provided by the English with as many vegetables of European and inland varieties as he wishes. In a court case held at Christiansborg on the Coast against a certain [Danish] governor, among the accusations was one of his having kept three Company slaves for his garden, and the governor was ordered to repay [the amount] the Company slaves had received as wages for several years. In this spirit [of meanness], the soldiers might be equally required to pay the female slaves for sweeping the quarters of the Guard. /**299**/ At Cape Coast more than a hundred slaves are kept for the gardens alone — gardens a good half mile long, with *allées* of orange, citron, and other trees. At the smaller [English] forts at least ten Company slaves are employed to tend the gardens.[81]

Our Ursue town, at Accra, was a large town in former times. Fifty years ago, Labode, Ursue, and Tessing, when combined, could muster an army of 12,000–14,000 men. But how they can [both] increase in size and diminish can be seen by the following. In 1739, at the time when [the Osu and their allies] were at war with the Dutch Negroes, scarcely 150 [could be mustered] to go into battle.[82] Yet in 1750 there were more than 500. So populous had their little boys and children [*sic*] grown in eleven years. Many families of Ursue Negroes still live in the Dutch town, and they are still registered with considerable debt in the Company's Debt-books.[83] The Dutch enticed away most of the Accras, by means of the outwork they built at their fort, into

---

[80] Gardens were established and kept by the Danes at later dates. However, the earlier Danish headquarters at Fredriksborg did have an excellent garden, which two French visitors commended (Nicolas Villault, *Relation des Costes d'Afrique* (1669) 380–1; Barbot [1732] (1992) 400). For the later gardens and plantations, see Monrad (1822) 317–25; H. Jeppesen, 'Danske plantageanlegg på Guldkysten', *Geografisk Tidsskrift* (1966) 48–72.

[81] For European gardens at Cape Coast, see Atkins (1735) 93–4; Davies (1957) 242; and for such gardens in general, Isert [1788] (1992) 105; Dickson (1969) 74–6.

[82] The reference is probably to the war that took place in 1737–1738, in which the Gã of Osu, La, and Teshi, and their allies the Danes and an Akyem chief, went into combat against the Accras and the Akwamu settlement in Accra, Otublohun (Nørregård (1966) 98; Irene Quaye, 'The Gã and their neighbours', PhD thesis, University of Ghana (1972) 218ff., 246–7; M.A. Kwamena-Poh, *Government and Politics in the Akuapem State* (1973), 75–6.

[83] The difficulty in collecting payment of debts was frequently recorded (Nørregård (1966) 111–2).

which the Negroes could flee when the Aqvamboes, or other enemies, suddenly fell upon them. Since we saw our Negroes running away from us to them, we also had to build an outwork if we wished to retain them, and ours was better and larger than those of the Dutch and English.[84] Those /300/ who were already in the Dutch town stayed there, but the rest remained where they were [with us].

We have four noble families in our town to which all of the town's inhabitants belong. The following are the Big Men living there at present: Adoui the broker, Ursa the caboceer, Ante-Grandees [? Big Ante], and Noyte, whose nickname is *Tooda* (Brandy-drinker or Drunkard, a title of honour among the Blacks).[85] Every New Year each one of these Big Men receives an anker of brandy and a piece of cotton cloth 24 or 25 *alen* long. In addition, Adoui receives four *rixdaler* from Christiansborg as a monthly tribute, but the Protector [sic] receives only 28 *rixdaler*. Caboceer Ursa receives four *rixdaler* monthly from the Company; Ante receives only two *rixdaler* monthly, as a Company slave; and *Tooda* receives nothing at all. In addition, the Company keeps two emissaries who, in 1750, were named Soja, the great emissary, and Abroe, the ordinary emissary, each of whom receives four *rixdaler* monthly.[86] It is necessary to bind the Black caboceers to fidelity with these salaries, not only those who belong immediately to us, but also those in the other lands where no other European has preceded us.

All the European nations are envious of each another in such situations, and if our /301/ correspondence with other nations were always recorded in the Copy-Letter-Books, it would appear especially ridiculous to those involved here in Copenhagen. They would read 'We, *N.N. Opperhoved* [Commander] and Council, etc. at such and such a time, solemnly protest that an Englishman, or a Dutchman, entices away or swindles His Majesty of Denmark and Norway of his Black subjects and Caboceer *N.N.*, and we assure them [sic] that if they do not desist we shall perform our duty by sacrificing life and blood to uphold Your Majesty's rights on the Guinea Coast.' As I say, it would appear comical here, since we indeed do not use any other methods of writing or speaking against the other nations that they do not use against us and against others in similar situations.[87] In 1747 we formed a union with a powerful Fante caboceer called Abonnam and promised him eight *rixdaler* monthly. He committed himself to act as protector for all the Danish Whites and Blacks, [especially] for ships' crews and passengers when they landed in Fante. He promised to provide us with

---

[84] Lawrence (1963) 206–8; Van Dantzig (1980b) 30–2.
[85] Presumably the four Big Men are the heads of the four families.
[86] Soja is mentioned as the Danish Company's linguist in a letter written by James Hopkins, the factor at James Fort (CRA, V-gK 888 (1746), 78). See also Nørregård (1966) 118.
[87] For example, the records contain an exchange of letters of complaint about Coyman's activities, letters involving the Danish, English and Dutch governors (CRA, V-gK 887, 2.9.1744; 888 (1746), 68–80).

millio[88] for the ships and for Accra, at the same low price others had paid before. He also promised, in the event of any war arising, to attack others, or defend us with his men, and to do whatever else we found useful, etc.[89] Since then quarrels have arisen on the Coast, increasing our expenses in that country, and [therefore] the /302/ association [with Abonnam] has been dissolved. If you should ask any of the traders living in that country if the association was not better in many instances than a garrison of fifty European soldiers, he would answer, 'Yes!' Thus, in that instance it was a case of being penny-wise and pound-foolish.

In former times, under the influence of their factors, the Dutch Negroes claimed a degree of mastery over our Negroes, and when this happened some of our commanders looked the other way. We cannot say what harm this has resulted in, and sensible people in the Government never speak of such shameful things.[90]

Little or nothing is cultivated in the fertile fields at Accra. Plots here and there, measuring a score of square *alen*, are all a family cultivates. When we advise the Negroes to cultivate more ground, and describe to them how rich they could become if they could provide the forts and ships with *millio* and other products of which they have need, they answer that it is not worth the trouble to cultivate the earth at the coast since they are not paid for their trouble, and their forefathers considered themselves too good for that. Yet, /303/ according to their own admission, they harvest two hundredfold normally, and never less than one hundredfold, even if the rain does not come when it is expected. Some of us Danes have cultivated a plot for a few years and have harvested five hundredfold. Admittedly, two or three miles inland, where the mountains begin, the land is more fertile than at the coast. More rain falls there because (as I believe) the clouds break on the mountains, and, when rain does not fall, nevertheless a heavy dew forms during the night, thus increasing the fertility. At the coast, and for a quarter of a mile from the sea, dew also forms, but it is very salty. However, the fertility inland is incredible as regards all varieties of plants, and *millie*. He who plants 10 *potter* [about ten litres] harvests 20 *tonder* [about 144 litres] and more.[91] How the Almighty has

---

[88] At this point *millie* becomes *millio*, and continues so, but probably this is merely a slip.

[89] Payments to Abonnam are recorded (CRA, V-gK 941 Omkostningsbøger 1746–1754, 29.2.1748; Nørregård (1966) 109).

[90] R. may be generalizing from an episode when a 'Dutch Negro' was given permission by Coymans to *panyar* the Danish linguist, Soya (Soja), because of a long-standing palaver between their families—according to a letter written by the English factor (CRA, Vg-K 888 (1746) 79).

[91] For modern peasant agriculture in Ghana, see Dickson (1969) 76–81. Many of the crops in R.'s day were forest or savannah plants, thus agriculture on the coast was not as productive as inland, whereas fishing and salt-making were available alternatives of livelihood. In the hills, farming and hunting were the normal occupations, and the output differences were the basis of trade between the coast and the interior. On agriculture in general, see Boateng (1970) 63–5. R.'s condemnation of the system of cultivating only small plots indicates that he did not understand the practice of bush fallowing widely in use, which required that plots be allowed to stand fallow for at least seven years (Dickson (1969) 76; Boateng (1970) 77).

blessed this land which these lazy natives do not know how to utilize! God has undoubtedly left them to their evil nature, and they consider good to be evil and evil good, since they consider all work too demeaning, and beneath them. To be thieves and murderers is, to their way of thinking, a most laudable craft. This finishes our description of Christiansborg and the Negro town called Ursue lying under it. That word *ursue,* in the Negroes' old language, means a tiger, but in the /**304**/ present language at Accra a tiger is called *lumo*. With this term *lumo* the Negroes name every commander of the Europeans. When an Accra wishes to ask, 'Where is the Governor?', he says, '*Nembæ lumo è bô?*', meaning, 'Where is the Tiger?'[92]

[Labode]

Next [after Ursue] we come to Labode, one-half to three-quarters of a mile east of Christiansborg. [This town] belongs to us, and no one disputes that.[93] Here you can see the remains of a very large Negro town, now so poor that it contains scarcely 600 people in all. The so-called Great Fetish or Oracle is here, and when the fetishes of the other Accra towns pronounce something which is completely incomprehensible and obscure, the Negroes come here from those places and ask about it. I believe that they remain just as wise then as they were before. When you ask why the Great Fetish comes to Labode and not to other places, the Negroes say it is because the Labode Negroes are more devout than the others — and among them, Putti is respected as a saint, whom no one wishes to rouse to anger. He, alone, is supreme in his town, and all the Accras and Mountain Negroes regard him with awe.[94] Otherwise the Labode Negroes are like all the others, just as lazy. They cultivate the land around their town /**305**/ among the ruins of the houses, and plant small *millio*, but this is done on the orders of the Fetish, because the Fetish eats no bread other than that made of small *millio*. Then, when they have enough for the Fetish, or perhaps a score of priests and priestesses, to eat, that suffices.[95]

---

[92] *Lumo* is a Gã term indicating a person of high status. Probably the correct form of R.'s phrase is *neegbe lumo ébà oo?* 'Where has the governor come, oh?' (although 'come' does seem out of place here) (p.c. Mary Esther Kropp Dakubu).

[93] Presumably R. means that the Danes had a locally-accepted monopoly of the marine import/export trade at Labadi, a privilege which excluded the other European trading nations from this trade. The extent to which they rented this privilege from the local polity, or otherwise merely enjoyed it by tolerance, is controversial, as is the extent to which they exercise any control over the local community.

[94] The respect and awe generated by the 'Labadi Great Fetish' (*La Kpa*) still obtained locally in the 1930s (Field (1937) 39).

[95] Small *millie*, known as *mah* (literally 'food'), is used for ritual feeding. The Labadi people are traditionally more farmers than fishermen. If in R.'s day they in fact limited their activities to the area close to home it may have been due to unrest and lack of safety in those areas suitable for farming farther away (p.c. I. Odotei).

At Labode many trees and bushes are considered to be sacred. A fence is usually raised around the trees to prevent any creature or human from approaching them too closely.[96] Putti offered as proof of the sacredness [of a particular tree] the fact that it had not died, as had all the other trees at the coast.[97] Our tree at Christiansborg could, then, with greater reason, be called sacred. The fetish hut and the area around it have been described earlier. Half a mile east of Labode is the Labode lagoon. This is also salty, as are all the coastal lagoons in that land. According to the claims of the Negroes, it extends three miles inland.[98] One and one-half miles from Labode is Tessing. This town is larger than Labode, and more than twice as many people live there. For the most part they are fishermen, and in earlier times they moved there from Labode because landing was better at Tessing than at Labode.[99] These three Negro towns belong to us Danes at Accra. We have /306/ often hidden the inhabitants of these towns in the outwork of Christiansborg when their enemies were about to attack them. All these towns are in great debt to the Company.

[**Ponni and Prampram**]

Two miles from Tessing we find Temma, where the Dutch have a small fort, much like our Prøvesteen at Ursue.[100] However, the Negroes at Temma have deserted their town and fled to Prampram or Ningo. This was after a Dutch factor at Accra, without the slightest cause or provocation, seized more than one hundred Mountain Negroes who had sought refuge there, and sold them.[101] Having done that, this same Dutchman established a lodge for defensive purposes at Ponni, three-quarters of a mile from there. When the Dutch first arrived there a number of Negroes came and built houses at Ponni. But that same Dutch factor at Accra, using his soldiers at Ponni, stole a number of [local] people and Mountain Negroes. [In return,] the Mountain Negroes, as was their custom, stayed close to the Dutch Negroes at Ponni and Temma as long as any were there, stealing and selling those they could seize. These European robberies were the work of a Dutch soldier named Adam Holland, who was *Baas*

---

[96] For fences around sacred places, see Isert [1788] (1992) 170.
[97] The coastal area around Accra is an anomalous vegetation zone, lacking the fairly dense tree cover of much of the rest of the coast of eastern Guinea.
[98] This is the Kpeshi Lagoon. It is noteworthy that R. appears not to have travelled the mere three miles inland which would have enabled him to confirm or deny the claim.
[99] For a tradition of the establishment of Teshie, see M.J. Field, *Social Organization of the Gã People* (1940) 207–8. This maintains that the original settlers were aboriginal 'Kpesi' and 'La' (from Labadi), as well as Fante fishermen, and a group of captives from Lagos (the last somewhat unlikely). Teshie is now one of the main fishing areas around Accra.
[100] For this Dutch fort, of which there are now no traces, see Van Dantzig (1980b) 55.
[101] The Dutch factor was Balthazar Coymans. See Chapter 2 above, note 22.

[Overseer] at Ponni.[102] He was [actually] a Danish deserter. Holland had blue linen sewn [as a dress for] his body in order to resemble a Negro, and in this military attire, together with some /307/ Blacks, he placed himself in the path of the Mountain Negroes. When he could not seize any of them, he seized Temma or Ponni Negroes and sold them or beat them to death. Such Dutch madness was bound to result in the blocking of routes by us and by the English, since the Mountain Negroes wanted to stay on the same side as all the Accras, consequently on the side of our Negroes as well. We Danes were the first to send a message up to the Mountain Negroes to assure them that the roads to our towns would be open to them, and if Adam Holland appeared on our roads we would send people out and have him beaten to death like a mad dog. Thereupon our roads were opened. The English at Accra did the same as we had done, and they too had their roads to the coast opened.

In these circumstances the Dutch factor made a decision worth recording here. He sent a serious complaint to Elmina, signed by each member of his European garrison, and including the signatures or signs of all the Grandes [grandees, Big Men] in his town, stating that the English factor had bribed the Mountain Negroes to lay siege to the Dutch at Temma and Ponni. He wrote that the Mountain Negroes were going to break down the fortification, decapitate the Whites, bring their jawbones to him (the Englishman), etc., etc. /308/ This was in fact entirely a fabrication, and one can see from this how shameless a Dutchman on the Guinea Coast can be, not only in order to cover up his own thievery, but to make his rascalry an issue involving the Dutch nation—an issue in which he would not only be praised for his good relationships, but also would make good the expenditure he had incurred in this matter. During a period of four years we were discomfited by this Dutchman at Accra, who nearly every month began causing this sort of disturbance.

The General at Elmina, who without a doubt knew the background of this matter, sent his factor's *species facti* [statement of the case], with half a hundred sworn signatures from Blacks and Whites, to the chief [English] agents at Cape Coast and demanded satisfaction. The chief agents sent a copy of that Dutch *species facti* to us at Christiansborg and asked the Governor and the Council to report our version of the matter. This was done, and we bore witness to the issue, describing it as it [really] was, and its background from the start. The chief agents received our explanation and waited for a

---

[102] A report from James Hopkins, the factor at James Fort, stated that Mr. Holland, Chief of the Dutch lodge at Kponi, 'has shot one of the English subjects from Prampram as he was busy fishing'. Hopkins complained to Factor Coymans at Crèvecoeur and was told that Holland was under orders 'to kill and exterminate all the subjects of Prampram whom he should meet close by Ponny'. He also warned Hopkins not to trouble him again (BLL, Furley N46, 23.2.1747; cf. CRA, V-gK 888, folder 1747, 105–12); see also for this episode, Van Dantzig (1980a) 249 ff.

time, until an English royal warship arrived at the Coast. The agents [then] asked the commander /**309**/ to take up the issue. He personally went to Elmina and showed them our explanation. The agents and the royal commander demanded satisfaction for such ungodly accusations, and this was promised them. *N.B.* The Dutch factor at Accra was poisoned and the issue was closed by this.[103]

Two miles east of Ponni, at Prampram, the English have built a small fort. The Negro town there was [originally] small, with [only] about a score of families, but since the Dutch, using the methods described above, made [the inhabitants] of Ponni and Temma flee their own towns, Prampram has become considerably larger than it was before. The English have their greatest trade here, ten times more than they have at the English [fort at] Accra. The factor here is always well provided with goods. In respect of that small fort, the only thing I can find fault with is its location, it being sited too far from the sea, with the result that the English cannot defend the landing place. This is a serious fault. Should the English at Prampram be at war with any Negro nation, a handful of Blacks could force them to starve to death.[104] /**310**/

[Fort Fredensburg]

We have a better fort in Fredensborg at Ningo, one and one-half miles east of Prampram. The building was begun in 1735, and in 1741 it was nearly finished, though the outwork was still lacking. The accompanying copper engraving was made from an on the spot sketch preserved at Fredensborg. The fort itself is in good condition, as seen here in drawing number 3, but an outwork remains just as necessary here as it is at Christiansborg and other places.[105] At Fredensborg, we have had at times to accommodate the Negroes and all their clutter in the courtyard and on the batteries of the fort. This is not only troublesome but also dangerous. You cannot, then, move forward on the batteries to load, manipulate, and fire a cannon without stepping on, or injuring, a Black woman or her child, who then screams and howls. We have a cistern in the Fort, and on such occasions we have seen the Blacks break the lock and take water themselves. They would not be satisfied with a *pott* of water a day, this being the ration to which the Europeans had to be limited. To avoid internal war, we had to look the other way, and not even ask who had done it, because if we did find out, that person would have had to be punished, and to start an argument with ten Europeans against /**311**/ 400 Blacks is not advisable. It is not exactly *partie égale* [an equal match].

---

[103] For Coyman's death, very likely by poison, see Chapter 2 above, notes 30–31.

[104] This is Fort Vernon, which also had the disadvantage of being poorly built (Van Dantzig (1980b) xii, 58. For a view of the fort, see Lawrence (1963) 84–5, plate 5.

[105] On Fredensborg ('Castle of Peace'), see Lawrence (1963) 67, 73, 76, 86, 90; Van Dantzig (1980b) xii, 56–7; Isert [1788] (1992) 34; Nørregård (1966) 96–7. See Plate 4.

Fort Fredensborg is a beautiful, regular fort, with a larger courtyard than Christiansborg, but it is, as we say, 'Nürnberger work'.[106] We have no vaulted warehouses there, as we do at Christiansborg. All the ceilings are of coconut logs, covered with plaster and flat stones on which the cannons stand. Every third or fourth year the ends of these coconut logs rot and fall down into the warehouses. We must then have the batteries removed, and fresh logs put in to replace the rotten ones. We usually do a patching up every other month.[107]

At the coast all iron rusts and dissolves in a few years — with your fingers alone you can break an iron rod which has been in place for five or six years. On the other hand, in the interior of the country a father can bequeath to his son a musket which he himself has used for forty years and it is still quite shiny and polished.

The masons we send to the Coast must normally be trained for a couple of years before they can work with the African stone. We quarry the stones from the rocks, and regardless of whether they emerge round or /312/ flat, the vaults, as well as any other necessary masonry, must be made of them. The stones we quarry at Fredensborg are as hard as marble, but those at Accra are as soft as sandstone.[108] We burn lime from beautiful seashells. A collector [of shells] would find many thousand among them worth saving.

In 1742 the Assiantes besieged this fort with 20,000 men, but could accomplish nothing.[109] However, suddenly, one night, they captured more than one hundred Negroes. The rest escaped into the fort. Had we had an outwork there, the Assiantes would not have captured a soul.

The landing place at Ningo is good, and rarely is the sea so rough that you cannot land or set out from there. The beautiful lagoon has been described earlier. Here too the Negroes produce a great quantity of salt, and this is sold to the Aqvamboes and carried to Crepe.[110]

---

[106] 'Nürnberger work' [modern Danish *nyrnberger*] means shoddy work, in contrast to R.'s earlier complimentary reference to the work of a specific Nuremberg artist (note 73 above).

[107] The Dutch also reported this problem. A letter was sent from Accra to Elmina stating that, their lodge having collapsed, the goods within had been damaged and had had to be moved to a native hut (BLL, Furley, 21.9.1749). On the disrepair of forts, see Lawrence (1963) 93.

[108] Lawrence (1963) 90–5; Niels Bech, 'Christiansborg i Ghana', *Architectura* 11 (1989) 107. For the quality of original stone and masonry at Elmina, see P.E.H. Hair, *The Founding of the Castel de São Jorge da Mina* (1994) 73, note 106.

[109] Reports on the size of the besieging force vary considerably. Dutch sources spoke of 4,000 men (BLL, Furley N45, 27 April 1742; Van Dantzig (1980a) 252). R.'s countryman, Christian Glob Dorph, the Commander at Fredensborg Fort), an eye-witness, reported an Asante force of 8,000 (J.K. Fynn, *Asante and its Neighbours* (1971) 74–5). All in all, an example of the difficulty in judging the numerical size of a crowd, as well as yet another instance of R.'s penchant for exaggeration.

[110] The local salt trade in the eighteenth century has been said to have 'rivalled the gold trade in importance and profitability' (Dickson (1969) 99–100); and was very important earlier, too (De Marees [1602] (1987) 201; Barbot (1732) (1992) 482; Bosman (1705) 308; Isert [1788] (1992) 81; Lars Sundstrøm, *The Exchange Economy of Pre-Colonial Tropical Africa* (1974) 122, 123).

A quarter of a mile from the fort entire herds of wild roe deer can be seen, the deer not in hundreds but in thousands. The Black hunters usually burn off the dry grass at night, and in the morning, when the grass has /313/ begun to shoot again, these roe deer and fallow deer come to eat the new grass. A hunter can sometimes shoot two animals at once.[111]

Earlier I said that each Negro town has a certain variety of animal which is considered to be sacred. The Ningo Negroes [revere] the wolf.[112] It is as if the African wolves know they are the idols of the Ningo Negroes, since they have been seen coming into town in daytime, yet you seldom hear of their having seized the lambs, etc. of their friends, the Ningo Negroes. An old wolf which had been living not far from the town for several years, and had visited the Negroes in town daily, walked close by our sentry, past the gate of the fort. This soldier was newly arrived in the country and he imagined he was doing no more than a public service when he killed the monster. His musket was not loaded but he struck the wolf on the head with the barrel, killing it immediately. A terrible din and alarm was heard in the town — young and old alike howled for their friend, the wolf. The fetish priest and all the Big Men came into the fort and threatened that they would run away if we did not sacrifice to the fetish, in order to avert the wolf's rage, otherwise it would certainly visit upon them all possible misfortunes /314/ to avenge this murder. The matter was settled by our having to spend one anker of brandy, one piece of *slees-lærred* [coarse cloth], in which the wolf was wrapped, and forty pounds of gunpowder to be shot off during his funeral. Then our Ningo Negroes made a wake for an entire day over the wolf, just as if it had been a prominent Negro, with drinking, dancing, shooting, and shouting.

At Fredensborg we have twenty cannon, but among them are one-pounders and half-pounders.

One and a half miles east of Fredensborg the English have their lodge at a place called Loy. There has never been a Negro town there, and in all probability no Blacks have settled there. Landing at Loy is particularly difficult, so sometimes the English have lost as much [in the value of the goods lost] at a single time, as they could have expected to earn in an entire year. When it is unsafe in the countryside the English withdraw from Loy to Prampram or Accra with all their goods. When the danger is over they return.[113]

---

[111] Smoking out the game is common today (p.c. I. Odotei).
[112] By 'wolf' R. means the hyena. In Adangbe it was called *gbete*, and at Ningo was an important deity. For *gbete/gbede* and attitudes to the hyena, see Isert [1788] (1992) 128–9 note cc; Zimmerman (1858) 436; R.G.S. Sprigge, 'Eweland's Adangbe', *Transactions of the Historical Society of Ghana* 10 (1969) 110–11; Field (1937) 39, 73, 77–8, 86.
[113] On his 1836 map Peter Thonning indicated Loi with the legend 'formerly inhabited'; and in 1783 Lai/Loi was deserted (Isert [1788] (1992) 35) For this locality, see Barbot [1732] (1992) 438–9, 451, notes 29, 30; Paul Ozanne, 'Ladoku: an early town', *Ghana Notes and Queries* (1965) 6–7; Fynn (1971) 127; Dickson (1969) 62, 65 (map), 104.

Four miles from Loy, at a place called Okko, the Dutch have built a lodge, although no Negro town existed there either.[114] Like the English, they /315/ have to move away at times. Not far from Okko is a spring that is the only source of spring water I have seen in Africa. I believe it is a mineral water, with a distinctive flavour, since it forms a reddish crust in the gully through which it runs. It would be worth having a physicist examine it. Perhaps the Creator has also placed there a blessing and remedy for the melancholy by which both the Blacks and the Whites are plagued.[115]

Two miles from Okko lies Tuberku, once a large Negro town, but in these troubled times all the Negroes have moved to Ada, and live better there than they could in their own town. Tuberku and all the area around it are sandy, whereas they have particularly fertile soil on the islands in River Volta, but they only cultivate it a little. Like all the coastal Negroes, they have to have all their food brought from the interior. Hence they consider the nations living up-country to be [mere] farmers and slaves, while the coastal Negroes consider themselves their masters. /316/

We have seen a period of unrest at Accra last an entire year, so that all the paths to the towns of the Mountain Negroes became overgrown. The Mountain Negroes, who were used to crawling through the openings made by wild animals, sent word to the Accras demanding their help in cutting through the bush the paths now overgrown. The Accras refused to do this, responding that the Mountain Negroes were farmers and if they wished to sell their fruits and *millio*, they would have to clear the bush themselves. We Danes wanted our Negroes to do it, but it was not possible to make them go, and meanwhile they ate grass, like beasts.[116] Our Negroes answered us like this: The nations living up-country had more need of them [*sc.* those on the coast] because of the salt [the former required] than the Accras needed the up-country nations. All the Negroes believe that if they do not have salt for their food they will become unwell, and the flesh on their bones will rot. When we receive slaves from the nations far inland, such as Dunko, Cassiante, etc. — which we identify from their faces — we must take good care that they are not given salt, because they take entire fistfuls, eat it, and become ill.[117] /317/

---

[114] *Oka*, inland and on the way to Tuberku, was shown on Thonning's 1838 map as 'formerly inhabited', but. a symbol nearby indicates a 'powerful fetish which gives refuge to runaway slaves'. *Okohwem* 'Oko Forest' is still well-known to the Adas, is regarded by some clans as their original settlement, and is revisited every ten years (p.c. Ivor Wilks). The Dutch were forced to abandon this lodge in 1747 (Nørregård (1966) 108).

[115] The reddish crust was probably only laterite (Dickson (1969) 63; A.T. Grove, *Africa* (1978) 12–13).

[116] This is a doubtful assertion. The 'grass' may have been a plant of which R. was ignorant. In times of drought the people may have eaten a plant they did not normally eat, dubbing it 'grass' (p.c. I. Odotei). Isert reports that the Africans refused to eat lettuce, telling him 'they do not eat grass as animals do' (Isert [1788] (1992) 127).

[117] *Dunko* [*Odonko*] is no specific place but the term was used in Asante to signify slaves from northern areas, recognizable by their scarification (Isert [1788] (1992) 83–4, 119; J.G. Christaller, *Dictionary of the Asante and Fante Language* (1881/1933) 92; R.S. Rattray, *Ashanti Law and*

[Export trade in slaves, etc]

The Europeans' trade on the Coast is in slaves, gold, and elephant tusks or ivory. Where the slaves come from has already been reported clearly, and all that remains is to describe how a European factor buys them. When the slaves have not been stolen by the Negro who brings them to the coast, the black merchant keeps them at the place where he has bought them. Using an iron clamp, he fastens the slave's right arm to a large log of wood which the slave can scarcely lift. The slave has to carry this on his head or shoulders. The black merchant does this so the slave will not run away from him on the way. In the case of a woman, a grown boy, or a girl-slave, he ties their right arm to their waist [sic]. Before a factor buys a slave, his black servants must examine the slave carefully to see if the individual has any injury, is ill, or has lost any teeth. The Negroes know how much the factor pays, and at what price each Black is valued. It is usually in accordance with Christiansborg's current price in 1749, /318/ for a male slave, six ounces of gold or 96 *rixdaler*.

Therefore we [may] pay [in a mix of goods]:

2 muskets @ 6 *rixdaler*	= 12 *rixdaler*
40 pounds gunpowder	= 16
1 anker Danish brandy	= 7
1 piece cotton [cloth]	= 10
1 piece *callavap*	= 6
1 piece *salempuris*	= 10
2 pieces gingham	= 10
2 iron rods	= 4
1 copper rod	= 1
4 pieces *plattilias* (coarse *sless-lærred* @ 12 a*l*.)	= 8
1 cabes beads	= 2
1 pewter basin	= 2
20 pounds bossies (cowries)	= 8
[total]	= 96 *rixdaler*[118]

Constitution (1956) 35; A. Norman Klein, 'The two Asantes', *IAS Research Review* (1980) 43–8). For over-eating of salt, it should be noted that salt from the coast was expensive for the northern areas, thus probably not commonly available. Furthermore, the slaves, having completed a long journey on foot, undoubtedly had a great physical need of salt on arrival at the coast.

[118] Later, at the end of the eighteenth century, the slave price had risen considerably, being 160 *rixdaler* for a male slave and 128 *rixdaler* for a female (Isert [1788] (1992) 82–3). Feinberg notes price rises at eighteenth century Elmina from 3 ounces of gold (= 48 *rixdaler*) for a male in the early century, to 12 ounces (= 192 *rixdaler*) by the 1760s (Feinberg (1989) 64). *Cabes* signified, at Accra, 2,000 cowrie shells (the small *cabes*) (Marion Johnson, 'The cowrie currencies of West Africa I', *Journal of African History* 11 (1970) 43). Presumably R. is using the term to signify a unit of 2,000 items—beads, in this case. The actual list of goods would be subject to change, depending on demand from the African side. At the end of the eighteenth century, Isert noted that in trading with the Asante they often demanded guns and powder exclusively, and occasionally fine cloth (Isert [1788] (1992) 83).

If the slave is missing a tooth you deduct four *rixdaler* from that sum; if two teeth are missing, eight *rixdaler*.[119]

The ship's-price which the factor receives for the slaves is usually eight ounces of gold or 128 *rixdaler*, [but] for a male slave it is sometimes ten ounces or 160 *rixdaler*. The difference between ship's-price and land-price /319/ for goods is as four to five; for instance, a piece of cotton cloth of 24 *alen* is, at ship's-price eight *rixdaler* and at land-price ten *rixdaler*.

It can be quite annoying when a Portuguese is in the process of buying slaves. Before the ship's captains see them we have the slaves shaved over their entire bodies, and then smeared with palm oil so that when they are going to be sold they will look at their best. A Portuguese captain may spend four hours examining a single slave. He sniffs down the slaves' throats, and feels them everywhere. A slave must perform antics for him, laugh and sing for him. Finally he licks them with his tongue around their chins to discover if they have beards. If a slave has the least scar on his body, the Portuguese thrusts him aside. An Englishman is also critical but not as unreasonably so as a Portuguese. A Frenchman usually takes anything black.[120]

When we take slaves from one place to another overland on the Coast, we use neck-rings, that is, rings normally placed around the legs are now placed around their necks. Through these we run a chain, each link being one and one-half spans long. With such a chain /320/ fifty slaves can be led, using only two or three men for an escort.

You must be constantly on guard that no slave gets hold of a knife or any other type of tool, in the fort as well as on board the ship. During the passage to the West Indies you have more than enough to do to keep the slaves in good humour. The ships' officers bring hurdy-gurdies and music boxes with them from Europe. Drums, pipes, and chewing-sticks are brought along from the Coast, and the slaves are allowed to dance at a certain place on deck, one group after another. We learn the most necessary phrases in their languages, assuring them that they are being brought to a good land where they will have many wives and good food, etc.[121]

On the Coast we have heard of deplorable incidents when slaves have overrun the ship's crew, murdered them, and let the ship drift in to land.[122]

---

[119] At the end of the century, one tooth missing reduced the price by 2 *rixdaler* (Isert [1788] (1992) 84).

[120] R.'s final sentence contradicts his earlier statement (/240/ above) about the French rejection of the children of slaves.

[121] An integral part of the treatment to 'keep slaves in good humour' was the frequent serving of brandy to the slaves (which also no doubt was also supposed to help to preserve their health). A rations list dated 1749 shows brandy served every Monday, Wednesday, Thursday, and Saturday (CRA, V-gK 62:239). For treatment of slaves on board ship, see Barbot [1732] (1992) 773–5, 778–83; Atkins (1735) 173, 175–6. For tobacco every day except Saturday, and brandy, as above, see Svalesen (1996) 112.

[122] Slave revolts when the ship was near land allowed any slaves who could swim to reach the shore (Isert [1788] (1992) 176).

At times the ships are becalmed at the equator for periods of six weeks or longer, and water and provisions are consumed. These circumstances are absolutely the worst in the world a person can experience, and [in such a situation] the ship's crew has been forced to mix poison in the food of a hundred or more slaves in order to save themselves.[123] /**321**/

Nearly all the ships taking on their cargoes from the Gold Coast or Lower Coasts go to the Portuguese island of São Tomé, or to Principe Island, in order to refresh the slaves. All the water taken on at the Gold Coast is thrown away, and better water taken aboard, since the water on the Gold Coast, as well as on the Lower Coast, is salty, always rank, and smells bad.[124] Our Copenhagen water has the particularly good characteristic that it only goes bad once, and then becomes [in taste] as sweet as nut kernels, and, in colour, that of old Rhine wine. The water of other nations can go bad four times a year.[125]

Elephant tusks are found in the interior of the country by the Blacks and brought down to the Europeans. The Negroes say that an elephant loses its teeth every seventh year. They [also] say that an elephant cow gestates for two years with calf; then she lets five years pass before she is ready to be mounted again; and elephants can be several hundred years old.[126] These creatures are said to live in Crepe in great numbers. The Negroes tell us that as many herds of elephants can be seen one hundred miles inland in Crepe as the number of hart and roe deer seen by us when we travel from Fredensborg to Ada. It is a pity that the Negroes have to saw the large tusks into two, or at times into three pieces, /**322**/ because otherwise they cannot carry them away, although two Blacks will carry a section of tusk on a pole. Once we weighed three pieces that had been a single tusk, and, if

---

[123] On being becalmed, see Tilleman [1697] (1994) 43. Granville Sharpe, writing in 1783, explains this macabre practice in economic terms — a choice between loss and remuneration. *Cf.* Thomas Fowell Buxton, *The African Slave Trade and its Remedy*, 1839 (1967) 130–32.

[124] The islands São Tomé, Príncipe, Annobon [Pigalu] were the natural last stopping and watering places for ships bound for the West Indies, following the ocean currents and prevailing winds. See Tilleman [1697] (1994) 44; Barbot [1732] (1992) 737; Bosman (1705) 400.

[125] The misconception that the drinking water aboard ships rotted several times and then became clear and good to drink was common among sailors in R.'s time. What seems to have happened was that a combination of bacteria and green algae absorbed many of the visible impurities and then sank to the bottom. This could occur several times as various kinds of organic matter rotted, in turn. The water appeared clearer but was still of very poor quality. Attempts to make it more potable were useless: boiling required the use of too much firewood; filtering through sand or porous stone took too long. Additions of countless varieties of metals, acids, salts, etc. were of little, or no, help. Straining the visible impurities (plant and animal), and a degree of aerating, was all they could reasonably do. A review of descriptions of the foul gasses and impurities collecting in the water make R.'s contention of the sweet flavour of Copenhagen water highly suspect. See H. Henningsen, 'Sømandens drikkelse', *Handels- og Søfartsmuseets Årbog* 36 (1977) 19–23. (I am indebted to Johan Kloster for supplying me with this information.)

[126] The gestation period is 20–21 months, so R. was not far off on that. But the life span is only about 60 years (p.c. Øystein Wiig).

I recall correctly, the tusk weighed 180 pounds. It would be a great curiosity in Europe if we could bring such a whole tusk back here.[127]

Gold is now so rare on the Coast that I believe the Europeans buy only a little, since what they do buy they must purchase from the Assiantes. Because the route has become so dangerous and difficult for them, forcing them to make a long detour far up into Crepe, they send only a little gold and slaves to the coast, in contrast to earlier times when they had the routes to Elmina open. At that time it was not unusual to hear that the Assiantes had, at a single time, bought three or four ship's cargoes of goods from Elmina alone.[128]

The gold weights we use on the Coast are called Troy weights, and are said to be Cologne weights. The Danish gold weight against the one used on the Coast is a ratio of nine to eight. It is necessary that the weight be heavier in Guinea, since the gold is never so pure.[129] In fact, small grains of sand are found mixed with it, so in smelting, or in *aqva fortis,* we usually lose 1/22 part. The Portuguese /323/ gold is much purer than the African. It is also of a deeper colour, but has small grains of steel mixed with it so it is difficult to smelt since it will not hang together.[130] An ounce of gold costs 16 rixdaler.

[Import trade]

We could dispose of many articles of our inland goods and manufactured products on the Guinea Coast. How praiseworthy are the English, who take care to do just that. More than a thousand English ships which come to the Coast annually have, as the greatest part of their cargoes, goods made in England, such as their woollen wares. Following is a list of woollen goods, from the sale of which many thousand people in England are fed, since not a ship comes to the Coast but has a thousand pieces of these goods.

long els, 24 *alen* long, 1 wide, ship- and land-price[131]	16 *rixdaler*
challong, 23 ½ *al.* long, 1 ½ *al.* wide	10 *rixdaler*
say [and] *rask,* 24 to 25 *al.* long, 1 ¼ *al.* wide	10 *rixdaler*
perpetuan, 13 *al.* long, 1 *al.* wide	5 *rixdaler*

[127] Large tusks had almost certainly been brought to Europe before 1760. For the trade and differences in sizes of scrivellos and tusks, see Atkins (1735) 181–3; Isert [1788] (1992) 85–6; Feinberg (1989) 59–60.

[128] On Asante routes to the coast see Wilks (1975) 24–5. R. probably underestimates the extent of the contemporary export of gold, although the trade had most likely diminished in importance since the seventeenth century, when gold represented the major export (in value) of Gold Coast.

[129] For different values for weights in Europe and Africa, see Bosman (1705) 85; Phillips (1732) 198, 206. Eight oz. troy weight = 1 mark gold. See also Tilleman [1697] (1992) note 181.

[130] Nitric acid (*aqua fortis*) would dissolve other metals, such as copper, but would not dissolve the sand, as R. seems to be implying (p.c. Mumuni Dakubu). Bosman preferred winnowing to the use of *aqua fortis* (Bosman (1705) 84–5.

[131] 'Long els' is Indian cotton cloth in long pieces (Robin Law, *Further Correspondence of the Royal African Company* [1681–1699] (1992) 63). However, R. later writes of Danish peasant cloth as being in 'long els' (/324/ below), so it may just mean a simple cotton cloth in long pieces. The length R. indicates is nearly 15 m.

How these goods are packed cannot easily be described, but we could acquire /324/ samples from London, and Knip's Factory is the best. We could do as the English do, by painting on each piece the Danish coat-of-arms instead of the English coat-of-arms, and take very good care that the colours on every piece of cloth are fast and do not fade because the Blacks test it with citron juice. If it changes we could hide it for many years in Christiansborg's magazines.[132] The Negroes wear these woollen cloths in travado and *oriental* times.[133] It becomes so cold at the seashore that some wear horse blankets. Farther up-country, and in the mountains, it is said to be even colder. A great quantity of woollen cloth is sent there.

Our Danish peasant cloth is [a sort of] *long els*, [but] even a little better. I think it is stronger than *long els*. In Denmark I have never seen such poor woollen cloth as *perpetuaner*, but we have cloth and manufacturing houses in almost all the provinces, and if a master weaver were given a piece it would be a simple matter for him to copy such a cloth. Our *rasks* and *chalonger* [sic] are now being sold for a tolerable price, and I think a manufacturer would agree to produce it [sic] if he knew, for certain, of places where it could be sold. /325/ The blue colour which we add to the cloth must not only be true but also dark blue. The Blacks do not like light blue at all. In like manner, red, green, and yellow colours must be true. Our striped and checked linens are also desired on the Coast, if only we could manufacture them somewhat looser and thinner, since the Blacks are not interested in tightly woven and fast linens. These loose linens could be expected to sell for a better price.[134]

Most of the time our gunpowder is ordered from Holland and sent to the Coast, although we have many powder mills [in Denmark]. It would be strange if we could not put just as much coal and less sulphur and saltpetre in our powder, as the Dutch do in theirs, making their powder desirable among the Blacks in Africa.[135]

---

[132] Here R. here first warns that the Blacks are canny merchants who test the cloth, then suggests a sly way to circumvent a failed test. The early writers often complained of the length of time it took for the prospective buyers to make up their minds, but they did recognize that it was difficult to cheat them. Cf. Atkins (1735) 158–9 and ff.; Isert [1788] (1992) 84. However, perhaps part of R.'s thinking was that fading would stop if cloths were stored in the dark, and that African fashion demands might change.

[133] A travado is a severe rain storm, hence by implication, the rainy season, while *oriental* indicates the NE winds which cause the *harmattan*, during the period of which the dust-laden air can block out some of the heat of the sun.

[134] For loosely woven cloth, see note 12 above. Could the preference be because it would be easier to unravel for re-weaving? For unravelling of cloth, see Isert [1788] (1992) 92.

[135] On the variations in the composition of gunpowder, see R.A. Kea, 'Firearms and warfare on the Gold and Slave Coasts', *Journal of African History* 12 (1971) 204–5. A smaller proportion of saltpetre to carbon would produce a weaker explosion, thus decreasing the chances of the muskets exploding.

[Danes and other Europeans on the Coast]

How careful we must be when we install people in some post down there, especially chaplains, who should be a guiding light for others! We have often had chaplains whom one could not praise, yet we have also had good ones, and it is with pleasure that we shall now identify them. I did not know the first three: Mr. Elias Swane, said to be a chaplain /326/ here in Seeland, is still blessed by many black heathens; Mr. Lange, who died wretchedly at Elmina; Mr. Trane, who died on the journey home. Mr. Oluf Dorph is at present the Dean in Falster.[136] Blessings are pronounced over these three to this day when their names are mentioned, both by Europeans and heathens.[137] Although these wonderful men could not accomplish anything concerning the temperament of the Blacks, by bringing them to lift their eyes to God and only to God, yet the heathens had a special respect for them — and were in no way disturbed in their idolatry.

I feel that God must first change the nature of the Blacks before they can be brought to an understanding and worship of God. Or, we must establish a *seminarium* on one of the islands in River Volta and place the children of the Blacks there when they are seven years old. They should be kept there until they have grown older, until we could be certain they would retain the Christian teachings in which they had been instructed. They must not only be taught Christianity, but they must also learn to work. In my opinion no other European nation would take offence if we established cotton and coffee /327/ plantations at River Volta so these Blacks could be of some service. To make the black youths accustomed to work is just as useful as bringing them to an understanding of God, since if they do not become accustomed to work they will soon begin to live in the manner of their forefathers again, which can in no way exist alongside Christianity. This [project] will certainly require great expenditures at the start, but within ten years, in my opinion, these young Blacks will be able to support themselves.[138]

Our civil servants are installed [with the titles] Sub-Assistants or Reserves. They are copyists, young people who have not (as we say) sown their wild

---

[136] Elias Svane: acted as chaplain at Christiansborg for six years, starting under Governor Herrn (1721–23). Svane established a school for mulatto children (C.C. Reindorf, *History of the Gold Coast and Asante* (1895/1966) 221/214; Nørregård (1966) 73, 169). Niels Thomsen Lange was chaplain at Christiansborg in 1728. Ole Dorph held the same post from 1738 to 1743, when R. was himself on the coast. Dorph's wife accompanied him to Guinea, being one of the few Danish wives on the Coast, and while there she bore four children, of whom only one survived. (I am indebted to Hans Jørgen Hinrup for the information on Lange and the Dorphs.) For a Johan Trane, not a minister but an effective company employee, see Nørregård (1966) 65, 94, 96, 132.

[137] R. knew Dorph as he did not know the others, and it is probably only clumsy wording that appears to exclude Dorph from being among those complimented.

[138] In his plan to link work and morality R. is being faithful to the biblical work ethic: 'In the sweat of thy face shalt thou eat bread.' (Genesis 3:19). This attitude lay behind many of the European complaints about Africans (supposedly) being 'lazy'.

oats. We do well, in that respect, not to send people there for high positions, or for trade, who do not know the nature of the country, since in that country they will measure everything according to European *alen*, and this will truly fall short. People who are too simple and inexperienced are not, in my view, suitable there, unless one can expect them to be somewhat crafty [in commercial ventures].[139] The Dutch do, indeed, send a treasurer to the Guinea Coast who is not acquainted with the country, but hardly ever an *Ober-Commis* or Factor, who must be trained. /328/ At least we should see to it that we have some staff at Christiansborg who can write a letter in French, who understand *jus nature*, and had done some reading, had education, etc.[140] Our surgeons there should be educated people who are acquainted with chemistry and botany, etc. A sensible and educated man will discover much in that country by which he can serve the public, and all mankind. We have no lack of people in Denmark who answer to this description, but thus far we have not given them encouragement.[141]

I wish in particular to recommend the music found in that country, as an innocent leisure activity and source of enjoyment. It would be a preventive measure against the surly moods which we Europeans experience when we have been in business, or in trade, on the Coast for two or three years, as well as against the depression and barbaric spirit to which we fall prey against our will. The mood is very infectious, and [in this respect] like a country illness for everyone.[142] The English give double salary to their employees who wish to take their European wives to the Coast, and we have seen that members of the English civil and /329/ military classes have taken European women there. At one time one could count six English women at Cape Coast, but a half-year later not a single one was to be found. They had all gone back, leaving their men to stay on.[143]

---

[139] People died in office, replacements from Europe took time, and temporary replacements were based purely on seniority, not necessarily an assurance of capability. Traders needed to learn their business on the coast, just as the masons did. This was amply proven by R.'s altercations with Governor Bilsen on trade practices. See Appendix B. See also Isert [1788] (1992) 157–8; Davies (1957) 255; Postma (1990) 65–6. On the necessity of understanding the nature of the places and people, see Atkins (1735) 166–68, 170–71.

[140] A fiscal was in charge of financial and legal matters (Feinberg (1989) 34; Postma (1990) 61–2). By *jus nature* 'natural law', a term in common use, presumably R. means 'natural justice', as distinct from specific national legal systems.

[141] Some forty years later, Isert filled this role with the qualifications R. felt to be necessary. R. must have felt that his colleague, Engmann, did not fit the bill. Perhaps Engmann became more involved in trade and administration than in practising medicine.

[142] On music played for recreation, see Isert [1788] (1992) 137–9. A later Dane claimed to experience a salubrious effect from a particular stringed instrument (Monrad (1822) 245). On melancholy and mad behaviour at the forts, see Feinberg (1989) 87–8.

[143] There are several instances of Danes having their wives and families with them at Christiansborg; among them Hendrich von Suhm (1724–27) and A.P. Wærøe (1728–1735). It was claimed that these Danish women did not survive long on the Coast (Barbot [1732] (1992) 409–10).

The English complain about their European women in the same way as the French do about their ships' priests, that is, they [*sc.* the wives] set people up against each other with gossip, causing disagreement among them. The French ships, according to rule, must have a chaplain aboard when their ships have 30 people or more as crew. This [rule] is subject to 400 *livres* fine to be paid to a to a certain monastery; but the captains pay their fine rather than take on the priest who has been assigned to them, because these priests usually cause disagreement among them.

When we first arrive in that land it is as if we have come to another world, where you can see other objects, other people, other ways of living. Everything is strange to us. We grieve, and wish that we were forced to seek our daily food at every man's door [at home] rather than to have had to come to such an uncomfortable land. The food does not taste good to us and we would rather starve than eat the food of the Blacks. The Blacks with whom we are to have close contact /**330**/ are surly and evil people who seek to cheat us or beg from us. And it is little better with the Europeans there. The European mildness, friendly manner of speaking, sensible behaviour, and innocent pastimes are totally lacking in that land. A barbaric spirit, a barbaric manner of speaking, barbaric pastimes and association have, instead, taken us and others over. The English men have fewer of these faults, but the Dutch have more than we do. A commander at a Dutch fort takes on the air of a Turkish sultan, or a bully. All of his orders to his lesser servants are given as if [disobedience] would cost the slacker his life. I should like to know if they can put aside these habits just as quickly when they return to Europe. They must certainly be able to adopt another attitude, otherwise I do not doubt there would come times in public company when they would be, if not beaten, at least ridiculed.

Those newly arrived in the land are shy, and do not know how to manage their salary, or how they should act. The old hands offer to feed them, and give them food as long as they have anything, and as long as they can receive reimbursement in their salaries from the /**331**/ government. After that, the newcomers must manage for themselves, if they can. The newcomer often grieves himself to death during the first year.[144] If he lives longer he learns to speak a little Negro-Portuguese. He then becomes acquainted with a Black in the town, who becomes his friend and gives him advice for his benefit. The black friend might lend him an ounce of gold with which our White buys brandy from a French or Dutch ship, or tobacco from a Portuguese. His black friend smuggles it in to land for him, and the White hucksters it. For the money (*bossies*) he receives he buys parrots, parakeets, monkeys, etc. These, in turn, are saleable goods for all the ships. If our

---

[144] For possible causes of such sudden deaths, see Isert [1788] (1992) 159. The first year was crucial, and was known among the English as the 'seasoning', which if an individual survived, he might then remain on the Coast without too much sickness.

White is lucky, there will be no lack of ships in the roads, so he can match his monthly salary by one hundred percent. He then repays his black friend, and he himself might [be able to retain] fifty *daler*, with which to carry on his trade. Finally, he earns enough, besides what he uses to continue his huckstering, for the purchase of a slave. His black friend, who has often been in Crepe and bought slaves, procures a slave for him. Our White gives him the goods he has, sufficient either for a male slave, or a woman, boy, or girl slave. The messenger sent [off on this errand] might be away in Crepe for one to four months, depending on circumstances. /332/ If he is lucky [in acquiring a slave] our White sells that slave to a ship, earning 50 percent. Then the messenger who was first sent to Crepe is off again. Should it happen that the Negro who was sent off drank up the goods, or gambled them away, or that the slave died, our White must begin again where he left off, by huckstering himself up to the surface again. At times our government would not permit an assistant to sell to a foreign ship a slave he had acquired by the method so described, but forced the servant to sell it to the Company at the Company price, even if the slave had cost just as much as the salary paid him by the Company, or even more.[145] The oft-mentioned country, Crepe, could be called the African *vagina gentium*, since all the nations inland acquire their slaves there. They are sold to pay a debt whose origin is a breach *in puncto sexto*.[146] When you see that Crepe is the country where nearly all the slaves come from in times of peace, and many thousand Fantes, Accras, English and Dutch black merchants go there with goods in order to buy slaves, why, then, should especially the Danish employee sell /333/ his slave at a loss? Another point is this. When the Company pays ship's-price, it is reasonable that everyone should help the ship to be filled, and in that case the government also pays a Fante, Dutch, or English Negro. Under the fortress no one dares to buy slaves, nor can he, since the black merchants who come so far will choose the goods they wish to have from our magazines.[147]

---

[145] The above description gives insights into various aspects of life for the European on the Coast, notably his learning to cope, his dependency on Africans, his conflict with the Company in trade, and his being in debt to African creditors. We have no way of knowing how large were the debts of Europeans to African creditors, but it was in the interest of the African merchant to keep the European in his debt.

[146] *Vagina Gentium*, 'vagina of the people', is a term with a double meaning, referring to both birth and sex. The slaves emerge there—in Crepe. But R.'s oblique phrase also points to his allegation of widespread sexual promiscuity among the Africans of the locality. The behaviour leads to adultery—the breach *in puncto sexto*, the Sixth Commandment—and that, in turn, leads to the punishment of being sold into slavery. Since he goes on, in the following paragraph, to explain that Crepe was an important entrepôt in the slave trade, the slaves were in fact not all locally produced.

[147] It is extremely difficult to extract any clear meaning from the last few sentences. The final sentence may mean that there would be nothing left for the merchants living near the fort.

When a European has come that far, as described above, then he can survive. He has become accustomed to Negro food, and though he may live sparsely, at times, for an entire month and longer, he knows that better times will come, and when there are good times it makes him forget the bad times he has endured. Yet we have almost no examples of them managing on their own, earning something, and returning to Europe. They wish to have one of the daughters of the country, or keep a black mistress. At times, however, circumstances do not permit this without their going into debt for it. The authorities permit this, since the Whites become naturalized, and it is apparent then that they are not so jealous, /**334**/ ill humoured, and desperate to leave the land as they were before.[148]

When the White's Negress has borne him a couple of Mulatto children he cares as much for her and his children as a man does who has his true wife and children in Europe. Some among the Europeans do not wish to leave their family on the Coast even if they know they could live better in Europe.[149] I have written above that this brings about both good and evil.[150] If the White is poor, he does not starve to death, but if he is wealthy you could not begin to describe how crafty these black women are in getting all they can out of their men at every opportunity. They know their man will soon die, or leave, so they must take care to use their time to trim him, which indeed they do — adequately.

A European leaving the Coast on his own initiative normally gives some slaves to his children, in order that they will not be of the poorest among the Africans. But we see that, later, as soon as the family needs something, these slaves are the first [property] they pawn or sell.[151] /**335**/ On several occasions I saw the testament of a European who died on the Coast, in which he remembered his black mistress with approximately this expression, "*I bestow and bequeath to my good Gire* [?girl] *N.N. one hounderd L. St.*[pounds sterling] *Furter I bestow to my good Gire N.N. –L. to bee taken of my Effects. And Goods after my decesse, both for their good service to my.*[152] The deceased had already appointed an *excutor* [sic] *testamenti*, who, in the presence of witnesses, distributed these *legata*.[153]

---

[148] The Mulatto Treasury provided for fixed sums to be paid monthly to the wives and children of the Danish staff, the sums being deducted from the individual's salary (Isert [1788] (1992) 157; Monrad (1822) 378–9). The system continued throughout the entire period of Danish establishment on the Coast (Georg Nørregård, *Guvernør Edward Carstensens Indberetninger fra Guinea* [1842–50] (1964) 41).

[149] An English governor at Cape Coast was unable to persuade his African wife to travel to Europe with him, but sent their mulatto children to England for their education (Atkins (1735) 94–6).

[150] The reference here is to Chapter 4, /246/–/248/, above.

[151] On inheritance at Elmina, cf. Feinberg (1989) 89, 91, and note 69.

[152] This appears in faulty English, either because the Englishman was semi-literate, or because R. has copied or remembered the text and his own written English was less than perfect.

[153] For another Will and Testament, that of Wulff Joseph Wulff, an Assistant at Christiansborg, see C.Behrens, *Da Guinea var Dansk* (1917) 293–4.

All the Europeans have an ugly habit of drinking at their gatherings, and their gatherings consist purely in excesses. Most of the time they drink punch, but the poorer Europeans drink brandy, as do the Negroes. If any one of them refuses to drink, he is considered to be obstinate and an evil person, who wishes to remain sober purely in order to philosophize over the others. And they consider that man to have a good temper who [thinks that], the earlier he drinks himself into drunkenness, the better – and all the others will assist him in going to bed.[154] I believe that punch is particularly harmful for us northern people, who have been raised on ale, and thus we weaken our health both on the Coast and in the West Indies — although most of the time /336/ the drink consists of half brandy and half water. The English, however, are accustomed to punch, and when they have been to a party on the Coast where it was necessary for them to drink, the next morning they take a dose of *tar. emetiq. sal. hyapsinth*, etc., and can begin anew, while we others suffer, our heads hanging [down] for full fourteen days.[155] If this ugly habit could be abolished at Accra, as it has been at Cape Coast where it has not been practised for many years, we would see that we could live longer and be healthier than we are. [But] we, and our assistants, look good in contrast to the Dutch at their forts. They look like bags of bones and withered people.[156] From the large *millio* the Negroes make a sort of ale, called *pitto*, but it is not fermented and is healthy to drink, if only it did not give us Europeans wind.[157]

[Fauna of Gold Coast]

It cannot be said that the air is unhealthy. I believe it is cleaner and healthier than ours in Europe. The warm climate is not subject to so many changes as is ours. Newcomers feel loathing when they see the many insects in that country — lizards which run around in our rooms, spiders, /337/ ants, many varieties of cockroaches, etc.[158] A lazy soldier at Christiansborg,

---

[154] On the drinking habits of the Europeans, partly caused by the extreme boredom of the life on the Coast, particularly in the case of the soldiers, see Isert [1788] (1992) 156; Monrad (1822) 355–6; Lawrence (1961) 58–9; Feinberg (1989) 87.

[155] *Tar. emetiq. sal hyapsinth* appears to be a recipe for an emetic cure for hangovers. Punch, traditionally with five ingredients (hence the name derived from Hindi *pāc* 'five'), contains sugar, fruit juice and spices, as well as brandy and water. In contradistinction to R.'s report, for a denunciation of the drinking habits of the garrison at Cape Coast, not least of their 'unwholesome mixture', see J.J. Crooks, *Records Relating to the Gold Coast Settlements* (1973) 8. The final sentence is another one of R.'s exaggerations — a fourteen-day hangover.

[156] R. perhaps hints that he, and he alone, observed temperance at Cape Coast. As for the claim of poor health and high mortality among the 'Dutch', it should be noted that the staff and soldiers at the Dutch forts and lodges were far from being exclusively Dutch, but included other Europeans; and also that the health hazards and high mortality were similar at all the European establishments. Cf. Feinberg (1989) 86–8; Postma (1990) 66.

[157] The term for this 'ale' among the Gã today is *made*; and among the Ewe *medah* (p.c. I. Odotei). Cf. De Marees [1602] (1987) 21b; Isert [1788] (1992) 127.

[158] Why R. includes lizards among 'insects' is unclear.

who had not made his bed for a long time, found a large snake which had made a nest under his bed and hatched four young. At night our soldier had felt something occasionally moving under him. In the morning he looked to see what it was and found the snake with four young. We like to have the lizards in our room because they eat other insects, and when we have none we go to our neighbour and, with his permission, catch a couple.[159]

It is a source of wonder to observe the ants in that land. At Fredensborg I have seen a variety of large ants which came from a distant field using a path they themselves had made. They crawled over the battery of the fort to our *millio* magazine, and [working] four by four, they took a *millio* grain and dragged it off to their nest. We had to search out the nest, which was a *fjerding* mile from the Fort, and (*s.v.*) urinate on it.[160] After that we saw no sign of them. Moreover, it appears they have a kind of language between them. I have frequently killed a fly and left it, or a small chicken bone, lying on my table. Within a minute an ant has come, run around the bone, gone away and come back with many hundred others, /338/ and they have truly dragged that bone along the floor, and up the wall, to take it to their nest. Sometimes the opening of their nest was been so small that they worked in vain for a full 24 hours to get it in.

Several times I have observed that small snakes appear with the travado. In our garden at Christiansborg, I have seen snakes lying in the broad leaves of the plantain trees, as if they were sunning themselves. In one Negro house, where the host had been away for several days and his door had been kept closed, I saw, under the roof, large snakes that had wound themselves around the rafters, or laths. They were sleeping so soundly that we killed them all with a sword. The Negroes must, therefore, always light a fire in their huts at night so that such vermin will not injure them, since they cannot stand the smoke.[161] I have seen scorpions in that country as large as a good-sized crayfish, and when you travel at night a Black must always walk ahead with a torch so such vermin run out of the way. The Negro hunters have assured me that they have seen snakes swallow a roe deer alive. The same variety of snake, they say, can, /339/ by attraction, with their jaws take hold of whatever animal they see. It is said that they are not poisonous.[162]

[159] R. is describing the gecko (*Hemidactylus*), a harmless, insectivorous lizard common in the tropics, which commonly inhabits the living quarters of humans, hanging on walls or hiding behind mirrors to catch insects. R. is also correct in noting that there are many species of cockroach (*Blattidae*). The story about the snake is probably true (p.c. A. Tye).
[160] For (*s.v.*), see Chapter 1, note 12.
[161] Snakes would appear with rainy weather because, in general, they do not like dry weather. Snakes in trees might be adjusting body temperature, but there are very common species which hunt in trees. The large snakes under the roof may have been green mambas (*Dendroaspis viridis*) (p.c. A. Tye).
[162] This is probably the python. It is true that pythons are not poisonous, and they do catch prey in their jaws, then throw their coils around it to asphyxiate it. The comment 'by attraction' probably repeats the myth about snakes hypnotizing their prey (p.c. A. Tye). See also Isert [1788] (1992) 105.

Wolves in that country are larger than the European variety, and dare to come into the Negro towns at night to fetch a deceased slave and drag him off. Our constable at Christiansborg was sleeping on a mat in a Negro hut in town one night, and a grown Negro boy slave was lying beside him. It was warm so our constable, who lay close to the door, opened the door to allow the breeze to cool him, and he and the boy fell asleep. A wolf came in there, stepped over the constable and took the head of the boy in its jaws and dragged him over the constable and out of the hut. This awakened the constable, who ran after the wolf, caught hold of the boy's legs and had to pull with all his might before he could recover the boy. The boy could not scream since his entire head was in the jaws of the wolf. The black boy is still alive but had been badly mauled, with one eye completely missing and his nose bitten quite flat.

[Another tale follows.] Once a Mountain caboceer came to the coast to visit his friend, an Accra. As is the custom, he had a drummer and a horn /340/ blower accompanying him. The Mountain caboceer, along with his followers, was well treated with brandy. When, in the course of [the party] they were all drunk, the Accra saw to it that the caboceer was carried into a hut. He assumed that the musicians would wake up and crawl into shelter themselves, but contrary to his expectations they slept until the middle of the night. A wolf came and seized the horn blower, throwing him across his broad back and running off with him. The hornblower did not awaken until the wolf had gone into the bush a quarter of a mile from the town, where the thorns tore at the hornblower so he woke up. He found that the wolf had his left arm in his jaws and he was lying across the wolf's back. In his alarm he took his horn, which he always keeps hanging over his shoulder, and blew into it. The wolf threw him down and the hornblower returned. The wolf had not harmed him at all, not even bitten him.[163]

Many have described crocodiles, but if I recall correctly, no one has written that the lower part of their mouth, or jaw-bone, is without joints, being fastened to their neck bone, and they move only the upper part. At Ada it once happened that a pregnant black woman wished to go to the lagoon in the morning /341/ and wash herself and her children, as was her custom. She had one child by the hand and a smaller one bound to her back. A crocodile, coming out of the water, seized the mother and both children. Having wrapped his tail around all of them, he lay for a long time in the lagoon with these people, and then disappeared with them.[164] This was an occurrence the like of which no old Negro has ever before heard of

---

[163] The so-called wolf is the hyena, frequently given this misnomer in the early sources. Hyenas have been known to drag people off but the picture of carrying his prey 'across his broad back' is probably untrue. Isert [1788] (1992) 128 n.cc repeats this tale, probably having borrowed it from R.

[164] R. is mistaken on two counts: the crocodile's lower jaw is indeed jointed; the crocodile does not wrap its tail around its prey. This is a physical impossibility, but the tail is used as a weapon to knock things over or into the water (p.c. A. Tye).

or seen. It has indeed been seen that when a Negro was travelling on the lagoon in a small boat resembling a dough trough, a sea elephant overturned the boat, and a crocodile seized the Black who was in it. But that a crocodile would come ashore and seize as many as four persons at once, the Negroes felt this must be case for exemplary punishment.[165] The Ada Negroes promised to combine forces and give a considerable gift to any fetish-maker who could entice that same crocodile ashore, in order that the Negroes could kill it. It so happens that our factor at Ada told us this, assuring us on solemn oath that he had seen the crocodile come out of the water to the feet of the fetish-maker. A score of other Negroes shot it to death, and, having cut it open, they saw human bones in the crocodile's stomach. Thus it was certain that this was the same crocodile which had taken those people. /342/

Many varieties of monkeys can be seen at Ada, as well as everywhere on the mainland. Most of these varieties cannot be transported over the sea since they die, and those who can be transported to Europe are just the most common sort. When the Negroes at Ada, Agona, etc. cannot get game meat they go hunting for monkeys. These animals, as well as dogs, cats, and rats, are very delicious dishes for all the Negroes.[166]

The Negroes also tell us, and some of the Europeans have seen it, that monkeys have a sort of government amongst themselves. They have caboceers, Big Men, etc. It is certain that they move in flocks of hundreds and more. When they come to a place where the *millio* the Negroes have planted is nearly ripe, or to fruit trees, and no Negro is present, the old monkeys send the young ones into the grain fields or trees. None of the young ones dare to eat the slightest amount themselves while they are picking, but must bring it all back to where the old ones are sitting in a circle. The old ones give notice when they have gathered enough [food], and the young ones then bring it into the circle. The old ones help themselves first, and the young ones last. /343/ Many Negroes assure us that they have seen monkeys sitting in a circle, holding court over one or more monkeys. Sometimes the accused is present and they beat him mercilessly, indeed some times they bite him to death and tear him into small pieces. When you ask the Negroes what they think the crime had been of those who were thus punished, they are of the opinion that those who are given the death sentence have committed a crime against a female monkey belonging to a caboceer or Big Man. Those monkeys who fell asleep on their watch received a lesser punishment. It is certain that where a flock of monkeys make their camp, either to forage or to rest, they place lookouts in the highest trees

---

[165] The mother and her two children were seized, but R. speaks of four persons here, so he must also have been counting the foetus.

[166] The most common sort of monkey would be the Green Monkey. The rats would probably be the Cane Rat ['Cutting Grass'] which is not a true rat (p.c. A. Tye). That 'all the Negroes' eat all these varieties of animals is not true. There were great variations in taste, totem and taboo.

around the camp. These howl as soon as they see people or wild animals. If you approach them more closely the lookouts retire to the camp, and if the gathering finds it wisest, they take flight. There have often been incidents of monkeys having violated a Negress.[167]

The animals called sea elephants by the Negroes resemble cows in every way apart from their having large tusks, yet only a span long, sticking out of their mouths. They are larger than our Seeland /344/ cows or bulls. Their forelegs are equally long, but their hind legs are much shorter, and it is as if they are lame, since, when these sea cows are on land and see a person, they will hasten to return to the water, and run, yet not more swiftly than one can usually overtake them. Their forelegs move quite swiftly, but they let their hind legs and the entire hindquarters drag behind them. They are usually blackish-brown with horns and ears like a cow. Some have a white spot on their foreheads and on their bodies. They are normally seen in pairs, as is the case with a bull and a cow.[168]

The large birds living at River Volta, which catch more fish than the Blacks do, are larger than a swan. On the Coast, there have been attempts to dry their large bodies and send them to Europe, but they have become rotten, perhaps because they were placed in a damp place. However, in the curios cabinet at the home of a certain gentleman in Lübeck, I have seen the head as well as the body of such a bird which came from America, but I think that the African variety is twice as large. At the request of the aforementioned gentleman I wrote to the Coast asking for a bird from River Volta, but the friend to whom I had written had already left to be repatriated.[169] /345/ The pretty crown pheasants found at Accra would be worth bringing to Europe, in order to begin breeding them.[170] It would

---

[167] Throughout, R. employs the term *Abekatter*, monkey, but clearly he was thinking of a larger primate, and the term should have been *Aber*. He may have been thinking of baboons or chimpanzees. Characteristics such as moving in 'flocks of hundreds' and eating grain are specific to baboons. The young bringing food to the elders is not true. They do gang up in alliances, can beat up individuals; and do have lookouts (p.c. A. Tye). The final statement repeats the myth that was common in the eighteenth century and crops up in nearly every account about chimpanzees, for example. (See, for a reproduction of a picture published in 1795, crediting an 'orang outang' with the act, J.N. Pieterse, *White on Black* (1992) 38). An English contemporary of R. wrote, 'it is said that the males [of 'mandrills'] often attack and use violence to the Black Women whenever they meet them alone in the woods' (William Smith, *A New Voyage to Guinea* (1744) 52). Cf. Phillips (1732) 211; Atkins (1735) 108. For a refutation of the myth, see Isert [1788] (1992) 120–1.

[168] The description of the hippopotamus is generally correct but they do use all four legs very well in running, and the two seen together were more likely a cow and calf, not a bull (p.c. A. Tye).

[169] The bird here described seems to be a pelican, of which there are two species in West Africa: the White Pelican (*Pelecanus onocrotalus*) and the Pink-backed (*Pelecanus rufescens*). R. is correct in stating that the African species are about twice the size of the of the American Brown Pelican (*Pelecanus occidentalis*) (p.c. A. Tye).

[170] This bird, the Great Blue Turaco (*Corythaeola cristata*), is mentioned in virtually all accounts that describe birds (p.c. A. Tye).

be still more interesting to bring some of the Labode crown-birds to Europe. These birds closely resemble a stork, but are larger, with a beautiful shining crown on their heads, and they have feathers of many colours. These birds are the idols, or godheads, of the Labode Negroes, and the fetish has taken them under his protection so no one dares to shoot or capture them. A Danish assistant who was a newcomer to the country caught one of these birds in the fields and brought it to the Fort. We really wished to keep it but were plagued for several days by all the Accra fetish-makers, male and female, so we finally had to deliver to them the 'fetish's hornblower' (as the Negroes call the bird). In addition we had to placate the fetish with a bottle of brandy.[171]

[Excursus]

This, then, is the account of the Guinea Coast, with descriptions I have not found in any author who has written from the Coast. Bosman, the best author to have written on the subject, reports little or nothing about these things, and other authors have filled their writings with untruths.[172] /**346**/ I have had it in mind to write about how our affairs on the Coast could be better arranged. Such a work would have to be extracted from conclusions based on the circumstances reported in this text. I shall leave that to others, since it could be done in many ways.[173]

I would like to say one thing to certain gentlemen on the Coast, if any of them are still alive, who, without a doubt, will blame me for having described matters much too clearly, and for having broken my promise, which was that when I left I would never think of the Coast any more. That [promise] has, indeed, been in my thoughts for several years, since I came here. I believed, just as did the others, that one could not write about this subject without offending decency and honour. Bosman did not dare to touch on the source of the slave trade and the Negroes' religion, and when he does write about these matters, you can see that he does not wish to dwell on them.[174]

---

[171] The 'fetish's hornblower' is the Crowned Crane (*Balearica pavonina*). See Isert [1788] (1992) 34 note c.

[172] If R. is referring to the descriptions above, he is wrong in claiming to have been alone in publishing such. Most of the creatures that he describes were mentioned by other authors, and although R.'s accounts contain some closely-observed original information (for instance, on termite nests and pelicans) many of his accounts are very similar to those given earlier, sometimes much earlier, by other Europeans.

[173] R.'s shorter text, *Negotien*, actually published four years before the present text, does precisely what he is suggesting here. Perhaps he drafted this passage before 1756.

[174] The slave trade had not achieved predominance in Dutch Guinea commerce during Bosman's time (1688–1702), its most active period being after 1720 (Feinberg (1989) 63). Bosman therefore said relatively little about the slave trade, but probably not because he did not 'dare to, as the Dane suggests. However, Bosman did write about African religion, at some length (Bosman (1705) 145–61). R.'s reference to breaking his silence appears to be a response to Engmann's complaint in the poem which R. nevertheless inserted at the beginning of the 1760 text.

[However,] a patron and learned gentleman here in the city has encouraged me to write this [book], in order to serve the public here, and perhaps in other places.[175] Gentlemen, I ask you, when /**347**/ I send several copies of this book to you with the first available ship, that you comment in respect of whatever I may have forgotten about the Negroes' history and their religion. I would have included more about both matters but could not recall the exact circumstances, and I have preferred to omit rather than present statements which, on most careful examination, could be challenged. It would be particularly welcome if anyone could send us [here] one or more of the speeches uttered by the Labode fetish — according to the claims of the Negroes — when the informant was himself present. I myself never heard, nor wished to hear, a Negro tell me, word by word, what the Labode fetish had said. What has been written here about the Fante fetish I heard by chance from the sons of Corrantryn, but I now regret not having been more inquisitive, in order to serve an inquisitive world. I assure those who are willing to take the trouble to write comments and send them here, that their remarks will be incorporated as soon as a new edition is published, and their names added to it.[176] On the Coast I have often had explained to me the rights of inheritance and accession to the throne among the Negroes, but I cannot recall this as perfectly as I ought to if I were to write about it. This information would also be welcome. /**348**/

Who can reach conclusions with any certainty in this world? Everything on which we humans build is only guesswork. [Nevertheless,] we can say, 'Such is this thing. That is not as it should be.' We can change every imperfect thing in many ways, or [at least] make suggestions for changing it. It is in the hands of the Almighty alone to give his blessings to our undertakings. It is in His hands to give each one of us love for king and country, in order that we do what we ought to do, namely, [ensure] that only the general good is our own good, and when it is served our own is served. We all have selfish intentions and [yet] believe that God blesses what we have earned with good conscience, and that God lays His curse on what we have brought about to the ruin and destruction of other people. Many reforms in respect of the present subject have been made in the past few years, but more still could be made. God grant that we choose the best.

---

[175] The learned gentleman was Bishop Erik Pontoppidan, who wrote the Introduction to R.'s book.
[176] I have not been able to find any other editions of the original Danish publication, although a German translation was published in 1769.

Appendix A

The West Indies trade of the French, English and Danes (1756)

[/**44**/...]¹ This must be sufficient about the Guinea Coast. Let us now see what empowers the French so markedly that they acquire great quantities of sugar. I mentioned earlier that persons of rank are sent to the [French] West Indies as governors.² Let us see what advantages the planters have there. When they start to work on uncultivated land they pay nothing. Their king has ordered them not to offer less than 1,200 *livres* for a healthy slave, and they are given twelve months' credit. If a slave is too old, the price is not lower but the planter is given a longer period of credit, for instance, 18–24 months, and so on. Then he pays up to a commissioner whom the captain has appointed on behalf of the shipowners. If the planter is unable to pay, it costs him 6%, and he is given a little more time. If he again fails to pay, the creditor dares not confiscate his plantation slaves, but he can take his domestic slaves, furniture, etc. If the planter has a house in town, the creditor can have it auctioned off. After a period of five years the creditor can sell the plantation and the plantation slaves. The merchants in France therefore employ a good correspondent in the West Indies who maintains a proper office. Some merchants join forces, build a warehouse, and send out bookkeepers, who always remain there. Rarely do the Englishmen from New England have permission /45/ to go to the [French] islands with provisions, and when it does happen the planter must give them no produce in payment but only money. Nor may the Dutch go there with their copper kettles, etc. Provisions are sent in great abundance from France. Since a slave ship has a capacity in excess of what five ships can load — unless it be coffee or indigo — the French are happy when they can acquire goods with which to load the ship, thus cutting down the expenses of the journey. Their Governor sets the prices on their provisions, so they earn about 10% in profit.

A Governor's income is large. He receives 40 *rixdaler* as 'anchor due' from each ship, and two *rixdaler* for every slave sold on his island, that is, one *rixdaler* from the captain and one *rixdaler* from the planter who purchases the slave. Legal cases are not decided according to the rules in France; but

---

¹ This appendix comprises the final section of Rømer's 1756 account. It is only lightly annotated.
² 1756, /28/–/29/, in Chapter 2 above.

the costs of the parties are double, and more in certain circumstances. As is the case with the captain of a French royal ship, a Governor has the power to examine the provisions provided by the ship owners. This is done as soon as a sailor reports that the provisions are rotten. The captains of merchant ships are [then] forced to purchase better provisions at the same place. The French know how useful sailors are and do not want them to die because of unhealthy and rotten food given them due to the misguided economy of the shipowners. The captain does not deliver his slaves to the government but sells them from the ship. He usually picks out the finest in order to receive prompt payment, and receives, sometimes, 14–16,000 *livres*. When he does not know the planter he frequently asks the shipowner's commissioner for advice — whether the planter is solvent, or if there exist /**46**/ doubts about his finances. In such cases he trades with two or three other planters [as well], all of whom, having bought slaves, must answer one for all, all for one.

The principal French islands are Martinique, Leogane[3] and Guardeloupe [*sic*]. None of these islands is as large as our St. Croix (I have been told), but the French own St. Domingo on the island of Hispaniola, which belongs half to France and half to Spain. On that last island, at times they suffer the same fate as the English at Jamaica and other places and the Dutch in Surinam, that is, their slaves desert them in droves [in favour of] the Spaniards and the mountains. Among the Spaniards the slaves are free as soon as they set foot on Spanish soil, and the planters dare not follow them to the mountains for fear of being beaten to death by the many deserters who live there.

When a captain has sold his slaves, he delivers a copy of his papers of sale to the shipowner's correspondent. If the correspondent has goods on hand which were delivered from the previous slave journey, he loads the captain with these. Of those goods the captain received for the finest slaves, not much goes to the shipowner. Then the captain collects [his payment] for freight [home], and if there is nothing else to be gained there, he takes on extra cargo, consisting of *pokkenholt, malogena-bræder*, dyewood, etc.[4] The shipowners know, by experience, that if they give their captains express orders to wait for cargoes, the repair of the ships will cost more than the profit they can earn from the cargo.

During the last war[5] the French would not allow any neutral nation to bring slaves to their islands, or their own products go to other lands, under whatever pretext, not even to obtain badly needed provisions. When the

---

[3] Léogane was not an island, but a French settlement on the island of Haiti ('Hispaniola').

[4] *Pokkenholt* is lignum vitae or guaiacum, the bark and resins from certain species of trees used for medicinal purposes; and here denotes the trees themselves. *Malogena-Bræder* translates as '*malogena* planks', but the first word is probably a misprint for 'mahogany'. 'Dyewood', otherwise 'logwood' or campeachy, was obtained at various points in the West Indies.

[5] Presumably the War of the Austrian Succession, ended in 1748, during which France and Britain fought campaigns against each other at sea and in the West Indies.

flour from which they baked bread was used up, /47/ the governors agreed with each other that they would serve at their table manioc (a root in that country normally eaten by slaves), and then no planter would feel ashamed at eating it. Yet the planters, with many supplications and gifts to France, sought flour. They kept an enormous quantity of products in store, and the French in Europe knew that some day the planters would be forced to go to them for something or other, a slave, or goods. Thus, it was the case that the French looked upon the West Indies as existing for their benefit, and not the case that the Europeans existed for the benefit of the planters. However, from no other [West Indian] islands do so many rich planters leave in order to finish their lives in Europe as from the French islands. Nevertheless, the French in Europe let the planters scream a bit, well aware that if they show them favouritism in some areas they will then demand it in others. Twenty years ago the French Company gained the right to ship East Indian and other goods abroad to the West Indies and the planters had to pay high prices for them. [In revenge,] on Martinique, the storage place for the whole of these goods, all the womenfolk [of the planters] assembled and set fire to the Company's warehouse, resulting in the loss of some 100,000 *livres* for the Company. Since then all French shipowners have been free to send these goods there, and the planters have purchased them at a better price.

It was mentioned earlier that the French send very civilized people to the Guinea Coast as captains and officers, but this does not apply to those who make their own way to the West Indies. Their livelihood is meagre. They receive not one-fourth the earnings of a Guinea merchant. A captain /48/ is paid 15 *rixdaler* a month, and nothing more, whereas great encouragement is given a Guinea merchant. In addition to his salary, the captain of a ship carrying 400 slaves is normally allowed the privilege of including 12–16 slaves of his own. The officers, depending on conditions, are given a *pistole* or five *rixdaler* per head brought to the West Indies. The captain and the officers may carry goods to sell for gold but not for the purchase of slaves. Up to the number permitted, slaves are purchased using the shipowner's goods, and the account books are kept in such a way that it is immediately apparent what a slave costs at European prices. Upon their arrival home this is deducted from their credit. When a fine slave is purchased the officers have the choice of the slave being theirs or the shipowner's. All the ships have irons for branding the slaves, usually with the name of the ship. For instance, if the shipowner has given orders that his slaves be branded on the right breast, the captain brands his own on the left breast, the second captain on the right arm, another on the left arm, and so on. Thus the officers will not take another man's slave instead of their own when one of the slaves dies.

In former times the French often overloaded their ships with slaves. It then frequently happened, when the journey to the West Indies was not fast enough, that the provisions or water were consumed. This circumstance is the most dangerous that anyone can experience. The Europeans strive to keep their slaves in good humour. They buy drums and pipes on the Coast, they bring games, whistles and music boxes on board, and a place is cleared on deck where the slaves can dance and play, one group after another. Even when the slaves have plenty [to eat], the Europeans are not entirely secure against revolts. Note /**49**/ that if the slaves are not given the usual [rations] or are given too small portions, it is impossible to say what desperate plans they may not make, in order to kill the Europeans. When such a ship has been at the equator for five or six weeks, with 4–500 slaves on board, they look miserable. If it lasts too long the Europeans readily mix poison in the food of, first, 100 slaves, and they die immediately. Later they treat more of them in the same way, and thus the Europeans are able to save themselves. In order to prevent this [situation] the French determine how many slaves they will take on board. Frigates leaving from Europe to the Coast are equipped for 450–500 slaves, more or less, but they are equipped differently from ours. Of what use are our long bulwarks reaching right to the main mast? If the ships were [intended] to be used at some time in war (may God forbid it) they could be refitted appropriately with very little cost, but [as they are] they are less suitable in the slave trade. The captain normally takes aboard a sufficient number of planks so that he can fit out his ship differently when he arrives at the Coast. Nearly all the ships, when they have taken on their load of slaves, sail to St. Thomae [S. Tomé] or Printzens Island [Principe] in order to obtain provisions for their slaves.[6] If they have been supplied on the Upper Coast this is not necessary since they will have as many provisions as they need, but if they call [only] at Gold Coast then they must go to St. Thomae and Printzens Islands because the water at Gold Coast is somewhat salty, causing it to deteriorate and smell bad within a few days. These islands at the equator are also on the route of the ships, and the captains remain there for as long a period as they think necessary for them and their slaves.

Now we come to the English colonies in the West Indies, /**50**/ passing over what the English own in the colder climates [of North America] since they are not relevant to our purpose. The English are no stronger in the warm climate than the French, but they carry on more trade than the Spaniards, and have more shipping there. Reflecting on this, you might think that the Spaniards and Portuguese own those rich gold and silver mines in Peru, Mexico and Brazil only for the benefit of the English. The Spaniards and Portuguese must go [mining] underground if they want to obtain clothing and food, since by merely discovering and exploiting rich

---

[6] The Portuguese islands of São Thomé and Príncipe in the Bight of Benin were often final provisioning points for slave ships from eastern Guinea before crossing the Atlantic.

underground veins of gold they neglect any form of agriculture. The English on Jamaica and the French on St. Domingo have just as rich mines as the Spaniards and Portuguese, but to open the earth, or attempt to do so, is to risk their lives. And they see, in the remarkable example of the Spaniards and Portuguese, that when people first acquire a taste for gold they forget everything else. And, in truth, among all their riches, the Spaniards and Portuguese are the poorest Europeans.

England acquires most of the American riches, as well as those from the West Indies, because they can deliver some 1,000 slaves annually under the Assiento [treaty]. The same [enrichment] applies to all varieties of goods brought to the Spanish coasts [of America] which, although strictly forbidden by the king of Spain, is still done. Jamaica is the entrepôt for all this trade, and it is an important colony. The other islands that the English own are of no great consequence. This island of Jamaica is the one that the English over many years have been settling, [while elsewhere] fearing their own slaves. The island is so large that no Europeans have yet been at the centre of the land. Slaves in droves run /51/ away from the Europeans and up to the mountains, where they reproduce so extensively that they are double the number of planters and their slaves. In 1744 the French sent several shiploads of ammunition to these Blacks so they could injure the English. The Blacks then so ravaged the entire land that the English were no longer safe in their forts and trading stations. I do not know what the result would have been had the English not made peace with them, declared them free men, and allowed them to bring their goods to the markets, etc. Thereupon the Negroes committed themselves to recovering and returning all the slaves who had deserted their masters. Knowledgeable people claim that they had foreseen that, after a period of twenty years, the entrepôts for West Indian goods would belong to England again. And this could be expected, because the French no longer brought Guinean slaves to their [own] islands. Slaves from Angola are hardly worth the trouble of transporting; and in Senegal the French purchase scarcely 500 annually. The planters, accustomed to treating their slaves inhumanely, would soon kill them off [they thought], which is what happened, and their plantations lie uncultivated.

The Dutch are the least important [nation] in the West Indies. We are better established than they are, and I do not know that they own anything legally other than Curassoe [Curaçao], which is about seven miles in length and three in width. I would not advise our nation to take over Surinam if the Dutch wished to be rid of it. How stupid, was it not, of the silly Dutch to establish sugar plantations on the mainland. They could easily (in my opinion) have foreseen that they must either treat their Negroes like the Spaniards and Portuguese have done, that is, teach them to say *Ave Maria* /52/ and hang a paternoster around their necks, or things would happen — as they actually did. The Dutch are hardly certain of their lives when they are outside the city. And even though, during the first twenty years, they established plantations some four to five miles inland, yet all that land has been ruined by runaway slaves and now lies waste, and the Dutch are scarcely able to defend the land a half mile from the shore. But what you might call a folly in that place has been compensated for by their St. Eustatius possession, usually called 'Statie'. It is a dry rock, not a half-mile in circumference, where no more than ten barrels of sugar can grow annually. It lacks fresh water which must be fetched from the English island two miles away. It looks like our Norwegian cliffs, with a little grass growing here and there, but in most places black stones are exposed. [However,] the greatest amount of trade is carried on at this place, and this rock might correctly be termed the Dutch entrepôt in the West Indies. Seldom are there fewer than one hundred ships in the road, which is in the open sea, and every time we hear of a hurricane in the West Indies, we hear that in the Statie road alone fifty vessels ran aground. From here as many as one hundred barques (or West Indian boats) sail to the Spanish coasts. And we do not hear that they are seized by the Spanish coast guards, because when they see their superior force they run away. On the other hand, the English trade in European ships which cannot sail so swiftly, therefore at times these are seized. Yet the English do not take these seizures too seriously. If the Spaniards seize [only] one ship out of one hundred they cannot injure the Englishmen greatly. The latter still bring /53/ more pieces-of-eight to England than the Spaniards do to Europe.

Anyone who has had the patience to read this so far will, without doubt, ask, *cui bono* [to whose benefit]? What does all this tell US? Then I must answer that I have heard that our most merciful monarch wishes to give all his subjects permission to trade. We have sensible men here in Copenhagen who understand how advantageous this would be for the country, and I simply wish to report how other nations carry on their trade and what advantages they draw from their labours. If you consider the situation of our own country, we are better off than Holland, and just as well off as England and France. We have the advantage of the Baltic Sea and of the many sailors raised in Denmark and Holsteen. Who does not know that Holland was incapable of equipping its ships for the Strait of Gibralter, Greenland, Davis Straits, etc. before our Norsemen, Jutlanders, and Holsteeners went to them and offered their services. Their practice was to earn money and return home in the winter. But I respond thus, would it not be better that these poor people were employed in the service of their own country? Moreover, if you investigated, you would find that one-third of them stay on in Holland or England, either because of being married there or of other enticements not found in their fatherland. It is indisputable that it would be of service [to us] if these men lived and worked in their own country, and equally indisputable that sailors are just as useful for a country as are farmers. When I have met ten captains from Holland, it is certain that eight of these were Danes, Holsteeners or Norwegians, but they rarely advance /54/ to such a post without being married in Holland. Yet I have met some from Föer and Sildt, whose wives live on these islands while they themselves travel from Holland.[7]

Is it possible that our Companies here in Copenhagen might employ as many as one thousand persons who [now] have to seek their bread abroad? You can well imagine how the Companies in England and Holland looked upon those merchants who, thirty or forty years ago, sent ships against the will of the Company to those places the authorities of the country had enfeoffed with charters and [the Company] kept as its own. They were undoubtedly looked upon as evil persons who would disturb the Companies in their trade. And if you note this *obiter* [*dictum*, i.e. passing reference], yet [find yourself] in agreement with these merchants, it would be all to the good. Consider how impossible it was for the Companies in England and Holland during that time to manage all their trade themselves, trade from both the Guinea Coast and the West Indies. And how impossible to employ all those people who nowadays make their living in this trade. And to send all those ships. That, I say, was quite impossible for them, and not the hundreds of Boards of Directors of Companies could argue with this. You may say they did this in earlier times. To this I answer, that whereas the [Danish] Company, in earlier times, sent one ship to these waters, I daresay there are now sent 1,000 ships from England and 500 from Holland. And [considering] how great and profitable a change has occurred in these countries in the course of fifty years, what could we not expect in our days, what great hope could we not nurture, if we allow our thoughts to toy with the idea [of freeing the trade]! Think of the opportunity we would have to supply the whole of Germany with West Indian products! Altona and Copenhagen /55/ are very conveniently located for this. Think of the great countries bordering on the Baltic Sea, Poland, Prussia, Moscow and Sweden—all those could be provided from our warehouses here in Copenhagen. Should anyone ask me, 'Where is all the sugar to come from?' I will answer, 'As yet, we do not receive here in Copenhagen one-fifth of our products. Never mind that the derelict plantations on St. Jean and St. Thomas could be cultivated properly. First, let half of St. Croix be settled and land be given free to those who will cultivate it, instead of demanding 500 *rixdaler* for a piece of land 3,000 feet long and 2,000 feet wide'. However, [you may say,] all the inhabitants who now are living on St. Croix came on those conditions. To this I answer that most of those who came during the last war were people living on the small islands with no fort to protect them, and they came to us out of fear of being ruined by the pirate ships of our enemies. And many of them have since left us. Let us make better arrangements in the West Indies so that no nation other than ours receives the West Indian products [from our islands].

---

[7] Føhr and Sylt are islands in Slesvig, near Flensburg.

Our governors marry the widows or daughters of rich planters, knowing that when they are relieved of duty they will become planters, and it is not to be expected that they should do anything not in their own interest. [But] if our all-merciful king himself owned the forts, and permitted the Danes freedom in trade, what articles of trade that are needful to us exist that could not be provided from here? Would not our wholesalers always have goods stored in their warehouses in the West Indies, so their ships could be provisioned? And goods for the trading correspondents overseas could always be kept in store here in Copenhagen. /56/ The planters complain about our Danish meat, saying it is lean and very poor when it arrives there. But let [those here] just have the freedom to ship it [themselves], then you will see that we can deliver just as good beef for four or five shillings a pound as the English do for ten to twelve shillings a pound. The same could be said for other foodstuffs they need, and I believe the Altona provisions would be better than the English, provided our merchants are informed immediately when the animals are about to be slaughtered, and it is known how much meat will be needed for one year. When our planters complain that our copper cauldrons, the ones they use for [making] sugar, are too expensive, they get no response. They therefore purchase them from the Dutch islands, and although they pay one to two shillings more per pound, they acquire these utensils at reasonable cost.

I believe that the entrepôts and other markets in the West Indies might cost more to maintain than the forts [in Gold Coast], but there would always be a sufficient surplus [from extended trade] to maintain our forts of Christiansborg and Friderichsborg [Fredensborg] on the Guinea Coast. The maintenance of our forts on the Coast might be taken over by a businessman here in Copenhagen, but I would not advise anyone to do it for less than 10,000 *rixdaler* annually. It would not be advisable for Your Majesty to do this, because it requires businessmen who could correspond with our people [there] and with our ships, to advise them for their own good, supporting them in word and deed and helping them in every way. It would not be advisable, either, to open the Guinea trade immediately to all our subjects. I think [the trading community of] Copenhagen would suffice at first. I know of no more than /57/ three cities in France, three in England, and two in Holland which are free to trade on the Coast,[8] and we would have enough to manage in Copenhagen before new arrangements were in place. Other than Reinhold, I know of no captain to whom can be entrusted both a ship and [the management of] trade.

I would also advise that we hire some of the ship's officers of the Dutch gold-traders, because no one is so well-acquainted with the entire Coast as they are, and such a man, having been three or four times a first mate on

---

[8] R. means Nantes, Rochelle, and probably St. Malo in France; London, Liverpool, and Bristol in England; Amsterdam and Zeeland in Holland.

these gold traders, could certainly be entrusted with a slave ship. You might say that these men are accustomed to trading Dutch goods, and that is true, and certainly we would have to be fair to such a man in many ways on his first trip out. But on the second trip we could say to him, 'Look here, my good captain, we are not well served if our money goes to Brabant for muskets, etc.' [Only] half of the goods obtained here are Danish and half are Dutch. In England the merchant, or his representative, accompanies the captain to select [goods for] the cargo. The owners do not buy a single piece without the captain's advice and agreement, and this is the system we should follow. On a ship in which they intend to carry 450 slaves to the West Indies, our captains must have a good cargo worth about 14,000–15,000 *rixdaler*. This would also ensure that the captain also brought home enough gold and ivory to cover the wages of the crew and the tax on the slaves. It should also be taken into consideration that the commission the Board of Directors now pays their ship's officers should not be paid by the owners [of non-Company ships]. That would be too expensive, /58/ amounting to 6,500 *rixdaler* for 400 slaves — yet that reward is not too large for those people to whom our welfare is entrusted and who risk their lives to gain some [profit] for their hard journeys. Let us look at the extremes of this economic aspect as practised, and let we Danes take a middle road. The French give too much, and the Dutch too little. We must arrange matters so foreigners will wish to work for us. There will be time enough to tighten up when our own people have learned the art. On a ship carrying 400–450 slaves the captain could be paid, besides his monthly salary of 24 *rixdaler,* eight slaves, the first mate four, the second mate three, the master three, the third mate and cooper two each. That makes 20 slaves for the officers,[9] yet these private slaves should not exceed in number those purchased for the owners, that is, for each 100 purchased for the owners the officers should be allowed to buy five, and so on. In addition the captain should be allowed two *rixdaler* for each slave he delivers to the West Indies, and the accompanying officers one *rixdaler* per head, of which the first mate would receive one half *rixdaler,* the master one quarter and the second mate one quarter, that is, [totalling] three *rixdaler* per head to be paid out to the officers. The ship's officers must have the same freedom [to trade] under us as they do under the French. When buying their quantity of slaves for the owner's cargo and wishing to earn more for themselves, they must arrange matters themselves to this end, either by bottomry or some other way. It would be an attractive encouragement for the Dutch officers to teach our sailors the slave trade, and [what is proposed] would be about twice as much as a Dutch captain earns, and half as much as a French captain is paid. /59/ It should also be determined how many pounds [of sugar] each officer should be permitted to

---

[9] The total is actually 22, not 20, unless the third mate and cooper are one and the same, or more likely, the cooper is not being considered as an officer.

bring to Copenhagen from the West Indies. It could be set according to the number of slaves, that is, each captain eight lb., the first mate four lb., etc.

All these arrangements are of little use as long as other nations come to our islands and are free to sell their slaves. Our planters insist that the Englishmen give them a better sale than we do, but they do not say what kind of slaves the Englishman sells them. They are Angola and Lagoon slaves, and in 1750 I saw a captain from Bristol sell a slave in St. Thomas for 160 and 180 *rixdaler* [sic] and an entire cargo which would not have brought him more [per slave] than £20 sterling [= 80 *rixdaler*] on the English islands.[10] Our planters themselves know that one of our slaves, those called Elmina slaves, is better than three of the English, and many of these [English slaves] have drowned themselves or hanged themselves before the captain left the West Indies. The planters wondered how I could tell one from another, that is, those our ships had brought and those who had been purchased from the English.

I see no reason why our slaves should be delivered to the government [in the West Indies]. Why cannot we do as the English do when they arrive, that is, the captain sells them from the ship and the ship owners set a certain price? When one of our ships belonging to the Company arrives at St. Thomas, the merchant immediately conveys them to the [official] warehouse. The Governor informs the planters, they come to him and ask to be allowed to purchase one or two slaves at auction. The Governor answers, 'Yes'. The planter goes to the Company warehouse where he sees the slaves /**60**/ who have already been branded, either by the Governor himself or by someone else who was given permission to do so. He also sees the ones who have not been branded, and among them he can pick out as many as the Governor has given him permission to buy.[11] This is done as long as there are unbranded slaves. The auction is then started. One planter does not bid on the branded slaves belonging to another. This would be an unchristian deed which would displease the Governor.[12] No. The merchant leading the auction outbids him several times, then the planter receives the branded slaves.[13] When you understand this you must admit that the government in the West Indies could take no measures which would be of greater injury to the Company than to allow other nations to go there and sell the slaves

---

[10] Law (1991) 174.

[11] For a description of a slave auction on St. Croix, see Isert [1788] (1994) 182.

[12] R.'s choice of words holds a mirror up to his milieu — auctioning human beings (Africans) is acceptable but bidding on another man's 'property' is unchristian.

[13] This passage is obscure but the procedure described seems to have been as follows. Whereas unbranded slaves are sold from the warehouse, branded slaves are sold at auction. Since 'one planter does not bid on the branded slaves belonging to another', he must be bidding only on the branded slaves belonging to the Governor. However, the auctioneer overbids the planter (by falsely announcing higher bids?), presumably on agreement with the Governor, until a price acceptable to the Governor is reached.

they do not take care to use on their own islands. And when our Company ships arrive the slaves are shared out among the planters in the method described above. All this would not happen if trade became free.[14]

I mentioned earlier the conditions under which the French sell their slaves, and should our planters wish to operate under the French conditions they would have to pay in the same way the French planters pay. If [instead] they want English or Dutch conditions, then they should ask if their situation is similar to that of the English on Jamaica and other places, and the Dutch on St. Statius. Everyone knows that all the merchants at those places where slaves are brought for sale are in debt to the ship-owners in England and Holland. Only a few merchants have accounts in banks in London and Amsterdam with credit for several thousand pounds sterling and guilders, /61/ some more and some less. At those places the captain's sale is just as reliable as if I had a promissory note of 1,000 *rixdaler* signed by three of our wealthiest merchants here in Copenhagen. But can this be said of our planters? Do we not know that they owe the Company some 100,000 *rixdaler* in debts? And far from the planters' debts decreasing, they increase every year. Let the planters themselves look upon the West Indies as a land where they have no intention of living until they die, but hope to leave there with enough to live from in Europe. And should circumstances not permit of such hopes, could they not reflect that their descendants may wish to live in Europe, indeed here in Denmark, on condition that trade is not so managed as to make Denmark a [mere] warehouse. That would not be advantageous, either. You cannot reason with foolish planters who do not think in this way. They see only the shell and leave the kernel; they only complain, 'The slaves are too expensive, and our goods must be sold at higher prices!' The most sensible answer that I have heard is this: 'You tell us that the French pay so much for the slaves, and this is true. But the French planters sort their sugar into three grades; thus they gain on one grade what they lose on another. That is to say, some grades of sugar are more expensive than ours on St. Thomas, some are the same price, and some are lower. Cannot one answer, 'Imitate them!"? [Moreover,] the planters say that our cloth is too expensive. But can these Messieurs be allowed to aspire to having cloth brought from England when our own merchants and manufacturers are dependent on goods [from the West Indies]? Do not these Messieurs make themselves quite unworthy of respect when they claim /62/ difficulties in paying one mark more for an *alen* of cloth while, in the evenings, they gamble away a couple of hundred *rixdaler* at the billiard houses, or they hold get-togethers costing sometimes 4–500 *rixdaler*, etc.?

All the French unanimously assure us that when a planter buys a slave the purchase price will be repaid with a single year's labour. Our planters say it

---

[14] R. seems to be pointing out that an influx of slaves from other nations would jeopardize the Governor's (and the Company's) monopoly.

takes eighteen months. Even if this is so, does it not encourage us [to follow the French system]? Obviously I believe the French method of trade the most advantageous for us. Who has been so wise and taught this to the French with such wonderful success? None other than their monks and priests — who are their spies and capitalize on their [religious] connections to discover if, for instance, a governor is competent or not, if products are sent out or not, and so on, and in what way trade can best be handled. The only thing the French court did [wrongly], causing so many bankruptcies in France, was neglecting to inform the traders that they no longer had free trade on the Coast. Thereafter, for four years, until 1749, we did not see a single French ship. After that, so many came that 340 Guineamen were said to have sailed from Rochelle alone. The French convinced them that they could buy slaves for baubles, but all of these ships were driven from the Coast by the English warships, and had to sail empty to the West Indies.

At some point earlier in this text, I stated that the Dutch had only inferior establishments in the West Indies. That is to say, most of their slave ships are required to sail to specific merchants on their islands, men who have contracted with the owners in Holland, and paid them in advance /63/. The result is that certain families, being able to afford such advances, become great capitalists. Then they peddle the slaves to the planters. But the ordinary planters, forced to buy slaves second hand, are at times oppressed and exploited, so they hardly ever get rid of their debts.

To conclude, it is my wish that the Almighty Himself will so manage affairs that the changes which should come about in the trade may be beneficial to Your Majesty and Your subjects.

Appendix B

The 1744 Christiansborg rebellion

In December 1744 Rømer fled from Christiansborg Fort, and on 28 February 1745, while in refuge at the English fort of Cape Coast, he wrote a 28-page explanation which subsequently he presented in Copenhagen to the Directors of the Company, to justify his actions before and during a rebellion at the Danish fort directed against the governor.[1] Governor Billsen had arrived in February 1744, and was to die only one month after Rømer's apologia, on 11 March 1745. No doubt his version of events was different from that of his dismissed Chief Trader, but if his final report was ever written, and if it reached Copenhagen, it has not yet surfaced in the archives. Despite the self-interested nature of Rømer's *Relation over tilstanden i Christiansborg* ('Report on Conditions at Christiansborg'), it is worth presenting in brief summary, as the fullest account of the rebellion and also for the light it throws on both the circumstances of the fort and the character of Rømer.

The years immediately before the rebellion had thrown up problems for the fort and its staff. In 1742 the Asante overcame the Akyem and their allies, thus changing the political and economic situation at Accra. Having reached the coast at Old Ningo, the Asante blockaded the Danish fort of Fredensborg, where the commander had to accede to demands for payment. The Asante advanced on Accra, sacking en route the English Fort Vernon at Prampram, and a Dutch lodge at Tema. Christiansborg came under siege and, packed as it was with refugees from the neighbouring areas, soon ran out of food. To relieve the siege, the Governor, Peter Nikolai Jørgensen, had to pay the Asante a considerable sum of money, and he had also to lend goods from the fort's stores to the distressed inhabitants of the local towns. These drastic events and the total change in alliances—from Akyem to Asante—evidently took a serious toll on Jørgensen's ability to manage affairs. He neglected trade, allowed discipline to lapse, and took to drink. His constable, Cornelius Petersen, appears to have had a free hand at Christiansborg, and the chaplain, Peder Meyer, joined the soldiers in carousing. Finally, on 26 May 1743, Jørgensen, apparently not daring to

---

[1] CRA, V-gK 189, 28.1.1745.

report the situation to the Directors in Copenhagen, handed over command to Christian Glob Dorph, the commander of Fort Fredensborg.[2]

Examining the accounts, Dorph found that there were enormous deficits. He initiated a much stricter regime and tried to reform matters. He sent the bookkeeper home, but was unable to increase trade. The Dutch company, having allowed its merchants to trade privately upon payment of a fee to the company, was now to be in control of the slave trade at Accra. Since it was known that the warehouse at Christiansborg was, in effect, empty, no Africans came to the Danes to trade, and hence food supplies were depleted. Dorph reported the situation to Copenhagen, and Rømer did the same.[3] The reaction there was immediate. A ship was hired to take a new Governor, Jørgen Billsen, to Gold Coast.

On arrival, Billsen recognized that he was expected to improve the situation, not least by exercising firm control.[4] It was later said that even before going ashore he announced that all private trade was henceforth to stop. This was a serious blow to the Company servants, who had always been able to supplement their meagre salaries by trading privately. The new governor immediately sent his predecessors, Jørgensen and Dorph, back to Denmark, the latter as a prisoner. He then to set to work to form local alliances, not only with the conquering Asante but also with what remained of the former rulers, the Akyem. But his personal relationships with his staff deteriorated rapidly.[5] The rebels later claimed that he not only deprived the soldiers of decent wages but also abused and humiliated them. The merchants were all old hands. Rømer was highly experienced in the fort's trade and seems to have had a profitable personal network in place locally. It is plausible, however, that he conducted himself towards Billsen at best in an untactful way, at worst with arrogance. His writings make it clear that he was impatient with Billsen's lack of flexibility in trade practices. In *Negotien* he makes much of the need for newcomers not only to adjust to tried and successful methods of trade on the Coast, but also to learn about the Africans and how to remain on good terms with them.[6]

Ashangmo, the king of Popo, a coastal polity east of River Volta, had invited the Danes to establish a lodge, or fort, at Qvitta. Billsen sent to Qvitta, in a company boat, Rømer and two other merchants, Esau Christensen Qvist and Johan Wilder, with instructions to establish trade contacts with

---

[2] This background to Rømer's account is from Nørregård (1966) 102–3; Fynn (1971) 74–5; and these sources also contribute to the interpretation of the account that follows.

[3] On 30 December 1743, Rømer wrote a letter in French to the Directors of the Company complaining about the failure of Jørgensen and Dorph to undertake trade, and calling them drunkards (*des hommes yvrongées*): CRA, V-gK 123, 30.12.1743.

[4] The situation of the Danish establishments at the time of Bilsen's arrival was stated in a report of 30 March 1744 signed by the new governor and others (V-gK 123, Generalbrev, 23.5.1744).

[5] See Nørregaard (1966) 105–06.

[6] E.g., 1756, /33/, in chapter 2 above.

the local chiefs there and to invite Ashangmo to take part in a palaver at Qvitta. But they were specifically ordered not to travel any further than Qvitta. However, after they arrived at Qvitta, Ashangmo invited them formally to hold the palaver in Popo itself, and the traders, perhaps unwisely, gave way. Disaster followed. Arriving at Popo at the end of July 1744, an overnight storm sank their boat and the goods and gifts for the king it carried were lost. Rømer had been ashore during the storm, but his companion, Qvist, had sought help from some Dutch who were also trading there, and Rømer seems to have believed that the Dutch, with the help of local people, had cut an anchor rope and then looted goods. Ashangmo, perhaps impressed by Rømer's competence in trading and his linguistic capacity, wanted him to remain and work for him, but eventually he gave both Danes leave to return to Qvitta, which they did on foot. Rømer began the construction of a lodge at Qvitta but was suddenly ordered back to Christiansborg by Billsen.[7]

The governor, angry at Rømer's ignoring of the original instructions and the consequent loss of goods, now had doubts about an establishment at Qvitta. Rømer, for whom the eastward move was a strategy he strongly believed in and had encouraged, did not return immediately to Christiansborg, pleading illness (perhaps correctly). Meanwhile the fort had other problems. Billsen brought charges of conspiracy against his constable, Cornelius Petersen, and rumours of rebellion had indeed circulated for some time, the major cause of discontent being allegedly Billsen's treatment of the soldiers. Rømer received a letter from his colleague, Simon Henrick Klein, Chief Merchant at Ningo, urging him to return immediately to Christiansborg in order to help in a stand against what he considered Billsen's unreasonable behaviour. Upon his return, Rømer had to explain to the Secret Council his actions in going to Popo, and though the other members of the Council were satisfied, only after a great deal of further discussion and correspondence did Billsen drop charges against Rømer. Another conflict arose when Rømer and Klein refused to sign a judgement condemning several soldiers — a judgement they felt was based on too little evidence and was too harsh. On 3 October 1744, Billsen suspended from service both traders, on the grounds of their bad conduct, indolence, and lack of experience in trade. The last charge was patently absurd.

Rømer and Klein promptly left Christiansborg and went to stay at the nearby Dutch fort, Creve Coeur. They insisted that Billsen put the suspension order in writing and that they appear before the Secret Council, but they also refused to accept a suspension which did not come directly from the Directors of the Company in Copenhagen. When Billsen produced a written order and made it public, the English asked Rømer to come and work for them at Cape

---

[7] These events were reported by Qvist (CRA, V-gK 887, 13.6.1744–4.1.1745m pp.32, 34).

Coast. On 19 October 1744, Rømer and Klein again sent their demand for a fair hearing to Billsen, but on that very day the rebellion took place.[8]

What follows is essentially Rømer's account of events at Christiansborg. The soldiers seized the keys to the main gate and the warehouse and claimed to have deposed Billsen. The oldest of the company employees, Joost Platfues, refused to accept the keys and take command, pleading his age, and Klein was then asked to take over. The entire Council met and agreed that Klein should keep the keys to the gate but return the warehouse keys. Klein then asked the English Chief Merchant at Accra, Andreas Detmer, and his Dutch analogue, Balthazar Coymans, to mediate between the parties; but the mediation failed. Billsen refused to be reconciled with his soldiers, calling them and the rest of the Council rebels. Since Klein declined command, Thomas Brock was called in from Fort Fredensborg. It was agreed that the fort's books should be examined by all concerned and their judgements registered.

Billsen himself now requested that the 'foreigners' — Detmar and Coymans — come and mediate. Both men being ill, Detmar sent his son and Coymans his assistant, and they were accompanied by the Chief Merchant from Winnebah, Mr. Graves. At the mediation hearing it was stated that the soldiers had been driven by sheer desperation and hunger to rebel against Billsen personally. While declaring their loyalty to King and Company, they refused to work under Billsen. They demanded that he produce the wage books for comparison with their own records. Billsen at first refused, and when a search for the books proved fruitless he declared that they must have disappeared or been destroyed during the rebellion. Further requests for delivery of the books and other records from Billsen proved futile, and it was widely assumed that they were with the governor's sister, who at the beginning of the troubles had been sent from Christiansborg to the English fort. It was decided that the keys to the warehouse should be in Platfues's keeping and that when Africans arrived, three Danish employees should accompany them to the warehouse and keep a separate record of sales and purchases. After more discussion in several meetings, and promises of improvement from Billsen, a reconciliation was effected between Billsen and the soldiers.

Several days later, having instructed Rømer and Klein to remain at the English and Dutch forts respectively, Billsen went to Cape Coast Castle. Rømer heard later that the purpose of the visit was to recruit soldiers, but the General at Cape Coast refused to allow this. Billsen then moved on to Elmina where, Rømer claims, the Dutch General, Jacob de Petersen, told

---

[8] The records relating to the inquiry into this rebellion are in CRA, V-gK 285, 1744–1745; also relevant is a long letter from Hackenburg (CRA, V-gK 123, 15.6.1745). Billsen does not appear to have written anything in his own defence, perhaps because he did not feel compelled to do so.

him that his suspension of staff without consultation with the Council was unheard of (a debatable point). According to Rømer, the Danish governor was anxious to tell the other nations that his entire garrison had rebelled against King and Company and deserved the death penalty. When Billsen returned, the rumour spread that he was planning to have his soldiers *panyarred* (seized) by the local Africans. Rømer thought this an unrealistic manoeuvre, since Billsen's only contact with Africans had been when he had had individuals beaten. Moreover, Billsen had given Africans uncomplimentary nicknames and ridiculed their palavers, he had been miserly in supplying them with brandy, and he had demanded deposits on loans even though the borrowers had had sufficient gold as security. (Whether this was truly Billsen's behaviour or not, we are informed how Rømer thought African-European relations should be conducted.)

After making promises to a broker to release a brother from prison and cancel his debt; and by payment to individuals, Billsen did finally succeed in recruiting a private guard of local Africans. The Danish soldiers felt so intimidated that they dared not go singly outside the walls of Christiansborg, or to the Governor's office to receive their wages, and they were virtually imprisoned. The Constable, Cornelius Petersen, took refuge at the Dutch fort (while Rømer was there) because the governor had given his new forces orders to *panyar* him. Petersen tried to acquire gunpowder from the English fort, but Rømer — so he claimed — talked the merchant there out of it, by indicating what a tragedy might occur if the soldiers had powder enough to effect an armed rebellion. On the pretext of drilling his men, now thirty strong, Billsen led them around the fort to inspect the guns belonging to the soldiers. But the brandy supplied to them ruined any discipline and attracted more Africans claiming to be part of the squad. Billsen had difficulty in stopping them from opening up the ammunition stores, and had finally to release his imprisoned Danish soldiers to help to restore order. Next, Billsen tried to hire an African guard from the Labode chief, Kpoti, but instead of the twenty to thirty men sought, Kpoti, after a number of refusals, sent only a handful. Billsen kept these new arrivals, together with a few whites, with him at all times, even insisting that they sleep in the same room as he did. The Africans he had imprisoned after the disturbances he now released. Rømer and Klein had been ordered to return to Christiansborg; Rømer refused, Klein returned and was arrested.

On 21 December 1744, now the subject of a written order of suspension, Rømer arrived at Cape Coast Castle, where he was welcomed. He aimed to return to Copenhagen, to lay the entire matter before the Company Directors, feeling certain he could clear his name. He heard that Billsen constantly spoke unfavourably of him, insisting that he was the cause of all the trouble. He was given passage on a Dutch ship, *Henrietta Suzanna Galei*, and he left Elmina for The Netherlands on 1 July 1745. Arriving in Vlissingen on 29 September, he made his way to Amsterdam, where he bought a passage on

Het Vergulde Lam, which sailed for Copenhagen on 19 October. On 4 November the ship was wrecked on the coast of Norway. He finally arrived in Copenhagen on 27 November where he stayed until the inquiry he had demanded was completed and he was cleared. He returned to the Gold Coast, now promoted to Chief Merchant, arriving there in June 1746.

In early 1745, Klein was held in a room that was sealed, apart from a small opening for the delivery of food; and other prisoners at Christiansborg were given only half the rations supplied to slaves. But Governor Billsen no longer dared leave the fort, because of the hatred the Africans felt for him. In the midst of some chaos, he died on 11 March 1745. The Dutch and Danish doctors said that his death was caused by improper diet while undergoing a treatment with mercury for a venereal complaint. Thomas Brock, named interim Governor, very soon discovered that both the Company's gold and Billsen's own gold (a considerable quantity of which he had seen Billsen weighing only a few days before his death) had disappeared. After searching Christiansborg, Brock interrogated at Cape Coast Billsen's sister, who admitted to possession of her brother's gold, but insisted that it was given her by the trader Wilder, to keep secret the fact that he had helped himself to all the gold at Christiansborg. A few hours after the interrogation, Brock fell ill and died, and the English doctor at Cape Coast diagnosed poisoning. Wilder then became the interim governor, but unaccustomed to the privileges of power he over-indulged in sex and drink (according to Rømer, who being still at Cape Coast no doubt kept his ears open for such scandal), and he, too, died, one month after Brock's death.

Wilder was succeeded by Friderick August Hackenburg, a young merchant from Fredensborg Fort.[9] The rebellion had extinguished itself, but Danish trade was in disorder. The Directors felt that Hackenburg was too young for the job, so appointed Platfues to the governorship. Platfues held the post until 1751 and was the governor during Rømer's final years in Africa.

---

[9] Since the father of the Gã historian, C.C. Reindorf was called Christian Hackenburg Reindorf, it seems likely that the young merchant was a male forbear of this illustrious Gold Coast family.

Appendix C

A 1760 Danish account of a Gold Coast warrior[1]
[Translated from Danish by S.A. Winsnes]

[*caption under the engraving*] Qvou, son of Eikoe, born in the town of Ursue, at Accra on the Guinea Coast. This [engraving] illustrates the manner in which a prominent Negro is equipped when he goes into battle.

[*text*]

Description
Of the fetishes and military attire shown in this copper engraving of the Free Negro, Qvou Ursou, and how these things are used, and how those of his nation, the Accra Blacks on the Guinea Coast, equip themselves when they are going into battle. As follows:

I. The use of fetishes or sacred objects, eight items.
1. *Ækkymi*. This is the band on the right temple, which according to their false beliefs (following formal offerings to the gods), is meant to be a protection against shot and other injury to the head.
2. *Ngámi*. This is a short fetish band around the neck, which by virtue of sacrifices made, will nullify spells cast by the enemy, avert dangerous enterprises, and refute all [their] lies.
3. *Mouü*. The long fetish band hanging down the right side of the neck makes the shot go past the wearers' sides and between their arms.

---

[1] See the illustration of a Gold Coast warrior on Plate 5. The printed text, in parallel columns in three languages, Danish, French and German, appearing below the illustration and then occupying four folio pages, accompanied the engraving, the whole item apparently published in Copenhagen in 1761. A copy is in CRA, and another in Kongelige Bibliotek, Copenhagen (cat. 30.2–285, folio). The translators of the French and German versions were named as J.N. Vilse and Christian Gottlob Mengel. The German version is close to the Danish but the French contains errors. The author of the text, Christian Lindholm Schmidt was a merchant at the Danish establishments in Guinea in the 1750s but was arrested at Fort Fredensborg in 1757, by Governor C.G. Engmann (Rømer's friend), for embezzlement. He then spent several years in Copenhagen, not only clearing his name of the charges but also suggesting ways of improving administration in Africa, and he was re-instated as Chief Merchant at Christiansborg in 1762. An inscription below the engraving names the artist: 'Mich. Rössler Reg. Dan. Calcogr. sculpsit et excudit Haffn. 1761' (see also engravings of Christiansborg and Fredensborg).

4. *Cabbra*. The shorter fetish band hanging around the neck on the left side is to ensure that the enemy warriors will not be able to speak to each other in order to plan, instead they will appear like deaf mutes; also that their muskets will not fire nor the primers light, even though their muskets are all charged.

5. *Abócca*. The fetish band on the left hand is to prevent shot from striking the hands, [protecting] both the skin and the flesh.

6. *Abócco egcó*. The fetish band fastened below the right knee-cap, is to ensure that, even after a dangerous fall, the wearer can stand up again, unharmed.

7. *Abócco enjó*. The band fastened below the left knee-cap has the same effect.

8. *Sissa*. The fetish bands above the right and left ankles are to prevent the enemy from coming up behind him and diverting his assault. The term *sissa* means 'devil', and the fetish has been so-named to prevent his hindering the advance

These are the fetishes or sacred objects with which this Negro, and [the other warriors of] the whole Accra nation, equip themselves; to varying extents, depending upon the time, place and situation, and what their special concerns and needs require. The other nations of Blacks [also] put on their fetishes and sacred objects, greater or fewer [in number], [worn] in many and various ways, and with various ascribed powers, all depending upon the degree of their superstition and worship of their gods.

II. Weapons [and military dress] **and how they are used.**
On his head he wears a military helmet called *louvvaa faï*, which wholly consists of the stretched skin of a tiger's head, with the ears still in place. No common Negro may wear this, but only those who are among the elders of the country, state, or settlement; those who have achieved fame in war or in [proving their] loyalty; and those who are wealthy. These are given special permission by their fetish (their god). The tiger, whom they call *louvvaa*, is held in high esteem because they consider it to be the most handsome and the strongest [animal]. They worship it so that it will not harm them or their families, and after its death the hide serves the elders and most prominent men as armour, bed covers, and so forth.

On top of the war helmet *louvva faï*, they place, as further ornamentation, a bundle of ostrich feathers, called *waa kjærre*, which, again, only the elders and most prominent men may make use of in war and in *brengaren* (celebrations). The ostrich, called *crupong*, is [the most] esteemed among birds, after the crowned crane, as being the most handsome and the strongest. It is used for riding on, as on a horse (which animal they do not know how to ride or control) but also its feathers are used as ornaments and signs of victory. They *dyrker* [raise/worship] ostriches because of their usefulness and service, while they despise horses and sell them as useless creatures.[2]

---

[2] Danish *dyrke* means both to raise or cultivate and to worship. It is difficult to know which meaning is intended here, especially since, in a postscript to the text, Schmidt admits that this statement is hearsay, and we do not know which vernacular term his informant used.

Below the waist, at the belt-line, is a sash or *pantjes* [cloth] called *crará*. This is made of linen, coarse or fine, or of Silesian cloth, called *plattilies* by us *Blanke* (Whites) on the Coast.[3] [It is worn,] so that they can move nimbly and swiftly; [also] to cover their private parts; to serve as a form of identification in battle; and as decoration when they *brengar*. Some wear red sashes or *pantjes* because red and white are the most sacred of all the colours, and no one is permitted to use them, other than their *lymo* (kings), *numbo* (elders), *gvôngkjæ* (priests) and *akjoyvoyu* (priestesses).

Boss, or [shells of] snails called *cauris tremma*,[4] which are the currency at most locations — although of different values along the Coast — also have their place in military attire, partly as sacred and blessed objects [to ensure] well-being and success, and partly as ornamentation and identification in the field of battle. They can be seen [on] a long fetish ribbon hanging around the neck, on the right side. Some also wear them on the helmet; some around the neck on a red or white thread which has been blessed; some on their cartridge pouch; and some on a belt around the waist; as well as in several other ways which in their own opinion will best serve them.

The cartridge pouch at the waist is called *baya*, and, like the helmet, is made of tiger skin, for the same reason and for the same purpose as described above. It is fashioned by their own craftsmen, as is the smaller cartridge pouch, called *toccu*, which hangs on the chest, and is comfortable, light, strong and a decorative part of their military attire. Another form [of the pouch] would not lend itself easily to their manner of fighting, [since with this one] they are able to keep their powder, shot, straw and flints suitably and satisfactorily protected. At the same place [i.e. at the waist] are fastened sheaths for from three to six small, sharp knives which they always use in the field, for eating, piercing and cutting, as well as for other uses, and finally, in a crisis, as hand weapons for their own protection when all the fetishes (as frequently) are no longer effective. Similarly, [they use] the large knife here depicted, the Negro Qvou holding it in his mouth, it being, in most instances, when not the work of their own cutlers and dagger makers, principally of Portuguese origin.

Accó kjærre, parrot feathers; *addu kjaaï*, ape hair; *ænerang*, red earth; *ajiraa*, white earth; *gnaaï*, red raffia; *tremma boss* [cowries], and other things are held to be sacred objects which are in part attached [just as they are] to the aforementioned fetish bands, and in part first smeared [with red or white earth]. Briefly, the reason why the Blacks use parrot feathers and ape hair, rather than other things is that they consider *acco*, the parrot, to be holy because of its willingness to learn to speak, since they say, 'Speech belongs to gods and humans'. Likewise, *addu*, the ape, is sacred because its

---

[3] For *plattilies*, see the Glossary. In the illustration the 'sash' (*Skarf*) is twisted to form a belt around the waist, with the ends hanging down full width, behind and before.

[4] That is, cowries, *Cypraea moneta*.

leaping and trickery show its willingness to learn to work. People say, 'They have been transformed from human form to what they are, the parrot because of its pride, and the ape because of its thievishness; yet in these forms they serve God's grace, by using their abilities as messengers, the one in the air and the other on the ground.'

In the caption to the copper engraving of the Negro Qvou shown above, he is identified by his full name, Qvou Ursou. The explanation is as follows. The name Qvou is the heathen Accra first name, which, eight days after birth, is given to him out-of-doors, in the presence of the elders among the Negroes, as well as relatives and friends. And the name Ursou is his second name, taken from the name of the settlement, Ursous, Ursu or Ussu, where he was born. This naming ceremony begins and ends, as usual, with a *brengaren* during which food and drink, brandy and tobacco, are offered according to the ability [of the family]. For this reason the name Qvov Ursov is used by me, as well as by all the others whom he has served on the Coast, since, although he has not been baptised nor admitted into Christendom, he has led a pure and virtuous way of life.

In the same caption under the copper engraving, he is called the 'Negro Qvov Ursov, son of the big woman Ejco', which is not to be interpreted as referring to the woman's physical size but to her noble status, since among the Negroes 'big' customarily means 'noble, so that as just explained, in accordance with the definition, 'the son of the big woman Ejco' in the Negro Accra language is translated into Danish as 'the son of the noble woman Ejco'.[5]

Certain terms which appear in this description, such as 'fetishes', 'fetish band', '*brengaren*', '*pantjes*', '*cassarerede*', 'fetish-box',[6] and suchlike terms, are not the Negroes' own but are a mixture of Portuguese with their language, and some come from other European languages, and are called [collectively] Negro-Portuguese.

Copenhagen
16 October 1760

Written, on request, by Christian Lindholm Schmidt

N.B. Concerning the practice mentioned above, that the Blacks ride on ostriches, this can be explained in the following way: A few years ago we heard from the Blacks on the Accra coasts that there lived in the interior a certain people who ride ostriches; but no European or Accra Black has ever seen such a rider.

End of text

---

[5] In fact, in the caption Ejco/Eikoe is not described as 'big woman', indeed it is not stated whether Eikoe is the mother or the father of Qvou.
[6] *Cassarerede* (see *callisiare* in the Glossary) and 'fetish-box' do not appear in the text.

Glossary

aggrey:	a particular type of bead of very high value, usually translucent blue in colour.
alen	Danish linear measure equivalent to 62.81 cm
anker	Danish liquid measure equivalent to 39–40 *potter* (see below)
benda	Akan gold weight, equivalent to 2 ounces of gold or 32 *rixdaler* (see below)
bossies	cowries (see below), from Portuguese *buzio* 'cowrie shell'.
brafo	Akan title, frequently employed to indicate an executioner, but also denoting a person of power, especially military (see McCaskie (1990) 136).
cabes	local unit of number at Accra in the eighteenth century, from Portuguese *cabeça* 'head', used to number thousands of beads and cowrie shells
callavap	otherwise *callowaypoos*, a patterned cotton cloth from South India, 14 yards long, of medium quality (K-N. Chaudhuri, *The Trading World of Asia and the English East India Company 1660–1760* (1978) 502)
callisiare	otherwise *callischare*, from Port. *casar* 'to marry', to set up house (a European with an African woman)
challong	? *cheilos*, striped medium quality cotton cloths from Gujarat; or ? *chillaes*, striped blue and white medium quality cotton cloths from Bengal (Chaudhuri (1978) 501, 503).
contreterre	a valuable bead, from Portuguese *conta da terra* 'bead of the earth/country'
cowries	sea shells (*Cypraea moneta*) imported from the Maldive Islands and used as currency in West Africa
factor	the European official in charge of all the trade of a fort or lodge, usually second in command to the governor of a fort
favn	Danish linear and depth measure, from finger-tip to finger-tip of arms outstretched, a fathom, approximately 1.8 metres
fiscal	title of a European official with certain legal powers at a fort, responsible for uncovering illegal trade by Company employees as well as preventing trade with interlopers
fjerding	Danish linear measure, one-quarter of a Danish land mile (1.9 kilometres)
føtter	Danish nickname for termites
harmattan	the season (December-February) on the Guinea coast when the normal westerly winds are replaced by NE winds, bringing dust from the Sahara to the coast and resulting in extreme haziness, dryness and relative cold
linned	Danish, 'linen', but seems to be used generically to denote certain varieties of cotton as well as linen cloth

266 *Glossary*

lod	Danish measure of weight, 15.6 grammes (14.6 grammes when used to weigh gold and silver)
long els	? 'long cloth', an Indian cotton cloth of unusual length, 37–40 yards long (Chaudhuri (1978) 502)
lærred	? coarsely woven cotton cloth, '*lærred*' and '*linned*' apparently to some extent interchangeable
mark	Danish unit of currency, 6 marks = 1 *rixdaler* (see below)
mil	Danish linear measure, the Danish mile in the eighteenth century equivalent to 7.5 kilometres
oriental times	season of the NE winds, the harmattan
palaber	'a talk, discusssion, argument, etc', from Portuguese *palavra* 'utterance, etc', wider than English 'palaver', used in Guinea to denote situations ranging from conversations, through arguments, to court cases
pantje/s	a cloth about 2 metres long and wide enough to reach from waist to knee when wrapped around a woman's hips
penjarte	'to pawn, seize in distraint', from Portuguese *penhorar* 'to distrain', but R. also applies it to a person possessed by a god, therefore under the god's control
perpetuan	a high quality woollen cloth (serge) made in England and Flanders, the name reflecting its durability
plattilias	a fine linen manufactured in Europe, the name supposedly from Portuguese *beatilha* 'nun's white veil' (Adam Jones, *Brandenburg Sources for West African History*, 1985, 318)
pott	Danish liquid measure of 0.968 litre
rask (rash)	a very fine worsted, sometimes containing silk, made in Europe (Jones (1985) 318)
rixdaler	Danish unit of currency, 1 *rixdaler* = 6 *mark* = 96 *shilling*, and 16 *rixdaler* = 1 ounce of gold
salempuris	otherwise *sallampores*, a plain white and blue dyed cotton cloth, named after the city of manufacture in India (M. Heiden, *Handwörterbuch der Textilkünde aller Zeiten und Völken* (1904) 452).
say	the same as rask, see above
sirts	chintz
skieppe	old Danish measure for grain, equivalent to 17.4 litres
slaplagen	form of poor cotton cloth from Europe, ? old bed sheets
slees-lærred	a coarse Silesian cotton cloth
span	linear measure, the distance from the tip of the thumb to the tip of the little finger or forefinger of the extended hand
Tie Tie	title of an Akan herald or messenger, from Akan *tié* 'hear'
travado	travado, sudden storm in Guinea, from Portuguese *trovoada* 'thunderstorm', now known as a line squall

Bibliography

Key to abbreviations

BLL	Balme Library, Legon, Accra
CRA	Rigsarkivet (Royal Archives), Copenhagen
IAS	Institute of African Studies, Legon, Accra
IFAN	*Institut Fondamental de l'Afrique Noire*, Dakar
THSG	*Transactions of the Historical Society of Ghana*
V-gK	Vestindisk-guinea Kompaniet (West Indies-Guinea Company)

PUBLISHED SOURCES

Ludewig Ferdinand Rømer
Tilforladelig Efterretning om Negotien paa Kysten Guinea, Af hvilke Nationer den drives, og paa hvilken Maade den er indretted af enhver Nation især, tilligemed Uforgribelige Betænkninger, hvorledes vor Negotie derhen og til Vestindien, bedre kunde indrettes
Copenhagen, 1756

Tilforladelig Efterretning om Kysten Guinea
Copenhagen, 1760

Abbiw, Daniel K.	*Useful Plants of Ghana*, London, 1990
Addo-Fenning, Robert	'The Akim or Achim in 17th and 18th century historical contexts: who were they?', *IAS Research Review* 4/2 (1988) 1–15
Adjei, A.	'Mortuary usages of the Ga people of the Gold Coast', *American Anthropologist* 45 (1943) 84–98
[anon]	*Africa Pilot volume I*, Hydrographer of the Navy, London, twelfth edition, 1967
Ajayi, J.F.A. and Crowder, M.	eds., *History of West Africa*, 3rd edition, London, 1985
Alpern, S.B.	'The European introduction of crops into West Africa in precolonial times', *History in Africa* 19 (1992) 13–43
Appiah, Peggy	*Tales of an Ashanti Father*, London, 1967
———	*The Pineapple Child and other Tales from Ashanti*, London, 1969
Asiwaju, A.I. and Law, R.	'From the Volta to the Niger, c.1600–1800', in Ajayi and Crowder (1985, above) I: 412–67
Assimeng, Max	*Social Structure of Ghana*, Accra, 1981
Atkins, John	*A Voyage to Guinea, Brasil, and the West-Indies*, London, 1735, reprinted 1970
Atkinson, Ronald R.	'Old Akyem and the origins of Akyems Abuakwa and Kotoku', in R.K. Swartz, Jr. and Raymond Dumett, eds., *West African Culture Dynamics: Archeological and Historical Perspectives*, The Hague, 1980, 351–369
Ayisi, Eric O.	*An Introduction to the Study of African Culture*, London, 1980

Azu, Diana Gladys	*The Ga Family and Social Change*, Leiden/Cambridge, 1974
Baesjou, R.	'The historical evidence in old maps and charts of Africa with special reference to West Africa', *History in Africa* 15 (1988) 1–83
Barbot, John [Jean]	*A Description of the Coasts of North and South Guinea*, in [Awnsham and John Churchill, publishers], *A Collection of Voyages and Travels*, 6 vols., London, 1732, V: 15–466 — see next item
[Barbot, Jean]	Barbot on Guinea. The writings of Jean Barbot on West Africa 1678–1712, trans. and ed., P.E.H. Hair, Adam Jones, and Robin Law, London, 1992
Beazley, C.R. and Prestage, E.	trans. and ed., *The Chronicles of the Discovery and Conquest of Guinea*, London, 1896
Bech, Niels	'Christiansborg i Ghana 1800–1850', *Architectura* 11 (1989) 66–111
Behrens, C.	*Da Guinea var Dansk: Wulff Joseph Wulff's Breve og Dagbogsoptegnelser fra Guldkysten 1836–1842*, Copenhagen, 1917. English translation by S.A. Winsnes forthcoming
Ben-Amos, Paula	*The Art of Benin*, London, 1980
Bjørn, A.R.	'Bjørn's Beretning 1788 om de Danske Forter og Negerier', *Thaarup's Archiv*, III (1797–8) 193–230
———	*Tanker om Slavehandelen*, Copenhagen, 1806
Blake, J.W.	*Europeans in West Africa 1450–1560*, London, 1942
———	*West Africa: Quest for God and Gold 1454–1578*, London, 1977
Blussé, Leonard, and Gaastra, Femme	eds., *Companies and Trade: Essays on Overseas Trading Companies during the Ancien Régime*, Leiden, 1981
Boateng, E.A.	*A Geography of Ghana*, London, 1970
Bosman, William	*A New and Accurate Description of the Coast of Guinea*, London, 1705, reprinted, with added notes, 1967
Bowdich, T.E.	*Mission from Cape Coast to Ashantee*, London, 1819
Boxer, C.R.	*The Golden Age of Brazil 1698–1750: Growing Pains of a Colonial Society*, Berkeley/Los Angeles, 1964
Bradbury, R.E.	*Benin Studies*, London, 1973
Brenner, Louis	'Religious discourses in and about Africa', in Karin Barber and P.F. de Moraes, eds., *Discourse and its Disguises*, Birmingham, 1989, 87–103
Broby-Johansen, R.	*Krop og Klær: Klædedragtens Kunsthistorie*, Copenhagen, 1975
Brown, S-D.	'From the tongues of Africa: a partial translation of Oldendorp's interviews', *Plantation Society in the Americas* 2 (1983) 37–61
Brun, Samuel	'Voyages 1611–20', in Jones (1983a below) 44–96
Buxton, Thomas Fowell	*The African Slave Trade and its Remedy*, London, 1839
Chaudhuri, K.N.	*The Trading World of Asia and the English East India Company 1660–1760*, Cambridge, 1978
Christaller, J.G.	*Dictionary of the Asante and Fante Language Called Tshi*, Basel, 1881, enlarged edition 1933
Claridge, W.W.	*A History of the Gold Coast and Ashanti*, London, 1964
Cole, Herbert M. and Ross, Doran H.	*The Arts of Ghana*, Los Angeles, 1977
Crooks, J.J.	*Records relating to the Gold Coast Settlements from 1750 to 1874*, Dublin, 1923

Bibliography 269

Curtin, P.D.	*The Image of Africa,* Madison, 1973
———	'The external trade of West Africa to 1800', in Ajayi and Crowder (1985, above), 2: 624–47
Daaku, KwameYeboa	*Trade and Politics on the Gold Coast 1600–1720,* Oxford, 1970
———	'Akan trade in the seventeenth and eighteenth centuries', in Claude Meillassoux, ed., *The Development of Indigenous Trade and Markets in West Africa,* London, 1971
Dakubu, M.E. Kropp	*Korle Meets the Sea: a Sociolinguistic History of Accra,* New York, 1997
Daniell, William F.	On the ethnography of Akkrah and Adampe, Gold Coast, Western Africa', *Journal of the Ethnological Society* 4 (1856) 1–32
Danquah, Joseph Boakye	*Akan Laws and Customs and the Akim Abuakwa Constitution,* London 1928
———	*The Akan Doctrine of God,* London, 2nd ed., 1968
Dapper, Olfert	*Naukeurige Beschrijvinge der Afrikaensche Gewesten,* Amsterdam 1668, cited second print 1676
Davies, K.G.	*The Royal African Company,* London, 1957
Debrunner, H.	*Witchcraft in Ghana,* London, 1961
De Corse, C.	'Beads as chronological indicators in West African archeology: a re-examination', *Beads: Journal of the Society of Bead Researchers* 1 (1989) 41–53
De Marees, Pieter	*Description and Historical Account of the Gold Kingdom of Guinea (1602),* trans. and ed. Albert van Dantzig and Adam Jones, Oxford, 1987
Dickson, K.A.	'Hebrewisms of West Africa: the Old Testament and African life and thought', *Legon Journal of the Humanities* (1974) 23–34
Dickson, K.B.	*A Historical Geography of Ghana,* Cambridge, 1969
Donnan, Elizabeth	ed., *Documents Illustrative of the History of the Slave Trade to America,* 4 vols., Washington D.C., 1930–1935
Ehrencron-Müller, H.	*Forfatterlexikon omfattende Danmark, Norge og Island indtil 1814,* Copenhagen, 1930
Ellis, A.B.	*A History of the Gold Coast of West Africa,* London, 1971
Ericson, J.M.	*The Universal Bead,* New York, 1969
Everts, N.	'Cherchez la Femme: gender-related issues in eighteenth-century Elmina', *Itinerario* 20, (1996) 45–57
Fage, J.D.	'Some remarks on beads and trade in Lower Guinea in the sixteenth and seventeenth centuries', *Journal of African History* 3 (1962) 343–7
———	'More about aggrey and akori beads', in *2000 Ans d'Histoire Africaine,* Paris (1981) 205–11
———	*A History of Africa,* London, 1995
Feinberg, H.M.	*Africans and Europeans in West Africa: Elminans and Dutchmen on the Gold Coast during the Eighteenth Century,* Philadelphia, 1989
Feldbæk, O.	'The organization and structure of the Danish East India, West India and Guinea Companies in the seventeenth and eighteenth centuries', in Blussé and Gaastra (1981, above) 135–58
Feldbæk, O., and Justesen, O.	*Kolonierne i Asien og Afrika,* Copenhagen, [1980]

Field, M.J. — *Religion and Medicine of the Gã People*, London, 1937, reprinted 1961
―― *Social Organization of the Gã People*, London, 1940
―― *Search for Security*, London, 1960
Fuglestad, F. — *Latin-Amerika og Karibiens Historie*, Oslo, 1994
Fynn, J.K. — *Asante and its Neighbours 1700–1807*, London, 1971
―― 'Asante and Akyem relations 1700–1831', *IAS Research Review* 9 (1973) 58–81
Garrard, Timothy F. — *Akan Weights and the Gold Trade*, London, 1980
Gayibor, Nicoué L. — 'Les Rois de Glidji: une chronologie revisée', *History in Africa* 22 (1995) 197–222
Geggus, D. — 'Sex ratio, age and ethnicity in the Atlantic slave trade: data from French shipping and plantation records', *Journal of African History* 30 (1989) 23–44
Gemery, H.A. and Hogendorn, J.S. — *The Uncommon Market: Essays in the Economic History of the Atlantic Slave Trade*, New York, 1979
Goody, J. — *Technology, Tradition and the State in Africa*, London, 1971
Gordon, A. and Kahan, L. — *The Tribal Bead: A Handbook of African Trade Beads*, New York, 1976
Gottlieb, A. — 'Sex, fertility and menstruation among the Beng of the Ivory Coast: a symbolic analysis', *Africa* 52/4 (1982) 34–47
Green-Pedersen, Svend E. — 'Om Forholdene på Danske Slaveskibe', *Handels- og Søfartsmuseet på Kronborg Årbog* (1993) 26–76
Grove, A.T. — *Africa*, third edition, London, 1978
Grove, J.M and Johansen, A.M. — 'The historical geography of the Volta Delta, Ghana, during the period of Danish influence', *Bulletin de l'IFAN* 30 (1968) 1376–1421
Gøbel, E. — 'Danish trade to the West Indies and Guinea 1671–1754', *Scandinavian Economic History Review*, 1 (1983) 21–49
Hagan, George P. — 'A note on Akan colour symbolism', *IAS Research Review*, 7 (1970) 8–14
Hair, P.E.H. — 'A further note on Oldendorp's interviews', *Plantation Society in the Americas* 2 (1989) 343
―― *Barbot's African Vocabularies*, Liverpool, 1992
―― *The Founding of the Castelo de São Jorge da Mina: An Analysis of Sources*, Madison, 1994
―― 'Heretics, slaves, and witches – as seen by Guinea Jesuits c. 1610', *Journal of Religion in Africa* 26 (1998) 131–44
Hargreaves, J.D. — *West Africa: The Former French States*, New Jersey, 1967
Heiden, M. — *Handwörterbuch der Textilkünde aller Zeiten und Völken*, Stuttgart, 1904
Hemmersam, Michael — 'Description of the Gold Coast 1639–45', in Jones (1983a below) 97–133, 356–83
Henige, D. — 'The problem of feedback in oral tradition: four examples from the Fante coastlands', *Journal of African History* 14 (1973) 223–35
―― 'Truths yet unborn? Oral tradition as a casualty of culture contact', *Journal of African History* 23 (1982) 395–412
Henige, David and McCaskie, T.C. — eds., *West African Economic and Social History*, Madison. (1990)

Henningsen, Henning	'Linje- og vendekredsdåb på norske og danske skibe op til 1814', in *Vestfold Minne*, Tønsberg, 1961, 35–63
——	Crossing the Equator, Copenhagen, 1961
——	'Sømandens drikkelse', *Handels- og Søfartsmuseets Årbog* 36 (1977) 7–67
Hernæs, Per O.	*Slaves, Danes, and African Coast Society*, Trondheim, 1995a
——	'Den balstyrige bergenser på Guldkysten', *Norsk Sjøfartsmuseum Årsberetning* (1995b) 127–38
Hogendorn, J. and Johnson, Marion	*The Shell Money of the Slave Trade*, Cambridge, 1986
Holsoe, Sv. E. and McCollum, J.H.	*The Danish Presence and Legacy in the Virgin Islands*, St. Croix, 1993
Idowu, E.B.	*African Traditional Religion*, London, 1978
Irvine, F.R.	*Woody Plants of Ghana*, London, 1961
Isert, Paul Erdmann	*Letters on West Africa and the Slave Trade*, trans. and ed. S.A. Winsnes, Oxford, 1992
Jefferson, L.E.	*The Decorative Arts of Africa*, London, 1974
Jeppesen, H.	'Danske plantageanlæg på Guldkysten 1788–1850', *Geografisk Tidsskrift* 65 (1966) 48–72
Johnson, Charles [Daniel Defoe]	*A General History of the most notorious Pyrates*, 4 vols., London, 1724–1726
Johnson, Marion	'The cowrie currencies of West Africa', *Journal of African History* 11(1970), 17–49, 331–53
Johnston, W.S.K.	'A list of seventy-seven tutelary gods of Cape Coast', *Ghana Notes and Queries* 12 (1972) 32
Jones, Adam	*German Sources for West African History, 1599–1669*, Wiesbaden, 1983 [1983a]
——	*From Slaves to Palm Kernels: A History of the Galinhas Country (West Africa) 1730–1870*, Wiesbaden, 1983 [1983b]
——	*Brandenburg Sources for West African History, 1680–1700*, Stuttgart, 1985
——	*Zur Quellenproblematik der Geschichte Westafrikas 1450–1900*, Stuttgart, 1990
Justesen, O.	'Aspects of eighteenth century Ghanaian history as revealed by Danish sources', *Ghana Notes and Queries* 12 (1972) 9–12
Kalkar, Otto	*Ordbog til det Ældre Danske Sprog (1300–1700)*, 5 vols., Copenhagen, 1881–1918 [important source for translation]
Kalous, Milan	'Akorite?', *Journal of African History* 20 (1979) 203–17
Kea, Ray A.	'Firearms and warfare on the Gold and Slave Coasts from the sixteenth to the nineteenth centuries', *Journal of African History* 11(1971) 185–213
——	*Settlements, Trade and Polities in the Seventeenth-Century Gold Coast*, Baltimore, 1982
——	' "I am here to plunder on the general road": bandits and banditry in the pre-nineteenth century Gold Coast', in Donald Crummey, ed., *Banditry, Rebellion and Social Protest in Africa*, London, 1986, 109–32
Kemp, Peter	ed., *The Oxford Companion to Ships and the Sea*, Oxford, 1994
Kilson, Marion	*Kpele La la: Ga Religious Songs and Symbols*, Cambridge, Mass., 1971

———	*African Urban Kinsmen: The Ga of Central Accra*, New York, 1974
Klein, A. Norman	'The two Asantes: competing interpretations of "slavery" in Akan-Asante culture and society', *IAS Research Review*, 12 (1980) 37–51
Klein, Herbert S.	'Economic aspects of the eighteenth-century Atlantic slave trade', in James D. Tracy, ed., *The Rise of Merchant Empires*, Cambridge, 1990, 287–310
———	*The Atlantic Slave Trade*, Cambridge, 1999
Klein, Martin and Lovejoy, Paul E.	'Slavery in West Africa', in Gemery and Hogendorn (1979, above), 181–212
Klemp, Egon, ed.,	*Africa: Maps dating from the Twelfth to the Eighteenth Century*, Leipzig, 1968
Kristiansen, V. [Michael Viggo Fansbøll)	*Ordbog over Gadesproget*, Copenhagen, 1908
Kwamena-Poh, M.A.	*Government and Politics in the Akuapem State 1730–1850*, London, 1973
Kyerematen, A.A.Y.	*Panoply of Ghana*, New York, 1964
Labat, Jean Baptiste	*Voyage du Chevalier des Marchais en Guinée, isles voisines et à Cayenne*, Paris, 1730
Larsen, Øivind	*Schiff und Seuche 1795–1799*, Oslo, 1968
———	*Eighteenth Century Diseases, Diagnostic Trends, and Mortality*, Oslo, 1979
Law, Robin	'Wheeled transport in pre-colonial Africa', *Africa* 50 (1980) 249–62
———	*The Horse in West African History*, Oxford, 1980
———	'Between the sea and the lagoons: the interaction of maritime and inland navigation on the pre-colonial Slave Coast', *Cahiers d'Études africaines* 29/2 (1989) 209–37
———	*Further Correspondence of the Royal African Company of England relating to the 'Slave Coast' 1681–1699*, Madison, 1992
———	*The Slave Coast of West Africa 1550–1750*, Oxford, 1991
Lawrence, A.W.	*Trade Castles and Forts of West Africa*, London, 1963
Lind, H.G.	'Undersøgelser, foretagne op ad Floden Volta i 1827 og 1828', *Archiv for Søvæsenet* 6 (1834) 1–6
Lovejoy, Paul E. -	*Transformations in Slavery*, Cambridge, 1983
Ly, Abdoulaye	*La Compagnie du Sénégal*, Paris, 1958
Lydenberg, Harry Miller	*Crossing the Line: Tales of the Ceremony during Four Centuries*, New York, 1957
McCaskie, T.C.	'Accumulation of wealth and belief in Asante history: 1. To the close of the nineteenth century', *Africa* 53 (1983) 23–43
———	'Nananom Mpow of Mankessim: an essay in Fante history', in Henige and McCaskie (1990, above), 133–150
———	*State and Society in Pre-Colonial Asante*, Cambridge, 1995
Maier, D.J.E.	'Military acquisition of slaves in Asante', in Henige and McCaskie (1990, above) 119–132
Manning, Patrick	*Slavery and African Life: Occidental, Oriental, and African Slave Trades*, Cambridge, 1990
Martin, Eveline C.	*British West African Settlements 1750–1820*, London, 1927

Menzel, Birgitte	*Goldgewichte aus Ghana*, Berlin, 1968
Metcalfe, George	'A microcosm of why Africans sold slaves: Akan consumption patterns in the 1770s', *Journal of African History* 28 (1987) 377–94
Meyer, Birgit	'If you are a devil, you are a witch, and if you are a witch, you are a devil', *Journal of Religion in Africa* 22 (1992) 98–132
Meyers, J.M. Bruce	'The connubial institutions of the Gãs', *Journal of the African Society* 30 (1931) 399–409
Molbech, Christian	*Dansk Ordbog*, 2 vols., Copenhagen, 1859
Monod, Théodore	*L'Ile d'Arguin (Mauritanie): Essai Historique*, Lisbon, 1983
Monrad, H.C.	*Bidrag til en Skildring af Guinea-Kysten og dens Indbyggere*, Copenhagen, 1822
Moore, David D.	'Henrietta Marie: an introduction to the first slaver in the New World', *Seafarers* 1 (1987) 200–4
Müller, Wilhelm Johann	'Müller's description of the Fetu country 1662–9', in Jones (1983a above) 134–259
Nketia, J.H. Kwabena	*Drumming in Akan Communities of Ghana*, Accra, 1963
Nørregård, Georg	*Guvernør Edward Carstensens Indberetning fra Guinea*, Copenhagen, 1964
—	*Danish Settlements in West Africa, 1758–1850*, Boston, 1966
Oldendorp, C.G.A.	*Geschichte der Mission der evangelische Brüder auf den caraibischen Inseln St. Thomas, St. Croix und St. Jan*, Barby, 1777
Olsen, Poul Erik	*Toldvæsenet i Dansk Vestindien 1672–1917*, Copenhagen, 1988
Opoku, A.A.	*Festivals of Ghana*, Accra, 1970
Opoku, Kofi Asare	*West African Traditional Religion*, Accra, 1978
Oxenbøll, Erik	*Dansk Økonomisk Tænkning 1700–1770*, Copenhagen, 1977
Ozanne, Paul	'Ladoku: an early town near Prampram', *Ghana Notes and Queries* (7 January 1965) 6–7
Parry, J.H., Sherlock, Philip, and Maingot, Anthony	*A Short History of the West Indies*, fourth edition, London, 1987
Pelton, Robert	*The Trickster in West Africa*, Berkeley, 1980
Perbi, Akosua	'The relationship between the domestic slave trade and the external slave trade in pre-colonial Ghana', *IAS Research Review* 8 (1995) 64–75
Phillips, Thomas	'A journal of a voyage made ... in 1693, 1694 from England to Africa', in [Awnsham and John Churchill, publishers], *A Collection of Voyages and Travels*, 6 vols., London, 1732 VI: 173–239, second print, 1746, VI: 206–55
Picton, John and Mack, John	*African Textiles*, London, 1979
Pieterse, Jan Nederveen	*White on Black: Images of Africa and Blacks in Western Popular Culture*, New Haven, 1992
Pietz, William	'Bosman's Guinea: the intercultural roots of an Enlightenment discourse', *Comparative Civilizations Review* 9 (1982) 3–22
—	'The problem of the fetish', *RES*, (Spring 1985) 5–17
—	'Fetishism and materialism: the limits of theory in Marx', in Emily Apter and William Pietz, eds., *Fetishism as Cultural Discourse*, Ithaca, (1993) 119–151

Postma, Johannes Menne	*The Dutch in the Atlantic Slave Trade 1600–1815*, Cambridge, 1990
Priestley, Margaret and Wilks, Ivor	'The Ashanti kings in the eighteenth century: a revised chronology', *Journal of African History* 1 (1960) 83–96
Priestley, Margaret	*West African Trade and Coast Society: A Family Study*, London, 1969
Quarcoo, A.K.	'The La-Kpa. Principal deity of Labode', *IAS Research Review* 3 (1967) 2–43
Quarcoopome, E. Nii	'Self-decoration and religious power in Dangme culture', *African Arts* 24/3 (1991) 56–65
Quartey-Papafio, A.B.	'The Gã Homowo festival', *Journal of the African Society* 19 (1920) 126–34
Rask, Johannes	*En kort og sandferdig Rejse-Beskrivelse til og fra Guinea*, Trondheim, 1754
Rattray, R.S.	*Ashanti*, Oxford, 1923
——	*Religion and Art in Ashanti*, Oxford, 1927
——	*Ashanti Law and Constitution*, Oxford, 1929, reprinted 1956
——	*Akan-Ashanti Folk Tales*, Oxford, 1930
Reindorf, Carl Christian	*History of the Gold Coast and Asante*, Basel, 1895, revised by C.E.R. Reindorf, 1950, 2nd ed., Accra, 1966
Reindorf, Joe	*Scandinavians in Africa*, Oslo, 1980
Richardson, David	'West African consumption patterns and their influence on the eighteenth century English slave trade', in Gemery and Hogendorn (1979, above) 303–30
——	'Slave exports from West and West-Central Africa, 1700–1810: new estimates of volume and distribution', *Journal of African History* 30 (1989) 1–22
Robertson, Claire C.	*Sharing the Same Bowl*, Bloomington, 1984
Roussier, Paul	*L'Établissement d'Issiny 1687–1702*, Paris, 1935
Ryder, A.F.C.	*Benin and the Europeans 1485–1897*, London, 1969
Sanders, James	'The expansion of the Fante and the emergence of Asante in the eighteenth century', *Journal of African History* 20 (1979) 349–64
Sanuto, Livio	*Geografia dell'Africa*, Venice, 1588, facsimile Amsterdam, 1965
Savary, Jacques	*Le Parfait Negociant ou Instruction Générale*, eighth edition, Amsterdam, 1726
Schmidt, Christian Lindholm	*Beskrivelse over Fri-Neger Qvou Ursovs Fetisserier og Krigsudrustning*, Copenhagen, 1761
Serle, William and Morel, Gérard J.	*A Field Guide to the Birds of West Africa*, London, 1977
Smith, Robert	'The canoe in West African history', *Journal of African History* 11 (1970) 515–33
——	'Peace and palaver: international relations in pre-colonial Africa', *Journal of African History* 14 (1973) 599–621
Smith, William	*A New Voyage to Guinea*, London, 1744, facsimile 1967
Snelgrave, William	*A New Account of Some Parts of Guinea and the Slave Trade*, London. 1734, facsimile 1971
Sprigge, R.G.S.	'Eweland's Adangbe', *THSG* 10 (1969) 87–128
Steensgaard, Niels	'The Companies as a specific institution in the history of European expansion', in Blussé and Gaastra (1981, above) 245–264

Bibliography 275

Sundström, Lars	*The Exchange Economy of Pre-Colonial Tropical Africa*, London, 1974
Svalesen, Leif	*Slaveskipet Fredensborg og den Dansk-Norske Slavehandel på 1700-Tallet*, Oslo, 1996
Teixeira da Mota, A. and Hair, P.E.H.	*East of Mina: Afro-European Relations on the Gold Coast in the 1550s and 1560s*, Madison, 1988
Tenkorang, S.	'The importance of firearms in the struggle between Ashanti and the coastal states, 1708–1807', *THSG* 9 (1968) 1–16
Thilmans, G. and de Moraes, N.I.	'Villault de Bellefond sur la côte occidentale d'Afrique. Les deux premières campagnes de l'*Europe* (1661–1671)', *Bulletin de l'IFAN*, série B, 39 (1976) 257–99
Thaarup, F.	*Archiv for Statistik, Politik og Huusholdnings-Videnskaber*, 3 vols., Copenhagen, 1797–1798
Tilleman, Erik	*A Short and Simple Account of the Country Guinea and its Nature [1697]*, trans. and ed. S.A. Winsnes, Madison, 1994
Ulsheimer, Andreas Josua	'Ulsheimer's voyage of 1603–4', in Jones (1983a above) 18–43, 340–56
Van Dantzig, Albert	'The Ankobra gold interest', *THSG* 14 (1973) 169–85
——	*The Dutch and the Guinea Coast 1674–1742*, Accra, 1978
——	*Les Hollandais sur la Côte de Guinée: À l'Epoque de l'essor de l'Ashanti et du Dahomey 1680–1740*, Paris, 1980 (1980a)
——	*Forts and Castles of Ghana*, London, 1980 (1980b)
——	'The Akanists: a West African Hausa', in Henige and McCaskie (1990, above) 205–16
Van den Boogaart, Ernst	'The trade between Western Africa and the Atlantic world 1600–1690', *Journal of African History* 33 (1992) 369–85
Vansina, Jan	*Oral Tradition as History*, London, 1988
Verger, Pierre	*Trade Relations between the Bight of Benin and Bahia from the 17th to the 18th centuries*, Ibadan, 1976
Villault, Nicolas, sieur de Bellefond	*Relation des Costes d'Afrique appellées Guinée*, Paris, 1669
Vogt, John	*Portuguese Rule on the Gold Coast 1469–1682*, Athens, 1979
Ward, W.E.F.	*A History of Ghana*, London, 1969
Westergaard, Waldemar	*The Danish West Indies Under Company Rule 1671–1745*, New York, 1917
Wilks, Ivor	'The rise of the Akwamu empire 1650–1710', *THSG* 3 (1957) 99–136
——	'Akwamu and Otublohum: an eighteenth century Akan marriage arrangement', *Africa* 29 (1959) 391–404
——	*Asante in the Nineteenth Century*, Cambridge, 1975
—	*Forests of Gold*, Oxford, 1993
Wilks, I., Levtzion, N., and Haight, B.W.	eds., *Chronicles from Gonja*, Cambridge, 1986
Winsnes, S.A.	'The jaundic'd eye: bias in the Danish sources for West African history', in Henige and McCaskie (1990, above) 217–26
Yarak, Larry W.	*Asante and the Dutch 1744–1873*, Oxford, 1990
Zimmermann, J.	*A Grammatical Sketch and Vocabulary of the Akra- or Gã Language*, Stuttgart, 1858, reprinted 1972

UNPUBLISHED THESES

Akrong, A.A., 'Sacrifice in Labode (Ga) [sic] Religion', MA thesis, University of Ghana, 1978
Greene, Sandra, 'The Anlo-Ewe: their economy, society, and external relations in the eighteenth century'. PhD thesis, Northwestern University, 1981
Kea, R.A.. 'Ashanti-Danish relations 1780–1831, MA thesis, University of Ghana, 1967
Quaye [Odotei], Irene, 'The Ga [sic] and their neighbours', PhD thesis, University of Ghana, 1972
Wilks, Ivor, 'Akwamu 1650–1750: a study of the rise and fall of a West African empire', MA thesis, University of Wales, 1958

MANUSCRIPT TEXTS

Meyer, Hartvig, [untitled, a history of Christiansborg Fort ?1698], CRA, V-gK 187
Rømer, Ludevig Ferdinand, 'Relation om tilstander i Christiansborg', CRA, Vg-K, 189, 28 2.1745
Thonning, Peter, 'Map of Gold Coast 1802 and revised 1838', CRA, Kortsamling, 227, and 337, XVII

Index to Rømer's texts

References to items in *Negotien* (1756) are italicized

Abonnam 216 powerful Fanti cabusee
Aborre 104 the Millie Cabusee from Accron, 104–5
Abroe 216 the ordinary messenger
Accra/Accras: 17 description from the road, 25, 39, *69, 71, 73, 75*, 80, 84 Dutch Accra has female fetish, 94, 99, 100, 105, 106, 110, 112, 113, 115 densely populated, 116, 117 Akwamu's demand for foreskin of king, 118 sister of Accra king, king hated, 120 became brokers for trade, 121, 122 purchase and holding of slaves -- delightful time, 122–23 as a 'fence', 128 increase in numbers, 129, 130, 131, 132, 133, 135, 136, 137, 138, 139 taken over by Akyem, surly, 140, 143, 145, 146, 148, 151, 155, 156, 159,169, 171 accompanied Opoku in 1744, 172, 173, 175, 178, 179, 181, 196, 198 red millie rare, 199, 201, 204, 206, 210 pester for loans, 211, 215 enticed by Dutch, 217 fertile fields, 218, 219, 220, 221, 223, 233, 235, 237, 239, 240
Acondo, King of Akwamu 130–31, 139
Acondo Chuma (Little Acondo) 139 temporary king of Akwamu, 175 lost everything to Oppoku Chuma
Acrofi 210 caboceer at Ada
Ada 151, 204, 205 lodges, attacked by Akwamu, Danes helped, 207 in times of flood, 207–08 lodge, new island, 208 one of the largest islands, 210 Adas more polite than Accras, 224 fertile, 227, 237, 238
Adampi/Adampees (Adangbe) 111 locus, 117 subjects of Accra, 118, 130, 132, 137, 139 under Frempung, 151, 173, 174, 199, 210 beg for loans
Adja (title of honour) 84 "fire", 85
Adjang 105 prominent Akwamu, 175 killed by Pobbi
Adoui 101 Danes' broker, 107, 163–4 conflict between families, 216

Afolli 186 (Foli Bebe/Ofori Bembeneen) Assiamboe's predecessor
aggreys 26 source unknown, royal regalia, 115, 156 worn by Opoku, 160
Agojo 208
Agona 111, 117, 119, 125, 128 ruined by Fante 129, 206, 208, 238
air 235 clean and healthful
Akims (the Akyem) 110, 112, 119, 120–1 tax to Asante, three kingdoms, sent women to Akwamu, 121 prohibited from coming to coast, 124, 125–6, 130 collect tax from Akwamu, 131, 136–40, 139 took over Accra, good-natured, 140 slaves became as native, 142, 143,144, 145, 146, 148–9, 150, 151, 152, 159, 168, 169, 170, 172, 173, 174, 175, 198 cannot eat millie, 199, 201
Akim (Akyem) 34 expert gold miners, *75, 77*, 95, 98, 105, 106, 108 Akim King Frempung, 120–1 deserted land, 120 women unwilling to return, 131, 136, 139 three kings and their territories, 140, 143, 144, 147, 152–3 description and destruction of, 152–4 battles against Asante 1741–42, 156, 174, 201, 208
Akotja, 'amputated' 116–7 Akwamu king circumcised
Akron (Akron/Gomoa) 104, 111, 112, 117, 119, 122, 125, 128, 131, 170, 172
ale 158, 235 *pitto*
Alexander 45–6, 50–1 Jewish hospital manager at Elmina
Alovi 210 caboceer at Keta
Altona *249*
America/Americas 17, *30*, 57, 189, 202, 203
ammunition 135, 137
Amsterdam 40, 44, *46, 48, 73, 253*
amulet 166 'emblem'
Ananse, see Nanni
ancestors see forefathers
Angola 32, 42, *252*

animals: 25 cows, sheep sacrificed, 27 whales reincarnation of people, 88 elephant ear, 88 rot in sun, 90 bones, 90 cows, sheep, 91 sheep, goat (cabrit), 94 heads of elephants, oxen, sheep, 95 sacrifice oxen, 96 goat sacrifice, 100 elephant taboo, 101 tails of elephant, cow, wolf, 105 fetish barked like a dog, 105 elephants, 108 reincarntion, 114 cat, dog, 121 European depicted as animal, 123 sheep, dog, cat, 139, 140, 141 monkey, 144 elephant as gift, 150 sacrifice, 162 crocodile, sea cow, 171 game meat, 182 wolf, 182 elephant tusks for horns, 194 hares, buffalo, hart, roe deer, 197 lamb, calf, sheep, cow, bull, domestic roe deer, 200 tiger, wolf paths, 210 amphibian, 211 sea elephants, crocodiles at Volta, 218 U*rsu*, tiger in old language, *Lumo* tiger in present language, 223 hunting methods, 223 sacred animal shot, lamb, 227 elephant gestation and numbers, 227 hart, roe deer, 232 monkeys for sale, 236 roe deer swallowed by snake, 237 'wolves' (hyenas), 237–8 sea elephant, crocodiles, 238–9 monkey society, 238 dogs, cats, rats eaten, 239 monkeys (apes) violate Negress, 239 sea elephants

Annamaboe (Anomabu) 63 French attempt at establishment, 67, 68, 69, 95 locus of Fante fetish, 170, 178, 179

anoint 192 Oppoccu's (Opoku's) body

Ante 216 Ante Grandees

antiscorbutics 199 in ship's medicine chest

antivenerics 199

ants: 19, 19–20 description of anthills and life of termites (white ants)

Antufi 151 Asante 'rebel'

Appau 150 succeeded Frempung in 1741

Appe 53

aqua fortis 228

aqua regia 148

Aquamboe/Aquamboes (Akwamu): 73, 74, 102–3, 105, 112 five miles NE of Accra, now deserted, 116–7 ancestress, young king raised in Accra, 118 successful battle against Accras, 119–120 captured slaves, 15 kings until 1734, 120 kings indebted to Akyem, women want to stay in Accra, 121 prohibited Akyem from coming to coast, 122 caught and sold their own, 123–5 became weaker as Accra became stronger, instituted decapitation, 128–9, 129 attack Labadi, 130 King Acondo, 131–2, 135–8 defeated by Akyem, 139 decimated, 139 surly, 140, 142, 146, 153, 169–70 new king on throne, 172–3, 174 cheat Asantes, 175, 200 steal from each other, 201, 204 favoured the Dutch, 205–6 Akwamu attacks Ada, 208 on islands in River Volta, 216, 222 buy salt at Ningo

Aqvando (Akwamu king) 130 succeeded Acondo in 1726, 130–2, 135 mediator, 136 hated by his people, 137 unsuccessful against Akyem

Arabian/Arabic 28, 171 books

Ascharri 154–5, 174

Asia 183, 210

assegai/spears/lances 24, 118, 172

Assiamboe (Ashangmo) King of Little Popo 176–7 swindled captains, 180 his residence, 186, 202 powerful, 209 agreement with

Assiantee (Asante): 94–5, 98, 106, 110, 112, 116 first conflict about a woman, 120 Akyem were tributary, 125, 136,139 after Akyem's war, 140, 143–4, 145, 150–52, 152–4 (1742) war against Akyem, 156, 157, 159, 167 do not mine gold, 169, 170–3, 173 Assiante Kottoko, 174, 199–200, 201, 208, 222 besiege Fredensborg, 228 source of gold

Atte 107 Adoui's brother

audience 140–2 with King Frempung, 156–9 with Oppoccu

Axania (Dutch Caboceer) 74

Axim 201, 49

Baas 219 at Kpone

Bahourd, Father 16

Baltic Sea 248, 249

bamboo 160

Bannana Island (Banana) 62

Bang (Bã Kwante, one of the three kings of Akyem) 111, 124 King of Akim, also 'planted' women, 139 rule over Dutch and English forts, 142–3, 144, 150, 151, 152, 154, 155, 178

Barbaric Custom 180

Barbary 171

barber 99

Baribi, see Bribi

Barovius, François 43

basin(s) 102 wooden for Labadi fetish 'head', 147–8 for panning gold, 156 gold basin for Opoku's feet, 225

Bassi 68–9 at the French court, 95 son of Corrantrin, 96, 97, 179

beads 23 *contreterre*, 99, 115, 192, 225. See also aggreys.

bean(s) 82, 114, 148 red *taqver* (tackies)

beard 87 on drums, 226 slaves examined for

becalmed 227 worst possible circumstance

bell(s) 90 in fetish hut, 177 blind musician wearing bells, 193

Benin (see also River Benin) 23–5 origin of Gold Coast families, 26 aggrey beads found there, 113 ruled in Golden Era, 114, 117

Index

Berkuse 210
Big Men (nobility) 223, 238 monkeys' Big Men
Billsen, Jørgen (Danish Governor) 76
birds: 81 chicken, 84, 85, 90 cock's tail, parrot's tail, 91 chicken, 99, 101 cock's feather, 108 reincarnation, 109 chickens, 123, 129, 144 hen stolen, 150 chickens, 161 pheasants, partidge, wild pigeons, 166 red cock used for amulet, 167 large bird seizes people, 196 partridge and pheasants, 197 chickens, 210 hatch on islands near Ada, large bird at Volta, 213 weaver birds/travat-birds, 214 turkey, 232 parrots, parakeets for sale, 239–40 large bird at Volta River, crown pheasants at Accra, crown birds at Labadi, 'fetish's horn-blower'
birth 180, 187
birthday 98–9 each week, 177 Assiambo's celebration
Bishop Worm 185 conditions of marriage to African women
black pepper 199 as medicine
bleeding (i.e. phlebotomy) 199
blood(y-ied) 88, 93, 98, 103, 122 bloody heads, 131, 134, 150, 172 Opoku spilled blood, 192
bloodthirsty 97–8 fetish in Fante
boats 192 small and large, 205 armed, 206 hundred armed boats, 207 up the Volta, 208 on Volta, 238 overturned by sea elephant
boat people 177, 192 boatsman, through the breakers, *remadorer*
bolle (bread) 196
bones 125, 127
book(s) 184 carried at funerals, 193 prayer books on ship
Borris, Enevold (Danish Governor) 74, 76
Bosman, Willem 19, 25 untrue description of Benin, 147 description of gold mining, 240
bossies (cowrie shells) 90, 101, 196 ten cowries = one Danish shilling, 208 twenty for red earth, 225, 232
Bourse 37, 51
bows and arrows 152
Box a Box ("Bugs-a-bugs") 19 English name for termites
Boye, Franz (Danish Governor) 71–2
Brabant 251
Brafo 97–8, 129 heads cut off, 201
branding of slaves 245
brandy 35, 56 *kieldyvel*, 84, 85 fetish can consume more than 200 Negroes, 86, 88, 90, 101, 103, 105, 107, 114 for acquisition of land, 116, 120, 122, 124, 127, 132, 137, 138, 142 Flensborger corn brandy, 143, 159, 160 distilling, 163 served to old men during a trial, 166, 169, 177, 180 used in building house, 183, 190, 192, 195, 201, 211 stored in sleeping quarters, 216 'brandy-drinker' as title, 223 at sacrifice, 225, 232 Whites buy for sale, 235 used in excess by Europeans, 237, 240 placate fetish
brass 102
Brazil/Brazilians 15, 30, 42, 43, *49*, 148, *246*
bread 162, 196, 197, 198 of millie, 218 of small millie for fetish
bribes 135
Bribi 84 'remarkable'
bric-a-brac 90, 93 trinkets, 94 knick-knacks, 104 trinkets
Bristol *57*, 252
Brunni 154–5 heir to Frempung's land, 174 Frempung's successor, conflict with Opoku
Buffalo Custom 180
burial of treasure 94
burning of towns/houses 94 by Asante

calabash 114, 166, 167
calendar 98
callisiare/callischare (to marry) 165, 185 marriage between European and Black woman
Canary Islands 30
cannibalism 28, 182 Blacks feared Europeans eat fatted slaves
cannon 16, 28 cannon balls, 119 shot for signal, 129, 135, 163, 181 four at Little Popo, 211 forty at Christiansborg, 212, 222, 223 twenty at Fredensborg
canoe 178, 208, 209 trip to Crepe
Cape (Cape of Good Hope) 15
Cape Cors (Cape Coast Castle) 16, 32, *51–2*, 56 English officers, 64, 68, *70, 71*, 111, 143, 215 gardens, 220, 232 European wives there, 235 on drinking
Cape la Hou (Grand Lahou) 33–4, 204
Cape Monto (Cape Mount) 17 flat land Cape Mount to Volta River, 21, war 22
Cape Palm (Cape Palmas) 21, 33
Cape Tres Pointes (Cape Three Points) 34
Captain/King Martin 22–3 war and its causes at Cape Mount
Captamarin (Cape St. Mary) 33
case (court case) 179 against Corrantryn. See also trial
cartridge 114 pouch for carrying
Cassiante 153–4 southeast of Asante, 154 Opoku had to have their permission to make war, 155 poor gold, 167, 200, 224 slaves from
cavalry 154, 171 Opoku's

ceremonies 87–9 New Year, 89 in honour of Putti and his ancestors, 107 at sunrise and new moon
chain(s) 99 as decoration, 176 sit in chains, 226 on slaves
Chalderian or 'fire worship' 25
chameleons 214 description
chaplains 230
Chaqvin (Jaquin/Jakin) *49, 53,* 201
charcoal 99 to blacken coiffure
cheese 197 'old cheese'
chest 38, 99, 114, 117, 119, 127–8, 199 medicine
chewing sticks 226
children: 114 a Negro's wealth, 118, 120, 122, 128, 129, 132 raised for sale, 136, 137, 139 child of royal Akwamu lady, 144 king's children distributed around the land, 148, 150, 152, 163 named after Europeans, 164 slave children, 169, 174 noble child, 179 child of Corrantryn, 180 slave child's 'custom' of no significance, 182 child of slave unwanted by traders, 185 mulattoes, 186 white child brings status, 187 black child killed, 215 grown to adulthood, 221, 230 *Seminarium* for black children, 234 mulatto, 237 eaten by crocodile
China 23, 26 porcelain, 30 emperor, 183 where cane grows, 193
Christian/-ity 16, 43, 86, 126, 134, 185, 197, 230 teach children
Christiansborg Castle (also 'the fort') 32, *48, 49, 70, 71, 72, 74, 77,* 84, 90, 93, 100, 104, 108, 111, 133, 134, 135, 137, 138, 139, 150, 153, 164, 165, 185–6 conditions of mixed marriage at, 191, 192, 197, 204, 205 main fortress, 210, 211–12 description, 214, 215 case about gardeners, 218, 219, 220, 221, 222, 229, 231, 235, 236, 237, 250
circumcision (male) 25, 100, 116–17 of the Akwamu king
cistern 212 at Christiansborg, both inside and outside the fort, 221 at Fredensborg broken open
civil servants 230–1 qualifications and requirements
clay 87 pot, 90 pot, 114, 160 pots, 180 pots, 180 in building houses
cloth *31, 52 silks, 65,* 81 creation of man from cloth, 99, 101, 103, 115 around the waist, 120, 156 brocade scarf, 156 taffeta, 160 cotton, taffeta, silk, wool, weaving, 162 bark cloth, 180 to decorate residence, 183 given as wedding gifts and as *pantjes,* 191 cotton, gingham, *salempuris, calavap,* 191 *slaplagen* used for menses, 216 as annual tribute, 220 to camouflage white body, 223 *slees-lærred* as shroud for 'wolf', 225 cotton, *calavap, salempuris,* gingham, *plattilias, sless-lærred,* 228–9 English and Danish cloth trade

clothing 22–23 Africans wear European clothing, conditions in peace treaty, 23 military clothing as gift, 93, 104, 108, 115 not needed, 134 removed, 135, 141, 229 wear horse blankets in cold periods
coat-of-arms 229 stamped on cloth
coffee 161 beans grow wild
coffin 172 of glass from Holland, 175 coffin and throne
colony(-ies) 175–6 Europeans could establish, 202
colour 229 on cloth must be true and fast, preferences
Como (Comedia del Arte) 167 theatre figure 'commanding wares' 190
complaint 220–1 letter
contraband 43
Contreterre, see beads 115
convulsions 91–2
Copenhagen 39, 64, *76, 77,* 186, 189, 191, 197, 206, 216, 227 water at Copenhagen good, *248, 249, 250*
copper 36 in adulteration of gold, 102 forbidden, 156 engraver, 160, 225 rod, *243* kettles, *250*
Coptic Christians 27
copy-letter-books 216 imagined text of a letter
Corrantryn (Caboceer at Anomabu: Koranting/Kurantsi/ John Currantee) 63 l'Empereur de la Côte de Guinée, 64 bound and robbed French, *68–9,* 95–6 makes sacrifice, *178–9, 241*
Costa de bonos Gentes/-de malos Gentes 33–34
council 41–2 Dutch, 45 salary of members, 94, 150, 220 at Christiansborg
court 238 monkeys hold court
coustyme (custom) 179–80, 180 in building a house, 204 as tax from forts, 223 for murdered 'wolf'
Coymans, (Coejmans, Balthazar) 39 Dutch factor at Creve-Coeur
Crepe (Anlo Ewe) 103 cheating the fetish, 129 entire country southeast of the Volta, 136, 139 Akwamu fled to Crepe, 144, 150, 173, 206, 208, 209–10 pleasure trip to Crepe, monstrous fish, 222, 227 elephants, 228 Asantes detour through, 233
crocodiles 210, 237–8 seized woman and child, then caught
crone(s) 90–1, 92 possessed, 105, 147 pan for gold, 148, 149, 163 (for history), 186
crops 31, 61, 62, 243, *244, 245*
crossroad 91
cultivation 217 of fields, Danes cultivate, 224 a little in fertile Volta islands, Mountain Negroes farmers
Curassoe (Curaçao) *247*
cutlass 194

Index

Daçon/Dacon 106 'Dutch Caboceer', 130 given royal wife, 139, 151, 153 killed
dagger 179
Dahomet (Dahomey) 181 enemies of Assiambo at Little Popo, 201-2, 209 killed Dutch at Keta
daler (coins) 99 as decoration
dance/dancing 87 to sacred drum, 88 at New Year, high priest Puttj, 180 in *Coustyme*, 182-3, 223, 226 on board ship
Dane guns 168
Danes/Danish 32, 69, *69-77*, 94, 104, 119, 128, 129, 133, 148 merchant dishonoured, 137 God's children, 138, 140, 142, 145, 146, 148, 153, 157, 160, 162, 165, 168 Dane guns, 171 messenger who accompanied Opoku, 176 own Volta River, 179, 185 in mixed marriage, 188, 191 cloth, 194, 195, 196 Danish shilling, 198, 202 future prospects, 204-5 Danes' right to Volta, 209 sole owners of Keta, 216, 217 cultivate a plot, 219 own three towns at Accra, 220 Danish desertor working for Dutch, 224, 228 Danish weights for gold, 233 sell slaves at loss, life and trade in West Indies
Dantziger Aqvavit 142
daughter 74, *75*, 86
Davis Straits 248
days (significant days) 98 good, bad, sacred, birthday, 99 Tuesday sacred, 100 Sunday's child, 129 *Bon Die*, 146 *Bon Die*
death 21 in rainy season, 42, 56 starve to death, 86, 103 if acted contrary to fetish, 105, 106 death of Dacon, 107 life after death, 118, 128, 133, 134 starving, 159 starved, 171 starved during campaign, 172 beaten, starved, 181 Qvaté shot to death, 187, 197 starve, 201, 205 beaten at Ada, 206, 220 beaten to death, 221 starve, 232 grieve to death, 238 monkeys bite others to death
De Borde, Martinus François (Dutch Director-General) 41-2 displayed his power, 43, *47*, 74
164 debt, interest and security, 165 explanation of *penjare* and palaver, 206 Adas registered in Debt Book, Danish leaders in debt to Company, 215 Ursu Negroes in Debt Book, 219 Accras in debt to Company, 234
De la Cour (French Governor at Anomabu) 69
Denmark 22, 200, 229
De Petersen, Baron Jacob (Dutch Director-General) 37, 45, *50*
De Garna, Wasco (Vasco Da Gama) 15
descendants 23, 24 of royal family, 119, 126 must take revenge for forefathers, 127-8 attempt recovery of ancestors' heads, 131, 138

devil 80 description, 126, 142 white as.., 159 sea-devils, 169-70 devilish temperament of Akwamus, 173-4 sea-devils
Diaz, Bartolom 15
dictionary 165 need for one of 'Negro-Portuguese' and Danish
Dinkero (Denkyira) 140 destroyed by Asante 60 years earlier, 201
doctor 40 English factor, James Hopkins (investigates poisoning)
Dorph, Oluf 230 chaplain in Denmark, 76
dragon 210
drink/drinking 42, 89, 109, 97 inebriation, 114 basins, 117 inebriated king, 123, 124, 127 intoxication, 143 drunken *kanalje* and drinking, 144, 150 Bang's drunkenness, 152, 158-9, 162 tea, punch, 165, 166 after palaver, 177 intoxicated, 180 in *Coustyme*, 211 'drinkage' brandy taken, 223, 233, 235 excesses, 340 'drunk'
drought 115
drowning 149 in mines, 192 risk of
drums/drumming 87 at New Year, description of sacred drums, 88 description of drums and drumsticks, 96 for Fante fetish, 96-7 a parable, 102, 125 skulls hung on, 127, 150, 167 head hung on drum, 226 on board ship, 237, *246*
duel 37-8 between two Dutchmen
dungeons 122, 178 slave dungeons
Dunko 224 slaves from
Du Puis, (?) 39 "A Frenchman from Bourdeaux" assistant to Dutch factor at Elmina
Dutch 19, 21 give names to Negroes, 32-4, 36-46, *46-55*, 87, 106, 119, 127, 128, 129-30, 133, 134 commander, Fort, 135, 138 town, Dutch fetish priest, Dutch Negroes, Dutch female fetish, 139, 142 Dutch muskets exploded, 145, 151, 153, 160, 165, 168, 172 Dutch general, 173 general and council, 181 fort, 188, 189, 191, 192, 194 captain and initiation tragedy, 196, 204, 205, 206 try to acquire foothold at Ada, 209 lodge at Keta, 215, 217 Dutch Negroes claim mastery, 220 madness, shameless, 221 have driven inhabitants from Kpone and Tema, 224 lodge at Okko, 231, 232, 233, 235 worse drinkers than Danes
Dutch Company (Dutch West India Company) 38-9, 40-1 goods priced lower than others, collect fees, seize interloper, 43 free trade for factors against 8 *rixdaler* fee, *46-54*, 189, *247-8*
Dutch fort 41, 43, 136 (Creve-Coeur) besieged, 137 siege lifted, *46-8, 50, 54*
Dutch Negroes 106 war against Danish Negroes, 135-6, 138

282   Index

earnest money 185 for bride
East India 15, 132, 193, 198
eat(-ing) fetish 100–01 description with snake skin necklace, 124 women 'planted by kings', 169, see also oath
eggs 27 petrified, 81, 82, 91, 94, 196, 210
Elmine (Elmina Castle) 33 chief castle of the Dutch, built of European bricks, 26 more recruits but more deaths, 39, 41 besieged by its own Negroes in 1740, 42 collect toll from Portuguese, 43, 44 book-keeping irregular, 46, *46, 48, 51, 52, 54, 70, 77*, 111, 112, 135, 143, 155, 159, 160, 170, 172, 173, 199, 204, 220, 221 complaint, 228, 230, *252*
embankment 214–5 as a catchment
England 40, 56, 164, 168, 228
English/Englishmen 19, 22, 24–5 as an informant, 33 learn Negro language, established on Upper Coast, 40, 55 high morals, 56, *57–62*, 64, 87, 119, 127 have severed heads at Cape Coast, received heads, 128, 129, 133, 134, 136 commander as mediator, 139, 142 English musket exploded, 145, 158 English ale, 168 copied faulty Danish guns, 173, 182, 188, 189 abolished monopoly, 190, 194–5 treatment on warships, 204 lodge near Fredensborg, 205, 215 depend on Danes for water, have gardens, 220, 221 greatest trade at Prampram, 224, 226, 228–9 great trade in woollen wares, 233, 235 accustomed to drinking punch,
English Company (Royal African Company) 55, 56 receives £10,000 annually for the establishment, *57–62, 59* Chief Agents, *62* established on Upper Coast, 168, *246–47 in* the West Indies
entertainment 43 in Brazilian mines
Eppe *53*
Europeans 231–3 description of ambience and reactions, 234 become accustomed and/or naturalized
evil 107, 125 evil habits only 100 years old, 126, 131, 141, 178 evil Black
execution 45 not allowed at Elmina Castle
executioner 157

factor 219 Dutch factor at Accra, 220 sent letter of complaint, 221 Dutch factor poisoned, English at Prampram well provisioned, 231 must be trained, 238 Danish factor at Ada, *et passim*
factory 160 weaving
Falster (in Denmark) 230 Mr. Dorph is dean there
family 163 conflict, 216 four noble families in Osu, 217, 234 of mixed marriage

famine 100 elephant eaten, although tabu, 132
Fante/Fantees 63, *67, 68*, 79, 95–7 most powerful fetish, 111 land and nations, 112, captured Asantes, 113, 128–9 war against Agone and Accron, 132, 170–3 conflict with Asante, 172 federation formed, 175, 179, 199 Union, 201 no leader, hate one another, 216–7 Danes' union with Fante, 233, 241
farmers 224 inland Negroes so called by coastal Negroes
fart/-ed 86 the fetish farted
feathers 90 from cock's tail, red from parrot tail, 93, 156 white, in Opoku's hat
fence 219 around sacred trees
'fence' (receiver of stolen goods) 122 Accra fence, 124, 145
fertility 217 of inland and mountain regions
fetish 16, 35, 78, 79, 81, 83, Chapter 3 *passim*, 129 Fante fetish stopped war, 138 pronouncement, 139, 145 on Danish muskets, 159 Labadi fetish, 168, 172 prophecies Opoku's death, 214 Tié Tié at Osu, 218 great fetish at Labadi, 238 fetish-maker to entice crocodile out of water, 240 fetish bird, fetish-maker, fetish's hornblower, 241 at Labadi, Fante fetish
Fetu 201
Fida (Whydah) 63 French fort, *69*, 201,
fire 96 symbol of Fante fetish permanently burning, 111, *245* fire set
firebrand 107 thrown at new moon
firewood 35, 83, 115 as fine for adultery
fish 21, 88–9 allowed to rot, 100, 108 reincarnation, 117, 196 *sardin,* 197 salted and dried, 198 plenty at Fredensborg, bream, herring, 'Old Crones', fresh lagoon fish, sea scorpions, 208 dried fish sold at Keta, 210 freshwater fish in Crepe, Berkuse, 214 change colour, *dorades*
fisherman 114, 219 at Teshie. See also *remadorer*
flag 163–4
Flensborger corn brandy 142
flint muskets 142 Danish did not explode, had double barrel. See also muskets
flintstones 142
Flood (biblical) 27
Foër *249*
food on board ship 64 cakes, biscuits, bread, rusks rotten, 199
forefathers 21, 26, 35, 79, 89 Putti's saved people, 94, 97, 100, 118 ancestress of Popo kings, 126, 127, 130, 150, 155, 168, 217 too good to be planters
foreskin 117 demand to replace after circumcision
forest 200
Fort Accada (?Akwida) *71*

Index

Fort Creve-Coeur 39, 204
Fort Fredensborg 139, 144, 173, 174, 197, 204 Dutch and English lodges nearby, 221–23 Fredensborg and surrounds, 222 besieged, 227
Fort Friderichsborg (i.e. Fredensborg) *70, 250*
Fort Nassau 33 Dutch fort at Mouré
Fort Royal (formerly Fort Frederiksborg at Fetu) *71*
fortresses/forts 36 Dutch have fourteen, 40, 50 English have only seven, 131 rents paid, 159, 180 residence in Little Popo, 189 cannot be moved to find trade, 203 suggests establishment in *Males Gentes* (Côte D'Ivoire), 208 at Ada, 216–7 tribute/protection fee
Fotter (Danish term for termites) 19–20
France 63, 96
Frempung 108 'great Akimist king', 139 ruled over Christiansborg, 140-2, 144 friend of Opoku, 149, 150 died 1741, 152, 154, 155, 174, 184–5 his burial
French 37 blacklist two Dutch generals, 39 a Frenchman from Bordeaux, 40, 63 thrice as many as Englishmen, no establishment, 64 robbed by Corrantrin, *65–69* on Guinea Coast, 168 ordered guns from England, 178, 182 captain throws slave infant away, 188, 189–90 charged higher prices by Africans, 197, 226 buy anything black, 231, 232 forced to have a chaplain on board, *243–46* in West Indies
From, 209 Dutch factor at Keta, killed by Dahomey Negroes
fruit 21, 96 plum-like fruit trees, 171, 199 prunes, citrons as medicine, 224, 229 citron juice to test colour
funeral customs 26 in Benin, 98 bury a body, 107 honourable funeral, 129 burial of heads, 144, 223 for the 'wolf
funeral speech, 154 speech over dead Ursue, 182–3 music, 183–5 funerals for ordinary people and for Frempung
Fyn (in Denmark) 193

gall 162 poison
gamble/gambling 181 lose all, 233 gamble away goods
game meat 21, 197
games *246*
gardens 215 at Cape Coast and Christiansborg, 236 at Christiansborg
garrisons 134 Dutch, 135, 197, 209 Dutch at Keta, 217, 220
geographer 27–8 map errors
geography 110–13
Giemawong 84 'God's Messenger', 84–7, 88, 102, 103, 106, 138 saved Danes,

gifts 84 at *Hɔmɔwɔ*, 85, 137 to Akyem, 142 slaves and gold, 144 elephant as gift, 179
glass 172 glass coffin for Opoku, 175
God 79, 81, 83, 85, 94, 106, 107, 108, 126 Creator angry at Blacks, 'Saviour', God's Word, 131 God and Supreme Being, 138, 154, 158, 162, 188, 189, 218, 224, 230, 241
gods 80, 121 sea gods give goods to Europeans, 138 sea god, 150 earth god, 240 large bird godhead in Labadi
gold 17 mines, 26 lower value than aggreys, 27 Akyem gold, 33, 34, 36–7 adulterated, 38, 38 false, 40–1 muskets for gold, 42, 43, 46 false at Elmina, *51 false, 52, 53,* 55 never adulterated by Englishmen, 56, 64, 89 balance/weight, 102 fetish made of, 115 tools of gold, 117 chest full, 119, 120 Akyem desert mines, 128, 130 tax payment, 139, 140 mines, Akyem thrifty, 142, 143 ransom for Bang, 145 for slaves in Crepe, 147–50 mining in Akyem, 155 Asante gold poorer than Akyem, 156 tree of gold, Asante, dust on Opoku's body, 159 Asante traders, 160, 167 from Cassiante, 174 ransom, 175, 200, 203 mining in America, 225, 228 gold trade, 232,
Gold Coast 17, 21, 24, 25, 34, 35 Whites brought evil to Africa, 63, 78, 111, 140, 203 need for new Gold Coast in future, 212, 227
'good days'/'bad days' (calendar) 98
Golden Era 113 under Benin rule
government 55–7 English system on Coast, 136, 238 monkey government, *57–62* English system, 46–8 Dutch system on Coast, *243–245* French in West Indies, *246–7* English in West Indies, *249–54* Danish existing system and suggestions for a new one
Graffi 205
Grandes 179 Fante Grandes, 220
grate 198 millie
Greenland(-ers) 21, 127, 162, *248*
greeting 85 clapping hands, 141 in European manner
Grönberg, (?) (Danish Director-General) *71*
Guard 215
Guardeloupe (Guadeloupe) 244
Guinea and West India Company 189, 190 Company ships must wait in West Indies until Dutch and English have loaded, 233 Company price
gun chest 194 on board ship
gunners 135
gunpowder/powder 41 one hundred pounds for sixteen *rixdaler* from Dutch, Dutch Company forbade sale, 116, 118, 121 Akwamu forbidden to sell to Akyem, 135, 142, 143, 145, 166, 172, 175, 184 at funerals, 190, 205 distribution, 206 sold to Adas, 223, 225, 229 for export

hair 90, 93, 99 women's hair styles, 101, 139 under cornerstone, 156 gold dust in Opoku's hair, 209 powdered with red earth
Hanover 168
harmattan, see *Oriental Tiid*
harrassment 194–5 treatment of crew and staff by authority
harvest 17 harvest twice a year
hat 156 Opoku's, 166 making for military use
head(s) 79 cut off in war, 91 cut off slaves, 98 cut off Brafos, 102 Labadi fetish like a head, 105, 106 Dacon's cut off, 125 cut off, flesh removed, hung on drums, 125–6 history of custom of collecting heads, in enemy hands, 127–8 in possession of English, recovery attempt, sign of victory, 129 of Brafoes and cabusees, 130 given back, of messengers, 134, 137 of Aquando, 137–8 beheaded, 152, 154 cut off, 156 collected near Oppoccu's residence, 157, 158 ale goes to his head, 160, 167, 175, 180 in 'Barbaric Custom', 181 shot off in cannons, kept in cellar and manhandled, 194 of the 'Man of the Line', 220 threat to decapitate Whites, 235 Danes' heads in a hangover
heir(s) 120, 139 none to Akwamu throne, 144 to Bang's throne, 154 made prisoner, 155, 169 to throne of Akwamu, 174, 175 to Asante throne, 186 mulatto children lose inheritance, 241 inheritance
heiroglyphic figures 25
Herrn, David (Danish Governor) *72–3*
Hispaniola *244*
hoes 115 of gold
Holland 41, 45, *51, 54, 65, 73*, 154, 164, 172, 191 cloth from, 229 gunpowder from, *248, 249, 254*
Holland, Adam 219–20 Dutch soldier, robberies
Hollander 40 high status over Zeelanders, 44 Dutchman, 145
Holstein/Holsteln 188 sailors from, *248*
honey 161–2
Hopkins, James 40 English factor and doctor in 1747
horses 171, 200 cannot be used in forest
horse tails 24 sign of honour
hospital 46
house 84 for fetish (oracle), 93, 94, 134, 156, 160, 163, 177, 180 making custom in building, 181 Qvaté's, 184 burial in own house, 208 Norwegian style, 218 cultivation around ruins, 219 at Kpone, 236 snakes in rafters
Hübner, Johannes, geographer 27
huckster(-ing) 232–3
hunter 82
hut 84, 85, 87, 88, 90, 97, 105, 114, 133, 179 for making custom, 219 fetish hut, 236 fire in hut to drive away vermin, 237

Iceland 162
illness 19 plague, 39 gout, 65 scurvy, 89–91 help from fetish, 172 Oppoccu fell ill, 178 Europeans infected by black woman, 199, 212–3 Guinea worm and treatment, 231 depression
In Puncto Sexto (Sixth Commandment) 114–5 is wife freeborn or slave, 164, 233 cause of debt
indigo 161 grows without trouble, not used for blue colour
insects 19, 19–20 white ants (termites), 161–2 bees, hive, honey, 235–6 ants, cockroaches
interlopers 40, 41, 43, 44, *55, 189*, 50 Dutch
interpreter 33, 143
iron 24 harder than in European, 103 shackles, 115 more rare than gold, 127 chest, 149, 159, 165, 167 Asante trade gold for iron, 175–6, 230 shackled, 181, 192 rods, 222 rusts at coast, not inland, 225 clamp on slave's arm, trade list
Italian (for bookkeeping) *72–3*
ivory/tusks 41, 225, 227–8 ivory trade, large tusks cut for carrying

Jacqueville (Grand Jack) 204
Jamaica *244, 247, 253*
Jancon (the Fort's drummer) 141 interview with Frempung
jawbone 125 wiped feet on, 128 foot on bone, 144 cut from living man, 180, 237 of crocodiles
Jew 45–6, *50–1*
jewels 160 skulls decorated
Judaism 25, 100 circumcision
Jus Manus 114
Jutland 193
Jörgensen (Councillor) 74

Kamp, Niels 141–2 bookkeeper, examined by Frempung
keys 99
kidnapped 116 the ancestress of Akwamu
kieldyvel 58, see also brandy
King Martin see Captain Martin (at Cape Mount)
King William 21–3 at war with King Martin, 34
kitt see musical instruments
knick-knacks, see bric-a-brac
knife/knives 25 not used for sacrifice, 88 stones instead of, 97, 101 in trial by ordeal, 114, 115 of gold, 226 keep from slaves
Knip's factory 229 cloth-makers in England

Index

Labode (Labadi) 78 has most important fetish, 79, 83 fetish is male, 86, 88, 89, 95, 96, 97, 101, 102, 105, 106, 129, 130, 138 fetish, 146 the fetish, 159 fetish, 175 fetish, 215, 218, 219, 240 fetish bird, 241
ladder 42
lagoon 17, 197 at Ningo, rich in fish, 214 salty, east of Christiansborg, 219 Labode lagoon, 222 Ningo, 237–8 crocodiles
Lagoon Negroes 205–6 attacked by Akwamu
land 113 4 acquisition, 120–1 Akims desert their land
land of milk and honey 196
landing 222 good at Ningo, 223 poor at Loy
Lange, Mr. 230 Danish chaplain, died at Elmina
language/-s 23–4 differ from each other, 32 Negro-Portuguese, Negro, 85 old-fashioned for fetish, 87 old language, 91 old language, 95, 108, 163, 218 old and present terms, 226, 232 Negro-Portuguese, 236 among ants; special phrases in local language: 87, 92, 100, 103, 165; special phrases after palaber, 218
Latin 135 letter in Latin, 210 Latin author
letters 45 personal letters returned to writer, 134 reports, letter in Latin
Leogane *244*
Liège 169 supplies guns
Linea Longitudinis 15
Little Popo 118, 176, 177, 180 residence of Assiamboe, 181 Popo, 186
Liverpool *57*
lizards 236 kept in rooms
loan 210
lock 94 padlock, 99, 127, 221 on cistern, broken open
lodges 204 Dutch and English near F'borg and Volta, 205 Dutch at Ada, Danes at Ada, 206 at Tuberku, 207 moved three times because of flood, 209 re-establish lodge in 1743, 219 Dutch at Kpone, 223 English, Dutch at Loy
London *57, 58, 60,* 189, 229, *253*
Lower Coast 21, 23, 40, 63, 86, 136, 178, 197, 201, 227
Loy 223
Lübeck 191 L. shillings
Lützow, Major 76

Madagascar 203
maintenance 55 English garrisons and forts, 56 English factor and fort
mallaget [malagueta] 199
Malos Gentes 34, 203 make new establishments
Mlefi 205, 208
Man of the Line 192–4 initiation on crossing Tropic of Cancer

market place 104, 105, 144 punishment for theft
marry/marriage 165 *callisiare*, 180, 183 marriage custom, 185–7 miscegenation, *callischare*
Martinique *244, 245*
masons 222 must train anew
mat (bed) 90 miniature for the fetish, 101 fetish carried, 107, 138, 181, 237
mechanic 133 the governor
medication 39, 199 European, African on slave ships
melancholy 224 plagues Blacks and Whites
menses 191 cloth used during m.
mercurium 148
Mexico 30, 147, *61, 246*
messenger/emissary 216, two salaried, 233
Middelburg *51*
military attire 166, 220 European camouflaged
milk 197 cows not milked
millie/millio 104 'Millie Cabuseer', 106, 114 Turkish grain, 144, 196 price varies greatly, 198 description and use, 217 *millio*, 218 small m. for fetish, 224, 235 make ale of, 236 ants eat it, 238 monkeys take it
mirror 114
mistress/es 104, 185, 234 Negress
Mogul emperor 30
Mohammedans 28
monsters 210 women, freshwater fish, 214 chameleon
moon 84 full moon, 98 calendar, 107 ceremony at new moon
Moors 171 still two in Asante
morals 55 Englishman have high morals, 109
mortality 36 among Dutch, 195 among Europeans on ships, 202 Europeans die out in West Indies, natives before 50 years old
Moscow *249*
mosquitoes 210 at Keta and Agona
Mountain Negroes 112, 113, 117 subjects of Accras, 118, 130, 137, 139 under Frempung, 151, 174, 201, 208, 218 in awe of Putti, 219 stayed with Dutch, 220, 224 to cut footpaths, 237 caboceer visits Accra
Mouré (Mori) 33
Mullaters (Mulattos) 56 as soldiers, *57, 58,* 86, 185 children, 234 children loved and cared for by Europeans
murder 35, 145, 156, 163, 164, 172, 175, 179, 181 fetish priest killed, 187 baby killed, 205, 218, 223 sacred animal killed, 226 slaves murder ship's crew
music 96–7, 177 musicians, birthday songs, 182–3 description of instruments, 226 on board slave ship, 231 relieves depression, *246* boxes

musical instruments 182–3, 243 *kitt* players, 237 hornblower saved by horn
muskets/guns (also flintlock muskets) 41 price in Europe, Dutch forbidden to sell, 104, 114, 116, 118, 121 sale to Akim forbidden, 133, 135, 139, 142, 143, 145, 152, 154, 161, 167 placed on fetish, loading and overloading, 168 faulty, redesigned, England copied, 172, 175, 190 in trade, 205 distributed, 222, 223, 225

Nanni (Ananse) 80–3, 179
Nantes *51, 52, 66*
neck ring 226 on slaves
necklace 101 stuffed snake skin
neighbours 21 kill each other
New England *243*
New Year (*Hɔmɔwɔ*) 84–9, 216 annual tribute from Fort
Ningo 197, 219, 221, 222 good landing place
Niumboo 80 name for God in Accra
Norwegian(s) 189, 193, 194 killed Man of the Line, 208 style of house
Noy 157–9 Danish Company messenger, long conversation with Opoku
Noyte 79 Caboceer at Teshie, 93–5 explanation of fetish stone, 97, 115 Noyte 130 years old, 216
numbers, see population
'Nürnberger' 213 artist, 222 "Nürnberger work" at Fredensborg

oath 43, 94, 100–1 description of eating fetish, other methods of swearing an oath, 205 Adas swear Volta R. is property of Danes, 220 signed complaint, 238, see also 'eating fetish
Ober-Kiøbmand [Chief Merchant] 195, 205
Ober-Styrmand 195
Okanie 106 general of 'our' army, bought Dacon's front teeth
Okko 204, 224 Dutch lodge
okraer [okras] 158 life-slaves, 184–5 buried with king
olive oil 197
Oppaqva or *Oppoccuaqva* 169 means Oppoccu's slave
opperhoved [commander] 197, 217
Oppoccu (Opoku Ware I) 112 Asante king, 136 demands 500 slaves from Akim, 137, 140, 143, 144, 150–9 *passim*, 155–6 physical description, tyranny, description for engraver, 157–9 description and conversation, 163 great names, 169 on the heir to Akwamu throne, 170–3 conflict with Fante, 174 conflict with Brunni, died in 1749, 178 great names, 201

Oppoccu Chuma 98–99 Akwamu king, 215 'Little Oppoccu', 227 killed by Pobbi
oracle (both prophecy and priest) 35, 78, 79, 86, 92, 138, 218 Labadi fetish great oration 60 description, 82 Fante fetish
Oriental Tiid (harmattan) 18–9, 229 cold
ornamentation 26 of an African king, full regalia, 98–9 for birthday each week, 156 Opoku
Oyo 202 have driven Dahomey away
Østrup, Peder (Danish bookkeeper) *71, 72, 73*

Pahl (Danish merchant) 73
palabres (palaver) 164–5
palm oil 180, 196, 197, 199 as medication, 208 on bodies, 210 in hair, 226 slaves smeared
palm wine 166, 180 in building of house
pantjes (cloth) 160 strips sewn together, 183, 183
pantomime 89 'pretence', acting out historical event, 104–5 Aborre's prophetic wife, 167 in war situation
parable 85, 96–7
paradise 126
Paris 63
Parliament *58, 59*
Passop, Peter 21
paternoster *247*
Patakai (Badagry) 201
patatos 114, 198
pawn 234
peace treaty 22 after war at Cape Mount
Peak of Tenerife 15
penjarte (panyarred) 91–2 possessed by fetish, 164–5
Peru 30, 147, *61*
Pescarallo 167 theatrical figure
Petersen, Cornelius (Danish Sergeant) 86
piles 208 to divert current
piment (pimiento) 197, 199 as medication
pipes 226, *246*
plaintiffs 156
plantation 22, 42, 117 in mountains, 119, 202, 230 cotton and coffee possible, *243, 247, 248, 249*
Pobi/Pobbi 105 Akim king, 146, 154, 174, 175
Point d'Espagne 156 on Opoku's hat
poison(ed) 39–40 case in point, 162 poison Europeans, 187 husband poisoned, 195, 221 Dutch factor, 227 poison slaves when becalmed, *246*
Poland *249*
pole(s) 93 painted and tied with raffia
Ponni (Kpone) 173 Dutch lodge, 204, 219 Dutch lodge, 220 Ponni Negroes, 221 English fort at Prampram

Pope 15
Popo 202, 208, 209, *53*
population/numbers 85 at fetish gathering; 107 Akims had 200,000 men in the field; 113 more during Golden Era than now; 115 a million at Accra earlier; 117 twenty times as many Accras as Akwamu, millions of Mt. Negroes and Adangbe; 118 thousands of archers, millions of inhabitants; 119 slaves/month, 500 families left after 1734; 126 4,000 heads collected in wars; 129 more than 2,000 captured by Akwamu; 132 Aquando 'ate' a couple of thousand/year; 135 1,000 armed Akwamus in escort; 137 many thousand surrendered to Accras; 139 Akwamu scarcely 1,000 men in arms; 142 1,000–2,000 come to trade; 143 200,000 Akims; 144 2,000 to 3,000 men to catch slaves; 146 census in Akim; 151 100,000 men for Akims, brigands, 10,000 to clear bush; 152 dead in war; 153 10,000 enemy sold, 20,000 Assiantes; 170 Akim with 10,000 men, Akwamu with 300; 171 Opoku and more than 300,000; 175 4,000; 215 army at Ursue from 14,000 down to 500 down to 150; 218 now only 600 at Labadi; 221 ten Europeans against 400 Blacks; 222 Assiante forces besiege Fredensborg
Portugal 17, 42, *49*
Portuguese 15, 16, 23, 32, 33 named Elmina, the mine, 36, 42, 43, *46, 49, 50 Portuguese pass, 51, 52, 54,* 81, 115, 116, 148, 157, 160, 164 Negro-Portuguese, 198 Portuguese millie, 204, 226 examining slaves, 227, 228 Portuguese gold purer than African, 232, *246, 247*
possessed/possession 87 drummer at New Year, fetish, 88, 90, 91, 92 detailed description, 93 avoided by passers-by, 97, 102, 104, 105
Prampram 173 English fort, 219, 221 description, 223 English must withdraw periodically
pranks 179 Nanni's (Ananse's)
pregnancy/pregnant 99 custom (naked), 191 when cloth rots, 237 pregnant woman eaten by crocodile
Prester John 27
priest/chaplain 16 French Father, 43, 78, 84, 85, 88, 96, 102, 108 Elias Swane, 117, 135 European, 148 Portuguese, 181 fetish priest killed, 218 priest, priestess, 223, 232 on French ships
prince 63 Corrantryn's son
Principe Island 227 for water, *246*
prophecies 105, 106, 107, 159, 175 pronouncement of Labadi fetish, 200, Rømer's prophecy
protector 216

Protestant 148
Prott, see Protten
Protten, Christian 186 (mulatto chaplain)
provisions 105, 135, 137, 153, 171, 172, 179 from Fante, 199 on ships, 212, 227 used up when becalmed
Prøvesteen 212 a watch tower with eight cannons, 219
Prussia *249*
punch 235
punishment 35, 42, 43 fine for contraband, 114, 123, 124, 144 jawbone removed, stand in market place, 178, 181 Qvaté's, 195 on ships, 201, 221, 238 of crocodile, in monkey society
Putti (Okpoti) 78 Caboceer of Labode, 79, 83, 86, 89, 97, 101 accused can buy his freedom, 105, 106, explains Dacon's death, 107 explanation of life after death, 108 on reincarnation, 129, 130 given royal wife, 137 had Giemmawong come, 138, 166, 218 held in awe, 219

Queen Anna at Cape Mount 22, 23
Qvacu 108 company slave
Qvahu (Kwahu) 208
Qvassi 86 Putti's brother, 112 successor to Asante King Oppoccu in 1751
Qvaté 181 killed fetish priest
Qvitta (Keta) 204, 208–10

raffia 42, 87, 90, 93
ragout 197 tasty 'Negro dish'
rain/rainy season 17, 21 July and August, 137, 147, 149, 162, 196, 207, 215, 217
red earth 87, 90, 102 smeared on fetish, 146 red clay, 208–9 from Mountain Negroes, 210 on hair in Crepe
reincarnation 108
religion 24 ceremonies, 37, 45, Chapter 3, 116
Reinhold (Danish skipper) *250*
remedorer (as fishermen) 100 not circumcised, 192. See also, boat people
reproduce 202 Europeans, natives in West Indies, Guinean slaves, 210 mosquitoes in stagnant water
residence 115–116 king/viceroy at Accra, 125, 156 Oppoccu's, 157, 158, 159, 160, 171, 176, 177, 180–1 Assiamboe's residence
rice 22
rifles 134, 154
River Benin 23, 23
River Galinhas (Gallinas) 21
River Gambia 23, 28, *60*
River St. Andres (Sassandra) 277
River Senegal *60,* 63,

288   Index

River Sess (Sester) 21
River Volta 17, 28, 34, *69*, 105, 111, 118, 129, 173, 176 Danes own it, 201, 202, 204–8 Danes' rights, description, history, 224 islands fertile, 230 *seminarium* for Mulatto children
road 122 ships' road, 135, 174 Fredensborg road, 192, 233
robbers/robbery 115, 145, 151, 173, 174, 175 thieves, 178 people stolen by Corantryn, 218, 219 by Dutch soldiers, 220 seized Negros
Rochelle *51, 66, 254*
rocks 197 reef at Fredensborg
root foods 198
Rotterdam *46*
routes 113, 136, 155, 160, 167 dangerous to Cassiante, 173 to Elmine and through Crepe, 199, 220 blocked, 228 from Asante to Elmine
rye 198

sacred object 102 Labadi fetish like head of gold, 219, 223 'wolf' sacred animal shot. See also bric-a-brac
sacred place 87, 95 above Anomabu, 138 in Labadi
sacrifice 25 of animals, 81, 84, 86, 88, 90, 91, 95–6 human being, to Fante fetish, 98, 129 slaves sacrificed, 138, 150 in gold mines, 223 on killing of sacred animal
sailors vs. landlubbers 192
St. Croix *31, 244, 249*
St. Domingo *244, 247*
St. Eustacius *248*
St. Jean (St. John) *31, 249*
St. Malo *51, 66*
St. Matheus 28 non-existent island in 'African Sea'
St. Thomae (São Tomé) 227, *246*
St. Thomas *31, 249, 252*
sal amoniacum 148
sal hyapsinth 235
salary(ies) 38 Dutch, *50* Dutch, 55–6 English, *58–9* English, *77* Danish, 231 English doubled if with wives, 232, 233, *245* French, *251*
salt 159, 196–7 salt fish, salty lagoon, 214 producing salt, 222 production at Ningo, 224 of great importance to inland people
Satan 104, 126, 194
scarf (cloth) 156 of gold brocade, 160 a *pantjes*
Schilderup, Severin Schielderup (Danish Governor) *74–6*
scorpions 236
seafood 208 dried shrimp
Seeland 85, 108, 193, 230
Seminarium 230 for black children

Senatu Gentium 114
seraglio 145 Ursue's wives
shells 27 mussel shells found inland, 222 beautiful, used for lime
shallop 192
ships 207 navigation of Volta, 208, 209, 215 dependent on Danes for water at Accra, 216–7, 228 English, more than a thousand annually, 233 ship's-price
shot 129 grapeshot, 135 grapeshot, 152, 163 grapeshot, 166
Siccadinger (crafty men) 121–2 Akwamu young men, 131
Sildt *249*
silver 17, 30, 99, 203 slaves for mining
singing 82, 87, 88, 96, 177, 180, 184, 226 for Portuguese
Sissa 80, see also devil
slaves 21, 28 Mohammedans from north, bite other slaves, one with pointed teeth sold hand-to-hand then killed, 30, *31* slave trade, *32,* 42 Portuguese, 43 price in Brazil, price for Dutch Company, 44, *50* 56, *66*–*7, 77,* 91 as sacrifice, 97 for sacrifice, 108 always slave in rebirth, 114 as wealth, 118, 119 by ambush, beginning of Accra trade, 121 Akims duped by Akwamu, 122 seized own countrymen, 124 men lured by 'planted' women, 128 skulls of, 129 sacrificed, 132 Accra's agreeable' trade, 136 500 promised to Opoku, 137, 139 son of slave woman as leader of Akwamu, 140 slaves married to native Akim slaves, 142 as gift, 143 criminal, 146, 155 bury treasure and then killed, 164, 165 debtor, 169 for purchase of a title, 174, 176, 177 young people pretending to be slaves, 178 ransomed by friends, 179 Company slaves, 180, 181–2 females with young, 190 French prices, 199 female slaves treat illnesses on board ship, 200, 202 future trade up Volta, 203 always necessary for mining in America, 205 Company slaves, 206, 209 unable to sell, 215 Company slaves, 224 seaside Negroes masters over inland Negroes, Dunkos, 225, 226 ship/land price, examined, 226 on board ship, 228, 233, 234 given to mulatto children by European fathers, 237 taken by 'wolves', *243, 252* on St. Thomas, *247* run away slaves
slave ships 41 special privilege, 44 forced to backtrack, 64–5, *et passim*
sloop 205, 207
smørballer (a porridge) 179–80
Smørball Coustyme ('Butter ball custom') 179–80 boys' puberty rite
snakes 20, 96–7 in parable, 101 stuffed skin as fetish, 236
Soja 166, 216 great emissary

soldiers 36, 38, *51, 54, 58, 74*, 86 a sergeant, 104, 127, 160 as distillers, 163, 196, 211, 215, 217, 219
soothsayer 93
South Pole 28
Spanish cane 183 for flutes, suggestions for cultivation
Spaniards/Spain 15, 16, 17, *30*, 42, *61, 244, 246–8*
Sparre, H.H. (Danish merchant) *74*, 205–6 helped Adas vs. Akwamu
spears 24 assegais, 118, 172 lances
species facti see 220–1 complaint
Spectacle de la Nature 19
spices 161 cloves and nutmeg, 197 (*piment*) Spanish pepper
spider 81, 235, see also Nanni
spikes 42
spirit/soul 80, 83, 84, 86, 125 of slain enemy
spurs 99 silver, as adornment
steam cabinet 178
steel 228 mixed with Portuguese gold
sticks 90 in fetish hut wall, 91 vs. illness, 99 chicken heart on stick for decoration, 135, 212 winding Guinea worm
stone 88 for slaughtering, 94–5 as fetish, 119 instead of gold in chest, 135 for loading cannon, 139 cornerstone of Fredensborg, 208, 222 quarried
stool(s) 88, 90, 141, 158
storyteller 81, 83
Strait of Gibralter *248*
sugar 161 cane, 162
Suhm, Hendrich von (Danish Governor) *73*
sun 107 ceremony at sunrise, 110
surf 192 strong along entire coast
surgeons 199 on slave ships, 231 requirements for Coast
Surinam 31, *244, 247*
Swane/Svane, Elias 108 chaplain at Christiansborg, 230
Svane, Frederik *72*
Sweden/Swedes 32, 204, *249*
swim 105, 192
swindle 38–9 Dutch worst, 81, 123–4 cheating each other, 174 swindle Asantes, 176, 177 Assiambo, 181–2 slaves' infants
swords 23 objects of splendour, 116, 118 swordsmen, 156, 167, 172

tallow 156, 161 from trees, collection and use
tar.emetiq. 235
tax/tribute 120 Akim to Asante, 121 tribute, 130 Akwamu to Akim, 131 from forts in Accra, 135, 140, 155, 216 annual and monthly from Fort
teeth 28 teeth like a tiger's, filed, points broken off, naturally pointed, 106 as trophy, 226 slaves missing teeth

Temma (Tema) 219 small Dutch fort, 220 Temma Negroes, 221 inhabitants gone
temperament 200 of the Blacks, 202 disposition, 218 Labadi Negroes lazy, 230 must be changed
Tessing (Teshie) 79, 93, 106, 115, 215, 219
testament 234 European husband to black mistress
The Hague 40
throne 157 Opoku's, 241
Tie Tie 84 messenger, 90, 214 name of lagoon and Ursue fetish
tiger 84, 218
Tiger Custom 180 description
time 98 calendar
tobacco 42, 197, 232 from Portuguese ships
toll 42 Portuguese pay at Elmina, *49*
Tooda 216 "Brandy-drinker"
torture 125 games with skulls, hung on drums
trade (general) 34 on *Costa de malos Gentes*, 40–1 Dutch goods priced lower, 41 private Dutch, 42 9–10 Portuguese ships every 3 months, 43 free for all factors, against fee, 102–3 wife for goods, 120 Accras became brokers, 129 Europeans buy 'own' Negroes, 132 European expertise, 133, 140, 142, 145, 146, 155, 168–9 Europeans copied faulty Danish guns for sale, 173–4 description of, 176–7 swindle at Little Popo, 188, 202–4 future prospects, 215 Danes in on trade because of fresh water, 221 English have most trade at Prampram, 225 list of goods and prices
Trane, Johan (Danish chaplain) 230
travados (line squalls) 18, 93, 147, 150, 152 bows and arrows better than guns during travat, 212, 213 travado-birds, 215, 229 cold in travado season, 236 snakes appear
treasure 64, 115, 119, 155 gold buried
trees 115 coconut, palm, 129 sacred, 156 made of gold, 161 roots for blue dye, tallow, 213 full of weaver birds, 215 orange, citron, 219 sacred, 222 coconut logs for ceilings at Fredensborg, 236 plantain, 238 monkeys on guard
trench 184 deep for burial of king, favourite wives and *okra*
trial 45 Dutch on Coast, 94–5 case before Council, 104–5 case between two prominent men, 178–9, 215 vs. governor for his gardeners
triangle (trade route) 145 Africa-America-Europe
trinkets, see bric-a-brac
Troy weights 228
Tropic of Cancer 193 initiation on crossing
Tuberku (Tubreku) 204, 206 lodge, 224 sandy area
Tuesday 99 sacred day

Tuffi 205, 208
Turkey/Turkish/Turks 24, 171 nation of Turkish religion, 198 Turkish corn (millie), *30*
turtles 197 at Ningo, 210

Ulenspeyl (*Til Eulenspiegel*) 80–1
union 216–7 Danes with Fante
Upper Coast 24, 29, 33, 44, 86, 134, 199, *52*
urine 87
Ursa (Osu Caboceer) 163–4 conflict between families, 216
Ursogrando (title of honour) 84 'Tiger'
Ursue (place name Osu) 84, 90, 100, 102, 106, 163, 211, 214, 215, 219
Ursue (Owusu Akim king) *75*, 94 111, 139 rule over Adampi, Mt. Negroes, and Fredensborg, his hair under cornerstone, 144–5, 145, 146, 151, 152 killed 1742, 154 honoured by Opoku, succeeded by Pobbi, 178
Ursue Afrie 153 Asante caboceer

Vagina Gentium 233 Crepe, all nations get slaves there
Van Ryk, Huybert (Dutch treasurer) 37–8 fraudulent sale of possessions
Van Voorst, Jan (Director-General at Elmina) 37–8 foiled Van Ryk's ruse, 40 a murderer, 46 successor to Petersen, *49, 50, 53*
vegetables 56, 215 from Cape Coast

war 22 on Cape Mount, peace treaty, 79, 94, 97, 105 battle Akim vs. Akwamu, 106, 109, 113 always means total destruction, 114, 117–8, 119 betrayal, 125–6, 127 waged by proxy, 128 Fante vs. Agona and Accron, 129, 135–6, 137 Akim vs. Akwamu, 146, 151–2 Asante vs. Akim 1741–42, 153, 154, 155, 159 Asante beaten, 170, 174, 190, 197 causes famine, 201, 206 Ada vs. Agona, 211–2 fortification at Christiansborg, 215 Ursue (Osu) vs. Dutch Negroes, 217, 221
warehouses 159 'emptied' thrice a year by Opoku, 222 at Fredensborg
warships 194–5 humane treatment on English ships, 221 English
water 17 fresh scarce, 57, 92 water pot, 110, 115, 123 for washing, 149 in mines, 150 in mines, 161 water hole, 162, 166, 180, 210 mosquitoes reproduce, 212 cisterns, 212 sea-water filtered through sand, causes illness, 215 collection, fresh for ships, 221 from cistern at Fredensborg, 224 spring at Okko, 227 used up when ship becalmed, best on S. Tomé, Copenhagen water, *246, 248*
wax 135 images
weaving 160 weaving and unravelling cloth
weights 228 gold weights Troy, Cologne, Danish: on Coast = 9:8
Werøe/Werrøe (Anders Pedersen Wærøe, Danish Governor) 71, *73–4, 75,* 132–8 *passim*, 206 in debt to Company
West Indies/India(n) 17, 30 trade, 39, 57, 133, 176, 188–90 Company and trade, West Indies Company, 193 ships, 195, 196, 198, 202–3, 226–7 the passage to, 235, *243–54*
West India and Guinea Company
wheat 198
whip 128
whisk 123
whistles *246*
white earth 99 on bodies, 166 on bodies at war, 184 at funerals
wife/wives 35, 82–3 *passim*, 84 wife of fetish, 86, 89, 103 wife traded for goods, 104–5 prophetic, bride, 115 adultery, 120–1 noble Akim wives, 130 noble, 131 earnings from, 136, 137 Akwamu fled, 141 a couple of hundred of Frempung's, 143 Bang's, 144 a thousand wives, 145 Ursue kept 400–500, 150, 151, 152, 155, 179, 183–4 eldest has highest rank, 184 limbs broken and buried alive with king, 185–7 in mixed marriage, 191, 226 promised to slaves, 231 Europeans on Coast, 234, *250* widows
wig 135, 141 pig-tailed
Willemsen, Andreas (Danish Governor) 73
wind 18 constant southwesterly on Coast, east wind, 96 whirlwind (Trompe de Mer) at sacrifice, 129 whirlwinds caused by fetish in Fante
wine 135, 158
witchcraft 187 cause of death
woman/women 120 whose sons would be kings in Akim, 120–1 married in Akwamu, 124 'planted' by Akwamu king, 141, 153 woman ruler, 163, 178 infected, 185 ff in mixed marriage, 186 royal woman marries a White, 198 grate millie, 210 ugly in Crepe, 221, 231 European women on Coast, 233 slave women, 234 married to European, 237 seized by crocodile
Worm, see Bishop
worms 64 in food on ships, 82, 199, 212–3 Guinea worm

Zeeland/Zeelander 40 low status, *46*
Zelle (Celle) 168 supplied guns
Ziel Ver Kooper 40

Addenda et Corrigenda

P. 18, footnote 12 should read: "R. inserts, here and in other places, '(s.v.)', apparently meaning something akin to 'pardon the expression', after having written the (vulgar?) gloss 'spit.' Thus, s.v. is an abbreviation of the Latin phrase *salva venia*, indicating his apology for his use of that word."

P. 70, line 5, replace "reckon up to four specier" with "could not manage the four rules of arithmetic."

P. 71, note 124, add "Fort Royal was not the chief fort then."

P. 152, line 11, after the sentence ending with the word "indecisive," insert: "The cowardly Bang wanted to have his Akims attack the enemy again, but they dared not look them in the eye."

P. 170, second line from the top, after "and," should read: "even though they had lost relatives and friends, and those remaining might expect the same fate, yet they praised…"

P. 188, third line from the bottom of the text: "twenty-four years" should be "forty years."

www.ingramcontent.com/pod-product-compliance
Lightning Source LLC
Chambersburg PA
CBHW071149070526
44584CB00019B/2720